What Is Cognitive Science?

What Is Cognitive Science?

Barbara Von Eckardt

A Bradford Book
The MIT Press
Cambridge, Massachusetts
London, England

153
V944w

Printed and bound in the United States of America.

Library of Congress Cataloging-in-Publication Data

Von Eckardt, Barbara.
  What is cognitive science? / Barbara Von Eckardt.
     p.   cm.
  "A Bradford book."
  Includes bibliographical references and indexes.
  ISBN 0-262-22046-6
  1. Cognitive science. I. Title.
  BF311.V624   1992
  153—dc20   92-10167
                                                                  CIP

TP

for Jeff, Alisa, and David

Contents

Acknowledgements

During the many years it took to write this book, numerous people and several institutions provided assistance and support. My biggest thanks go to my husband, Jeffrey Poland, who not only talked philosophy with me for hours on end, and critically went over the entire manuscript with a fine-tooth comb, but also put up with all the anguish that goes with a major intellectual undertaking. I am also very grateful to Nancy Nersessian, Owen Flanagan, Joe Mendola, Phil Hugly, Pat Manfredi, Pat Franken, Carol Slater, and an anonymous referee for reading and providing helpful comments on either the full text or a substantial portion thereof. In addition, a number of people gave me helpful feedback on sections of the manuscript. These include—in no special order—Bill Bechtel, Sander Gilman, Linda Waugh, Robert Meyers, Michael Devitt, Ruth Millikan, John Post, Scott Berman, Al Casullo, Robert Audi, Charlie Sayward, Ed Becker, Martha Farah, Tyler Burge, Dick Boyd, Jerry Samet, R. J. Nelson, Bob Van Gulick, Donna Summerfield, Dan Little, Jerry Fodor, Rob Wilson, and Ross Mandel.

In doing the figures, I received invaluable assistance from Fadi Joueidi of the University of Nebraska-Lincoln Humanities Research Center and from Travis Wagner, Stacy Wagner, and Ken Jensen of the UNL Instructional Design Center. Doug Weber helped with the index.

I had the opportunity to present some of the book, especially early versions of chapters 1, 2, 7, 8, and the appendix, to audiences at Wellesley College (1984), the University of Rochester (1985), Hamilton College (1985), Rice University (1985), the State University of New York at Albany (1986), the University of Indiana (1986), Rutgers University (1986), Bielefeld University, (1986), Princeton University (1988), Cornell University (1986, 1988, 1989), the University of South Carolina (1989), and the University of Nebraska at Lincoln (1989, 1991), and also at meetings of the Society for Philosophy and Psychology (1988, 1990). The discussions that followed these presentations were invariably stimulating, oftentimes jarring loose new thoughts or convincing me that old ones required revision.

I was also fortunate to receive considerable financial and institutional support for this venture. The book began as a project on "Explanation and Theory in Cognitive Psychology" supported by a National Science Foundation Fellowship during 1980–82 and by a Yale University Morse Fellowship during 1980–81. By 1984–85, when I was the Henry R. Luce Associate Professor of Language, Mind, and Culture at Wellesley College, it had taken its present form. The appendix and a draft of most of the first half of the book were written that year and during the subsequent two years, when I held a National Endowment for the Humanities Fellowship for College Teachers (1985–86) and a Society for the Humanities Postdoctoral Fellowship at Cornell University (1986–87). During 1987–89 I was a Visiting Scholar in Cognitive Studies and Philosophy at Cornell University, where I finished the first draft of chapters 5–8. I am extremely grateful to Frank Keil for helping to arrange that affiliation (and office space) at a time when I was otherwise unattached. In addition. I would like to thank my mother, Marianne Horney Eckardt, for financial support during those lean years.

And last, but by no means least, my thanks go to wonderful staff members at The MIT Press—Betty Stanton, who exhibited the patience of a saint in waiting for me to finish and who was encouraging and cheerful to the end, Teri Mendelsohn, who steered me through the final stages of the submission process, and Paul Bethge, who polished my prose with an eye for detail that was truly awe-inspiring.

What Is Cognitive Science?

Introduction

One of the most dramatic scientific developments in recent years has been the emergence of a new field called "cognitive science"—a field that studies cognition by drawing on the resources of a number of disciplines, including cognitive psychology, artificial intelligence, linguistics, philosophy, neuroscience, and cognitive anthropology. (See figure i.) Within the relatively short span of 30 years, this fledgling science has gone from being a bright idea in the minds of a handful of researchers to being an established sociological fact. The Cognitive Science Society, founded in 1977, now has more than 1350 members and holds internationally attended research meetings each year. There is at least one journal explicitly devoted to the dissemination and discussion of research in the field (appropriately, it is called *Cognitive Science*), and numerous others publish research results from one or another of the contributing disciplines. Several major publishers now have cognitive science series. There are graduate programs, undergraduate majors, and research centers. And, last but certainly not least, millions of dollars have been contributed to the cause.

Yet, despite all this activity, it is possible to be skeptical about whether cognitive science exists as a coherent intellectual enterprise. Perhaps there is no such thing as cognitive science, really. Perhaps there are just cognitive *sciences*—perhaps we have psychologists, AI researchers, linguists, philosophers, neuroscientists, and anthropologists studying cognition from their own disciplinary perspectives and with their own particular disciplinary methodologies.

Such skepticism is not unheard of. In fact, two recent, widely read general books on cognitive science make a closely related point. In *The Mind's New Science*, Howard Gardner (1985, p. 37) suggests that in cognitive science "there is as yet no agreed-upon research paradigm—no consensual set of assumptions or methods." A similar statement is made by Miller, Polson, and Kintsch (1984, p. 16) in the lead paper of *Method and Tactics in Cognitive Science*: "There is very little, if any, consensus concerning a set of more specific goals and metatheoretical assumptions that could define a coherent field of inquiry." Given this supposed lack of consensus, Miller, Polson, and Kintsch go on to suggest that what makes a piece of research "cognitive science research" is simply that it is concerned with intelligence, that it makes use of results or methods characteristic of at least two of the subdisciplines of cognitive science (as, for example, psycholinguistics does), and that it is produced by researchers who accept the relevance of problems and results from the various other subdisciplines

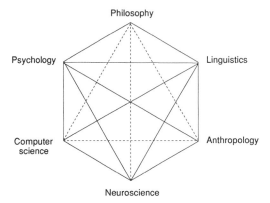

Figure i
The cover of the 1978 "Report of the State of the Art Committee to the Advisors of the Alfred P. Sloan Foundation" showed the disciplines standardly included within cognitive science. (From Walker et al. 1978; reprinted by permission of the Alfred P. Sloan Foundation.)

of cognitive science (p. 17). In other words, no constraints are imposed on *how* intelligence is to be theorized about. Anything goes, as long as it concerns the nature of intelligence and is properly interdisciplinary.

The existence in the literature of disagreements over the basic goals and commitments of cognitive science is undeniable. In particular, there appear to be no agreed-upon answers to the following questions: Is the domain of cognitive science restricted to the study of cognition in humans, or does it extend to nonhuman machines and animals? What is it, more precisely, about cognition that cognitive scientists want to explain? What sorts of computational mechanisms underlie cognition? Is cognitive science committed to the existence of mental representations? If so, what sorts of properties do mental representations have? Does cognitive science presuppose folk psychology? What sorts of explanations do we find in cognitive science?

Despite the undeniable existence of certain disagreements, one can question whether they reflect a widespread lack of consensus within the cognitive science community. I would like, in fact, to argue a contrary thesis: that there is far more *implicit* agreement among cognitive scientists (of all disciplinary stripes) as to their goals and their basic assumptions than the skeptics would have us believe, and that where genuine disagreement exists—and it certainly does on a number of points—there are rational grounds for adjudicating it. In other words, I would like to argue that a coherent, transdisciplinary framework of shared commitments for cognitive science can be reconstructed, and that this reconstructed framework is substantially in accord with what everyone considers to be the clear cases of cognitive science research. The aim of this book is to characterize this framework of shared commitments.

There are several reasons why such a characterization may prove useful to both practitioners and proponents of cognitive science.

First, of course, for readers interested in the question with which I began—whether cognitive science exists as a coherent, intellectual enterprise—the characterization provides an answer.

Second, foundational characterizations of a scientific field are often useful in educating students to become members of the corresponding scientific community. This function of foundational descriptions seems particularly important in the case of cognitive science because of its multidisciplinary character. The student of cognitive science must spend so much time learning the literature and the methodology of one or more of its subdisciplines that there is a real danger of not seeing the forest for the trees. A characterization of the sort I am about to present may help the student to keep the forest more clearly in view.

Third (and this was my original motivation for tackling this project), cognitive scientists will be in a better position to defend themselves against their critics if they have a clear conception of what they are and aren't committed to as a community. As cognitive science has begun to flourish, a number of critics have objected that the cognitivist approach to the nature of mind and cognition cannot succeed. It has been claimed, that there are certain important aspects of cognition that cognitive science is unlikely to be able to handle, that cognitive science is committed to untenable assumptions about the nature of mind, and that cognitive science is based on a faulty methodology.[1] Clearly, an important part of evaluating such objections is ascertaining whether or not they are "on target" in the sense of taking issue with assumptions to which cognitive scientists are in fact committed. But, obviously, this is impossible unless one knows what the commitments of cognitive science are.[2]

A fourth reason why this project may prove useful is that developing a characterization of the type envisioned here turns out to be an excellent way to sort, in a systematic way, through a host of issues and controversies with respect to the foundations of cognitive science that have appeared in the literature in recent years. Thus, even if when all is said and done some readers do not buy my description of the fundamental assumptions of cognitive science, they may still find the process of arriving at that description illuminating.

The kind of foundational consensus I am going to articulate is sometimes regarded as unscientific.[3] Two points can be made in reply. First, for what it is worth, there are certainly a great many historians, sociologists. and philosophers of science who believe that scientific research does, in fact, typically proceed within a framework of commitments of roughly the sort I will be attributing to cognitive science.[4] Second, the framework hypothesis is entirely defensible from an epistemological point of view. When a scientific community adopts a framework of assumptions within which to conduct its research, it is not engaging in some dubious *a priori* practice, nor is it taking the stance that such-and-such an approach to its domain must be right, come what may. Rather, the community is adopting these assumptions as a general working hypothesis about the character of its domain. In opting for the cognitive science approach to the study of mind, for example, a cognitive scientist is not saying that the mind must be an information-processing device. Rather, he or she is saying: This looks like a promising approach. Let's see where it takes us. If things go wrong, we can always give it up and try something else.

The foundational assumptions that make up what I have been calling the framework of shared commitments of a field are often deemed "metaphysical," where a metaphysical claim is taken as one for which no empirical result could ever be relevant. This label is highly misleading, on my view. The foundational assumptions of a scientific research program can clearly be either supported or undermined by confrontation with nature. This does not happen directly, as when scientists test specific theoretical hypotheses against data, but it happens nonetheless. It happens because what the world is like (or, in this case, what the mind is like) affects— though it does not totally determine—whether a given research program will be successful. The nature of the world influences success because it affects whether a research program will be able to come up with empirically well-supported answers to basic questions of the sort specified by its framework of shared commitments. In particular, one would expect that, *ceteris paribus*, if the foundational assumptions are wildly off base, the research program will eventually fail no matter how ingenious or strenuous the research effort. In addition, one would expect that, *ceteris paribus*, if the foundational assumptions are close to the mark and the research effort is sufficiently ingenious and strenuous, the research program will eventually be successful. The point is that these two principles allow us to use the evidence of actual success or failure to support the truth or the falsity of the foundational assumptions in question.[5] And if we can do that, then the foundational assumptions are not metaphysical. I conclude that scruples about commitment by a scientific community to a framework of basic goals and assumptions are unfounded.

I said earlier that the aim of this book is to characterize a transdisciplinary framework of shared goals and assumptions for cognitive science. Let me now try to formulate this aim more precisely. What sort of commitments are shared by practitioners of a field like cognitive science? I attempt to tackle this problem in section 1.1. One of the most important facts about cognitive science is that it is an immature field. Thus, section 1.1 takes up the problem of developing a general metascientific schema for characterizing the shared commitments of an immature science. Specifically, I propose that an immature science is best characterized in terms of a schema consisting of four components: a set of domain-specifying assumptions, a set of basic questions, a set of substantive assumptions which constrain answers to these questions, and a set of methodological assumptions. I call any realization of this schema a *research framework.*

In earlier drafts of this book, my research-framework proposal was preceded by a lengthy discussion of why several of the prominent existing units of analysis for science (specifically, the logical positivist notion of a "theory," Thomas Kuhn's notion of a "paradigm," and Larry Laudan's notion of a "research tradition") are not adequate to handle the case of cognitive science. Since that discussion threatened to get in the way of the main business rather than set the stage for it, I have relegated it to an appendix. It is still available to those with an appetite for philosophy of science, but it can be treated as optional by readers whose main interest is in the foundations of cognitive science.

Given the metascientific schema laid out in section 1.1, my aim, then, is to characterize the transdisciplinary research framework of cognitive science—that is, to describe cognitive science in terms of its domain-specifying assumptions, its basic questions, its substantive assumptions, and its methodological assumptions. This formulation is still not quite right, however, for it turns out that the project just described is simply too ambitious for a book of reasonable length.

For the sake of manageability, therefore, I restrict my attention to what one might call the central component of cognitive science's research program: the study of the human adult's normal, typical cognition (ANTCOG for short).[6] However, for ease of exposition, I will occasionally lapse into a less precise way of speaking and refer to my characterization as a characterization of "the" research framework of cognitive science.

ANTCOG is central in two respects.

First, its inclusion in the overall research program of cognitive science is completely uncontroversial. Scientific domains do not come ready-made. Rather, we begin with a working hypothesis as to what set of phenomena will be susceptible to the same theoretical approach; we then gradually refine or modify this hypothesis as the construction of a theory proceeds. Everyone agrees that the domain of cognitive science should include human cognition or intelligence. However, there is disagreement as to whether it should include more (and, if so, what). There are three major areas of uncertainty: whether cognitive science includes the study of the cognition (or intelligence) of man-made computers,[7] whether it includes the study of the cognition (or intelligence) of nonhuman animals, and whether it includes the study of human mental phenomena other than cognition (such as the emotions).[8] I will not have anything to say about any of these areas of controversy.

The second respect in which ANTCOG is central is this: Uncontroversially, the subject matter of cognitive science is human cognition or intelligence. This subject matter, however, has many different aspects and dimensions and hence can be studied from many different points of view. Cognitive scientists want to know how cognition typically works in normal adults, how it varies across individuals, how it varies across different populations, how it varies across cultures, how it develops, how it goes wrong in neurologically impaired patients, and how it is realized in the brain. (See figure ii.) ANTCOG plays a central role within this research structure. It is standardly used as a *reference point* by each of the other approaches to cognition. Much of the study of development is conceptualized as the study of *development toward* the adult normal state. Individual and group differences (within the normal range) are often explored as *differences from* the typical. Cognitive deficits are usually analyzed as *deviations from* the norm. And, finally, the study of neural realization, to a large extent, focuses on the *realization of* typical, normal adult structures

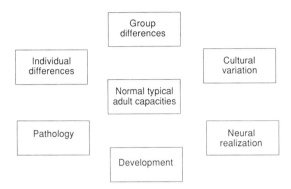

Figure ii
The current research structure of cognitive science.

and processes. Of course, by calling ANTCOG the "central" subsidiary research framework of cognitive science I do not mean to suggest that it is more important or more interesting than any of the others.[9]

Although a complete characterization of the research structure of cognitive science is clearly preferable to a partial one, the partial characterization I shall provide should suffice for my purpose, which is to respond to those who doubt the existence of a common framework of assumptions in cognitive science. One reason for this is that ANTCOG is itself a transdisciplinary program of research. Thus, to demonstrate the existence of ANTCOG is to demonstrate the existence of *a* (if not *the*) common research framework. In addition, because of its centrality, once ANTCOG is articulated, it is relatively easy to see (at least roughly) how the rest of the research structure might be generated.

Precisely formulated, then, the project of this book is to provide a characterization of the subsidiary research framework of cognitive science that concerns adult, normal, typical cognition. What does such a characterization involve? Clearly, if I am to make my case that cognitive scientists of all disciplinary stripes have something important in common, more than mere articulation of the research framework's commitments is needed. Thus, I take on two further tasks. First, I attempt to justify the choice of commitments selected to be part of the characterization. Second, I attempt to clarify the meaning or significance of the included assumptions. The first task is necessary because not everyone agrees on what the fundamental commitments of cognitive science are. The second is necessary because it turns out that, even where there is near-unanimous agreement that some particular assumption constitutes a commitment of the field, it is not always clear what that commitment comes to.

Current disputes about the commitments of cognitive science use arguments of two sorts: those designed to show that cognitive science is (or is not) currently committed to some foundational assumption and those designed to show that cognitive science ought (or ought not), on rational grounds, to be so committed. In developing my characterization, I was faced with the problem of how to handle this dual mode of argumentation. Four responses were possible: fudge the distinction, ignore normative considerations, consider both descriptive and normative arguments but opt for one or the other in cases of conflict, or consider both but reflect differences in cases of conflict. Since this book was written with an interest in furthering the enterprise of cognitive science, the fourth seemed the option of choice. On the one hand, if cognitive science is (is not) currently committed to an assumption that is not (is) defensible on normative grounds, surely this fact should be reflected. On the other hand, from an evidential point of view, the distinction should be preserved. Therefore, in dealing with each proposed assumption, I considered both descriptive and normative arguments relevant to its acceptance. And in presenting the results of my assessment, I note whether acceptance of a proposed assumption is based primarily on descriptive or on normative considerations.

The work of presenting, clarifying, and justifying my research-framework characterization (in the sense of justifying the inclusion of an assumption within the research framework, not in the sense of justifying the assumption itself) takes place in chapters 2–9. In addition to developing the notion of a research framework, chapter 1 takes on two further preliminary tasks. It describes what I take to be a paradigmatic example of research in cognitive science: Stephen Kosslyn's work on mental imagery. It also provides an overview of my proposal, so as to head off the problem of losing sight of the main points in the thicket of detailed discussion and argumentation. Chapter 2 begins the process of instantiating the research-framework schema developed in section 1.1 by considering what the domain and the basic questions of cognitive science are.

The two major substantive assumptions—that the cognitive mind is a computational device and that it is a representational one—are discussed in chapters 3–8. Although there is near-unanimous agreement that these are the two fundamental assumptions of cognitive science, it turns out on close inspection that it is not so clear what is being assumed. The problem is not, on my view, that most cognitive scientists are unclear about something that is inherently clear. The problem is, rather, that the relevant concepts themselves are (for the present, at least) quite open-ended and vague. I have two different responses to this problem, one for each of the two assumptions. Since there is currently no definitive theory of what a computer is, and I am certainly in no position to supply one, I try to do the next best thing and say something about how cognitive scientists conceive of the computer at the present moment in the history of cognitive science. Chapter 3 tackles this task at both a general and a specific level. On the one hand, I attempt to characterize cognitive science's concept of a computer in general. On the other, I describe two kinds of computational devices—so-called conventional machines and connectionist machines—that are now influential in cognitive science research.

My approach to the lack of clarity of the notion of mental representation is somewhat different. It seems reasonable to suppose that we will gain a more systematic picture of what cognitive scientists think about mental representation if we consider it against the background of a theory of representation in general. But since cognitive scientists do not share (at least, explicitly) any common view of representation in general, I attempt to supply one. In chapter 4 I sketch Charles Sanders Peirce's views on the subject. The central point that emerges from my consideration of Peirce's theory is that a representation of any sort has four essential aspects: the nonsemantic entity to which representational properties are attributed (the "representation bearer"), what the representation represents (the "representational object" or "content"), what determines the representational object of the representation (the "ground"), and what gives the representation significance for whoever or whatever considers it meaningful (the "interpretant").

In chapters 5–8 I attempt to sort out what assumptions cognitive science makes about how these four aspects are manifested in mental representation. In general, my position is that working out a detailed theory of the representation bearer, the content, the ground, and the interpretant of our mental representations is a task for future cognitive science research. However, cognitive science does currently impose certain constraints on that theorizing. In chapter 5 I discuss the nature of these constraints with respect to the representation bearer and the content of our mental representations, in chapters 6 and 7 I take up the question of constraints on the ground, and in chapter 8 I discuss cognitive science's view of the interpretant.

In chapter 9, I tie up some loose ends. I spell out what I call the *explanatory strategy* of cognitive science—namely, how the substantive assumptions are brought to bear to answer the basic questions of the field. And I discuss a number of methodological assumptions, including three somewhat controversial assumptions about the role of neuroscience in cognitive science. In the epilogue I offer my own list of foundational challenges that cognitive science must meet if it is to remain viable.

I have tried to make this book intelligible to anyone interested in the foundations of cognitive science, including philosophers and nonphilosophers. That means, in particular, that I have tried not to presuppose knowledge of the background literature. However, since many of the issues are complex, subtle, and fairly abstract, I have found it necessary to introduce an occasional technical term or acronym. To aid the reader in keeping the meaning of these terms and acronyms in mind, I have provided a glossary.

Suggestions on How to Read and Teach This Book

There is a shorter (although by no means short) way and a longer way to read this book, depending on how much philosophical dispute the reader has an appetite for. The shorter way focuses on the portions of the book in which I lay out and clarify my proposal concerning the research framework of cognitive science. The longer way also includes the portions in which I present and evaluate descriptive and normative arguments for and against assumptions that are, ultimately, either not included in my characterization or considered controversial.

To take the shorter way, read chapter 1, the first few pages of section 2.1, section 2.2, the first page of section 2.3, section 2.4, chapter 3, chapter 4, the first half of section 5.2, section 5.3, chapter 6, section 7.1, sections 8.1 and 8.2, section 8.4, chapter 9, and the epilogue.

The book can also be used as the basis for a graduate course (or perhaps even an upper-level undergraduate course) on the foundations of cognitive science. Many sections of the book deal fairly exclusively with one particularly important journal article or book chapter in the literature. A natural way to structure a syllabus is to assign that primary material in conjunction with the corresponding section of this book. A list of suggested supplemental readings follows the references, at the back of the book.

1 Some Preliminaries

The thesis of this book is that a transdisciplinary *framework of shared commitments* (henceforth FSC) for cognitive science can be reconstructed that is substantially in accord with what cognitive scientists believe and with how they conduct their research. Most of the book will be devoted to articulating and discussing this framework in detail. However, before we begin to consider the ins and outs of cognitive science, a bit of preparatory work is in order. First, we must ascend to the metatheoretic level and think about what sort of FSC can appropriately be attributed to cognitive science. Second, a fairly detailed description of an example of cognitive science research will help keep the subsequent discussion from getting too abstract (always a danger for a philosopher). And, third, an overview of the characterization to be presented will, I hope, keep the reader from losing sight of the main points while reading the many pages of detailed discussion and argumentation.

1.1 Research Frameworks

In attributing a framework of shared commitments to cognitive science (or, more precisely, to the cognitive science community), I am buying into what I shall call a roughly Kuhnian picture of science. This picture came to the attention of philosophers of science primarily through the work of Thomas Kuhn. However, the version I have in mind does not accept all the details Kuhn lays out in *The Structure of Scientific Revolutions* (1970a). Rather, it adopts the general outlines of Kuhn's story while leaving a number of crucial details open. The picture is this:

(1) Scientific activities and processes are typically carried out by scientific communities.

(2) Such activities and processes are of two distinct kinds*:

(a) those that take place *within* a framework of assumptions shared by the community

(b) those that take place *outside* of this framework and concern themselves with whether the community should remain committed to the prevailing FSC or whether an alternative FSC should be adopted.

---

*Kuhn calls (2a) "normal science" and (2b) "scientific revolution," but since I am trying to abstract away from his specific conceptions of these two kinds of scientific activities I have relabeled them in a neutral way. I will call activities of type (2a) "FSC-guided science" and activities of type (2b) "FSC-choosing science."

(3) Precisely what it means for FSC-guided science to take place "within" an FSC is not clear. However, as our relabeling implies, in some sense, an FSC "guides" or constrains the FSC-guided science that takes place within it; and the coherence of a body of FSC-guided science can be at least partly accounted for by appeal to the associated FSC.

(4) FSC-choosing science happens infrequently. This is largely because FSCs are not rejected easily. In particular, their adherents often exhibit great tenacity in the face of apparently falsifying evidence.

The canonical description (or "reconstruction") of science has been one of the ongoing projects of the philosophy of science since its inception. In aid of such description, philosophers of science have proposed a host of units of analysis, including "theories," "paradigms," "exemplars," "disciplinary matrices," "explanatory ideals," "research programmes," "fields," and "research traditions."[1] For lack of a better term, let me call these notions *PS units of analysis* ('PS' standing for 'philosophy of science'). Although such notions can be viewed simply as descriptive devices employed by theoreticians of science, they can also be assigned a deeper psychological or sociological meaning. In particular, those who adopt a roughly Kuhnian picture of science can view the various PS units of analysis as proposals concerning the *form* taken by the FSCs of all or some scientific communities.

These considerations provide a number of working assumptions for my project. In particular, I will be assuming that there is such a thing as a community of cognitive science, that this community shares a framework of commitments, and that those commitments function as a framework for research and thus contribute to the coherence of the scientific activities that fall under the label 'cognitive science'.

These working assumptions raise a number of crucial preliminary questions:

• What sort of framework of shared commitments can most suitably be attributed to the cognitive science community?

• In particular, are any of the existing PS units of analysis appropriate ?

• How is the suitability of a proposed PS unit of analysis to be assessed?

Let me take the last question first. For a PS unit of analysis to be suitable for describing the framework of shared commitments of cognitive science, it must satisfy the following five desiderata.

(D1)   The unit of analysis itself and its accompanying theory of science must be free of internal difficulties such as excessive vagueness and inconsistency.   (the "soundness desideratum")

Proposed units of analysis typically carry with them a minitheory of how FSCs of the proposed type function in science. Both the units of analysis themselves and these minitheories need to be evaluated on *internal* grounds. That is, one needs to ask whether the concepts being utilized are defined clearly enough and whether the claims that make up the minitheories are internally consistent, make sense, and so forth.

(D2)   The unit of analysis must be such that it can be adopted by an *immature* scientific community.   (the "immaturity desideratum")

What all cognitive scientists share over the course of time is a commitment to something like an *approach* to the study of mind rather than to some specific set of theories, explanations, or laws. It is not that the latter do not exist—surely they do. The point is, rather, that commitment or loyalty to such theories, explanations, or laws varies from research laboratory to research laboratory and from year to year (even from month to month). I take it that this feature of cognitive science—that it is still in search of a set of more permanent theoretical commitments—is what makes it an immature rather than a mature science. While a science is still immature, the theories that it generates are still tentative. They are on probation, so to speak, and they may become outmoded and be replaced by a new set of theories in the very near future. Yet when this happens the science does not change in any essential way. We do not stop doing cognitive science, for example, just because we decide that the specific theories of memory or language production that we accepted yesterday are wrong.

(D3)   The unit of analysis must fit the specific kinds of explanations and theories typically found in cognitive science.   (the "applicability desideratum")

Neither the soundness desideratum nor the immaturity desideratum has much to do with cognitive science *per se*. Occasionally, however, congruence with more specific features of the field under study becomes relevant to a judgment of suitability.

(D4) A suitable unit of analysis must be such that a scientific
      community's commitment to a framework of shared commitments
      of the proposed kind contributes in some significant way to the
      coherence of research associated with the FSC in question. (the
      "coherence desideratum")

Despite its richness and diversity, research in cognitive science exhibits
considerable coherence and like-mindedness, on my view. That is, there is
something importantly similar about how researchers in different subdisciplines of cognitive science and those in different subsidiary research programs of cognitive science conduct their research: how they ask and answer questions about cognition. The reason for this, I suggest, is that
cognitive scientists, *qua* cognitive scientists, share a framework of commitments that, in some sense, gives rise to these similarities. Note, however,
that in order for me to make this point the FSC I attribute to the cognitive
science community must be one that can, in principle, contribute to the
coherence of research.

(D5) A suitable unit of analysis must identify those properties of an
      FSC that are normatively relevant for assessing the adequacy of
      frameworks of the type in question. (the "assessment
      desideratum")

One motivation for undertaking this project is to develop a characterization of cognitive science that will be useful for assessing recent challenges and critiques. Usefulness for this purpose requires two things: that
the characterization bring out those features of cognitive science that are
addressed in the various challenges and critiques and that the unit of
analysis used for the characterization can be supplemented with norms of
the sort being appealed to in the challenges and critiques. Desideratum 5
ensures that both of these requirements will be fulfilled.

An example will make the point clearer. In note 2 to the introduction I
mentioned P. S. Churchland's (1980a,b; 1986) criticism of a certain conception of cognitive psychology on the grounds that cognitive psychology (on
this conception) is committed to sententialism and to commonsense foundationalism. The reason this attribution counts as an objection to cognitive psychology for Churchland is that she is implicitly invoking something
like the following norm: A framework of shared commitments is adequate
only if there is no reason to seriously doubt the truth of any of its "founda-

tional" assumptions. Since she takes it that cognitive psychology (on the conception in question) is committed to sententialism and to common-sense foundationalism and that both of these doctrines are open to seriously doubt, she concludes that cognitive psychology is inadequate. The point of the assessment desideratum is to suggest that if our characterization of cognitive science is to be useful in evaluating critiques such as Churchland's, it must be couched in terms of a unit of analysis that can be meaningfully conjoined with norms of the sort appealed to by critics of the field.

Now that I have figured out a way of determining the suitability of a proposed unit of analysis, the next task is clearly to use these desiderata for the purpose of assessing existing views. In the early stages of writing this book, I did just that. In particular, I surveyed proposals by the logical positivists, by Kuhn, by Toulmin, by Lakatos, and by Laudan. I concluded that none of the proposed units of analysis, taken "as is," was suitable for developing a characterization of cognitive science. I will not present the detailed arguments for this conclusion here, since that would take us too far afield, but let me at least note the basic reasons for my negative conclusion.*

The views of Kuhn, Lakatos, and the logical positivists can be ruled out fairly quickly as not applying to immature science. In addition, both Toulmin's and Kuhn's proposals suffer from some soundness problems. Laudan's conception of a "research tradition" is relatively free of internal difficulties and can, in principle, be applied to an immature science; however, without fairly substantial modification, it faces other difficulties with respect to applicability, coherence, and assessment.

The conclusion I drew from my survey of existing proposals was that none of the existing PS units of analysis would do for my purposes. A new, more suitable alternative was clearly required. It turned out, however, that this "new" alternative didn't have to be radically new. Kuhn, with his conception of a disciplinary matrix, and Laudan, with his notion of a research tradition, were definitely on the right track. Building on these existing units of analysis, I developed the notion of a *research framework* and the minitheory of research frameworks described in the remainder of this section.

---

*The views of Kuhn, Laudan, and the logical positivists are discussed in the appendix.

A research framework consists of four sets of elements: a set of assumptions that provide a pretheoretic specification of the domain under study (prefixed with the letter **D**); a set of basic empirical research questions, formulated pretheoretically (prefixed with **Q**); a set of substantive assumptions that embody the approach being taken in answering the basic questions and that constrain possible answers to those questions (prefixed with **SA**); and a set of methodological assumptions (prefixed with **MA**). These four sets of elements make up a quadruple that can be abbreviated thus: $\langle D, Q, SA, MA \rangle$. I shall refer to these assumptions collectively as the "foundational assumptions" of a research framework.

Research frameworks can evolve. To understand in what sense they can evolve, we must distinguish between a research framework *per se* and *versions* of a research framework. Strictly speaking, quadruples of the sort I have just described are versions of research frameworks (although in the interest of smoother prose I will often ignore this distinction). The foundational assumptions of any such version of a research framework are classifiable into *unrevisable* and *revisable* assumptions. Two versions will count as versions of the same research framework if they differ only with respect to their revisable assumptions. The research framework itself can then be thought of as a schema for a set of versions with the unrevisable elements specified and the revisable elements either left blank or specified in terms of a range of options. See figure 1.1 for an abstract example. Given the distinction between a research framework and its versions, we can then say

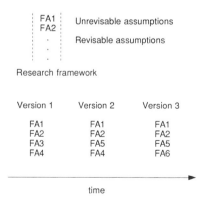

Figure 1.1
How a research framework can evolve.

that a particular research framework is evolving if there exists a historical series of research-framework instantiations (a research framework at a time) such that each instantiation in the series is a version of that research framework and such that the foundational changes from one instantiation to the next are always relatively small.

Let us now take a closer look at each of the elements of a version of a research framework.

The *pretheoretic specification of the domain* includes three different kinds of assumptions:

• An *identification* assumption, claiming that the domain of the research framework consists of phenomena of such-and-such a kind. Implicit in this assumption is the existential claim that such-and-such phenomena are either actual or nomologically possible.

• *Property* assumptions, claiming that the phenomena picked out by the identification assumption have such-and-such properties. Property assumptions may be fairly minimal, since we may not "know" very much about the domain phenomena before we do research.

• A *grouping* assumption, claiming that the phenomena picked out by the identification assumption make up a theoretically coherent set of phenomena, or a *system*. That is to say, with sufficient research it will be possible to arrive at a set of answers to the basic empirical questions of the research framework (about these phenomena) that constitute a unified theory and that are empirically and conceptually acceptable.

The function of these domain-specifying assumptions is to "fix" a particular *domain of inquiry*.[2] Such assumptions are "low-level" in the sense that the phenomena they posit can be assumed to exist relatively independently of any specific conceptual or theoretical apparatus that one adopts in order to answer questions about such phenomena. Thus, for example, commitment to the existence of the human cognitive capacities leaves open the question of precisely how such capacities are to be studied. It is important to preserve the "low-level" nature of domain-specifying assumptions so that it makes sense to talk about two research frameworks' being in the business of investigating the same phenomena (roughly speaking) and yet approaching those phenomena in different ways. It is also important to note that the domain-specifying assumptions (especially the property assumptions) are subject to revision as scientists attempt to answer the basic questions of the research framework. As originally specified, these assumptions constitute the starting point of inquiry. But precisely what is included in the domain and what low-level properties domain phenomena are assumed to have may change as investigation proceeds.

The second component of a research framework is a set of *basic empirical questions* that research in the field is designed to answer. These are questions about the domain that, in a sense, give the research associated with the framework its direction. These basic questions should be distinguished from the *derivative empirical questions*, which arise once we add in the substantive assumptions or once data have been collected and specific hypotheses have been formulated.

Laudan (1977, p. 15) suggests that the empirical questions of a research tradition are about phenomena that "strike us as odd, or otherwise in need of explanation." More specifically, his view is that any given research tradition operates against the background of a certain context of inquiry that, among other things, tells us "what to expect and what seems peculiar or 'problematic' or questionable." The putative empirical phenomena that constitute the focus of the empirical questions of the research tradition will be limited to those that violate these expectations and, hence, count as peculiar or problematic in the light of these expectations.

This requirement strikes me as all wrong. In the first place, many of the phenomena explained by classical examples of scientific theorizing were not regarded as odd or unexpected by the scientists proposing the theories. For example, Galileo explained free fall and Newton explained the motions of the planets and the swing of the pendulum, but I seriously doubt that these phenomena were regarded as odd or peculiar at the time.

More to the point, Laudan's oddness requirement is not consistent with the sorts of empirical phenomena on which cognitive science has focused attention. As we shall see in the next chapter, cognitive science is primarily interested in explaining the human cognitive capacities—perception, memory, language, reasoning, and so on. But it is certainly not correct to say that cognitive scientists regard such capacities as odd or peculiar in the light of some background theory. For one thing, there is at present no accepted *scientific* background theory at all. Furthermore, the folk psychological theory we possess actually countenances these capacities in a straightforward way. This is not to say that cognitive scientists don't regard the cognitive capacities as mysterious or in need of explanation. They certainly do. But to say that they regard the cognitive capacities as mysterious and in need of explanation is not the same as to say that they regard them as odd or peculiar.

There are two further commonly advocated restrictions on the nature of the empirical phenomena studied by science that, on my view, do not apply to the basic empirical questions of a research framework.

It is often held that scientific explanation is a species of explanation-why (i.e., explaining why an event occurred, or why such-and-such is the case). Since explanations sought within a particular research framework are closely connected to the questions posed within it, the claim that all scientific explanation is why-explanation is equivalent, in my terms, to the claim that all the basic questions of a research framework are why-questions. I reject such a restriction for the simple reason that with it the notion of a research framework would not apply to cognitive science. As we will see in chapter 2, the basic questions of cognitive science are not why-questions at all; rather, they consist in two what-questions and two how-questions. Furthermore, cognitive science does not represent an isolated case, on my view. For although it is clear that why-explanations play a very important part in science in general, philosophers of science have been mistaken in thinking that this is the only form that scientific explanation can take.

The second restriction I want to deny is that the basic questions of a research framework are all questions about data, in some narrow sense. By "data in some narrow sense" I mean pieces of information gathered deliberately, either by careful observation or by controlled experimentation, for the purpose of advancing scientific understanding of some set of phenomena. There is no question that during the course of scientific research scientists want to answer questions—and here the questions usually are why-questions—about the data they have gathered. But it is important to realize that this aim is a secondary one. Their primary aim is to understand and explain (and, hence, answer) questions about some set of phenomena whose existence is known (or, at least, believed) before the research process associated with the framework has even begun.

Shapere (1977, pp. 531–534) offers us a useful specification of the types of questions ("problems," in his terminology) that scientists typically ask about domains. He distinguishes between *domain questions* ("domain problems") and *theoretical questions* ("theoretical problems"). Domain questions concern the extent and the precise nature of the domain, whereas theoretical questions call for a "deeper" account. For example, we may want to explain properties of the phenomena in the domain in terms of properties of their parts (a "compositional" problem); in contrast, we may be more interested in explaining these properties in terms of the development of the objects (an "evolutionary" problem).[3] We shall find that the basic questions of cognitive science fall nicely into Shapere's scheme, for there will be both domain questions and theoretical questions; furthermore, the latter will turn out to be primarily of the compositional kind.

Giere (1979, 1988) has argued that scientific theories consist of two components: "theoretical models," which are idealized systems of a sort, and "theoretical hypotheses," which tell us that some *real* system (or set of real systems) is similar (in certain respects and to a certain degree) to the idealized system in question. For example, the following is a theoretical hypothesis, according to Giere: that the solar system is a classical particle system (i.e., a system of objects satisfying Newton's three laws of motion and the law of universal gravitation). The real system here is the solar system; the theoretical model is a Newtonian classical particle system.

The substantive assumptions of a research framework have a similar structure. That is, like Giere's scientific theories, each consists of two components, one analogous to a theoretical model and one analogous to a theoretical hypothesis. However. there are two important differences between such substantive assumptions and Giere's scientific theories. Giere (1988) treats a theoretical model as *identical to* an idealized system of a sort.[4] In contrast, the substantive assumptions of a research framework are propositions, some of which define or describe such an idealized system.[5] Furthermore, the substantive assumptions do not specify the relevant idealized system in any detail; rather, they simply outline, often with very broad strokes, a *kind* of system—specifically, the kind relevant to the research project at hand.

To be more specific, the substantive assumptions fall into two groups:

• *Linking* assumptions, which claim that the domain picked out by the domain-specifying assumptions of the research framework constitutes, or is substantially like, a system of type X. These are like Giere's theoretical hypotheses.

• *System* assumptions, which claim that systems of type X have such-and-such properties. Such assumptions specify something like a schema for one of Giere's theoretical models.

The role of such substantive assumptions is this: The domain-specifying assumptions of a research framework identify a certain class of phenomena as the phenomena of interest and as constituting a system or a theoretically coherent set of phenomena. The basic empirical questions specify what scientists committed to the research framework want to know about these phenomena. The substantive assumptions indicate how these questions are to be answered. In particular, they tell us what kind of system the domain phenomena are thought to be, and hence they constrain the sorts of answers to the basic empirical questions that are relevant.

Both the Kuhnian paradigm and the Laudanian research tradition contain a set of assumptions analogous to the substantive assumptions of a research framework, and in both cases these assumptions are described as "metaphysical" (Kuhn 1970a, p. 41; Laudan 1977, p. 79). I believe that this label is very misleading. Walsh (1967, p. 301) claims that there are three main features of metaphysics as traditionally practiced: First, metaphysics deals with "the real nature of things"; it is preoccupied with questions of ontology. Second, it is commonly presented as the most comprehensive of inquiries because of its extreme generality and its concern for the world as a whole. Third, metaphysical propositions have a special epistemic status; they are generally regarded as certain or "exempt from intellectual challenge" by virtue of being derived from reason alone.[6]

Why Kuhn and Laudan call the substantive assumptions of their respective units of analysis "metaphysical" is not clear; however, my sense is that it is the third traditional feature of metaphysics that is most relevant to the attribution. In any case, I would like to contend that of the three features only the first applies—or at least that it is the only one that applies to the substantive assumptions of a research framework. In classifying a real system as a system of a certain sort, the substantive assumptions are claiming that systems of that sort exist. The solar system can be a classical particle system only if there are systems of objects satisfying Newton's laws. In particular, neither the property of comprehensiveness nor the property of special epistemic status applies. Typically, a scientific research framework is associated with a restricted domain (such as the human cognitive capacities) rather than with the entire universe.[7] Furthermore, insofar as empirical considerations such as success or failure and progressiveness or nonprogressiveness are relevant to the acceptance or rejection of an FSC, and hence to the assumptions it includes, such assumptions are not certain, nor immune from revision, and not solely the products of reason. I conclude that the substantive assumptions of a research framework ought not be considered "metaphysical."[8,9]

Thus far I have discussed three components of a research framework: the domain-specifying assumptions, the basic empirical questions, and the substantive assumptions. The fourth and final component is a set of methodological assumptions concerning the appropriate ways to go about studying the domain in question. These methodological assumptions will be of two kinds: those that are shared with much or all of the scientific community (that is, the sort of commitments Kuhn [1970a, p. 184] refers to as "values" in discussing the elements of a disciplinary matrix) and those that are specific to the research framework in question. Both sorts of assumptions must, of course, be suitably fundamental in the sense that abandoning the assumption would entail abandoning either the research framework as a whole or the operative version of that framework, depending on whether the assumption was unrevisable or revisable. Thus, there may be many particular research methods or techniques (such as the use of reaction-time data in cognitive psychology) employed in a field at a given moment in time, commitment to which would not count as a methodological assumption of the research framework in the sense currently being defined.[10]

We now have some idea what research frameworks are. How do they function? Following Laudan (1977), it is useful to think of the research activity that takes place within a research framework as, essentially, problem-solving activity. This idea can be made more precise as follows: A problem, in general, is a task whose solution is both subject to certain fairly well-defined constraints and not obvious. Intellectual problems, including many scientific problems, are question-answering tasks. That is, the task a scientist sets for himself or herself is to answer certain sorts of questions about the world, or at least about what he or she takes the world to be. The fundamental problem associated with any research framework is to answer each of the basic empirical questions of that framework in such a way that the following constraints are satisfied:

• Each answer is scientifically acceptable in light of the scientific standards set down by the shared and specific methodological assumptions of the research framework.

• Each answer is consistent with the substantive assumptions of the research framework.

• Each answer to a theoretical question makes significant reference to the entities and processes posited by the substantive assumptions of the research framework.

The fundamental problem of a research framework is obviously a problem consisting of many "parts." We can treat each of these "parts" as a problem in its own right. Thus, corresponding to each of the basic empirical questions of the research framework there will be a smaller problem— namely, the problem of answering that question in a way that satisfies the above constraints. How to individuate problems at a finer grain than this is not at all obvious and may well depend on the specific character of the research framework involved. Undoubtedly, however, there will be a complex interplay of hypothesis formation and hypothesis testing that will give rise to numerous derivative problems.

Stephen Kosslyn's work on mental imagery (to be described in the next section) provides a nice illustration of such derivative problems. Kosslyn began his research with the working hypothesis that visual mental images are like computer-generated displays on a cathode-ray tube. This working hypothesis then gave rise to a rough picture of what representational and computational resources are involved in imaging. In particular. Kosslyn posited two kinds of representations—"surface" representations and "deep" representations—plus numerous distinct computational processes. This picture, in turn, gave rise to a host of more specific questions: What is the format of the functional surface representation underlying the experience of "having an image"? Is it quasipictorial, or propositional? What are the properties of the medium in which surface representations occur? And so on. Kosslyn performed various experiments to try to answer these more specific questions, and the findings generated by these experiments once again gave rise to a new set of questions. For example, he found that when subjects scanned a memorized and imaged map, scanning time was a linear function of the distance scanned. This result clearly raised the question of why this was so.

It is natural to think of a research program, in the nontechnical sense, as seeking explanations for the phenomena in its domain. This commonplace claim about research programs can easily be accommodated by my technical conception of a research framework if we adopt what some philosophers have called the "erotetic" approach to explanation (Bromberger 1965; Achinstein 1971, 1983)—that is, the view that explanations are basically answers to questions.[11] For given this approach, the fundamental explananda of a research framework are simply its basic questions.

On the erotetic view of explanation, the "explanandum" of an explanation consists of the question itself; the "explanans" consists of the answer. Here questions are conceived of as nonlinguistic entitles bearing the same sort of relation to interrogative sentences (linguistic items) that propositions are taken to bear to declarative sentences. Although we generally pick out questions by interrogatives, it is important to note that interrogatives, like declarative sentences, can be both vague and ambiguous. A more precise way of individuating a question is in terms of its *possible answer set*. Thus, the fact that the interrogative "How does John play the violin?" can be answered in at least two distinct *types* of ways (by saying something about the quality of his playing and by telling a complicated causal story about the events inside John that issue in his playing) suggests that the same interrogative ambiguously expresses two distinct questions.

In talking about explanations, it is useful to draw a distinction between a possible explanation and the correct or actual one. This distinction is mirrored in a straightforward way in the domain of questions and answers. A possible explanation relative to some explanandum is simply a possible answer to the question that constitutes the explanandum. The correct or actual explanation is, then, an answer that is both possible and true. It is also useful to talk about *kinds* of explanations. One can do this, on the erotetic view, by talking about kinds of questions.

Precisely what distinguishes ordinary explanation from scientific explanation is not clear. It is certainly not that all scientific explanation is why-explanation, as so many authors have maintained. As we shall see in section 2.4, none of the basic questions asked by cognitive science are why-questions. (Two are what-questions, and two are how-questions.) One possibility is that scientific explanation always takes place within an FSC and is, hence, more constrained that ordinary explanation. According to Kuhn's general picture of science, scientific research always proceeds within an FSC which, in some sense, guides its development. This means, among other things, that questions posed by this research are asked within this guiding framework and answers to these questions are sought within it. Insofar as a question posed within such a framework is posed in a language, it will have associated with it a set of linguistically possible answers. However, it will also have associated with it a smaller possible answer set: the set of answers that are not only linguistically possible but also in keeping with the set of assumptions that constitutes the FSC. For example, if the question "How does John play the violin?" were asked within the research framework of neurophysiology, we would clearly be looking for an answer of the second type mentioned above (a causal story about the internal events that issue in John's playing). But we would also be looking for an answer framed in neurophysiological term—that is, one that made reference to the kinds of entities and properties posited by the framework of assumptions constitutive of present-day neurophysiology.

It is clearly important to distinguish any given research framework, in the sense of a set of assumptions, from the research activity that takes place within it. This research activity has many dimensions and manifests itself in many ways. For our purposes, the most interesting manifestations involve intellectual commitments and "products" that stem from the scientific community's commitment to the research framework. At any moment in time, these intellectual commitments and products include

a set of questions directly motivating specific research investigations,

a research methodology currently being employed (including techniques, procedures, methods of testing, and so forth),

a set of proposed hypotheses, models, and theories currently under serious consideration, and

a set of data or empirical "findings" generated by the research methodology.

One of the interesting facts about an immature science is that, even though it is not associated with a body of accepted theory, its research activity nevertheless exhibits considerable coherence. One of the questions driving my choice of a suitable unit of analysis for cognitive science is: Why is this so? The minitheory of research frameworks proposed here allows us to answer this question quite nicely.

Loosely, what makes the research activity associated with a research framework coherent is that it is all produced under the "guidance" of that research framework. More precisely, what happens is this: Research frameworks function as FSCs for scientific communities. Commitment to a given research framework means that the community takes it as a goal to solve the fundamental problem posed by the research framework—that is, to

answer the basic questions of the research framework subject to the constraints imposed by the methodological and substantive assumptions of
the framework. This goal is then acted upon, and the result is a body of
research activity that "hangs together" in important ways.

More specifically, the coherence of the research activity generated within
a particular research framework (call it "RF") amounts to the following:

• Any research question posed by the community committed to RF is
typically either one of the basic questions of RF or a question that is
derived from one of them once the research process gets underway.

• The research methodology currently being employed by the scientific
community committed to RF will be a methodology that is consistent with
the methodological assumptions of RF and is deemed relevant for finding
or adjudicating answers to the basic questions of RF.

• Any hypothesis, model, or theory ("hypothesis" for short) put forward by
the community committed to RF is typically either a possible answer to
one of the basic or one of the derived questions or a claim intended as a
constraint on such a possible answer. In addition, all hypotheses will be
consistent with the substantive and methodological assumptions of RF,
and any hypothesis that constitutes a possible answer to one of the basic
theoretical questions of RF (or one of the questions derived from a basic
theoretical question) will make reference to the entities and processes
posited by the substantive assumptions of RF.

• The research findings arrived at by the community committed to RF will
typically be either partial answers to one of the basic domain questions (or
one of the questions derived from a basic domain question) or evidence
relevant to deciding the adequacy of some proposed hypothesis of the sort
described in the preceding point.

The principal norm for the assessment of a research framework is
whether it is rational to pursue. Laudan (1977) makes the rational pursuability of an FSC largely a matter of its empirical track record (as measured by its changing problem-solving effectiveness). (See section A.3 of the
appendix for a more detailed discussion of Laudan's view.) I believe the
issue is much more complicated than that. This is not the place to develop
a detailed theory of assessment for research frameworks. I would, however,
like to make a few suggestions as to how Laudan's track-record picture
might be enhanced.

Ideally, we would like to identify the various considerations that are either necessary or sufficient for it to be rational for a scientific community to pursue a particular research framework, RF.

What these considerations are, how they are to be weighted, and how they interact may depend on the circumstances under which the decision is being made. Research frameworks are not pursued in a vacuum. Rather, they are adopted by particular scientific communities at particular moments in time under particular historical and sociological circumstances. In deciding whether it is rational for a scientific community to pursue RF, it is clearly important to look at questions like the following: What is the scientific goal of the community? Is the scientific community adopting RF for the first time, or is it trying to decide whether to continue to pursue it? Is there some overriding reason not to pursue any research framework at all at the time? Are there alternative frameworks available with roughly the same domain as RF?

Furthermore, though the track record of RF is certainly a relevant consideration in deciding its rational pursuability, there are other considerations. Any of the following may be relevant under some circumstances:

• the degree of empirical success of RF—that is, the extent to which the scientific community of RF has succeeded in solving the fundamental problem of RF (in other words, the extent to which it has succeeded in finding answers to the basic questions of RF that satisfy the constraints imposed by RF's methodological and substantive assumptions)

• the rate of progress of RF—that is, the degree of empirical success of RF over time

• the promise of RP—that is, the likelihood that the scientific community of RF will solve the fundamental problem of RF

• the foundational adequacy of RF—in particular, the conceptual soundness of the foundational assumptions, the plausibility of the foundational assumptions in the light of other theories to which we are committed, and the explanatory adequacy of the substantive and methodological assumptions (that is, whether, in principle, the substantive assumptions provide for sufficient conceptual resources and the methodological assumptions provide for a rich enough methodology that the basic questions of RF can be answered).

I take what I have said about research frameworks to constitute a sketch of an FSC theory, analogous to the theories of Kuhn and Laudan, that describes a particular realization of Kuhn's general image of science. In other words, it is a theory of a particular sort of FSC that tells us what that sort of FSC is like, what FSC-guided science amounts to (that is, how the proposed type of FSC contributes to the coherence of research done within it), and what is involved in FSC-choosing science at least to the extent that it is rational (that is, how the proposed type of FSC ought to be evaluated).

Kuhn and Laudan both claim that their particular FSC theories have wide applicability in the history of science. My claims are far more modest. Like the substantive assumptions of a research framework, claims about the applicability of a type of FSC are best thought of as theoretical hypotheses (like those of Giere [1979, 1988]) claiming that some piece of the world is similar to a given theoretical model. In this case, the FSC theory constitutes a "theoretical model" describing a certain sort of scientific system (such as a paradigm-centered system or a research-tradition system) and the theoretical hypothesis claims that certain *real* scientific systems are FSC systems of the type in question. On this view, then, what I have done so far is develop a theory of a research-framework "system" without, as yet, having advanced any theoretical hypothesis about the applicability of that theory.

The theoretical hypothesis I want to advance has several parts.

First, cognitive science is clearly a research-framework system. I can assert this with great confidence since the notion of a research framework was expressly developed with an eye to its applicability to cognitive science and the remainder of this book constitutes an application of the theory to cognitive science.

Second, it is quite probable that immature sciences (or fields, subfields, and areas of specialization) in general are research-framework systems. This second claim is weaker (insofar as it is probabilistic) than the first because I have not tried to apply the notion of a research framework to any other immature science (field, subfield, or area of specialization) besides cognitive science. However, since many of the features of the notion were developed with *characteristic* properties of immature science in mind, it is quite likely that the theory of research frameworks has wider applicability than simply to cognitive science.

Third, the theory of research frameworks may also apply to mature sciences. The conception of a research framework I have developed was devised with immature science, and especially cognitive science, in mind. However, it may have occurred to the reader that there is nothing about this conception that prevents its application to a mature science. And, in view of its origins, this makes perfect sense, for the antecedent notions of a paradigm and a research tradition from which the theory of research frameworks drew its inspiration were both designed to apply to mature science.

But if a mature science as well as an immature science can be fruitfully characterized as a research framework, what distinguishes the one from the other? I believe the fundamental difference is a genetic one. Within any domain, scientific activity always begins with questions raised by our ordinary life experience. But once scientific activity gets underway, it evolves and builds on itself. In particular, work carried on within one research framework can sometimes result in the development of another research framework. For example, hypotheses formulated in terms of the gene in the framework of Mendelian genetics gave rise to questions concerning the biochemical structure of the gene; and these questions, in turn, led to the development of the research framework of molecular genetics. The distinction between an immature and a mature scientific research framework is clearly one of degree. A research framework rooted in our ordinary conception of the world and without any scientific ancestors is clearly immature. A framework that has evolved out of a long line of other scientiful research frameworks is clearly mature. A framework with some scientific lineage but not much will be an unclear case.

This way of drawing the distinction allows us to make sense of a number of other contrastive features often associated with mature and immature sciences[12]:

• A mature scientific community tends to have more confidence than an immature community in how it conceives of its domain of study. Because a mature research framework has evolved out of a previous framework, its domain-specifying assumptions and its basic questions will typically be formulated in terms drawn from the theories adopted to answer the basic questions of the ancestor framework. As a result, the level of confidence in the parsing of nature inherent in these assumptions and questions will tend to be fairly high. In contrast. the domain-specifying assumptions and the basic questions of an immature research framework are typically drawn from our ordinary conception of the world. But since scientists are generally aware of the fact that, in the past, scientific theorizing often induced major conceptual changes in this ordinary conception, the question of whether or not it will be necessary to revise the domain-specifying assumptions as research progresses will loom larger than it does in the case of a mature research framework.[13]

• Research within a mature framework is, typically, more highly constrained than research within an immature framework. This is because a mature research framework inherits many of the empirical findings and theoretical results of its ancestors. In contrast, in an immature science there is no such established backlog. There may be constraints; however, insofar as these constraints are derived from our ordinary conception of the world or constitute "hunches" about the domain, they tend to have the status of working assumptions rather than accepted findings and hypotheses.

• Research within a mature framework is typically more technologically advanced than research within an immature framework. Again this is because the former comes into the world with an inheritance—in this case, an inheritance of methods and equipment. In contrast, an immature framework often needs to invent its technology from scratch.

• A mature scientific community is, typically, more entrenched than an immature scientific community. For example. a mature community can usually boast of more journals, communication links, and sources of funding; a clearer sense of professional identity; and more agreement about the locus of expertise. Again, the root of these differences is the genetic difference between mature and immature research frameworks. Although a mature research framework differs from its ancestor sufficiently to constitute a new framework, it may nevertheless inherit some of the sociological structure associated with the old scientific community. In contrast, an immature scientific community often must develop itself from scratch.

1.2   An Example of Cognitive Science Research

As my example of research in cognitive science. I will use Stephen Kosslyn's work on mental imagery.[14] There are two reasons for this choice. First. Kosslyn's work is often regarded as a paradigmatic example of research in this field (Gardner 1985, pp. 323–339; Stillings et al. 1987, pp. 39–42).

Second, as we will see, the richness and the systematicity of this research nicely illustrate many of the points I will be making in the chapters to come. In this section, I will simply describe the work in its own terms. In section 1.3, where I will be presenting an overview of my characterization of cognitive science, I will occasionally refer back to specific features of Kosslyn's research to illustrate particular aspects of cognitive science's research framework.

The core of Kosslyn's research[15] concerns the normal adult capacity to form and use mental images. This work has three major components: the experimental study of human imaging capacities, a general theory of mental imaging that outlines the representational structures and processes underlying these capacities, and a number of specific, dynamic models of how our imaging capacities are exercised.

The Experimental Study of Human Imaging Capacities

According to Kosslyn (1980) and Kosslyn, Pinker, Smith, and Shwartz (1979), Kosslyn's program of research was conceptualized as a two-phase strategy. In the first phase, guided by the working hypothesis that visual mental images are like displays on a cathode-ray tube generated by a computer program from stored information, experimental data were collected to constrain the class of possible models relevant to human imaging capacities; in the second phase, a detailed theory and a model were proposed, to be tested and elaborated by further experimental work.

During the first phase, the CRT metaphor suggested a number of hypotheses. The first was that two kinds of representations are involved in imaging: quasipictorial "surface images," which occur in a spatial display medium and are subject to the limitations of such a medium, and "deep" representations, which consist of information stored in long-term memory that can be converted into a surface image. A second hypothesis was that there were a number of different kinds of processes involved, including processes that generate the surface display from the deep representations and processes that can interpret the surface display once it is generated.

Another guiding idea of the first phase of research was to use experimental evidence to answer a series of basic questions raised by the CRT metaphor. These included the following:

What is the format of the functional surface representation underlying the experience of "having an image"? Is it quasi-pictorial or propositional?

What are the properties of the medium in which surface representations occur? Does it have a grain? Is it of fixed "size" and "shape"?

What is the nature of the underlying representations in long-term memory from which surface images are formed? In particular, are surface images generated by being simply retrieved, or are they in some sense constructed?

If they are constructed, does the imagery system have the capacity to store information in separate encodings that can later be amalgamated to form a single image in active memory?

If they are constructed, can descriptive information be used in forming images, or are they formed solely on the basis of nondiscursive information?

One of Kosslyn's most famous experiments was carried out in order to address the first of the above five questions. In particular, Kosslyn was interested in whether the surface representation underlying the experience of "having an image" had anything akin to the spatial characteristics that seem to be a feature of phenomenal images.

Kosslyn et al. (1979, pp. 536–537) describe the task of this experiment as follows:

Ss first learned to draw a map of a mythical island that contained seven objects (e.g., a hut, a tree, a rock). These objects were located so that each of the 21 interobject distances was at least 0.5 cm longer than the next shortest. After learning to draw the map, Ss were asked to image it and to focus mentally on a given object when it was named (each object was used as a focus point equally often). Following this. a probe word was presented; half the time this word named an object on the map, and half the time it did not. On hearing the word, S was to look for the object on his image. If it was present, he was to scan to it and push a button upon arriving at it. If it was not found on the imaged map, he was to push another button.

In general, the longer the distance on the imaginary map (depicted here in figure 1.2) subjects were required to "scan," the longer their reaction times. These results are summarized in figure 1.3. From this and a number of other related experiments, Kosslyn et al. (1979, p. 537) concluded that the surface representations underlying our experience of having an image depict metric distance and that this property affects real-time processing of images.

During phase I of his research, Kosslyn conducted a variety of other experiments designed to reveal something about how humans generate

Figure 1.2
The fictional map used in Kosslyn's map-scanning experiment. (From Stephen M. Kosslyn, *Image and Mind*, © 1980 by the President and Fellows of Harvard College. Reprinted by permission of the author and Harvard University Press.)

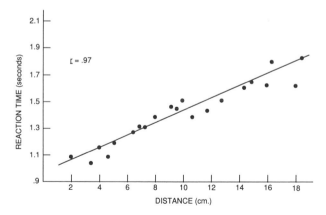

Figure 1.3
The time to scan between all pairs of locations in Kosslyn's map-scanning experiment on an image of the map illustrated in figure 1.2. (From Stephen M. Kosslyn, *Image and Mind*, © 1980 by the President and Fellows of Harvard College. Reprinted by permission of the author and Harvard University Press.)

images. For example, he claims to have found support for the following findings:

• Larger images require more time to form, as do images of more detailed line drawings.

• When subjects are shown parts of animals on separate pages and then asked to mentally "glue" them together, the time to form an image of the composite drawing increases linearly with the number of pages used to present it.

• Subjects are shown 3 × 6 arrays of letters. The arrays are labeled either "three rows of six" or "six columns of three." When subjects are later asked to image the arrays, more time is required for image generation if the array had been described in terms of six columns rather than three rows.

Recall that all the questions and findings mentioned so far were parts of phase I of the research. In phase II, a computational theory and a computer simulation model were developed that both satisfied the experimental constraints laid down in phase I and provided explicit computational accounts for the data collected in phase I. This work took two forms: a general theory of mental imaging and a number of specific, dynamic models for the various capacities that involve the imagery system.

A General Theory of Mental Imaging

The theory posits that a number of representational structures and processes underlie the human ability to image. There are three kinds of representational structures. The first, a short-term memory structure, consists of quasipictorial "surface images" which occur in a spatial display medium and are subject to the limitations of such a medium. The second and third, called "deep" representations, consist of information stored in long-term memory that can be converted into a surface image. Here we find "literal" encodings (which contain information about how the represented object looks) and propositional representations (which contain factual information about the represented object, including such things as how the parts are put together, the sizes of the parts, and the names of the superordinate categories).[16] Figure 1.4 is a schematic representation of the structures posited by the theory.

In addition to these representational structures, the theory posits a number of processes that operate on these representations and specifies

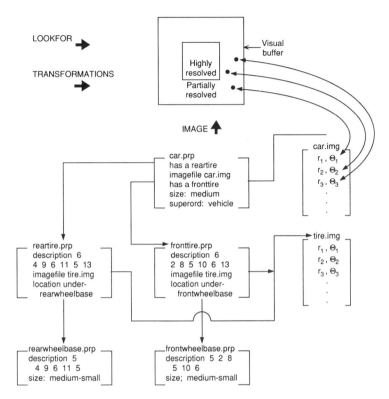

Figure 1.4
A schematic representation of the structures posited by Kosslyn's theory of mental imagery.
The words in capitals indicate major processes and the locus of their action. (From Stephen
M. Kosslyn, *Image and Mind*, © 1980 by the President and Fellows of Harvard College.
Reprinted by permission of the author and Harvard University Press.)

them in terms of well-defined input-output functions. These include processes that generate the surface display from the deep representations as
well as processes that can interpret and transform the surface display
once it is generated. Table 1.1 outlines these processes and their functions.

Specific Dynamic Models of Human Imaging Capacities[17]

The general theory of imaging describes the various representational structures and processes that supposedly underlie the human ability to image.
In addition, because it specifies the input conditions required by each
operation and the results of executing any particular operation, the general

Table 1.1
Theory-relevant processes included in Kosslyn's model of mental imagery. (From S. M. Kosslyn, *Image and Mind*, © 1980 by the President and Fellows of Harvard College, pp. 150–151. Reprinted by permission of the author and Harvard University Press.)

Name	Type[1]	Input[2]	Operation	Output
PICTURE	P	r, θ file [size, location, orientation]	Maps points into surface matrix; mapping function may be adjusted to vary size, location, and/or orientation.	Configuration of points depicting contents of an IMG file (produces new format; if mapping function adjusted also produces new content).
FIND	C	Name of sought part	Looks up description; looks up procedures specified in description; executes procedures on surface matrix.	Passes back Locate/Not Locate; if Locate, passes back Cartesian co-ordinates of part.
PUT	P	Name of to-be-placed part	Looks up name of image file, location relation, and foundation part; looks up description of foundation part and relation; calls FIND to locate foundation part; adjusts mapping function; calls PICTURE.	Part integrated into image (produces new content).
IMAGE	P	Name of to-be-imaged object(s) [size, location, orientation, level of detail]	Locates IMG file; calls PICTURE [if size, location, or orientation specified, adjusts mapping function; if detail required, searches for HASA entries, calls PUT].	Detailed or skeletal image at specified or default size, location, and/or orientation (produces new content with different format, organization).
RESOLUTION	P	Surface image	Computes density of points in image.	A number indicating dot density of image (produces new format).
REGENERATE	A	Surface image	Works over surface matrix, refreshing most-faded parts first until all parts are refreshed.	Image reactivated, with sharpness relations among parts altered (alters content).

LOOKFOR	P	Command to find a named part or property on an image	Calls REGENERATE; looks up description and size of part; calls RESOLUTION; if density not optimal, calls ZOOM or PAN; checks whether image overflows in direction of part, if so calls SCAN; calls FIND; if part not located searches for relevant HASA entries, calls PUT to insert regions, calls FIND.	Found/Not Found response.
SCAN	A	Image, direction of required shift [rate]	Moves all points in surface matrix along vector; fills in new material at leading edge via inverse mapping function.	Image repositioned (alters content).
ZOOM	A	Surface image, target resolution [rate]	Moves all points in surface matrix out from the center; fills in new material via inverse mapping function; calls RESOLUTION; calls PUT to insert new parts as resolution allows.	Scale change in image, higher resolution, and new parts (alters content).
PAN	A	Surface image, target resolution [rate]	Moves all points in surface matrix in from the center.	Scale change in image, lower resolution (alters content).
ROTATE	A	Image, angle, and direction [rate]	Moves all points in bounded region in specified direction around a pivot.	Reorients image (alters content).

1. A indicates alteration transformations, which alter the *initial* data-structure; P indicates production transformations that do not alter the initial data-structure but produce a new one from it; C indicates comparison operations that compare two data-structures or parts thereof.
2. Optional input is indicated in brackets.

theory also, in effect. specifies the ways in which these operations can be put together. It does not, however, actually give a blow-by-blow account of how we exercise our imaging capacities or how we carry out particular imaging tasks. Thus. Kosslyn supplements his general theory with various specific models for these individual capacities and tasks. Figures 1.5 and 1.6 show two of these specific models, one depicting Kosslyn's hypothesis on how surface images are generated from deep representations and one depicting his hypothesis on how images are searched to determine whether the object being imaged has a named part.

In both phase I and phase II of his research program, Kosslyn relied on experimental evidence from normal subjects to support his hypotheses. For example. Kosslyn's theory that image generation involves the PIC-TURE, PUT, and FIND modules (a view first advanced in Kosslyn and Shwartz 1977) is supported by three classes of empirical findings: the fact that image-generation time is proportional both to the number of "parts" the imaged object or scene has and to its complexity, the fact that humans can construct images on the basis of descriptions of how parts are to be arranged, and the fact that image-generation time is proportional to the "subjective size" of the object being imagined (smaller objects take less time). (See chapter 6 of Kosslyn 1980 for a more detailed discussion of the evidence relevant to this part of the theory.)

In recent years, additional evidence for Kosslyn's theory of the imagery system in normal humans has been obtained from the study of neurological patients. Roughly speaking, the arguments go like this: If the best explanation for a patient's pattern of behavior is the hypothesis that there is selective impairment in a particular component or "module" of the imagery system as conceptualized by Kosslyn, then that pattern of behavior is taken to be evidence for the existence of that component or module in normal individuals. Arguments of this kind have been advanced to support Kosslyn's positing of distinct components for image generation (Farah, Levine, and Calvanio 1988; Farah, Gazzaniga, Holtzman, and Kosslyn 1985), long-term visual memory, and image inspection (Farah 1984). In addition, the study of several split-brain patients provides support for Kosslyn's theory that image generation involves the PICTURE, PUT, and FIND modules (Kosslyn, Holtzman, Gazzaniga, and Farah 1985).

Kosslyn and his co-workers have also begun to study the human imagery system from a number of other perspectives:

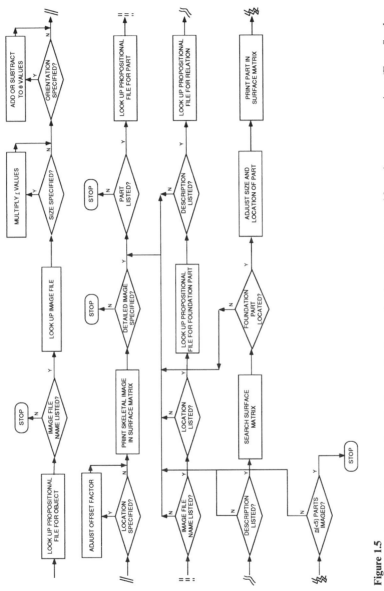

Figure 1.5
Flow chart describing Kosslyn's hypothesis regarding how surface images are generated from deep representations. (From Stephen M. Kosslyn, *Image and Mind*, © 1980 by the President and Fellows of Harvard College. Reprinted by permission of the author and Harvard University Press.)

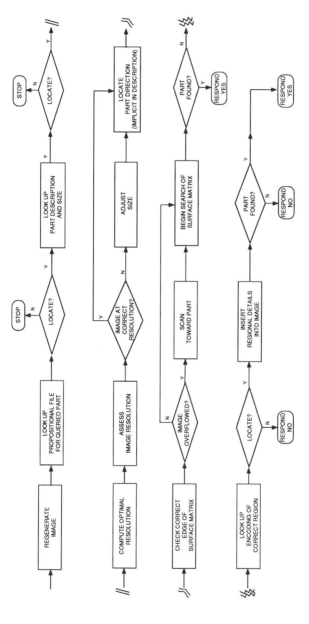

Figure 1.6
Flow chart describing how images are searched to determine whether the object being imaged has a named part. (From Stephen M. Kosslyn, *Image and Mind*, © 1980 by the President and Fellows of Harvard College. Reprinted by permission of the author and Harvard University Press.)

The study of developmental changes in the nature and use of the imagery system in children   Kosslyn has begun to use his work on the nature of imaging in the adult to define more precisely and study more effectively various claims made in the literature about the development of imaging in children. In particular, his work on adults contributes in two ways. First, it provides a detailed formulation of the "endstate" of the developmental process in the way that grammars do for the study of language development; second, it provides a battery of tasks to use for age-comparison purposes. Kosslyn has conducted a number of experiments designed to study the "representational-development hypothesis"—the view that children rely more heavily on imagery when accessing information stored in memory than do adults. Kosslyn (1980) reports on an experiment in which first-graders, fourth-graders, and adults were compared on a property-verification task. Half the time, the subjects were explicitly instructed to use imagery; half the time they were not. The major finding was that the younger children's response times were very similar whether or not imagery instructions had been given, whereas the adults' response times varied enormously. There is considerable evidence to suggest that the variation in adult time is due to the fact that when not explicitly instructed to use imagery, adults will respond on the basis of propositional information. Hence, the similarity in the first-graders' response times seems to indicate that younger children use imagery even when not instructed to do so. In addition to this experiment. Kosslyn, Margolis, Barrett. Goldknopf, and Daly (1990) examined age differences in four separate aspects of imaging (image generation, maintenance, scanning, and rotation), comparing 5-year-olds, 8-year-olds, 14-year-olds, and adults. That study suggests that younger children are relatively good at maintaining images but relatively poor at scanning, rotating, and generating images.

The study of individual differences in the human capacity to image   In another study, Kosslyn, Brunn, Cave, and Wallach (1984) tested 50 subjects on a wide variety of tasks involving mental imagery and obtained individual measures for each subject. For any given subject, performance on the battery of tasks varied considerably. Each task was then analyzed in terms of Kosslyn's general theory of imaging and each pair of tasks was assigned a similarity score based on the number of shared processing components (according to the theory). It turned out that these similarity scores were a fairly good predictor of observed correlations among task performances.

The study of pathology in the human imagery system   Kosslyn's work on mental imagery was extended to the study of imagery deficits in neurologically impaired patients by Farah (1984), who studied 27 descriptions of cases of loss of imagery that contained relatively detailed information concerning the tasks the patient could and could not perform. These tasks included question-answering tasks, introspection tasks, drawing and construction tasks, recognition tasks, and sensory and perceptual tasks. Three distinct patterns of abilities and defects emerged. Using analyses of each of the tasks in question based on Kosslyn's general model of imaging. Farah formed the following three functional-deficit hypotheses: that patients who exhibit the first pattern of abilities and defects suffer from a deficit in the generation process, that those in the second group suffer from a deficit in long-term visual memory, and that those in the third group suffer from a deficit in the inspection process. In addition, Farah, Levine, and Calvanio (1988) administered their own set of tests to a patient (R.M.) with a deficit in imaging ability due to a cerebral artery infarction and obtained results indicating a selective disfunction of the image-generation component.

The study of the neural realization of the human imagery system   Considerable evidence exists that imaging, in general, involves the use of cortical visual areas (Farah 1988). Recently, Kosslyn and Farah conducted a number of studies designed to investigate the localization and lateralization of various components of the normal imagery system. Contrary to the received view in neuropsychology, several studies provide converging evidence that the left hemisphere is critically involved in the image-generation process. Of the twelve cases studied by Farah (1984) that had been diagnosed as having an image-generation deficit, ten were reported to have had either primarily or exclusively dominant posterior damage. Lesion data (based on CT scans) from the patient reported by Farah, Levine, and Calvanio (1988) point to involvement of the occipito-temporal region of the left hemisphere. The split-brain patient (J.W.) studied by Farah, Gazzaniga, Holtzman, and Kosslyn (1985) could not perform a task requiring the generation of a multipart image with his right hemisphere alone. Finally, Farah's (1986) use of a lateralized, tachistoscopic stimulus-presentation technique with normal subjects produced the result that the effect of imagery was greater when the stimulus was presented in the right visual field (that is, to the left hemisphere).

In more recent work, Kosslyn has attempted to collect evidence on the lateralization of the imagery system at an even finer grain of analysis. For example, Kosslyn, Holtzman. Farah, and Gazzaniga (1985, p. 339) argue that the split-brain patient J.W. cannot perform tasks requiring the generation of multipart images with his right hemisphere because "the PUT processing module has selective difficulty in operating in the right hemisphere." The lateralization of the subsystems involved in imagery is discussed further in Kosslyn 1988.

1.3 The Characterization in Brief

In this section I present a summary of my characterization of cognitive science. Since the various framework assumptions are presented with very little accompanying explanation or interpretation (this will come), and since they often make use of technical notions, I do not expect the reader to grasp them fully at this point. However, I do hope that the summary will provide both an overview of what is to come and a reference point for putting later discussion in perspective. In other words. the summary will function something like a road map with points of interest named but not described. The one bit of elaboration I will provide is to indicate, where appropriate, how Kosslyn's work illustrates the various abstract assumptions.

Cognitive science is a complex and constantly developing enterprise. Even if we abstract away from the details of actual research and attempt to capture only the foundational framework within which such research is carried out, we are still left with a research-framework structure of considerable complexity and fluidity. My characterization will, thus, inevitably simplify matters. Before proceeding, therefore, let me attempt to pin down more precisely what *claims* I want to make regarding the characterization to be presented. There are four:

• What I am characterizing is the *current version* of the research framework of cognitive science rather than the framework itself. Hence, I allow for the possibility that there may be an instantiation of the research framework at some time in the future that will be similar but not identical to the one I will present (because it will involve the addition or deletion of certain revisable assumptions) but that will still be classified as cognitive science.

• This research framework (version) is intended to be *transdisciplinary*—that is, common to all cognitive scientists no matter what their primary disciplinary home.

• This research framework is, in fact, technically only a subsidiary research framework of the field—namely, the subsidiary research framework devoted to the study of adult, normal, typical cognition (ANTCOG). The framework of ANTCOG can, however, serve as a reasonable proxy for the total framework of cognitive science, for two reasons. First, as I noted in the introduction, it plays a pivotal role vis-à-vis the other subsidiary research frameworks. Second, it turns out that most of the assumptions associated with the framework of ANTCOG are assumptions that all the subsidiary research frameworks of cognitive science share. In fact, only the basic questions and two methodological assumptions are specific to ANTCOG. For stylistic reasons, I will often not acknowledge this point explicitly. That is, I will often speak of "the research framework of cognitive science" when, strictly speaking. I should be referring only to "the research framework of ANTCOG."

• The characterization is more like a rational reconstruction than a straightforward description. This is because assumptions will be accepted or rejected on the basis of two sorts of considerations: descriptive arguments (that is, arguments that muster evidence to the effect that most cognitive scientists in fact endorse (or do not endorse) the assumption in question) and normative arguments (that is, arguments to the effect that cognitive scientists ought (or ought not) to endorse the assumption in question). However, as I mentioned in the introduction, when including an assumption as part of the proposed framework. I will indicate its epistemic status. The convention will be this: An assumption included primarily on the basis of normative considerations will be labeled with an alphanumeric string followed by a superscript n (e.g., $R2.2^n$), whereas an assumption included primarily on the basis of descriptive considerations will be labeled with an unsuperscripted string. There will also be two assumptions whose status is indeterminate because there are good arguments both for and against including the assumption as part of the framework. In these instances, I will mark the assumption with a question mark to indicate that further deliberation is necessary.

Given the fact that my characterization of cognitive science is partly reconstruction, the reader may wonder how I can claim that the assumptions in question are, in fact, assumptions of the cognitive science community.[18] The answer is twofold. Although I will engage in a certain amount of adjudication regarding foundational disputes, this adjudication will be relatively local. Hence, it will not threaten the basic claim that there is widespread foundational consensus in the field and that the proposed research-framework characterization is substantially in accord with what cognitive scientists believe and with how they conduct their research. In addition, even the normative arguments typically begin with some descriptive premise. That is, the form of these arguments is usually "Given that cognitive scientists are, in fact, committed to X, they ought (if they are rational) also be committed to Y." Thus, there is a sense in which the assumptions attributed on the basis of normative arguments—the Y assumptions—are also (implicitly, at least) assumptions of the researchers who hold the X assumptions.

The Research Framework of Cognitive Science

Like any science, cognitive science begins by selecting from the myriad phenomena that exist in the world a certain small subset of phenomena as its domain of investigation. Because it is an immature science, both the properties of this domain and the questions raised about it are conceptualized in ordinary, commonsense terms. On my view, the domain-specifying assumptions and basic questions of cognitive science are the following.

Domain-Specifying Assumptions

D1 (IDENTIFICATION ASSUMPTION)   The domain of ANTCOG consists of the human cognitive capacities.

D2 (PROPERTY ASSUMPTION)   Pretheoretically conceived, the human cognitive capacities have a number of important properties. I shall refer to these as the *basic general properties* of cognition.

(a) Each capacity is *intentional*; that is, it involves states that have content or are "about" something.

(b) Virtually all of the capacities are *pragmatically evaluable*; that is, they can be exercised with varying degrees of success.

(c) When successfully exercised, each of the evaluable capacities has a certain *coherence* or cogency.

(d) Most of the evaluable capacities are *reliable*; that is, typically, they are exercised successfully (at least to some degree) rather than unsuccessfully.

(e) Most of the capacities are *productive*; that is, once a person has the capacity in question, he or she is typically in a position to manifest it in a practically unlimited number of novel ways.

D3 (GROUPING ASSUMPTION)   The cognitive capacities of the normal, typical adult make up a theoretically coherent set of phenomena, or a *system*. This means that, with sufficient research, it will be possible to arrive at a set of answers to the basic questions of the research framework that constitute a unified theory and that are empirically and conceptually acceptable.

Kosslyn's research illustrates each of these assumptions. D1 tells us that the domain of ANTCOG is the human cognitive capacities. Kosslyn's work has focused on one particular cluster of our cognitive capacities: those involving visual imagery. In particular, he has empirically investigated the human capacities to generate images, search images, and transform images. (I will occasionally speak of "the capacity to image" to cover all of these.) Kosslyn's research illustrates another related point about the domain of cognitive science: In the introduction, I suggested that the overall research framework of cognitive science is made up of various subsidiary research frameworks, of which the study of adult, normal, typical cognition is only one. Among the other subjects of study are individual differences, group differences, cultural variation, pathology, neural realization, and development. In recent years, Kosslyn and his co-workers have extended the original work on mental imagery into four of these areas: individual differences, pathology, neural realization, and development.

Each of the imagery capacities studied by Kosslyn exhibits the basic, general properties of cognition described in D2. Consider the capacity to generate images. Images have content; they are images *of* things (a house, car, map, your grandmother). Hence, the capacity to generate images is intentional. This capacity can be carried out with varying degrees of success. Hence, imaging is pragmatically evaluable. If I set out to form an image of my car but image my cat instead, I will not exercise my imaging capacity correctly. When exercised successfully, imaging exhibits coherence in the sense that the image formed will correspond to my intention. Imaging is also reliable, in the sense that, typically, within the limits of our individual capabilities, we are able to form images accordance with our intentions. I am probably an average imager (there is a great deal of individual variation in the ability to generate and use images), but when I decide to exercise my imaging capacity in a way that is within my capabilities, I can usually do what I intend to do. Finally, imaging is productive. Once a person has the capacity to image (a capacity that seems largely innate), he or she can form a virtually unlimited number of images.

Although Kosslyn has focused on only one aspect of cognition, his work clearly presupposes that our capacity to image belongs to and is integrated with a larger set of cognitive capacities. In other words, his work reflects an assumption very much like D3. The last section of his book makes this point quite evident. He writes:

I have been struck time and time again by how our model-building enterprise has forced us to expand the range of our inquiry in selective ways. I have noted repeatedly in this book that a "front end," a perceptual processor, is necessary to fill in many of the details in our model.... it seems to me that cognitive psychology parses neatly into three main areas: language, perception, and reasoning.... Imagery is interesting because it recruits all three of these "primary faculties," and thus studying imagery illuminates the nature of each of them. Note that since imagery utilizes these faculties in special ways, it makes sense to study imagery as a distinct domain. But if a theory is ever to have explanatory adequacy, we must understand the relevant aspects of the primary faculties it recruits. (Kosslyn 1980, pp. 478–479)

The Basic Questions

Q1   For the normal, typical adult, what precisely is the human capacity to _____?

Q2   In virtue of what does a normal, typical adult have the capacity to _____ (such that this capacity is intentional, pragmatically evaluable, coherent, reliable, and productive)?

Q3   How does a normal, typical adult typically (exercise his or her capacity to) _____?

Q4   How does the capacity to _____ of the normal, typical adult interact with the rest of his or her cognitive capacities?

One reason Kosslyn's research provides such a nice example for my purposes is that he has addressed questions about imaging of each of the basic kinds (Q1–Q4). The experimental work carried out in the first phase of his research revealed numerous things about what the human capacity to image, in fact, consists in,—about what people can and cannot, typically, do on imagery tasks. It thus addressed an instantiation of Q1: What precisely *is* the cognitive capacity to visually image? The relevant Q2 question is answered in Kosslyn's general theory of mental imaging, which claims that certain kinds of representational structures and certain kinds of computational processes underlie the human ability to image. The relevant Q3 question is addressed by Kosslyn's specific dynamic models of the human imaging capacities. Kosslyn has begun to investigate two questions about imaging that fall under Q4: How do people typically use visual images to answer questions? How does our capacity to image interact with our capacity to visually perceive?[19]

What gives cognitive science its identity is more than that it is interested in answering questions about the human cognitive capacities. It is also that it seeks to answer these questions in a quite specific way. In particular, it seeks to answer these questions in accordance with the following substantive assumptions.

The Substantive Assumptions

SA1: THE COMPUTATIONAL ASSUMPTION

C1 (linking assumption)   The human, cognitive mind/brain is a computational device (computer); hence, the human cognitive capacities consist, to a large extent, of a system of computational capacities.

C2 (system assumption)   A computer is a device capable of automatically inputting, storing, manipulating, and outputting information in virtue of inputting, storing, manipulating, and outputting representations of that information. These information processes occur in accordance with a finite set of rules that are effective and that are, in some sense, in the machine itself.

SA2: THE REPRESENTATIONAL ASSUMPTION

R1 (linking assumption)   The human, cognitive mind/brain is a representational device; hence, the human cognitive capacities consist of a system of representational capacities.

R2 (system assumption)   A representational device is a device that has states or that contains within it entities that are representations. Any representation will have four aspects essential to its being a representation:

it will be realized by a representation bearer; it will represent$_o$ one or more representational objects: its representation$_o$ relations will be grounded somehow: and it will be interpretable by (that is, it will function as a representation *for*) some currently existing interpreter.

In the mind/brain representational system, the nature of these four aspects is constrained as follows:

R2.1 (the representation bearer) The representation bearer of a mental representation is a computational structure or process, considered purely formally.

?(a) This structure or process has *constituent structure.*

R2.2^n (representational content) Mental representations have a number of semantic properties.

(a) They are semantically *selective.*
(b) They are semantically *diverse.*
(c) They are semantically *complex.*
(d) They are semantically *evaluable.*
?(e) They have a *compositional* semantics.

R2.3 (the ground) The ground of a mental representation is a property or relation that determines the fact that the representation has the object (or content) it has.

(a) This ground is *naturalistic* (that is, nonsemantic and nonintentional).
?(b) This ground may consist of either internal or external factors. However, any such factor must satisfy the following restriction: If two token representations have different grounds, and this ground difference determines a difference in content, then they must also differ in their causal powers to produce relevant effects across nomologically possible contexts.

R2.4 (the interpretant) Mental representations are significant for the person in whose mind they "reside." The interpretant of a mental representation R for some subject S consists of the set of all possible determinate computational processes contingent upon entertaining R in S.

There are various ways in which the "theoretical" questions Kosslyn poses about our capacity to image might be answered. Kosslyn, as a cognitive scientist, chooses to answer these questions in computational and representational terms. That is, he predicates his theorizing on the working assumption that the mind/brain is both a computational and a representational device (assumptions C1 and R1), and goes on from there.

It is characteristic of empirically oriented work in cognitive science (just as, I suspect, it is in other disciplines) that fundamental theoretical notions are often used without being explicitly explicated or grounded in a foundational way. Taking the foundations of one's field for granted is perfectly good science so long as someone else (such as a more theoretically or foundationally inclined practitioner) eventually does worry about the foundational issues. Kosslyn adopts just such an attitude with respect to the notions of computation and representation. He posits the existence of computational processes and representational structures without worrying too much about such questions as 'What is a computer?' or 'In virtue of what do representations have content or significance?'. Thus, there is nothing explicit in Kosslyn's work corresponding to C2, R2.3, or R2.4.

Kosslyn does, however, concern himself with the formal and semantic aspects of the mental representations he posits (R2.1 and R2.2). In a "conventional" computational theory (see section 3.3) of the sort Kosslyn advances, the "bearer" of a representation is a data structure. Such data structures have two formal properties, according to Kosslyn: format and organization. Furthermore, any given data structure will be supported by a computational "medium" with certain characteristic formatting properties. Kosslyn describes each of the three kinds of representations posited in his theory—surface representations, literal encodings, and propositional encodings—in terms of the above formal properties. (See section 5.2 for a more detailed discussion.)

The representations involved in mental imaging also have semantic properties. Although Kosslyn does not make use of the terminology employed in the formulation of R2.2, each of the semantic properties (a)–(e) is a property of one or more of the representations he hypothesizes. Consider a surface representation R of my dog Sydney. The content of this representation is quite specific. It is of a dog rather than a cat, a cloud, a fire engine, or something more nebulous. Hence, R is "semantically selective." It is also "semantically complex." R not only represents Sydney; it represents her in a certain way or under a certain aspect—as viewed from a certain distance at a certain angle under certain lighting conditions. This semantic complexity permits R to be "semantically evaluable." There is a sense in which my representation of Sydney can be true or false, or accurate or inaccurate. R might represent Sydney as smaller than she is, or with fur of a different color. In that case, it would be inaccurate; it would not be "true to" Sydney. Finally, a surface representation is "compositional." It is not all of a piece. It is a complex image made up of smaller representational parts that can be moved around and exchanged for other parts. I can transform my image of Sydney by imagining that she has rabbit ears. I can also imagine these same rabbit ears on a rabbit or on a person, or floating in space.

The semantic diversity of our representations consists in the fact that, as a class, they possess many different kinds of representational objects. Surface representations, by their very nature, can represent only phenomena that are visualizable. Hence, taken in themselves, they do not manifest much "semantic diversity" (although they do exhibit some). One can imagine not only objects but also states of affairs or events. And one can imagine not only actual phenomena but also possible or fictional ones. Propositional encodings introduce a further element of diversity, for these are representations which are supposed to represent such abstract objects as "facts" or propositions.

The Methodological Assumptions According to the substantive linking assumptions, the cognitive capacities consist, to a large extent, of a system of computational and representational (i.e., information-processing) capacities. These assumptions constrain what counts as a possible answer to each of the basic questions. Thus, in endorsing the substantive assumptions, cognitive scientists limit themselves to entertaining only answers to the basic questions that are, roughly speaking, formulated in information-processing terms. Since, on my view, questions are individuated by their possible answer sets, the subset of possible answers cognitive scientists are willing to entertain can be captured in another way: by *transforming* each original basic question into a revised basic question that will admit of only information-processing answers. The resulting transformation looks something like this:

The Revised Basic Questions

(Q1′) For the normal, typical adult, what precisely is the narrow information-processing function that underlies the ordinary capacity to _____?

(Q2′)   When a normal, typical adult has the capacity to _____, in virtue of what computational and representational resources is he or she able to compute the associated narrow information-processing function (such that the ordinary capacity is intentional, pragmatically evaluable, coherent, reliable, and productive)?

(Q3′)   When a normal, typical adult typically exercises his or her capacity to _____, how is the associated narrow information-processing function computed?

(Q4′)   How does the information-processing capacity associated with the capacity to _____ of the normal, typical adult interact with the rest of his or her information-processing capacities?

Because cognitive science is an umbrella field, encompassing a number of methodologically distinct subdisciplines, its methodological assumptions are rather general in character. In particular, each of them seems to either ground or further specify the various other components of cognitive science's research framework. There are a total of ten assumptions. The first three concern the domain of cognitive science, grounding both the exclusive focus on individual human cognition and the subdivision of cognition in general into individual cognitive capacities.

M1   Human cognition can be successfully studied by focusing exclusively on the individual cognizer and his or her place in the natural environment. The influence of society or culture on individual cognition can always be explained by appealing to the fact that this influence is mediated through individual perception and representation.

M2   The human cognitive capacities are sufficiently autonomous from other aspects of mind such as affect and personality that, to a large extent, they can be successfully studied in isolation.

M3   There exists a partitioning of cognition in general into individual cognitive capacities such that each of these individual capacities can, to a large extent, be successfully studied in isolation from each of the others.

Most of the assumptions that make up the research framework of ANTCOG, including most of the methodological assumptions, are inherited from cognitive science in general. What is peculiar to ANTCOG are the basic questions. The next two methodological assumptions concern those basic questions (and, hence, are also specific to ANTCOG).

M4   Although there is considerable variation in how adult human beings exercise their cognitive capacities, it is meaningful to distinguish, at least roughly, between "normal" and "abnormal" cognition.

M5   Although there is considerable variation in how adult human beings exercise their cognitive capacities, adults are sufficiently alike when they cognize that it is meaningful to talk about a "typical" adult cognizer and it is possible to arrive at generalizations about cognition that hold (at least approximately) for all normal adults.

The remainder of the methodological assumptions have to do with the cognitivist "approach" to the study of cognition One assumption simply defends the explanatory strategy of the field; the rest articulate features of that approach that go beyond the explanatory strategy: its scientific and multidisciplinary character and its relation to neuroscience.

M6   The explanatory strategy of cognitive science is sound. In particular, answers to the original basic questions can, to a large extent, be obtained by answering their narrow information-processing counterparts (i.e., the revised basic questions).

M7   In choosing among alternative hypothesized answers to the basic questions of the research framework, one should invoke the usual canons of scientific methodology. That is, ultimately, answers to the basic questions should be justified on empirical grounds.

M8   A complete theory of human cognition will not be possible without a substantial contribution from each of the subdisciplines of cognitive science.

M9[n]   Information-processing answers to the basic questions of cognitive science are constrained by the findings of human neuroscience.

M10[n]   The optimal research strategy for developing an adequate theory of the cognitive mind/brain is to adopt a co-evolutionary approach—that is, to develop information-processing answers to the basic questions of cognitive science on the basis of empirical findings from both the non-neural cognitive sciences and the neurosciences.

M11[n] Information-processing theories of the cognitive mind/brain can explain certain features of cognition that cannot be explained by means of lower-level neuroscientific accounts. Such theories are, thus, in principle, explanatorily ineliminable.

Kosslyn's research presupposes most of the methodological assumptions described above. In studying the human capacity for visual imagery, the focus of attention is on the individual cognizer (M1), on cognition in isolation from other aspects of mind (such as affect and personality) (M2), on a single capacity or a cluster of capacities (M3), and on normal and typical cognition (M4 and M5). Kosslyn's work also exhibits several aspects of the cognitivist "approach." Insofar as Kosslyn seeks to answer the basic questions about imaging in information-processing terms, he is assuming that that the "explanatory strategy" of cognitive science is sound (M6). He justifies his theoretical claims by appeal to data in accordance with the usual canons of scientific methodology (M7). He also makes use of the empirical and theoretical resources of subdisciplines of cognitive science other than cognitive psychology (M8). His general theory is complemented by an AI-style computer-simulation model, and his study of the pathology and the neural realization of the human imagery system relies on findings from neuropsychology and neurology. Furthermore, such neuroscientific findings have been employed to provide additional support for his theory of imaging in normal people, suggesting a commitment to M9 and M10. Whether Kosslyn would embrace M11 is not clear.

2 The Domain and the Basic Questions

The domain-specifying assumptions and the basic questions of a research framework tell us what scientists committed to that framework are interested in understanding and explaining, at least at the outset of their inquiries. Cognitive scientists are not entirely in agreement as to the nature of the domain and the basic questions for cognitive science (or, to be more precise, of the subsidiary research framework of cognitive science that deals with adult, normal, typical cognition). In this chapter, I will chart and attempt to adjudicate the various disagreements, and will present what I take to be the most defensible conception.

The domain-specifying assumptions of a research framework include three kinds of claims: an *identification* assumption, which indicates what kinds of phenomena are to be included in the domain; *property* assumptions, which specify essential or particularly important properties of the phenomena identified by the identification assumption; and a *grouping* assumption, which indicates that the phenomena picked out by the identification assumption make up a theoretically coherent set of phenomena, or a *system*. Each of these three kinds of claims will be discussed in turn. Section 2.1 will take up the identification assumption, section 2.2 will discuss various property assumptions, and section 2.3 will discuss the grouping assumption. Most of the disagreements will concern the precise nature of the identification assumption for ANTCOG. However, one further area of controversy will emerge; this will concern the best way to formulate the grouping assumption.

2.1 The Identification Assumption

Everyone agrees that the domain of cognitive science is human cognition or intelligence. However, there is controversy regarding precisely what aspects of cognition (or intelligence) are or should be the focuses of study. On my view, the best way to state the identification assumption of cognitive science is this:

D1 (IDENTIFICATION ASSUMPTION) The domain of ANTCOG consists of the human cognitive capacities.

Although it is not very clear in the pretheoretic scheme of things precisely what a cognitive capacity is (and, in particular, what distinguishes cognitive from noncognitive capacities), there does seem to be fairly widespread agreement on what constitutes the clear cases within the general class. They include our capacity to use language (perceive it, comprehend it, produce it, translate it, communicate with it, etc.), to perceive visually, to apprehend music, to learn, to solve problems (reason, draw inferences), to plan action, to act intentionally, to remember, and to imagine. Each of these subclasses can, of course, be broken down into far more specific capacities; for example, the capacity to remember includes the capacity to remember faces, episodes from the past, lists of nonsense syllables, facts, concepts, and so on. There are also several borderline phenomena whose membership in the domain of cognitive science is, at present, unclear. These include our capacity to acquire skills with a significant motor component and our capacity for nonlinguistic auditory, tactile, olfactory, and gustatory perception.

I said above that there was controversy over D1. This does not mean, however, that I think the evidential basis for is D1 weak. To the contrary, I believe that if one looks at what cognitive scientists actually study—the subject matter of their research—it becomes evident that every clear case of cognitive science research focuses on one or another of the cognitive capacities. To provide a completely persuasive descriptive argument in support of this contention would require counting and categorizing every piece of cognitive science research that has been done to date. For obvious reasons, I do not propose to do that here. However, short of such an exhaustive survey, a compelling inductive case can be made by inspection of any of the currently available surveys of the field. Consider, for example, Gardner's 1985 book *The Mind's New Science*, in part II of which Gardner discusses several research efforts that, on his view, "qualify for the label *cognitive-scientific*, ... involve the central questions in cognitive science [,] and ... are considered by the cognitive-scientific community to be of high quality" (pp. 293–294). These include David Marr's work on human visual perception, Stephen Kosslyn's research on visual imagery, the work of Eleanor Rosch, Brent Berlin, and Paul Kay on color naming and categorization, and the research of Amos Tversky, Daniel Kahneman, and Philip Johnson-Laird on human reasoning. Note that each of these research efforts focuses on one or another of the cognitive capacities—specifically, the capacity to perceive visually, to use visual images, to categorize colors, and to reason.

Despite the fact that the nature of cognitive science *research* clearly supports D1, one does occasionally find somewhat different (though closely related) *characterizations* of the domain of cognitive science in the literature. That is, cognitive scientists' *metascientific* claims sometimes diverge from D1. There are four principal alternatives:

Alternative 1   The domain of cognitive science is human intelligent behavior or action.

Alternative 2   The domain of cognitive science is the human propositional attitudes.

Alternative 3   The domain of cognitive science is human knowledge representation and use.

Alternative 4   The domain of cognitive science consists only of those human cognitive capacities that are *unencapsulated*—that is, those whose exercise is sensitive to the subject's goals and general "knowledge."

None of these alternatives is radically off-base. However, let me indicate why I think that none of them really fits the bill.

Alternative 1

The view that the domain of cognitive science is human intelligent behavior or action tends to go hand in hand with the position, adopted by many people in artificial intelligence, that the domain of cognitive science is intelligence *in general*, including the intelligence of nonhuman machines.[1] As I noted in the introduction, I shall not be dealing with the question of extending cognitive science's domain to nonhuman subjects. I would, however, like to consider whether, given that we restrict the domain to the human species, the aim of cognitive science is best conceived of as the study of human intelligent behavior.

Clearly, from the point of view of someone who endorses D1, there is something right about alternative 1. The *exercise* of any given capacity can be viewed as a piece of intelligent behavior or action (albeit sometimes a mental one), and D1 claims that the domain of cognitive science is the human cognitive capacities. For example, the exercise of my capacity to read constitutes an act of reading, and the exercise of my capacity to answer questions about a text constitutes an act of question-answering; and both of these are surely instances of intelligent behavior.

Nevertheless, there are several things that trouble me about conceiving of the domain in this way. First, I have been unable to discover a conception (or a theory) of intelligence that does not subject alternative 1 to fairly obvious counterexamples. Second, alternative 1 naturally gives rise to several unfortunate methodological tendencies. And third, it raises false expectations about the aims of cognitive science's research program.

What, then, is intelligent behavior supposed to be? If one examines what has been said on the subject, one immediately notices that there are two quite different conceptions of intelligent behavior at work. Intelligence is a comparative notion, and it appears that the comparison can either be interspecies or intraspecies. When people within the field of cognitive science (such as Simon [1981a,b] or Haugeland [1985]) write about studying intelligence, they seem to be thinking about the various properties of mind (and the behaviors to which they give rise) that distinguish human beings (and certain nonhuman machines) from lower species. Presumably this is also the notion of intelligent behavior that Pylyshyn (1984, p. 3) has in mind when he gives the following as an example of the sort of "phenomena" cognitive science seeks to explain:

A pedestrian is walking along a sidewalk. Suddenly the pedestrian turns and starts to cross the street. At the same time, a car is traveling rapidly down the street toward the pedestrian. The driver of the car applies the brakes. The car skids and swerves over to the side of the road, hitting a pole. The pedestrian hesitates, then goes over and looks inside the car on the driver's side. He runs to a telephone booth at the corner and dials the numbers 9 and 1.

In contrast, when psychologists (such as Sternberg [1984]) speak about intelligence, they have in mind studying only those properties of mind (and the behaviors to which they give rise) that make a person "smart." Let me call the former the "democratic" conception of intelligent behavior and the latter the "elitist" conception.

Any version of alternative 1 formulated in terms of an elitist conception of intelligent behavior will clearly result in too narrow a view of the domain of cognitive science. This is because cognitive scientists are interested in studying cognitive capacities—such as the capacity to perceive or perform an intentional action—that all normal human beings have in common, no matter how intelligent (in the sense of smart) or unintelligent (in the sense of stupid) they might be.[2] Unfortunately, the concept of intelligent behavior in the democratic sense (in which all normal human beings are intelligent) has received very little attention in the literature. I have come across only two treatments (there may, of course, be others), neither of which is very satisfactory.

In his book *Artificial Intelligence: The Very Idea*, Haugeland (1985, p. 6) raises the question of what intelligence is only to dismiss it: "Doesn't everything turn on this? Surprisingly, perhaps, very little.... For practical purposes, a criterion proposed by Alan Turing (1950) satisfies nearly everyone."[3] The final remark is a perplexing one, for the Turing test was proposed as a criterion for when a *machine* thinks. It does not, in and of itself, speak to the question of what the explanandum of cognitive science should be, and Haugeland does not tell us how to adapt it for this purpose.

What Haugeland may have in mind is something like this: The aim of cognitive science is to explain the sort of intelligent verbal behavior in humans that, if generated by a machine, would allow it to pass the Turing test. But surely this won't do. In the first place, not everyone believes that passing the Turing test ought to be taken as a sufficient condition for a machine's being intelligent (see, for example, Block 1981b and Bieri 1988). Second, even if one believes that the Turing test constitutes an adequate criterion for a system's being intelligent, what is criterial is that the system generates a *body* of behavior sufficiently rich to induce a "judge" to believe that the system is a human being. However, no individual piece of behavior need be part of this larger body of behavior. Hence, the adapted criterion does not really speak to the question of when an individual piece of behavior is intelligent. Finally, the suggestion (in adapted form) would restrict us to verbal behavior, whereas we surely want to include nonverbal intelligent behavior in the domain of cognitive science.

The question of what intelligent behavior is fares somewhat better in Simon's hands, but there are still difficulties. Simon (1981a, p. 15) writes:

Intelligent systems exhibit their intelligence by achieving goals (e.g., meeting their needs for survival) in the face of different and changing environments. Intelligent behavior is adaptive, hence must take on strikingly different forms when the environments are correspondingly different.

Several points in this passage require clarification. First, Simon uses 'environment' to mean either an external or an internal environment. Second, although the reference to "goals" might appear to be mentalistic, Simon seems to have nothing more in mind than the notion of a system's "function"—the function that a device can be designed to have or that a biological organism can acquire by evolution. I infer this on the basis of a passage on page 15 of Simon 1981b in which goals are attributed to a relatively simple machine (a so-called motor controller). Finally, Simon (1981a, pp.

15–16) takes it that adaptation can occur on three time scales:

> On the shortest time scale, intelligent—hence adaptive—systems continually change their behavior in the course of solving each problem situation they encounter....
>
> On a somewhat longer time scale, intelligent systems make adaptations that are preserved and remain available for meeting new situations successfully. They learn. There are many forms that this semi-permanent adaptation can take, and correspondingly many forms of learning. One important form is the accumulation of information in memories and the acquisition of access routes for retrieving it....
>
> On the longest time scale, intelligent systems evolve. Their evolution may be Darwinian.... It may equally well be social, through the discovery of new knowledge and strategies and their transmission from one system to another.

There are two questions that might be raised about Simon's account: Is his conception of intelligent behavior intuitively plausible—that is, does it properly delineate between intuitively clear cases of intelligent behavior and intuitively clear cases of nonintelligent behavior? Does it correspond to the class of phenomena cognitive science studies, or ought to study? Since I doubt that we have an intuitively clear idea of what intelligent behavior is, I will consider only the second of these questions.

Alternative 1, formulated in terms of Simon's conception of intelligent behavior, seems too broad, for there are cases of adaptive behavior (in Simon's sense) mediated by fairly low-level biological mechanisms that are not in the least bit cognitive and, hence, that do not belong within the domain of cognitive science. An interesting example is the phenomenon called "conditioned taste aversion." It has been experimentally demonstrated in rats (Garcia, Ervin, and Koelling 1966) and in children (Bernstein 1978) that if a subject eats something and becomes ill shortly thereafter, he or she will tend to avoid that food in the future. If we consider the goal of the organism in this example to be something like to ingest food conducive to health and survival, the case fits Simon's conception quite nicely. The goal is to ingest food conducive to survival; the changing environment consists of changing food options: the behavior consists in responding to one of those food options (an apparently unhealthy one) by rejecting it. That rejection is adaptive with respect to the goal in question. But although this fits Simon's conception of intelligent behavior, it is clearly outside the domain of cognitive science as the latter is currently construed. Moreover, there is reason to believe that this is how matters should be: In the experiments with the children, even when the children knew perfectly well that the nausea they were experiencing was not caused by the ice cream but was only associated with it temporally, they still rejected the ice cream. Their cognitive apparatus could not overrule the biological mechanism responsible for the avoidance response (Mook 1987, p. 239).

The idea of intelligent behavior rests on two notions: the notion of intelligence and the notion of behavior. Thus far, my objections to alternative 1 have turned on the fact that there is currently (to my knowledge) no conception of intelligence that makes the claim a plausible one. I should now like to point out that, even if an adequate conception of intelligence were to be found, alternative 1 would still not be optimal, because it restricts the domain of cognitive science to certain forms of *behavior*.

An obvious difficulty is that alternative 1 seems to rule out the exercise of all capacities that are either purely input capacities (such as perception) or purely "inner" capacities (such as memory). There is, however, a way around this difficulty, although it is not very satisfactory. Alternative 1 restricts us to the exercise of capacities with an output component only at the level of the explanandum. Phenomena such as perception and memory could still be part of the picture at the level of the explanans. For example, although we are barred from regarding perception as part of the domain, we are free to include perceptual discriminative behavior. And in giving our explanations of discriminative behavior, we are free to invoke our perceptual capacities. Although this move probably works to preserve most of what we want within the "grasp" (if not, technically, within the domain) of cognitive science, it points up two unfortunate methodological features of conceiving of the domain in this way. The first is that a research framework dedicated to explaining behavior rather than the cognitive capacities may have some tendency to overlook (and, hence, never account for) one of the central properties of those capacities namely, their intentionality. This is because *behavior* is an unclear notion, sometimes meaning bodily movement and sometimes meaning something akin to intentional action. In contrast, if the cognitive capacities (in all their intentional glory) are taken as our explanandum, there is no danger of overlooking the property of intentionality, since the object of the game becomes, in part at least, to explain in virtue of what the capacities have this seemingly mysterious property.

Another unfortunate tendency fostered by alternative 1 is the tendency to approach cognition in a holistic way. Intelligent behavior, whatever that may be, is clearly the product of a complex interaction among our various cognitive capacities. If we take the point of cognitive science research to be the explanation of intelligent behavior, then we are confronted with the problem of capturing this interaction right from the start. If, on the other hand, we adopt the view that I have been pushing (i.e., that the objects of our explanations are the various cognitive capacities), it is far easier to adopt a "divide and conquer" strategy. And only the latter, I submit, makes any methodological sense. Our capacities are difficult enough to explain one by one. If we are faced with the task of describing them in interaction at the outset, the job becomes completely daunting.

Finally, there is also a sense in which alternative 1's focus on behavior is misleading with regard to the aims of the research framework of cognitive science. To say that one is interested in explaining an action or a piece of behavior usually means that one is interested in explaining *why* it occurred. For example, to say that we are interested in explaining the phenomenon described in Pylyshyn's example would usually be to say that we want to know why the pedestrian ran to the phone booth and dialed the numbers. That is, talk about the explanation of behavior is usually construed as a call for reasons or causes. But this is not at all the sort of explanation that cognitive scientists are typically after. Kosslyn, for instance, is certainly not interested in *why* his subjects performed the map-scanning task. (Presumably the answer to that question is either that he paid them for participating in his experiment or that they were required to do so in order to pass the introductory psychology course they were taking.) Rather, he wants to know *how* they did it and *in virtue of what* (mental resources) they did it.

The point about the lack of why-explanations requires some qualification. When cognitive scientists seek to explain their data, they certainly are trying to answer why-questions of a sort—namely, questions of the form "Why, in this experiment, did such-and-such a pattern of data result?" Kosslyn is certainly interested in explaining why, when subjects performed the map-scanning task, their reaction times were typically a linear function of the "distance" between points scanned on the imagined map. But although this is a why-explanation, it is very different from explaining why the subjects performed the map-scanning task in the first place. Furthermore, I would submit that such why-explanations of the data are important only because they give us a way of adjudicating among alternative answers to one of the how- or what-questions designated as the basic questions of the research framework.

Alternative 2

The view that the domain of cognitive science is the propositional attitudes has been most vociferously advocated by Fodor, as in the following passage:

I assume that what we want—and what a successful cognitive science ought to give us—is a propositional attitude psychology.... That is: propositional attitudes constitute the main subject-matter of the theory: the theory purports to tell us what propositional attitudes are and what sorts of things they do.   (1985a, p. 1)

What is a propositional attitude? A propositional attitude is a mental state that can be analyzed into an "attitude" component (such as perceiving, remembering, intending) and a "content" component, where the content is propositional in form (e.g., that there is milk in the refrigerator). States with the same attitude component can differ in content (for example. I can both perceive that the sky is blue and perceive that the poppies have bloomed). Conversely, states with the same content can differ in attitude (for example, I can both perceive and remember that there is milk in the refrigerator).

As with alternative 1, there is something right about this view. Pre-theoretically conceived, our cognitive capacities do involve propositional attitudes. Exercising our capacity to perceive culminates in a state of perceiving, exercising our capacity to remember (recall) culminates in a state of remembering, exercising our capacity to speak a sentence begins with an intention to speak that sentence, and so on. Furthermore, part of explaining precisely what any given cognitive capacity *is* and how we exercise it may well involve providing a theory of the sort Fodor envisions. For example, if the capacity to perceive involves a propositional-attitude state of perceiving, then saying what that capacity *is* at (say) an information-processing level of description will involve saying what the propositional-attitude state of perceiving comes to at that level of description. And the latter is precisely Fodor's program.

There are, however, a number of difficulties with alternative 2. First, even though it is true that, in some sense, cognitive science must give an account of some of the propositional attitudes in order to accomplish its aims (that is, in order to answer its basic questions), providing such an account is only a small part of what cognitive scientists want to accomplish. They also want to know what mental resources are required for a person to have the capacities in which those propositional attitudes figure, how those cognitive capacities typically get exercised, and how those capacities interact. Thus, to say that the domain of cognitive science is the propositional attitudes is misleading at best.

Furthermore, alternative 2 as formulated above contains no explicit quantifier, but the phrase 'the propositional attitudes' clearly suggests that what is intended is that the domain of cognitive science encompasses *all* the propositional attitudes. There are good reasons for believing, however, that not all the attitudes are appropriate candidates for this role. In the first place, though it may be true that any cognitive capacity (as ordinarily conceived) involves a propositional attitude, the converse is false. Many a propositional attitude is not a "part" of any *cognitive* capacity and hence not uncontroversially part of cognitive science's research program. Searle (1983, p. 4) generated the following list of states that can be intentional states:

belief, fear, hope, desire, love, hate, aversion, liking, disliking, doubting, wondering whether, joy, elation, depression, anxiety, pride, remorse, sorrow, grief, guilt, rejoicing, irritation, puzzlement, acceptance, forgiveness, hostility, affection, expectation, anger, admiration, contempt, respect, indignation, intention, wishing, wanting, imagining, fantasy, shame, lust, disgust, animosity, terror, pleasure, abhorrence, aspiration, amusement, and disappointment.

Note that many of these are not, in any way, part of what constitutes the uncontroversial cases of cognitive science research. In particular, at the present time, cognitive science has little to say about either states of affect (joy, elation, depression, remorse, sorrow, anger, etc.) or states that figure in motivation (hope, desire, aversion, aspiration, etc.). In sum, then, while it is certainly not wildly off-base to say that the domain of cognitive science is the propositional attitudes, such a characterization does not capture the focus of the field in a completely accurate way.

Alternative 3

The view that the domain of cognitive science is human knowledge representation and use can be found stated on page 6 of Gardner 1985:

I define cognitive science as a contemporary, empirically based effort to answer long-standing epistemological questions—particularly, those concerned with the nature of knowledge, its components, its sources, its development, and its deployment.

There are several reasons why I do not think this accurately captures the domain of cognitive science.

In the first place, Gardner's statement of this alternative is much too broad. Human beings represent and use their "knowledge" in many ways, only some of which involve the human mind. What we know is represented in books, pictures, computer databases, and so forth. Clearly, cognitive science does not study the representation and the use of knowledge in all these forms. Thus, at a minimum, alternative 3 must be amended to read: The domain of cognitive science is human knowledge representation and use *in the mind.*

But even with this amendment alternative 3 is not quite right, for now it looks too narrow. Narrowness is certainly a consequence if we accept the standard philosophical conception of knowledge as being "factive," for cognitive science studies more than those representations which are true in some sense. For example, it is interested in misperception, the acquisition of false belief, and the use of the imagination. Perhaps, then, we ought to modify alternative 3 once more so as to get rid of the factive component and speak about something like the representation and use of *beliefs* rather than the representation and use of knowledge. But again the characterization is too narrow. Although many of our cognitive capacities (pretheoretically conceived) involve beliefs, there are aspects of these capacities, and even other entire capacities, that are of interest to cognitive science and that are not captured by speaking of the representation and use of beliefs. The exercise of any productive capacity, such as the capacity to speak or write sentences, starts with an intention. But intentions are not beliefs. Nor are mental images, although they may certainly have beliefs associated with them.

An advocate of alternative 3 might try one more move. We have seen that talking about the representation and use of knowledge is problematic because knowledge is factive, and that talking about the representation and use of beliefs is too narrow because it introduces constraints on the type of propositional attitude to be studied (namely, just beliefs). But there seems to be an obvious way around both of these difficulties. The solution is simply to talk about representation *per se*. Such talk is not factive, because there can be false representations. And we have simply left out any mention of an attitude. But this too is off the mark. Although cognitive science certainly concerns itself with mental representations and their use, such phenomena do not constitute the *domain* of the field (namely, what theorizing in the field is designed to explain). Rather, talk about representations and about their use belongs to that theorizing itself. In particular, representations and their use are posited to explain such things as how we perceive, understand, and produce language, how we remember, and how we reason. Therefore, they do not constitute the domain of cognitive science; they are designed to explain it. I conclude that alternative 3 is unsatisfactory.

Alternative 4

The fourth alternative is that the domain of cognitive science consists of only those human cognitive capacities that are unencapsulated. To say that a capacity is unencapsulated is to say that the exercise of that capacity is sensitive to the goals and the general "knowledge" of the person exercising the capacity. To say, in contrast, that a capacity is encapsulated is to say that its exercise will always proceed in a certain way without regard to those goals or that general "knowledge." Note that only *general* knowledge is relevant to characterizing an encapsulated or an unencapsulated capacity. It is quite possible for an encapsulated capacity (such as "early vision" seems to be) to have recourse to a form of "tacit" knowledge as long as that knowledge is available only to the processes underlying that capacity.

Of all the alternatives we have considered, this one is, in some sense, the most interesting. Most people agree that the domain of a science ought, ultimately, to be picked out on theoretical grounds. Alternative 4 attempts. in effect, to anticipate what these grounds will be. It is thus interesting because it is principled in a way that the other alternatives are not. Nevertheless, I would like to argue that, at this point in the history of cognitive science, alternative 4 ought to be rejected along with alternatives 1–3.

Something very like alternative 4 is suggested in Pylyshyn's book *Computation and Cognition* (1984). I say "suggested" because Pylyshyn never quite comes out and says directly and explicitly that this is what he has in mind. Nevertheless, a fair bit of textual evidence points in this direction.

My reading is most explicitly supported by some passages in Pylyshyn's final chapter whose point, we are told, is to raise the question of "what the term *cognition* applies to exactly, hence, what the domain of cognitive science includes." First, on page 258, in summarizing "the ideas discussed and the claims made" in the book, Pylyshyn says the following: "All indications are that certain central aspects of human behavior depend on what we believe and what we desire—on our knowledge, goals, and utilities and on our capacity to make inferences from our beliefs and desires and turn them into intentions to act." Although he does not explicitly say at this point that it is these aspects of behavior which constitute the domain of cognitive science, it is clear that this is where his focus is. Second, on page 266, in taking up the question of what phenomena might fall outside the boundaries of cognitive science. Pylyshyn talks about phenomena falling outside "the semantic principles I claim characterize cognition." This, in itself, is open to several different readings, of course; however, what he has in mind becomes quite clear when we put this statement together with passages which indicate what Pylyshyn takes these semantic principles to be—namely, principles formulated not only in terms of representations and representation-governed processes but also in terms of such notions as knowledge, belief, desire, and rationality (pp. 130, 210ff.)

The other aspect of *Computation and Cognition* that supports attributing alternative 4 to Pylyshyn concerns his notion of "functional architecture." The functional architecture of a computational system consists of the basic computational resources available in the system: its primitive symbol-manipulation operations, its storage and retrieval mechanisms, its control structure, and so on (p. 92). The significance of the functional architecture, for Pylyshyn, is that it marks the point in the system (the "level of aggregation," as he calls it) where we must move from semantic explanatory principles to nonsemantic ones. Mental processes that *make use of* the functional architecture and that are defined in terms of it can always be described semantically or in terms of the subject's beliefs, desires, and inferences. Processes that occur *within* the functional architecture cannot (p. 130). To explain how a primitive operation works, for example, one must appeal to nonsemantic biological or physical principles.

Given that Pylyshyn holds that the domain of cognitive science consists only of those phenomena explainable in terms of semantic-level principles, and given that the functional architecture is, by definition, not so explainable, it would follow that apparently cognitive phenomena that seem to require explanation in terms of the inner workings of the functional architecture ought not fall within the domain of cognitive science. Pylyshyn does seem to accept this as a consequence of his position, and I take this to support my reading of him. For example, he hypothesizes that both the capacity of children to acquire a grammar of a certain sort and the human capacity to form "knowledge-independent, low-level, visual representations" are primarily dependent on features of the functional architecture; hence, he classifies them as noncognitive and takes them to fall outside the proper domain of cognitive science.[4]

How does alternative 4 fare as a characterization of the domain of cognitive science? In view of the current state of the art, the answer with respect to descriptive considerations is clear. Many researchers currently believe that significant aspects of the human perceptual capacities—both visual and linguistic—are encapsulated. But such capacities and the theories being developed to explain them are not for that reason considered to be outside the domain of cognitive science. For example, Marr and Nishahara's work on "early" vision (Marr 1982) is considered by many to be a paradigm of good work in cognitive science.

Recall, however, that, in weighing whether an assumption should be considered part of the research framework of cognitive science, what the field actually does or does not subscribe to at the current time can be overridden by normative considerations. Pylyshyn may have this sort of strategy in mind, for certain passages in his book can be read as forming an argument against the view that the domain should include both encapsulated and unencapsulated capacities and in favor of the view that it should contain only the latter. I would formulate the first part of the argument as follows:

Pylyshyn's Negative Argument

(1) Phenomena that belong to the same domain should be subject to uniform principles of explanation.

(2) Nonencapsulated capacities can be accounted for only in terms of "semantic principles of explanation."

(3) A "semantic principle of explanation" is one that refers to the beliefs, desires, and rationality of the organism.

(4) Encapsulated capacities can be accounted for only in terms of nonsemantic principles of explanation (either purely formal or biological).

(5) The conjunction of semantic and nonsemantic principles of explanation is not uniform.

(6) Therefore, encapsulated and nonencapsulated capacities should not be included in the same domain.

This establishes Pylyshyn's negative thesis. The argument for his positive thesis then continues as follows:

Pylyshyn's Positive Argument

(7) *Ceteris paribus*, the domain of cognitive science should include only those phenomena that either are paradigmatically cognitive or require the same kind of principles of explanation as the paradigmatically cognitive phenomena.

(8) Only the nonencapsulated capacities are paradigmatically cognitive.

(9) Therefore, the domain of cognitive science should include only the nonencapsulated capacities.

Although questions can certainly be raised regarding premises 1, 7, and 8, the chief difficulty with Pylyshyn's total argument lies with his conception of the semantic (premise 3). There are two levels of description relevant to cognitive science that might be characterized as "semantic," and it is important not to confuse them. There are commonsense descriptions of the human cognitive apparatus in term of knowledge, belief, desire, rationality, etc., and there are theoretical descriptions in terms of mental representations and representation-governed computational processes. If we accept Pylyshyn's somewhat nonstandard usage, as stipulated in premise 3, and restrict the term 'semantic principle of explanation' to a principle of explanation that refers to the beliefs, desires, and rationality of the organism, then the argument is in trouble because premise 2 becomes false: in cognitive science, non-encapsulated capacities not only can be but are accounted for by reference to mental representations and representation-governed processes, and, hence, by principles of explanation that are not semantic in the requisite sense. On the other hand, if we revise Pylyshyn's third premise and take a semantic principle of explanation to be one that refers to content-bearing objects at either the ordinary or the theoretical level of description, then we see that the semantic/nonsemantic distinction and the encapsulated/nonencapsulated distinction cross-cut one another. In particular, there can now be capacities that are encapsulated but that require explanation in terms of representations and representation-governed processes.

As it turns out, this is not merely a conceptual possibility. Indeed, a number of current theories of low-level vision (i.e. those aspects of visual processing that deal with "problems related to the recovery of physical properties of the visual environment" [Yuille and Ullman 1990, p. 6]) treat such processes as virtually encapsulated and representation-governed. According to Yuille and Ullman (1990, p. 6), "low-level vision is believed to act in a manner almost independent of the domain and task." Yet theories of early vision certainly posit representations. For example, as Yuille and Ullman (1990, p. 10) note, Marr's landmark 1982 study posits two stages of representations: the *primal sketch*, "a symbolic representation obtained directly from the image by detecting and describing significant features in the image, such as intensity edges and texture boundaries," and the $2\frac{1}{2}$-*D sketch*, a representation that describes "the surrounding surfaces and their properties, such as their depth, surface orientation, color, and texture."

Thus, revision of premise 3 leads to the falsity of premise 4. I conclude that Pylyshyn's argument does not go through and, hence, does not constitute a good reason for overriding the fact that alternative 4 fails to capture the clear cases of cognitive science research.

2.2   The Property Assumptions

Thus far we have ascertained that the domain of cognitive science is the human cognitive capacities. Do these capacities have any properties that are particularly important from the point of view of cognitive science research? There are five basic general properties, on my view. Thus, we need to include five property assumptions as part of our domain characterization. (The point of articulating these properties is not to define what a cognitive capacity is. Rather, the point is to identify a number of properties *in fact* shared by all or most of the cognitive capacities that, *prima facie*, should be explained by any adequate scientific theory of cognition.)

D2 (PROPERTY ASSUMPTIONS)   Pretheoretically conceived, the human cognitive capacities have a number of important properties.

(a) Each capacity is *intentional*; that is, it involves states that have content or are "about" something.

(b) Virtually all of the capacities are *pragmatically evaluable*; that is, they can be exercised with varying degrees of success.

(c) When successfully exercised, each of the evaluable capacities has a certain *coherence* or cogency.

(d) Most of the evaluable capacities are *reliable*; that is, typically, they are exercised successfully (at least, to some degree) rather than unsuccessfully.

(e) Most of the capacities are *productive*; that is, once a person has the capacity in question, he or she is typically in a position to manifest it in a practically unlimited number of novel ways.

Let us now consider each of these properties in turn.

D2(a) Each of the human cognitive capacities is *intentional*; that is, it involves states that have content or are "about" something.

In order to see in what sense the cognitive capacities are intentional, it is useful to make a distinction between *basic* and *complex* cognitive capacities. A complex capacity is one that can be analyzed into subcapacities, relative to our ordinary conceptual scheme; a basic capacity is one that cannot. Our capacity to name objects, for example, is complex. There is an answer (though a crude one) to the question how we do it. First, so the story goes, we perceive and recognize the object (the precise relationship between these two subcapacities is unclear); then we think of its name: then we utter its name. In contrast, consider any one of those subcapacities— say, our capacity to utter some specific word. How do we do it? Before doing some scientific psychology, we haven't the slightest idea.

Cognitive capacities are often described in the literature as input-output functions of a special sort (Haugeland 1978; Von Eckardt Klein 1978b; Cummins 1983). At the level of our ordinary conceptual scheme, it is most appropriate to talk about beginning events (or states) and end events (or states). For example, visually perceiving a dog takes us from something like a beginning event of dog-like light rays impinging upon the retina (or, perhaps, just the presence of a dog in our field of vision) to the end state of a perceptual experience, and inferring that Socrates is mortal on the basis of the premises that Socrates is a man and all men are mortal takes us from the beginning state of simply considering the premises to the end state of reaching a judgment about the conclusion. Intentionality seems to enter the picture as follows: Each of the basic human cognitive capacities involves some intentional state at the beginning point, at the end point, or at both points. Exercising the capacity to perceive culminates in a state of perceiving, exercising the capacity to remember (recall) culminates in a state of remembering, exercising the capacity to speak a sentence begins with an intention to speak that sentence, and so on.[5]

Roughly speaking, what makes these states intentional is that they have content—they are "about" something. Beyond this, there is considerable philosophical disagreement. However, cognitive scientists seem to agree on the following additional points:

• The intentional states relevant to cognitive science are propositional-attitude states. Note that this is not true by definition. As Searle (1983, p. 7) points out, not every intentional state has an entire proposition as intentional content. To argue for this point thus requires showing that, in each case where an intentional state *seems* (on the basis of its expression in natural language) to take something other than an entire proposition as intentional content, either the natural-language expression is misleading and the intentional state has an entire proposition as intentional content after all or the intentional state is not one within the purview of cognitive science. Searle (1983, pp. 30, 41) argues quite persuasively that intentional states such as wanting and perceiving, which seem to be able to take a simple object rather than a proposition as intentional content ("I want some apple juice"; "I see the tree"), really always have full propositional content as intentional content (I want that I have some apple juice, I see that there is a tree before me). The remaining, genuine cases, such as loving and hating, are not currently within the purview of cognitive science, although of course this may change.

• Propositional attitudes are semantically evaluable. Beliefs can be true or false, perceptions can be veridical or nonveridical, intentions can be carried out or not. One of the properties Searle (1981, 1983) attributes to propositional attitudes is *direction of fit*. Intuitively, the direction of fit of an intentional state is determined by which side is amiss (the mind or the world) if "the fit doesn't come off" (Searle 1981, p. 207). The kind of term we use to express the relation of satisfaction between a propositional attitude and the world depends largely on the direction of fit of the attitude in question. 'True' and 'false', according to Searle (1981), are used to assess success in representing states of affairs in the mind-to-world direction of fit; in contrast, terms such as 'fulfilled' and 'realized' are used to assess success in representing states of affairs in the world-to-mind direction of fit.

• Furthermore, what makes such states semantically evaluable is that their content specifies (under certain aspects) what Searle calls *conditions of satisfaction* that can either be satisfied or not, depending on how the world is. It is this property of intentional states which allows them to be "directed" at objects which do not, in fact, exist.[6]

• Propositional attitudes are "intrinsically" intentional. Objects or states with content can have this content in virtue of different sorts of "grounding" properties or relations. The notion of intrinsic intentionality taxonomizes such "grounding" properties into two groups: those whose content is determined (in part, at least) by the conscious mediation of some intentional agent and those whose content is not so determined. Objects or states whose content is determined (in part, at least) by the conscious mediation of some intentional agent are said to lack intrinsic intentionality (they are, instead, "derived"): those whose content is not so determined are said to possess it. On the standard view, intentional mental states have intrinsic intentionality, whereas expressions in natural language and conventional signs and symbols are derived.[7]

• Propositional attitudes have significance for their subjects. Not only does a belief or a desire involve a certain attitude toward a content, but both the attitude and the content make a difference to the subject's activities (mental and nonmental) and, hence, to the subject. In other words, propositional attitudes are not "inert": they have consequences that are experienced by the subject who has them. At a minimum, they typically manifest themselves to us at the level of consciousness. In addition, they are capable (under the right circumstances) of influencing both the character of our cognitive processes and our actions.

D2(b)   Virtually all of the cognitive capacities are *pragmatically evaluable*; that is, they can be exercised with varying degrees of success.

We can perceive either "veridically" or "nonveridically." We can be successful in saying or doing or imagining (all cases of production) what we intended to, or we can merely make an attempt and fall. We can reason correctly or incorrectly. We can successfully recall a fact, a face, or a concept, or we can "wrack our brains" and come up with nothing or the wrong thing.

The successful exercise of a cognitive capacity seems to require four things:

The beginning state must be of the right kind.

The end state must be of the right kind.

The beginning state must bear the right sort of relation to the end state.

The end state must be arrived at by means of the right kind of causal chain.

For example, in the case of veridical perception, the beginning state is a distal perceptual stimulus and the end state is a perceptual experience. However, this is not sufficient for a process to count as veridical perception. The end state must bear the right relation to the beginning state; in particular, the perceptual experience must be an experience *of* the perceptual stimulus and, further, must reflect the properties of that stimulus reasonably accurately. And, finally, the right sort of causal chain is required. Even if the first three conditions are satisfied, if the end state is produced in some deviant way—say, by the insertion of microelectrodes into the brain of the subject—the process does not count as veridical perception.[8]

We still classify processes that satisfy most but not all of these four conditions as perception, but as unsuccessful perception. Illusion, for example, involves the right sort of beginning and end states but a relationship and a causal chain that have gone wrong (though not radically wrong). In contrast, where none of the conditions are satisfied we clearly do not have perception at all.

There are also, of course, things that the mind can do to which the notions of success and failure seem to be inapplicable. Most of these (such as dreaming, daydreaming, fantasizing, and engaging in loosely structured, meandering sequences of thoughts) are not, at present, studied by cognitive science, although they certainly might be. In his popular textbook *Psychology*, Henry Gleitman (1981) puts the point this way with respect to the phenomenon of thinking; Psychologists who study thinking are mainly interested in thinking in the sense of reasoning, pondering, or reflecting. To distinguish this sense from the other senses, "they refer to *directed thinking*, a set of internal activities that are aimed at the solution of a problem, whether it be the discovery of a geometric proof, of the next move in a chess game, or of the reason why the car doesn't start. In all these activities, the various steps in the internal sequence are directed and dominated by the ultimate goal, the solution of the problem." (p. 312)

D2(c)   When exercised successfully, each of the evaluable cognitive
        capacities has a certain *coherence* or cogency.

This coherence property is equivalent to the third condition for the
successful exercise of a cognitive capacity mentioned above. It is, however,
important enough to merit a separate discussion.

If we consider the beginning and end points of any of the cognitive
capacities when they are exercised successfully, we note that they are far
from arbitrarily related. In fact, they typically bear a fairly well-defined
relationship to one another. Moreover (and this is an important point), this
relationship holds in virtue of the *contents* of the intentional states involved. Thus, the evaluability of our cognitive capacities rests on the fact
that some exercises of these capacities exhibit coherence; that, in turn,
could not be the case unless some of the states involved in these capacities
were intentional.

Although it seems to be very difficult to say what this relationship
amounts to in general (that is, what it is that holds true of all the cognitive
capacities), we have fairly clear intuitions regarding what form it takes in
the case of any specific cognitive capacity. There seem to be at least two
important kinds of cases: input and/or output capacities in which either
the beginning or the end state is intentional, but not both; and purely
mental capacities in which both the beginning and end states are intentional.

The principal basic input and/or output capacities are perception and
intentional action. (Learning is also an important input capacity, but it is
not basic; it can be broken down into various subcapacities, such as
perception and memory.) On the basis of Searle's (1983) analysis of the
intentional states involved in these two capacities, each capacity can be
viewed as a capacity to bring it about that the relevant intentional state
is satisfied. The capacity to perceive, when exercised successfully, brings it
about that the conditions of satisfaction (in the sense of requirement) of the
perceptual experience are, in fact, satisfied by the perceptible state of affairs
in the world that brought that experience about. It does this by getting
the experience to fit the world. In contrast, the capacity to act intentionally,
when exercised successfully, brings it about that the conditions of satisfaction (in the sense of requirement) of the intention are, in fact, satisfied by
the ensuing behavior by getting the behavior right. In other words, the
coherence relation involved is the notion of satisfaction.

Searle's analysis of the satisfaction relations relevant to perception and intentional action is, actually, more complicated than this. He holds that the conditions of satisfaction relevant to perception and intentional action not only say something about a person's immediate environment and behavior, respectively, but also say something about the causal relations holding between the world and the relevant intentional states. For example, on his view, the conditions of satisfaction of X's seeing a yellow station wagon are "that there is a yellow station wagon in front of X and the fact that there is a yellow station wagon in front of X is causing the visual experience" (Searle 1983, p. 61). In other words, the fact that the visual experience is caused by the state of affairs that the visual experience is an experience of, is, for Searle, a component of the conditions of satisfaction of that visual experience. A similar claim is made for intentional action. The intentional component of intentional action, on Searle's account, is an experience of acting. The conditions of satisfaction of this experience of acting are not only that there be certain bodily movement or states of the agent, but also that these have certain causal relations to the experience of acting.

Haugeland (1978) suggests an alternative approach for revealing the coherence of capacities that involve either perception or action. In particular, he attempts to deal with such capacities by comparing an appropriate *description* of the relevant nonmental state (rather than the state itself) with a description of the content component of the intentional state. Thus, in considering the human capacity to perceive, we are supposed to compare a description of what a person is "looking at" with a description of the content component of the person's perceptual state. And, in considering the capacity to act intentionally, we are supposed to compare a description of the content component of a person's state of intending to do something with a description of what that person actually does. If we choose the right descriptions, the resulting coherence relation will be something akin to synonymy.[9]

Let us now turn to a consideration of the purely mental capacities. The first point to notice is that many of these capacities are strongly analogous to the cases of perception and intentional action just considered. That is, we have "inner" perception (that is, introspection) and "inner" action (what Gleitman, in the quote above, had in mind when he mentioned "directed thinking"). Here again the relation of satisfaction plays a significant role. Note, however, that in cases of directed thinking the coherence relation often involves more than satisfaction. This is so for two reasons: First, such capacities are intentionally imbedded; one intends to exercise a mental capacity that is, itself, intentional. Second, what is intended is usually (perhaps even always) underspecified.

An example should make the point clear. In discussing memory retrieval, Gleitman (1981) describes a situation in which a person is doing a crossword puzzle and needs to find an eight-letter word for 'African anteater'. To do this part of the puzzle, the person must exercise his or her capacity to retrieve semantic information. We might analyze the successful exercise of this capacity as follows:

Beginning state   X intends (that X recalls (what an eight-letter word for 'African anteater' is))

End state   X recalls (that an eight-letter word for 'African anteater' is 'Aardvark')

Clearly, a relation of satisfaction is involved, for X does, in fact, carry out X's intention: X does, in fact, recall an eight-letter word for 'African anteater'. Note, however, that the coherence relation involves more than this. In addition to satisfying the original intention, the end state fills a certain gap in the beginning state—the gap marked in the above formulation by the interrogative element 'what'. One way to see this clearly is to reformulate the beginning state thus:

Beginning state   X intends (that X recalls (that an eight-letter word for 'African anteater' is ——————)

If we consider the propositional object of the beginning state to be something akin to an "open sentence" in logic, then the relationship between the beginning state and the end state is one of *true closure*. The end state fills in the blank in such a way as to make the proposition true. There is more to be said, however. What makes the end-state proposition true is something quite specific. The proposition being recalled makes an identity claim; furthermore, the blank being filled in is one of the relata of that identity claim. We initially identify the intentional object only by *description* (i.e., "an eight-letter word for 'African anteater'"). Once recall has been successful, however, we can *name* it ('Aardvark'). The end-state proposition is true if what was inititally described is identical to what is eventually named.

As far as I can tell, all human mental capacities can be analyzed in a similar way. Consider problem solving. Any problem can always be formulated in terms of a question. For example, in the introduction to their section on problem solving, Johnson-Laird and Wason (1977) discuss seven sample problems, all of which are formulated as questions. For instance:

Problem no. 1   You are in a hotel room in Tibet, and you want to have a wash. You go to the wash-basin and discover indecipherable symbols on the taps. Which tap do you turn on for hot water? (p. 13)

Problem no. 2   Given a human being with an inoperable stomach tumor, and rays which destroy organic tissue at sufficient intensity, by what procedure can one free him of the tumor by these rays and at the same time avoid destroying the healthy tissue which surrounds it? (p. 15)

Problem no. 3   How can one construct four equilateral triangles out of six matches, where each side of a triangle is equal in length to the length of the matches? (p. 17)

If we can formulate any problem as a question, then the beginning and end states of the capacity to solve problems can always be described thus:

Beginning state   X intends (that X thinks (that the answer to such-and-such a question is _____))

End state   X thinks (that the answer to such-and-such a question is thus-and-so)

(Of course, any particular instantiation of this schema would replace the 'such-and-such' and 'thus-and-so' (but not the '_____') with the name of a particular question and a particular answer, respectively.)

Here is a sampling of how this analysis might apply to various other mental capacities:

Deductive reasoning

Beginning state   X intends (that X thinks (that, given such-and-such premises, the conclusion which follows logically is _____)

Game playing

Beginning state   X intends (that X thinks (that, given such-and-such a current position in game G, the next "good"—i.e., conducive to winning—legal move is _____)

Imagining

Beginning state   X intends (that X imagines (that the front of his house looks like _____)

And so forth.

D2(d)   Most of the evaluable capacities are *reliable*; that is, typically, they are exercised successfully (at least to some degree) rather than unsuccessfully.

We are all acutely aware of the fact that the exercise of human cognitive capacities often goes wrong, even for adults considered normal. We suffer perceptual illusions, forget things, make slips of the tongue, reason illogically, and so on. And, clearly, some of our capacities can be counted on more than others. On the whole, however, we do quite well when it comes to perception and production, whereas purely internal capacities such as remembering and reasoning seem to exhibit more variability. Nevertheless, it is a fact that most of the cognitive capacities of the normal adult (that is, an adult who by standard criteria is not considered retarded, neurologically impaired, and so forth) work remarkably well most of the time. And this is a fact that seems to demand explanation.

D2(e)   Most of the capacities are *productive*; that is, once a person has the capacity in question, he or she is typically in a position to manifest it in a practically unlimited number of novel ways.

For example, once I have the relevant capacity, I can perceive scenes I have never seen before, reason about problems have never thought about before, appreciate music I have never heard before, generate images I have never imagined before, remember things I have never remembered before, and so forth. Contemporary linguistic theory, especially of the Chomskian variety (see Chomsky 1968), has emphasized the productivity of the capacity for language. Chomsky, however, often has a stronger notion of productivity in mind. D2(e) characterizes the productivity of a cognitive capacity in terms of the psychological possibility of *novel* exercises. In contrast, Chomsky claims that once a person acquires knowledge of a particular natural language, he or she can in principle understand and produce an *unbounded* number of sentences, where the "in principle" clause is meant to bracket resource constraints such as limited attention, limited memory, and limited time and where the unboundedness of the capacity stems from the recursive character of syntax in natural language. (For example, the grammar of English permits any two sentences to be conjoined by 'and' to form a new sentence.) I prefer the weaker notion of productivity because it carries with it less theoretical baggage. At least on Chomsky's view, talk about what we can do "in principle" presupposes that we can distinguish empirically between aspects of the mind underlying our competence and aspects of the mind underlying our performance. But this assumption may be empirically false, and it certainly does not belong to the framework of cognitive science *per se*—especially not to the component characterizing the domain of study.[10]

2.3 The Grouping Assumption

D3 (GROUPING ASSUMPTION)   The cognitive capacities of the normal, typical adult make up a theoretically coherent set of phenomena, or a *system*. This means that, with sufficient research, it will be possible to arrive at a set of answers to the basic questions of the research framework that (a) constitute a unified theory and (b) are empirically and conceptually acceptable.

Pylyshyn (1984, p. 113) seems to have something like assumption D3 in mind when he writes that "cognitive phenomena are a 'natural kind' explainable entirely in terms of the nature of the representations and the structure of programs running on the cognitive functional architecture." To formulate the point in terms of the notion of a "natural kind" is not quite right, however. It is worth a brief side excursion to see why this is so.

Considerable attention has been devoted to the topic of natural kinds in the recent philosophical literature. Most of it, however, has been concerned with the semantics of natural-kind *terms* rather than with the kinds themselves. That is, the question: 'What distinguishes natural from non-natural kinds?' has received less attention. Everyone, however, seems to agree on the following:

(a) Natural kinds either are or determine a set of actual and possible individuals (depending on one's view of universals).

(b) What these individuals have in common is that they resemble each other or are similar to each other in some respect.

(c) Which kinds constitute the natural kinds and what the similarity relations are that underwrite the natural kinds are questions to be answered ultimately by science. In other words, the natural kinds will be those kinds picked out by predicates (though, possibly, not all—see below) which appear in our scientific laws and theories.

(d) Hence, if one is a realist about science, natural-kind facts are objective facts.

(e) Natural-kind terms are "projectible predicates" (Goodman 1955); hence, natural-kind attributions are counterfactual supporting. For example, 'is gold' is a projectible predicate and a natural-kind term, whereas 'is my grandmother's favorite metal' is not; the reason for the latter is that "there are no laws that apply to things in virtue of their being metal of my grandmother's favorite kind" (Fodor and Pylyshyn 1981, p. 146).[11]

Within this framework of agreement, however, there is disagreement about whether there are any additional constraints on something counting as a natural kind. At least three views can be discerned in the literature:

(1) The *liberal view* (clearly held by Fodor and Pylyshyn [1981]; also attributable to Quine [1969]). On this view, a natural kind is any kind picked out by a predicate in a scientific law of our ultimate science. And any "level" of scientific law will do, including, in particular, laws from the special sciences. In other words, no additional constraints are imposed on (a)–(e) above.

(2) The *explanatory-primacy view* (Copi 1954; Platt 1983; Linsky 1982; de Sousa 1984). This view is more restrictive than (1) but less restrictive than (3). Here, X is a natural kind just in case (a) there exists a set of explananda, of interest to some community of scientists, associated with X; and (b) there exists a set of properties shared by all and only instances of X, the attribution of which (in conjunction with appropriate true auxiliary hypotheses) truly explains those explananda. For example, let us say that biologists are interested in explaining various behavioral and anatomical facts about tigers. Suppose, further, that they identify what the "essential" genetic property of being a tiger is and that the attribution of this genetic

property explains (in conjunction with appropriate true auxiliary hypotheses) the behavioral and anatomical facts in question. Then, on this view, *being a tiger* will constitute a natural kind. In contrast, the properties picked out by the various behavioral and anatomical facts (e.g., having a particular pattern of stripes, having particular eating habits) probably will not constitute natural kinds, even though predicates expressing both kinds of properties will appear in the constituent laws of our eventual true tiger theory. (This is assuming, of course, that explanatory-primacy conditions (a) and (b) do not hold independently of these properties.)

As both Copi (1954) and Platt (1983) point out, this conception of natural kinds involves a certain amount of relativism. In particular, natural kinds are relative to a selected "explanation space" determined by the interests of the scientists involved. That is, we cannot say what property or set of properties has explanatory primacy until we have decided what we want to explain (that is, until we have fixed our "explanation space").

Even though the explanatory primacy view restricts the class of natural kinds considerably more than the liberal view does, the restriction still does not rule out the possibility of natural-kind attributions in the special sciences. Platt (1983, p. 139) recognizes this consequence explicitly:

A form of argument commonly encountered in recent philosophical writings seeks to establish that some class of phenomena—say, that of seeings or that of rememberings—is not the membership of any natural kind by invoking the fact that within the membership of that class we find a variability in the "structural realisations" of those members. But that does not establish the presumed conclusion. The possibility remains open that the class of phenomena concerned is the membership of some higher level natural kind, a kind which allows of ("species-specific") variation within the lower level varieties of that kind.

Presumably, the reason this possibility remains open is that the two conditions for explanatory primacy may still be satisfied despite the supposed structural variability in how seeings and rememberings are realized. That is, there may well be a set of explananda associated with seeings (rememberings) and a set of properties shared by all and only seeings (rememberings) the attribution of which (in conjunction with suitable true auxiliary hypotheses) truly explains those explananda. If this is the case, then, on the explanatory-primacy view, seeings (rememberings) can constitute a natural kind.

(3) The *microstructure view* (held in one form or another by Mellor [1977], Putnam [1975a], Sterelny [1983], and Lewis [1983]). There is

a certain amount of variation in the ways this last position has been formulated. One version is formulated in terms of the notion of explanation, one in terms of causality, and one in terms of laws. Since for present purposes these variations make no difference, I have chosen a formulation in terms of the notion of explanation, thereby, making (3) a more restrictive specification of (2). Accordingly, the microstructure view is identical to the explanatory primacy view except that the relevant "explanation space" is restricted to the causal powers of things (including their power to cause certain observations in us) and the set of properties with explanatory primacy is restricted to those that are structural in a physical, chemical, or biochemical sense. On my reconstruction, the view looks like this: X is a natural kind just in case (a) there exists a set of explananda concerning the causal powers of instances of X and (b) there exists a microstructure shared by all and only instances of X, the attribution of which (in conjunction with appropriate true auxiliary hypotheses) truly explains those explananda. For example, water is a natural kind, on this view, because the chemical theory that water is H_2O explains a host of facts concerning the causal powers of water (that it produces steam at 212°F, causes sugar to dissolve within a certain temperature range, etc.).

In contrast to the explanatory-primacy view, the microstructure view of what a natural kind is may have the consequence that there are no (or very few) natural kinds picked out by the terms of the special sciences, as Sterelny (1983) notes. This is because, supposedly, most special-science kinds are functional and, hence, admit of multiple (microstructural) realizations: "In the natural sciences, all the members of a kind share a structure that can be defined physically.... Notoriously, the same is not true of the predicates of the special sciences." (Sterelny 1983, p. 122)

The same sort of reasoning lies behind P. M. Churchland's (1982, p. 223) claim that "for a substantial number of contemporary philosophers, *thinker* is not a natural kind at all." The philosophers he has in mind are those committed to functionalism. Since functionalists believe that "a thinker is just any organization of matter that instantiates a certain functional organization" which can be "realized ... in a variety of quite different physical systems," and since "one can exploit quite different materials governed by quite different laws in order to achieve distinct instantiations of the same abstract functional organization" (p. 224), the conclusion follows, according to Churchland.

To my knowledge, no functionalist has ever drawn this specific conclusion, but that is a minor quibble. (Churchland can claim that he is
attributing a belief that in fact follows from beliefs a functionalist would
acknowledge even if the functionalist doesn't realize that it so follows.) The
important point is that the argument works only if 'natural kind' is used
in its most restrictive sense. If it is used in either the liberal sense or
the explanatory-primacy sense, the premise about multiple realization
provides no grounds for the conclusion, as the quote from Platt (1983)
made clear. There may very well be sets of explananda (detailing, for
example, the behavioral properties of intelligence) that can be explained
perfectly well by some functionalist conception of what a thinker is.

We come now to the point of this whole excursion into the literature on
natural kinds. Is it appropriate to say that the cognitive capacities constitute a natural kind if what we really want to say is that they constitute an
appropriate domain for scientific research? There are two reasons why we
should answer "no" to this question.

First, assumption D3, in fact, makes two claims, one implicit and one
explicit. It says (implicitly) that there *exists* a set of answers to the basic
questions of the research program that meet conditions a and b of D3. This
is an ontological claim. And it also says (explicitly) that, given sufficient
research, we will be able to arrive at those answers. This is an epistemological claim. Substituting a natural-kind claim for a domain claim is
wrong because claiming that the cognitive capacities constitute a natural
kind (in whatever version) makes only an ontological claim: namely, that
there exists a natural kind of a certain sort. Nothing is said about our being
able to discover this natural kind.

Second, even if we focus our attention solely on the ontological part of
assumption D3, a natural-kind claim won't suffice. Depending on how we
construe natural kinds, either the claim that the cognitive capacities constitute a natural kind is almost certainly false or it does not capture what we
want to say. In either case, formulating the final domain-specifying assumption in terms of the notion of natural kinds is incorrect.

To see this last point, we must consider each of the natural-kind claims
in question. For ease of discussion, let us abbreviate them as N_L ('L'
for 'liberal'), N_{EP} ('EP' for 'explanatory primacy'), and N_{MS} ('MS' for
'microstructure').

Consider first the microstructure version, N_{MS}. Although all the facts are
not yet in, it strikes me as extremely unlikely that all and only instances of

all the various kinds of human cognitive capacities (visual perception, language production, music understanding, remembering, etc.) will have some one microstructural property in common, at least at a neurophysiological level. The hard part is not finding a structural property that they all share—since all the human cognitive capacities exist in virtue of structures and processes in the brain, they will all share various neurophysiological and anatomical properties. The hard part is finding some set of neural properties that distinguishes the realization of *just* the human cognitive capacities from the realization of two other classes of capacities: human noncognitive capacities (such as our capacities to swim, jump, and sleep) and nonhuman cognitive capacities (such as a chimpanzee's ability to solve problems).

Despite the persuasiveness of these considerations, P. M. Churchland (1982) has argued for the apparently contrary thesis, that *thinker* is a natural kind in a fairly restrictive sense. Churchland construes a natural kind as "a kind that figures in some one or more natural laws" (p. 223, note 1). At first blush, this sounds like the liberal view; however, the only way to make sense of his argument that functionalism is committed to the thesis that thinker is *not* a natural kind is to read 'natural' here as meaning 'physical'. On this reading, Churchland's conception comes very close to the microstructure view. There are, however, minor differences. Insofar as the physical laws exclude the biological ones, it is narrower in scope; and insofar as the physical laws concern more than just the microstructure of things, it is broader. For present purposes, though, these non-negligible differences don't really matter.

Churchland's argument trades on certain presumed similarities between the notion of a living thing and the notion of a thinking thing. It goes like this:

1. Living thing is a natural kind. "While it is no doubt true that metabolic activities can manifest themselves in a nomically heterogeneous variety of substrates—governed by sundry chemical principles, or by mechanical principles, or by electromagnetic principles—it is also true that there is a deeper level of physical law that comprehends all of these cases as instances, and in whose terms the fundamental activities of living matter can be characterized. The theory that achieves this remarkable result is non-equilibrium thermodynamics, a theory of great generality whose concern is with the dynamics, quality, and distribution of *energy*." (p. 232) To

be more precise: "a living thing is a dissipative system, a semi-closed local entropic minimum, whose internal negative entropy filters out further negative entropy from the energy flowing through it" (p. 233).

2. There are important parallels between vital activity and cognitive activity. Specifically: "Both the vital economy and the cognitive economy appear to maintain a fairly uniform identity or character despite being instanced in a wide variety or physical systems. Both economies come in continuously varying 'grades'.... Further, both economies display a very strong *developmental* aspect.... Both economies require a continuous flux of quite specific kinds of high-quality energy. Both economies represent the evolved accumulation of enormous amounts of information, and both economies play an essential role in the reproduction of this accumulated information in other individuals." (p. 234)

Rather than simply concluding at this point that *thinker,* like *living thing,* is a natural kind, Churchland chooses to complicate matters somewhat. He advances the suggestion that what all these parallels point to is that vital activity and cognitive activity are continuous rather than distinct. "They are both instances of the same form of activity, instances that differ only in degree. Cognitive activity, we might say, is just a high-intensity version of that of which vital activity is a comparatively low-intensity version." (p. 235)

It is far from clear what to say about this argument. First, bracketing for the moment the question of its success, I am not certain that Churchland even ends up with the claim he initially intends to make (viz., that *thinker* is a natural kind). This is because, as de Sousa (1984, p. 565) points out, one of the main demands "typically made of a well-behaved theory of natural kinds" includes the demand that natural kinds manifest sharp boundaries—that they not shade into each other. If this demand is taken seriously, then, insofar as cognitive activity is continuous with vital activity, cognitive activity will not constitute a natural kind. Second, if the conclusion is tantamount to a natural-kind claim, it is not clear how successful it is. There is at least one reason to be wary. From a formal point of view, Churchland's argument is an instance of what the logicians call an "argument from analogy"—a form of inductive argument that easily lends itself to fallacious reasoning. Typically, the structure of an analogical argument looks like this (Salmon 1984, p. 64):

1. Objects of type X have properties F, G, H, etc.
2. Objects of type Y have properties F, G, H, etc. and Z.
3. Therefore, objects of type X have property Z as well.

In assessing how good such an argument is we must look not only at the truth or falsity (or plausibility) of the premises but also at whether possession of the common properties is *relevant* to possession of the inferred property. Is maintaining a fairly uniform identity despite multiple realization relevant to the existence of an underlying shared microstructure? Is coming in continuously varying grades, displaying a strong developmental aspect, requiring a continuous flux of high-quality energy, etc. relevant? I have no idea. And Churchland certainly does not help us out on this score.

I have suggested some reasons why Churchland's argument is not completely persuasive. In the end, however, whether we are persuaded or not does not really matter to the issue at hand. Even if it were true that the human cognitive capacities constitute a natural kind in the most restrictive sense, *saying* that they do is not tantamount to saying that they constitute an appropriate domain for cognitive science—and it is the latter claim that we want to make. Suppose that Churchland's suppositions are correct—that the human cognitive capacities constitute a natural kind in the sense that there exists a (microstructural) theory true of all and only the human cognitive capacities that is capable of explaining the causal powers of those capacities. Still, the existence of this state of affairs would not guarantee us answers to the basic questions of the research program of cognitive science that pertain to the various, distinct *kinds* of cognitive capacity (such as language understanding, visual perception, and imaging) rather than to all the capacities taken together. For example, knowing what biological or physical properties are shared by all and only the human cognitive capacities will not help to explain how we understand sentences, or plan actions, or generate images. And this is because answering questions about the latter requires knowing about the *distinguishing* features of these subkinds, rather than about their commonalities.

A similar argument applies to N_L the natural-kind claim formulated in terms of the liberal view. Suppose all we require for something to count as a natural kind is that a predicate picking out this kind appear in some lawful generalization of the field. In other words, suppose that all we need is at least one true, counterfactual-supporting generalization in which the predicate 'human cognitive capacity' appears. Surely cognitive science will be able to offer us that. In fact, several candidates spring immediately to mind: 'Visual perception is a human cognitive capacity', 'All human cognitive capacities are intentional in character', and 'People are typically unaware of how they exercise their cognitive capacities'. Note, however, that when we assert that the cognitive capacities constitute an appropriate domain for scientific research we intend to say much more than that cognitive science will be able to come up with generalizations like the above. We intend to say what we in fact have said: that a theoretically coherent set of answers will be forthcoming to all the basic questions of the field. Thus, even the most liberal conception of a natural kind is not suitable for our fourth domain-specifying assumption.

On both the most restrictive and the most liberal conception of a natural kind, claiming that the human cognitive capacities constitute a natural kind falls short of what we want to say for similar reasons. Each of the three claims we have considered thus far—domain-specifying assumption D3, N_{MS}, and N_L—involves both an explanans and an explanandum. In D3, the explanandum is fixed by the basic questions of the research program. The ontological claim being made is a relative one: that there exists an appropriate explanans for this explanandum. In contrast, the ontological claim made by N_{MS} and N_L is not relative. N_{MS} asserts the existence of a certain kind of microstructure theory. N_L asserts the existence of a certain set of laws. The problem is that, having started with the explanans rather than the explanandum, the posited explanans turns out to be inadequate to the *desired* explanandum (namely, answering the basic questions of the research program).

The situation with respect to N_{EP}, the explanatory-primacy version, is in a sense just the reverse. Here we start with the explanandum rather than the explanans; furthermore, our choice of explanandum is unrestricted. Thus, we are free to choose the basic questions of the research as the desired explanandum. The problem arises with respect to the explanans. Recall the second requirement for something's being a natural kind, on the explanatory-primacy view: X is a natural kind only if (b) there exists a set of properties shared by all and only instances of X, the attribution of which (in conjunction with appropriate true auxiliary hypotheses) truly explains those explananda. It is the existence of such a *shared* set of explanatory properties that is highly doubtful.

In section 2.4 I will suggest that among the basic questions of ANTCOG are questions of the form 'In virtue of what does a typical normal adult have the capacity to _____?'. Suppose now that we raise this question about each of our cognitive capacities: perception, memory, language understanding, language production, and so on. Is it even remotely plausible that the cognitive capacities have *in common* some set of properties appeal to which would answer *each* of these distinct questions? Certainly not on a cognitivist approach, for (as we shall see) cognitive science attempts to answer these questions by appeal to a person's representational and computational resources. But it is precisely because these resources are different for each capacity that the capacities themselves are different.

In sum, then, the situation is this: N_{MS} either is false or (if we accept Churchland's argument) does not say what we want to say. N_L is probably true, but it also does not say what we want to say. And N_{EP} is almost certainly false. Thus, each version either is certainly false or makes the wrong claim.

Note, however, that this argument in no way impugns the existence *in general* of natural kinds in cognitive science. What I have been calling the "subkinds" of cognitive capacities are probably natural kinds. No matter what our science of the mind eventually looks like—that is, even if we end up with something very unlike a computational theory of mind—we will probably still have laws about visual perception, language production, remembering, etc. Thus, each of the subkinds will constitute a natural kind, at least on the liberal view. It is also quite likely that all and only instances of each subkind will share some underlying properties sufficient for explaining most of what we want to explain about the subkind in question. If so, then each subkind will constitute a natural kind, on the explanatory-primacy view. It is even possible that the explanatory properties will be microstructural properties (this is certainly the assumption of neuroscience), thus vindicating the microstructure version of the natural-kinds claim for the subkinds as well.

2.4   The Basic Questions

A research framework gets its direction, on my account, from the questions it attempts to answer. I have already suggested that the domain of cognitive science consists of the human cognitive capacities. But exactly what about human cognition do cognitive scientists want to know? More precisely, what questions are they asking about human cognition?

There are four kinds of basic empirical questions that motivate research in cognitive science. Questions of each kind can be raised for each of the cognitive capacities included in the domain. I will express these kinds of questions in the form of interrogative schemas in which the blank is to be filled in with an expression referring to some particular cognitive capacity (such as 'recognize words' or 'perceive a scene').

Recall that the basic empirical questions of a research framework are anchored in our pretheoretic conception of the domain (as characterized by the domain-specifying assumptions). They are vague in the sense that, for any basic question Q, it is not entirely clear what should count as a possible answer to Q. The "approach" adopted by a research framework is specified by its substantive and methodological assumptions. The substantive assumptions, in particular, function as constraints on possible answers to the basic empirical questions. Because the identity of any given question is determined by its possible answer set, in constraining the basic questions, the substantive assumptions, in effect, define a new set of questions. I shall call these the *revised basic questions*. To put the matter slightly differently: The questions of a research program are initially posed in a "theory-neutral" fashion so that, in principle, they can be shared by competing research frameworks and answered in radically different ways. The role of the substantive assumptions of the research framework is then to constrain the set of possible answers to those answers that are theoretically appropriate for that research framework (for example, those that are framed entirely in information-processing terms). In this section, I will characterize the original basic questions of ANTCOG. The revised basic questions will be discussed in chapter 9 after I have had a chance to lay out the substantive assumptions of the research framework.

The basic question schemas of the research framework of ANTCOG are the following.

Q1   For the normal, typical adult, what precisely is the human capacity to _____?

At the outset of the research process, we can describe the cognitive capacities of interest in a rough-and-ready manner. However, we do not know precisely what they are, either empirically or theoretically. The first question is a request to sharpen our understanding of each of the capacities so that questions Q2–Q4 can be posed more precisely. Deeper understanding can be gained in four ways.

First, there is the route of philosophical reflection on our commonsense conception. My characterizing the bulk of our cognitive capacities as intentional, pragmatically evaluable, coherent, reliable, and productive is precisely the result of such reflection, but much more can be said along these lines. For example, if the object of investigation is our capacity to use images, we can ask the following about this specific capacity: *In what respects* (if at all) is it intentional, pragmatically evaluable, coherent, reliable, and productive?

Second, cognitive scientists—especially, cognitive psychologists and linguists—seek greater empirical understanding of our cognitive capacities. How does the capacity manifest itself in particular circumstances? For example, what are the temporal characteristics of exercising a given capacity? Recall, for example, Kosslyn's map-scanning experiment. Information about such temporal characteristics is not at all part of our ordinary knowledge of cognition, and it can be very revealing when it comes to answering questions of the form exhibited in schemas Q2–Q4.

A third route for gaining deeper understanding of the capacity under study is to reconceptualize it in terms of the approach adopted by the research framework. How, for example, might we understand the human capacity to use mental images in information-processing terms? Kosslyn's use of a CRT metaphor at the outset of his research is an example of answering Q1 in this second way.

A related approach is to investigate the scope and the limits of the capacity under study. When a person fails to exercise a capacity successfully (under normal circumstances), what form does this failure take? To put the question another way: Under what conditions do errors begin to manifest themselves, and what is the nature of these errors? Both Simon (1981b) and Pylyshyn (1984) have emphasized the importance of observing a device in atypical circumstances in order to make inferences about its internal structure. In discussing a motor as an example of an artificial system, Simon (1981b, p. 16) writes: "In a benign environment we would learn from the motor only what it had been called upon to do; in a taxing environment we would learn something about its internal structure— specifically, about those aspects of the internal structure that were chiefly instrumental in limiting performance." It is for just such reasons that cognitive scientists have attached much importance to "error data" in trying to understand the cognitive capacities.

Q2   In virtue of what does a normal, typical adult have the capacity to
_____ (such that this capacity is intentional, pragmatically evaluable,
coherent, reliable, and productive)?

People do not have their cognitive capacities magically. There is something about the mind/brain in virtue of which they have the capacities they
do. The second question is a request for a description of the mental
resources that make any given capacity possible, in either its successful or
its unsuccessful form. Of course, when this question is posed in the context
of a particular research framework, researchers have a general idea of
what the resources in question are like. Thus, to pose this question in the
context of cognitive science is to assume that the resources in question are
representational and computational. An example of answering this question about our capacity to use visual mental images from a cognitive
science perspective can be found in Kosslyn's general theory of mental
imagery. (See figure 1.3 and table 1.1 above.)

Q3   How does a normal, typical adult typically (exercise his or her capacity to) _____?

Whereas Q2 is after a static description of what underlies any given
capacity, Q3 seeks a dynamic account. How are the mental resources
described in answer to Q2 actually deployed when a person *exercises* the
capacity in question? What stages or steps does a person typically go
through when the capacity is exercised successfully? What exactly goes
wrong when the capacity is exercised unsuccessfully? Cummins (1975,
1977, 1983) provides a nice account of this sort of explanation in his
discussions of "functional analysis." Kosslyn answers this sort of question
when he develops specific dynamic models for the various subcapacities
involved in the imagery system. (See figures 1.5 and 1.6 above.)

Q4   How does the capacity to _____ of the normal, typical adult
interact with the rest of his or her cognitive capacities?

Thus far, each of the capacities has been treated in isolation. This
question is a request for a more integrated account. How does our capacity to perceive interact with our capacities to remember, and so on? Here
I might also introduce the distinction embodied in Q2 and Q3. That
is, I might ask what it is about our mental resources that allows our
capacities to interact (a question akin to Q2), and how our various cogni-

tive capacities interact when they are being exercised (a question akin to Q3).

I have now completed my discussion of the domain and the basic questions of cognitive science. The next task—one that will occupy me for the remainder of the book—will be to get clear on how cognitive science goes about trying to answer those basic questions. In chapters 3–8 I will explore the conceptual and theoretical resources invoked by cognitive science for this purpose. Finally, in chapter 9, we will see what happens when these conceptual and theoretical resources are combined with the basic questions I have just outlined. In particular, we will see how the basic questions are transformed when it is assumed that the cognitive mind is an information-processing system.

3 The Computational Assumption

What distinguishes cognitive science, as a research program, is more than that it is interested in answering questions about the human cognitive capacities. It is also that it seeks to answer these questions in a quite specific way. In particular, it seeks to answer these questions in accordance with what I have called the "substantive assumptions" of its research framework. Precisely how these assumptions constrain the project of answering the basic questions of the field will be discussed in chapter 9. However, before we are in a position to understand this constraining role of the assumptions we must have a deeper understanding of the assumptions themselves. The principal task of the next six chapters is to develop such an understanding.

As was noted in chapter 1, the substantive assumptions of a research framework fall into two kinds. "Linking assumptions" claim that the domain picked out by the domain-specifying assumptions of the research framework constitutes (or is substantially like) a system of some designated kind X; "system assumptions" characterize the kind of system being attributed.

There is substantial agreement among cognitive scientists that the research framework of cognitive science in general, and that of ANTCOG in particular, is committed to two fundamental linking assumptions, one concerning the computational nature of the human cognitive capacities and one concerning their representational nature (Fodor 1975; Newell 1980; Haugeland 1981; Pylyshyn 1984; Gardner 1985; Stillings et al. 1987).[1] In this chapter. I will consider the first of these linking assumptions and the associated system assumption. I shall call the conjunction of these two assumptions "the computational assumption." The chapter will focus on two questions: Is it appropriate to consider the computational linking assumption a metaphor? What do cognitive scientists have in mind when they claim that the human cognitive capacities are computational, or that the mind/brain is a computer?

3.1 The Computational Linking Assumption

The "linking" part of the computational assumption can be formulated as follows:

SA1: THE COMPUTATIONAL ASSUMPTION

C1 (linking assumption)   The human cognitive mind/brain is a computational device (computer); hence, the human cognitive capacities consist, to a large extent, of a system of computational capacities.[2]

This assumption, or some variant thereof, is often referred to as "the computer metaphor," although there are some writers who explicitly deny the correctness of that label (see, for example, Pylyshyn 1979 and Newell 1980). I would like to begin my discussion by considering whether it is appropriate, in view of the current commitments and practices of the cognitive science community, to regard C1 as a metaphor rather than as a literal working hypothesis.

What is a metaphor? As one might expect, there is no simple, agreed-upon answer to this question. The nature of metaphor has been explored for roughly 2000 years, since the time of Aristotle, and the literature on the subject is both vast and varied. Nevertheless, since the publication of Max Black's famous essay "Metaphor" in 1954, the opinions of analytic philosophers and cognitive scientists have converged on a number of points. It will be sufficient for present purposes if we can get a handle on these areas of agreement.

There are numerous questions that can be (and have been) asked about metaphors. For example: What are the functions of metaphors in everyday speech, in literature, and in science? How do we identify metaphors? How do we understand metaphors? What is the semantics of metaphor? The convergence of opinion I alluded to above seems to be centered primarily on questions concerning the cognitive function and understanding of metaphor; in contrast, there is considerable disagreement as to whether there is such a thing as metaphorical meaning and, if so, what it is like.

Metaphors are, by definition, figures of speech. They come in a variety of "sizes," ranging from phrases to sentences to significant chunks of text. Since the purpose of this discussion is to shed light on C1, I will focus exclusively on simple sentential metaphors of the form 'A is B', where the A term is being used literally and the B term metaphorically. Standard examples include 'Man is a wolf', 'Sally is a block of ice', and Wallace Stevens' line 'The garden was a slum of bloom'. In each of these cases, the surface form of the metaphor involves an identity or an attribution rather than an explicit comparison (e.g., 'Man is like a wolf'). This is what distinguishes metaphors from similes.

A number of different terminological conventions have been proposed for talking about metaphors. Since none of the proposed terms wears its meaning on its sleeve (so to speak), I find them confusing rather than helpful.[3] I thus propose to use the following patently obvious terminology: I will call the A term ('man') the *nonmetaphorical term* and the B term ('wolf') the *metaphorical term* of the metaphor. The object designated by the A term will be called the *nonmetaphorical subject*; the object designated (or the property expressed) by the B term will be called *metaphorical subject*.

It is generally agreed that we identify metaphors as metaphors on the basis of a perceived tension or incongruity between the metaphorical term and either the nonmetaphorical term or the surrounding (explicit or implicit) context (Beardsley 1958, 1962; Henle 1958; Goodman 1968; Mathews 1971; Black 1977; Kittay 1987). Precisely what the nature of this incongruity is remains a point of controversy,[4] but at a minimum we can say this: In the simple sort of case we are considering, what prompts the recipient (the reader or hearer) to try to understand a metaphorical statement metaphorically is that if the statement were to be taken literally it would be obviously false. Human beings are obviously not wolves, literally speaking. Thus, given the conversational implicature to always tell the truth, when a reader or a hearer is confronted with a metaphorical statement, he or she infers that the statement was not intended to be understood literally and proceeds to try to construe it metaphorically.

Black's principal contribution to the literature on metaphor was to argue for an "interaction view" of metaphorical understanding, as against the commonly accepted "substitution view."

According to the substitution view, a person who uses a metaphor has in mind a proposition that could, in principle, be expressed literally. If the metaphor has the form 'A is B', the proposition may be that A has such-and-such B-like properties or that A is like B in such-and-such respects. For example, in the case of the metaphor 'Man is a wolf', the intended proposition might be either that man is fierce or that man is like a wolf in being fierce.[5] Metaphorical understanding, on this view, consists in the recovery of this underlying, intended proposition.

On the substitution view, the act of metaphorical understanding is "like deciphering a code or unravelling a riddle" (Black 1962, p. 32); on the interaction view, it is far more creative and open-ended. Black assumes that both the nonmetaphorical and metaphorical terms of a metaphor are associated with "systems of commonplaces"—that is, commonly held beliefs about the nonmetaphorical and metaphorical subjects, respectively. Understanding a metaphor then consists in using the set of commonly held beliefs concerning the metaphorical subject in order to shed new light on the nonmetaphorical subject. This is accomplished by using the commonplaces associated with the metaphorical subject to select, emphasize, suppress, and organize "features of the principal subject [nonmetaphorical subject] by *implying* statements about it that normally apply to the subsidiary subject [metaphorical subject]" (Black 1962, pp. 44–45). In the case of 'Man is a wolf' the metaphorical interaction works like this:

The effect ... of (metaphorically) calling a man a "wolf" is to evoke the wolf-system of related commonplaces. If the man is a wolf, he preys upon other animals, is fierce, hungry, engaged in constant struggle, a scavenger, and so on. Each of these implied assertions has now to be made to fit the principal subject (the man) either in normal or in abnormal senses.... A suitable hearer will be led by the wolf-system of implications to construct a corresponding system of implications about the principal subject.... The new implications must be determined by the pattern of implications associated with literal uses of the word "wolf". Any human traits that can without undue strain be talked about in "wolf-language" will be rendered prominent, and any that cannot will be pushed into the background. The wolf-metaphor suppresses some details, emphasises others—in short, *organizes* our view of man. (Black 1962, p. 41)

In other words. according to Black, the essence of metaphorical understanding is not recovery but creation—creation of a new, nonstandard representation of the nonmetaphorical subject on the basis of the interaction of the two systems of associated commonplaces.

I have been focusing on the substitution and interaction views of metaphor as theories of metaphorical understanding because it is this aspect of metaphor that is relevant for our purposes and it is this aspect of metaphor that has generated a significant consensus in the literature (viz., that the interaction view is roughly correct). It should be noted, however, that both the substitution view (especially the comparison version) and the interaction view are also standardly taken as proposals regarding the existence and the nature of metaphorical *meaning*.[6] In this respect, they are far more controversial. I will not have anything to say about this aspect of the two views.

It is also worth noting that there is a marked compatibility between the interaction view of metaphorical understanding, as discussed in the philosophical literature, and current computational work on analogical reasoning in cognitive science circles.[7] To my knowledge the latter research was not directly influenced by Black's 1954 paper (a number of the major review papers do not even cite it), yet it requires very little imagination to regard many of the computational models being proposed as detailed elaborations of Black's vague suggestions regarding "systems of associated commonplaces" and "interaction." There are, in particular, two striking similarities:

• As we have seen, a prerequisite to metaphorical understanding on the interaction view is the existence of two systems of "commonplaces," one associated with the nonmetaphorical subject and one with the metaphorical subject. Current computational models posit the existence of "knowledge" representations of a *target* domain and a *source* domain.

• On the interaction view, the act of metaphorical understanding itself involves the "interaction" of the two systems of commonplaces to yield nonstandard implications concerning the nonmetaphorical subject. In cognitive science research on analogical reasoning, this interaction is conceptualized as a process of *mapping* from the source representation to the target representation in order to yield a set of analogical inferences. This mapping has two aspects: the generation of a set of hypotheses regarding possible ways in which elements of the source might map onto elements of the target and the evaluation of these hypotheses. As Holyoak and Thagard (1989, p. 297) describe it, "The mapping implicitly defines a set of inferences that could be made about the target, based upon correspondences with predicates and objects in the source domain. Thus if predicate P and object O in the source map onto P′ and O′ in the target, and the proposition P(O) holds in the source, then the proposition P′(O′) can be constructed as a candidate inference about the target. Whether a candidate inference will in fact be seriously considered as a plausible hypothesis about the target will depend upon such pragmatic factors as whether the inference is relevant to the analogist's goals in using the analogy and whether the inference is consistent with what is already known about the target domain."[8]

Thus far, we have been discussing the nature of metaphors as they appear in ordinary and literary speech. What about the use of metaphors in science? One of the most illuminating treatments I have come across builds explicitly on Black's interaction view. In his article "Metaphor and Theory Change," Boyd (1979) argues that certain kinds of metaphors—he calls them "theory-constitutive" metaphors—have a very important role to play in science.[9] In particular, such metaphorical attributions have the function of introducing theoretical terminology where none has existed. Like interactive metaphors, theory-constitutive metaphors are open-ended. But they differ in certain important respects from literary metaphors. The point of using a literary metaphor is to direct attention to hitherto unnoticed, but in principle known, properties of the primary subject. In contrast, scientific metaphors are used in order to encourage scientific exploration of previously *unknown* similarities and differences between the nonmetaphorical and the metaphorical subjects.[10] Thus, on Boyd's view, the aim of scientific metaphor is discovery, whereas the aim of literary metaphor is insight.

One way of bringing out this contrast is to consider the distinction within computational theories of analogical reasoning between generating possible analogical inferences and evaluating or justifying those inferences. In the case of literary or ordinary metaphor, the evaluation stage is relatively trivial (from a phenomenological point of view, although perhaps not from a computational, point of view). All the information required for evaluation of the target domain and the goals of the speaker or writer is, in principle, available; it simply needs to be utilized in the evaluation process. In contrast, in the scientific case we are concerned with whether candidate analogical inferences are *true* rather than simply whether they are consistent with currently available information. And since the inferred properties of the target domain are usually unobservable (and, hence, only indirectly testable), evaluating such inferences typically involves a long and arduous process of *obtaining* the information relevant to evaluation.

Another interesting feature of the scientific case is that full knowledge of the metaphorical subject is not required for a theory-constitutive metaphor to be useful. Such metaphors can have programmatic importance not only with respect to exploring similarities and differences between the nonmetaphorical and metaphorical subjects but also with respect to expanding our knowledge of the metaphorical subject itself.

Boyd (1979) emphasizes several other points of difference between literary and scientific metaphors. Literary metaphors are typically associated with a single author or work, whereas theory-constitutive metaphors can become the property of an entire scientific community. In addition, when a literary metaphor is repeated too often its force is lost, since once we have noticed the points of similarity the metaphor loses its interactive quality. In contrast, because exploring the points of similarity between the nonmetaphorical and metaphorical subjects of a theory-constitutive metaphor is a much more difficult and time-consuming process, such metaphors can be "explored by hundreds of scientific authors without their interactive quality being lost" (Boyd 1979, p. 361). Finally, it is often said that a literary metaphor can never be adequately captured by a literal paraphrase. Just the opposite is true of theory-constitutive metaphors. If the program of research generated by a theory-constitutive metaphor is completely successful, then we will eventually understand exactly in which respects the nonmetaphorical and metaphorical subjects are like one another, and this knowledge will be literally expressible.

There is no question that much of what Boyd has to say about theory-constitutive metaphors applies to C1—a point that is hardly surprising, since Boyd regards the computational metaphors of cognitive science as paradigmatic instances of theory-constitutive metaphors.[11] More specifically, there are at least five ways in which C1 functions like a Boydian theory-constitutive metaphor:

• The "computer metaphor" plays the role it does in current cognitive science because many scientists interested in cognition believe that no other theoretical terminology for describing the mind/brain at a *functional* level is as fruitful.

• The attribution that the mind/brain is a computer is clearly open-ended in ways that are characteristic of Boyd's "theory-constitutive" metaphors: No one, at present, knows in what ways the mind/brain may be a computational device. Furthermore, the concept of a computer is itself surprisingly vague (as we shall see in the next section), and it may well be that exploration of the similarities and differences between minds and computers will lead to an expansion of our knowledge of computers.

• In order to determine whether there are points of similarity between mind/brains and computers, we must use a scientific methodology, not a literary one. That is, the relevant properties of mind—if they exist—are not simply apparent; they must be experimentally determined in the usual scientific ways.

• C1 is also theory-constitutive in Boyd's sense in that it is a property of a group (namely, the scientific community of cognitive scientists) rather than of a single individual.

• The force of C1 is certainly not lost upon repeated use within that group.

Clearly, C1 is theory-constitutive in many respects. And yet, despite the fact that Boyd's analysis of theory-constitutive metaphors seems to fit C1 like a glove, there remains the question as to whether C1 ought to be understood as a *metaphor*. This question remains because theory-constitutive metaphors, whatever their methodological role in inquiry and however they differ from literary and everyday metaphors, remain *nonliteral* attributions. They are, as Boyd (1979, p. 360) says, "metaphors which scientists use in expressing theoretical claims for which no adequate literal paraphrase is known." Thus, to say that C1 should be regarded as a metaphor, albeit a theory-constitutive one, is to imply that cognitive scientists assume not that mind/brains are literally computers but only that they have some properties in common with them. But is this what cognitive scientists, in fact, assume? To answer this question we obviously need to know something more about what cognitive scientists mean by the term 'computational device'. In particular, we need to ascertain whether cognitive scientists believe that a computational device is the sort of thing that the mind/brain could not literally be or whether they regard the notion of a computational device as broad enough and abstract enough to include both man-made machines and the human mind. It is to this question that we now turn.

3.2   The Computational System Assumption

What do cognitive scientists mean when they assume, as in C1, that the mind/brain is a computational device? To put the question another way: What system assumption should accompany C1? Presumably, it will take the following form:

C2 (system assumption)   A computational device is a device with such-and-such properties.

What is the appropriate way to substitute for 'such-and-such' in order to best reflect the current commitments and research of the cognitive science community? For ease of exposition, I shall refer to the concept of a computer that C2 is designed to explicate as "the cognitive science concept of a computer."

Two approaches to capturing the cognitive science concept of a computer can be found in the literature. The first is to characterize a computer in terms of notions developed in the mathematical theory of computability and automata theory. This is the approach taken by Newell (1980, 1990). Haugeland (1981, 1985), Nelson (1987, 1989). Pylyshyn (1984), and Johnson-Laird (1988). The second approach is to characterize a computer in the way that standard reference books in computer science do: as a data-processing or information-processing device. This is the approach taken by Boden (1981) and by Stillings et al. (1987). I shall argue that if our goal is to specify the notion of a computer relevant to C1, the second route is clearly the most appropriate one. My argument will rest on a number of considerations:

(1) The cognitive science concept of a computer is not idiosyncratic. It did not originate in cognitive science: rather, most of its notions and claims came from fields outside cognitive science and were taken over by cognitive science in the hope that they would elucidate the nature of mind. The original sources of the concept are various and well known: work in mathematical logic on computability by Gödel and Turing; the technological development of electronic computers, which began during World War II and which is continuing: and the postwar explosion of research in computer science.

(2) The cognitive science concept of a computer is broad enough to encompass both "conventional" and "connectionist" machines.[12] Computers come not only in all shapes and sizes, but also with different kinds of inner workings. When cognitive scientists first began to theorize about the human mind/brain in computational terms, they had in mind a particular kind of computer (akin to the electronic devices most of us are familiar with) known as a "conventional" or "von Neumann" computer.[13] More recently, however, another kind of computer, which relies on the connection and the parallel actitivity of many small computing units, has captured the imagination of many cognitive scientists. I will describe these types of computers in sections 3.3 and 3.4, respectively. Although there is currently a hot debate concerning which sort of computer—conventional or connectionist—will prove to be the best model for human cognition, the important point for our purposes is that both conventional and connec-

tionist theorizing clearly fall within the purview of cognitive science. Thus, any adequate formulation of the computational assumption must reflect that fact.

(3) The cognitive science concept of a computer is specific enough to capture what distinguishes the cognitive science approach to human cognition from other approaches. One of the things that sets cognitive science apart from other approaches to cognition is that cognitive scientists are interested in developing computational models, theories, and hypotheses. In accordance with the metascientific views developed in chapter 1, this feature of cognitive science theorizing results from the fact that the research framework of cognitive science includes the substantive assumption that the cognitive mind/brain is a computer and from the fact that a research framework guides research at the theoretical level in the sense that researchers committed to the framework attempt to develop theories which make reference to the entities and processes posited by the substantive assumptions of the framework. The point is that if the *source* of cognitive science's distinctive computational mode of theorizing is the computational assumption, then this assumption must be formulated in a way that is specific enough to capture this theoretical distinctiveness. In other words, the substantive assumption must actually mention the kinds of entities and processes that typically show up in the computational models and theories characteristic of cognitive science research.

(4) The cognitive science concept of a computer is broad enough to constitute a theoretical basis not only for ANTCOG but also for the other subsidiary programs of cognitive science. To make the task of describing the foundations of cognitive science manageable, I have restricted myself to a description of the subsidiary research program concerned with adult, normal, typical cognition (ANTCOG). It is clear, however, that although the various subsidiary research programs described in the introduction (see figure ii) may differ with respect to basic questions (and, possibly, some methodological assumptions), they share the substantive assumptions I am attributing to ANTCOG. Thus, the concept of a computer invoked for ANTCOG must also be applicable to the other subsidiary research programs.

Let us now consider each of the two approaches to capturing the cognitive science concept of a computer in the light of these four considerations.

Consider first the computability approach. The starting point of computability theory is the idea of an *effective procedure*—"a set of rules which tell us, from moment to moment, precisely how to behave" and which are so explicit they can be "followed" mechanically (that is, without the use of "understanding" or "interpretation") (Minsky 1967, p. 105). Since 1936, a number of attempts have been made to capture the idea of an effective procedure more precisely. These attempts fall into, roughly, three groups: First, effectiveness has been equated with a certain class of functions, the general recursive functions: second, it has been identified with computability on machines that are infinite in certain ways, including Turing machines and program machines; third, it has been defined in terms of certain kinds of symbol-manipulation systems. (See Minsky 1967 for more detail.) The astonishing thing, and the central finding of computability theory, is that all these precise ways of capturing the intuitive idea of an effective procedure turn out to be equivalent! There are, thus, good inductive grounds for believing that effectiveness, in the intuitive sense, is nothing but computability, in one of the above technical senses. This is the gist of the so-called Turing/Church thesis.

There are two ways to use computability theory in order to specify the system assumption associated with C1. The first is to characterize a computer purely *behaviorally*—that is, as a device with certain input-output capacities, and specifically as a device that can "compute" computable functions. The second is to characterize a computer as one or another kind of abstract automata, such as a Turing machine. Both ways are inadequate, on my view.

The first problem we run into if we try to characterize a computer solely in terms of its computational capacities (that is, without any reference to internal structure) is the problem of making the characterization precise. How many computable functions does something have to be able to "compute" in order to be considered a "computer"? There are three obvious possibilities: at least one, all, or some significant number.

Suppose we adopt the minimal characterization and formulate the system assumption like this: A computer is any device that can "compute" at least one computable function. This obviously won't do, for the simple reason that on this formulation practically any physical object will turn out to be a computer—a consequence that is radically at odds with the way the term 'computer' is standardly used. Suppose that the function in question is some constant function $f(x) = 0$, where x is defined for some range of numbers. Then a stone in my yard that is subjected to varying amounts of rainfall is a computer. Simply take the input to be the amount of rainfall and the output to be some constant property of the stone (say, its hardness). No matter how much rain falls on the stone, its hardness always stays the same. Its behavior thus satisfies the constant function in question. Admittedly, the standard conception of a computer is vague and imprecisely defined, but it certainly is not meant to encompass stones! In sum, the one-computable-function formulation won't do because it violates consideration 1.

Suppose now we go to the opposite extreme and claim that the relevant sense of 'computational device' in C1 is that of a device that can "compute" any computable function—that is, a device that is, in the technical sense, universal. In this case we no longer have to worry about the extension of the notion being too wide and including things like stones. But we may have to worry about it being too narrow. For one thing, restricting the notion of a computer to that of a universal machine again flies in the face of the way the term 'computer' is standardly used in computer science, for although many computers are universal machines, there are certainly things called "computers" that can compute only a special range of functions. A chess-playing machine is a case in point.

It appears, then, that if we adopt a behavioral approach to characterizing a computer we are left with the third option: that a computer is any device that can "compute" a significant number of computable functions. This is the approach adopted by Newell (1990). Newell begins with the notion of a *machine* as something that defines a function from input to output. A *computational system* can then be defined as "a machine that can produce *many* functions", where some of its inputs are viewed as providing the specification of the function to be produced. An example is a hand-held calculator.

Computing a significant number of computable functions is plausibly a necessary condition for something's belonging to the cognitive science concept of a computer; however, it is not sufficient, on my view. The reason turns on the third consideration above. In articulating the substantive assumptions of cognitive science's research framework, we are trying to get at what distinguishes this approach to the study of cognition from other approaches. But if nothing is said about what sorts of mental structures and processes are supposed to "underlie" our cognitive (and computational) capacities, then cognitive science is not distinguished from other approaches (such as attempts to explain cognition in purely neurophysio-logical terms). In short, even the most plausible version of a characteriza-tion solely in terms of computational capacities won't do for our purposes, precisely because it is behavioral.

What about using one or another sort of abstract automaton as the basis for saying what a computer is? For example, one might say that what cognitive scientists have in mind when they claim that the mind/brain is a computational device is that it is a finite-state automaton or a Turing machine. The trouble with resorting to this sort of specification is that it is too specific. To see why this is so, consider the following brief descriptions of these kinds of machines.[14]

Finite-State Automaton As I shall use the term, a finite state automaton is a "black box" that takes in input and generates output as a function of its internal states. These machines are sometimes known as "finite trans-ducers" (Nelson 1968; Hopkin and Moss 1976) and "finite state automata with output" (Nelson 1987) to distinguish them from machines with input but no output ("acceptors") and machines with output but no input ("gen-erators"). Any FSA can be precisely defined by specifying the following:

an input set I

an output set O

a set of internal states S with a designated initial state s_0

a *transition* function m: $I \times S \rightarrow S$ that tells you what the next internal state of the machine will be given that it receives a certain input while in a certain present internal state

an *output* function n: $I \times S \rightarrow O$ that tells you what output the machine will generate given that it receives a certain input while in a certain present internal state.

See figure 3.1 for an example of an FSA.

Turing Machine A Turing Machine is a finite-state automaton associated with an external storage or memory medium. This external memory me-dium takes the form of a tape with squares from which input symbols are read and on which output sumbols are written. This tape is indefinitely long in both directions. The FSA is linked to the tape by a "head" which can point to only one square of the tape at a time but which is capable of moving both right and left on the tape. To specify a TM precisely, we

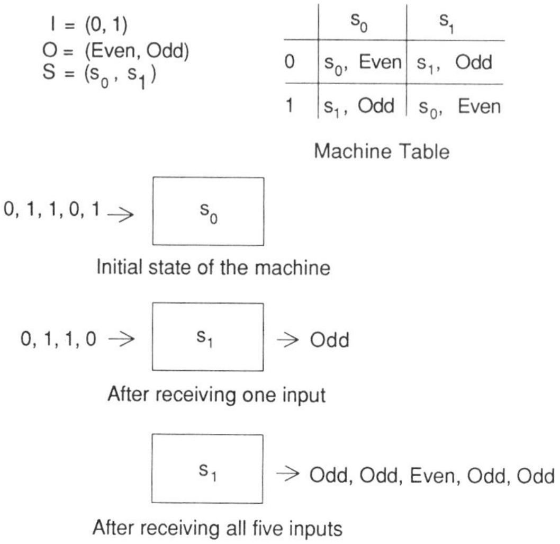

I = (0, 1)
O = (Even, Odd)
S = (s_0, s_1)

	s_0	s_1
0	s_0, Even	s_1, Odd
1	s_1, Odd	s_0, Even

Machine Table

0, 1, 1, 0, 1 $\rightarrow$ | s_0 |

Initial state of the machine

0, 1, 1, 0 $\rightarrow$ | s_1 | $\rightarrow$ Odd

After receiving one input

| s_1 | $\rightarrow$ Odd, Odd, Even, Odd, Odd

After receiving all five inputs

Figure 3.1
A finite-state automaton. The transition and output functions have been combined in one "machine table." This machine keeps track of whether it has received an odd or an even number of ones. The final output is 'Odd', corresponding to the fact that there were a total of three ones. The machine works because its state and its output change only when a 1 is input. (Based on an FSA described in Minsky 1967, p. 20.)

need, as in the case of a finite-state automation, an input set I, an output set O, a set of internal states S with a designated initial state s_0, a transition function, and an output function. In addition, the following new elements are required:

a special *blank* symbol belonging to the input and output sets, so that symbols on the tape can be "erased"

a new set D consisting of the directions right (R) and left (L), so that the head can "move" in either direction on the tape

a direction function d: I × S → {L,R} specifying the direction of movement as a function of the input symbol that is "read" and the present internal state of the device.

See figure 3.2 for an example of a Turing machine.

A *universal* Turing machine is a Turing machine that is capable of "imitating" any other Turing machine by, in effect, getting a description of that machine as part of its input.

$I = \{ (,), A, X \}$
$O = \{ (,), A, X, NWF, WF \}$
$S = \{ s_0, s_1, s_2, STOP \}$

	s_0	s_1	s_2
)	s_1 X L	s_1) L	Never occurs
(	s_0 (R	s_0 X R	STOP NWF -
A	s_2 A L	STOP NWF -	STOP WF -
X	s_0 X R	s_1 X L	s_2 X L

Initial state of the machine and the tape

After three cycles

Final state of machine and the tape

Figure 3.2
A Turing machine. The machine table indicates the next state, output, and direction of movement given a current state and input. This machine determines whether a sequence of left and right parentheses is well formed. It searches to the right for ')', then searches to the left for '(', and then replaces each by an 'X' until it comes to the end of the expression (designated by an 'A'). If any unmatched symbols remain, it prints 'NWF' (for 'not well formed'). If no unmatched symbols remain, it prints 'WF' (for 'well formed'). (Based on a Turing machine described in Minsky 1967, pp. 121–122.)

My contention is that expanding the C2 schema in terms of some particular kind of abstract automaton—say, a Turing machine—will result in an assumption that is too specific for our purposes. One way to support this contention is by pointing out that each kind of abstract automaton is distinguished by a particular sort of architecture. That is, its computational capacities are due to its having a certain "fixed structure" of parts, which work in certain ways and are interrelated in certain ways.[15] A Turing machine has a two-way tape, for example, whereas a finite-state automaton does not. If one chooses to specify C2 in terms of a specific sort of abstract automaton, one is saying that cognitive scientists assume the mind to have a specific kind of computational architecture. But, in fact, nothing could be farther from the truth. Cognitive scientists assume that the mind has some kind of computational architecture, but what kind is left as a matter for research. In fact, as Haugeland (1985, p. 164) has so aptly pointed out, "the mind could have a computational architecture all its own. In other words, from the perspective of AI, *mental architecture* itself becomes a new theoretical "variable," to be investigated and spelled out by actual cognitive science research."

There is a reply to the above argument that has a certain amount of plausibility but that ultimately misses the point. The reply is this: The above argument rejects the claim that an abstract automaton description of a computer is appropriate for C2 on the grounds that it is too specific, but in fact such descriptions are not specific at all. Granted that there may be any number of mutually exclusive ways of answering the question "What is the computational architecture of the mind/brain?", there are also complementary ways of answering this question. In particular, abstract automaton descriptions are so abstract that they will always or often be true of a concrete object that has the requisite computational capacities, no matter how we might describe its computational architecture at a less abstract level. The mind/brain is subject to many different "levels" of description, including more than one mode of description at the computational level.[16] Thus, no matter what mental architecture is like, at a fairly detailed level of description the mind/brain will always be describable as a Turing machine, or a finite-state automaton, or a production system, etc. at a more abstract level, even though the mapping from the more "natural," more specific architectural description of the mind/brain to its more abstract automaton description may not be at all obvious.[17]

The response to this reply is that the concepts relevant to C2 are not simply concepts that might be *applicable* to the cognitive mind/brain but concepts that cognitive scientists believe will have some *explanatory* power. The substantive assumptions of a research framework are supposed to be formulated in terms of entities and processes that actually play a role in answering the basic questions of the framework. Thus, in the end, the charge that invoking some particular kind of automaton is too specific is correct. It is too specific not so much because it flies in the face of the fact that the computational architecture of the mind/brain is still an open question (although this is true) as because developing specific explanatory theories about the computational architecture of the mind/brain is not limited to thinking about the mind/brain as some particular kind of automaton, such as a Turing machine. In fact, few researchers think about the mind/brain this way when they are developing models of specific cognitive capacities.[18] The most explanatory level of description seems to be quite a bit less abstract.

Thus far we have considered the computability approach to capturing the cognitive science concept of a computer and found it wanting. Let us now consider the alternative, data-processing approach.

If one looks up the term 'computer' in any standard reference book on computer science, one finds a characterization that goes something like this: A computer is a device capable of accepting, storing, manipulating, and outputting data or information in accordance with a set of effective rules (Rodgers 1970; Gould 1971; Sippl and Sippl 1972; Maynard 1975; Chandor et al. 1977; Weik 1977; Spencer 1980; Godman 1984; Meadows et al. 1984; Oxford University Press 1986; Freedman 1989). Two further necessary conditions are sometimes imposed: that the operations of the device be automated and that the set of rules governing the behavior of the machine be, in some sense, *in* the machine (Gould 1971; Weik 1977; Freedman 1989). For our purposes, it doesn't much matter whether these two additional conditions are imposed or not. However, since minds, if they are computers at all, are automatic computers with internalized rules,[19] I will use the term in the stronger sense—that is, with the addition of the two necessary conditions.

The standard characterization is fine as far as it goes, but it obscures an important point relevant to our discussion. As they are used in computer science, the terms 'data' and 'information' are systematically ambiguous, referring both to the *content* of what is received, stored, manipulated, and output and to the formal *bearers* of that content. For example, the terms 'data' and 'information' may be used to refer to numbers, or characters, or propositions; insofar as that is true, the terms are being used in a semantic sense. However, they may also be used to refer to representations designating those numbers, or characters, or propositions, and insofar as *that* is true the terms are being used in a nonsemantic, purely formal sense.[20]

The ambiguity is tolerated within computer science for two reasons.

First, the operation upon data (information) in the semantic sense is contingent upon the operation upon data (information) in the formal sense and everyone knows this. For example, the computer adds two numbers (data in the semantic sense) *in virtue of* manipulating representations of those numbers (data in the formal sense).

Second, fudging the distinction between the objects being represented and the representations themselves seems to make no difference to questions of concern in computer science, such as how to build a faster, more efficient machine. It does, however, make a difference to questions of concern in cognitive science, for one of the questions that must be addressed if cognitive science is to be a viable enterprise is this: *In virtue of what* do mental representations have the informational content they have? (This question will be discussed in chapter 6.) And without making the distinction between information (in the semantic sense) and the bearers or that information, this fundamental question cannot even be raised. For that reason, I shall be scrupulous in distinguishing between the two senses. Specifically, I shall use the terms 'data' and 'information' only in the semantic sense—that is, only to refer to objects (abstract or otherwise) being represented by the machine. When I wish to refer to what is doing the representing. I shall talk about symbols or representations.[21]

If we now imbed the above distinction between representation and information in the standard definition of a computer, we get the following:

C2 (SYSTEM ASSUMPTION)   A computer is a device capable of automatically inputting, storing, manipulating, and outputting information in virtue of inputting, storing, manipulating, and outputting representations of that information. These information processes occur in accordance with a finite set of rules that are effective and that are, in some sense, in the machine itself.

How does the above characterization fare with respect to the four considerations enunciated earlier? There appear to be no difficulties with respect to the first, third, and fourth considerations. C2 is certainly not idiosyncratic, since it is clearly derived from computer science's standard conception of a computer (consideration 1). In addition, it defines a computer in terms of its internal workings rather than simply in terms of its behavior; thus, it seems to provide a basis for distinguishing cognitive science from other approaches to cognition, such as neurophysiology (consideration 3). And, finally, there is nothing about C2 that conflicts with the aim of cognitive scientists to include the developmental and pathological aspects of cognition within the domain of the field (consideration 4).

Satisfaction of consideration 2 is not so straightforward, however. It is quite evident when one begins perusing computer science reference books that the typical characterization of a computer, upon which C2 is based, is formulated with only conventional machines in mind—probably because widespread interest in connectionist machines is very recent and because such devices have, as yet, no commercial applications. (They are also, by and large, still simulated on conventional computers.) However, since cognitive science's concept of a computer clearly includes both conventional and connectionist machines, it is important that our formulation of C2 can encompass both sorts of computational devices.

There is a *prima facie* tension between consideration 2 and two aspects of C2: that C2 characterizes a computer as a device that *manipulates* representations and that it requires a computer to have rules that are, in some sense, in the machine. As we shall see in the next section, both of these requirements are satisfied by conventional machines in an obvious way. However, their applicability to conventional machines is less evident. Nevertheless, I shall argue that there is a sense in which they hold true for connectionist machines as well. I shall thus regard C2 as an acceptable formulation of the computational system assumption of cognitive science.

Before proceeding to a discussion of the distinction between conventional and connectionist computers, let us return to the question of whether the linking assumption, C1, is a metaphor. At the end of section 3.1 I arrived at the conclusion that, although C1 has many of the properties Boyd attributes to "theory-constitutive" metaphors, the fact remains that it is not appropriate to consider C1 a metaphor unless it is clear that cognitive scientists take it to be obviously false. Thus, I raised the following question: Do cognitive scientists assume that mind/brains are not literally computers but are merely like them in certain (possibly unknown) respects?

I have taken no polls on this question. But if we consider C2 in conjunction with what we know about the structure and functioning of the human brain and in conjunction with the kind of research cognitive scientists do, there is every reason to believe that most cognitive scientists take C1, when conjoined with C2, quite literally. Not only are proposed answers to the basic questions of cognitive science framed in information-processing terms; in addition, there is nothing that is known (or that cognitive scientists believe) about the structure and functioning of the brain that makes it impossible or even implausible that the mind/brain is a computer in the sense of C2. I take it, then, that cognitive scientists do not think that C2 is obviously false, and that, hence, C2 should not be regarded as a metaphor.

Why then the widespread allusion to the "computer metaphor"? The most obvious explanation is that when people consider C1 to be a metaphor they are thinking of a computer as an essentially man-made, electronic device. This is certainly the ordinary, popular conception of a computer, and it is even to be found in several standard computer science reference books. For example, Weil (1977, p. 91) writes that "a computer is a piece of machinery [and a] person is no longer implied by that term," and Ralston (1976, p. 463), Meadows et al. (1984, p. 44), and Godman (1984, p. 8) all define computers as electronic. The point is that if a computer is by definition a man-made, electronic device, then C1 is clearly a metaphor, for the human mind/brain is neither man-made nor electronic.

It should be clear, however, that, although this restricted conception of a computer may be part of our "folk computer science," it is not the conception accepted by most experts in computer science *per se*. And if we formulate C2 in terms of the latter (correct) conception, then the metaphorical status of C1 is highly dubious.

3.3 Conventional Machines

One of the most striking features of C2 is that it is so vague. C2 tells us that for something to count as a computer it must, roughly speaking, be an information processer, but it leaves completely open *how* this information processing is to be accomplished (other than that it must be in accordance with effective, internal rules). One might wonder, then, whether C2 is really the sort of assumption that can function as a guide to theory construction in the way that the substantive assumptions of a research framework are supposed to. The answer turns out to be "It depends." In particular, it depends on the level of theoretical detail one is after and the level of detail one believes that cognitive science (or one's particular subdiscipline within cognitive science) currently has the methodological resources to support.

The computational assumption, as articulated above, has guided cognitive science research in two ways. On the one hand. many psychologists and most linguists engage in what can arguably be called "architecturally neutral" research. This mode of research accepts the lack of architectural specificity of C2 and restricts itself to asking questions about cognition that presuppose no (or very few) architectural assumptions. Research designed to answer questions concerning the precise nature of one or the other of our cognitive capacities (in other words, questions that fit my schema Q1—see section 2.4), such as Kosslyn's map-scanning experiment, falls in this category. So also does research that makes claims about the kinds of representations involved in the exercise of a given capacity, where these representations are characterized purely semantically. (This corresponds roughly to what Newell [1990] calls the "knowledge level.") One might even argue that certain very "high-level" empirical claims about processing are architecturally neutral in the same way. This is because they don't tell us in any detail how a certain capacity is exercised. Rather, they simply provide (empirically motivated) constraints on any adequate processing model. An example is Swinney's (1979) claim that when a person understands a sentence containing an ambiguous word, he or she "looks up" both meanings of the term, irrespective of context.

In contrast to the architecturally neutral research of the above sort, classical AI researchers and connectionists are interested in developing models of the mind/brain that involve greater computational detail. Such "architecturally specific" research clearly requires going beyond the conceptual resources of C2. In particular, this sort of research typically involves two further steps: Researchers must develop a more specific working hypothesis regarding the nature of the cognitive mind/brain's computational architecture, and they must raise and attempt to answer questions about cognition in terms of that working hypothesis.

Two more specific conceptions of a computer have guided architecturally specific research to date. The first is that the cognitive mind/brain is a conventional computer; the second is that it is a connectionist computer. In the next two sections, I will briefly describe the most salient features of each of these kinds of devices. By way of completing the discussion in the previous section, I will also indicate how each satisfies the general characterization of a computer given in C2.

Before I begin, it will be useful to have certain standard terminological distinctions under our belts. Computer science has not yet developed a systematic taxonomy of kinds of computers. However, it has developed a number of categories for classifying computers into kinds. It should be borne in mind that these categories were developed before there was any widespread interest in connectionist devices; hence, they are not always clearly applicable to such machines. Nevertheless, because they embody distinctions that have become standard in the computer world, they constitute an important backdrop for our discussion.

The most important of these categories are the following:

Analog vs. digital   A computer is analog or digital depending on what form its representations take. If it represents information (usually, real numerical values of a variable) by means of a continuously varying magnitude (such as a voltage), where any change in the value of that magnitude is computationally significant,[22] it is an analog device. If it represents information by means of discrete units, such as zeros and ones, it is digital.

Serial vs. parallel   A computer is serial or parallel depending on the character of its processes. If it is only capable of performing its operations one at a time, it is serial. If it is capable of performing more than one operation at a time, it is, to some extent, parallel. There may, of course, be mixed cases. A computer may have one component that functions serially and another that functions in parallel. Some computers give the illusion of being parallel when, strictly, they are not. This is because a large number of processes are potentially active although at any one instant only one is being executed. Strictly speaking, this is called *concurrent processing*.

Special-purpose vs. general-purpose   A special-purpose computer is designed for a limited class of applications. An example is a chess-playing machine. It can accept only certain kinds of data, for example, and it can perform only a limited number of operations. In contrast, a general-purpose machine (such as a mainframe or a personal computer) can, in principle, imitate any special-purpose computer. That is, it can, in principle, compute any computable function, and hence it is universal in the technical sense. In practice, of course, because of temporal and memory limitations, no actual general-purpose computer is universal in this sense, but it comes close enough for all practical purposes to be considered a universal machine.

Stored-program vs. wired-program   This distinction is straightforwardly applicable only to conventional computers. C2 includes the condition that the program governing the behavior of the computer must, in some sense, be in the machine. We can now unpack the phrase 'in some sense'. A conventional computer can have a program in itself in two senses. The program can be explicitly represented in memory. Alternatively, the program can be wired into the hardware of the machine in such a way that it cannot be altered by the computer itself. The requirement of non-self-alteration is important because when a program is stored in memory it is also, in a sense, in the hardware of the machine. However, a program stored in memory can be altered by the computer itself.

All conventional computers with stored programs are, to some extent, wired-program machines. That is, even if a computer is capable of accepting a specific program as input and subsequently storing it in memory, it must have a wired-in program that "tells" the machine how to "interpret" this stored program. The distinction between a machine's being stored-program or wired-program is, thus, not whether it has one sort of program or the other but rather whether it can have a stored program at all. If a conventional device can have a stored program (even if it may also have a wired program), it is called a "stored-program machine"; if it cannot have a stored program, it is a "wired-program machine." Thus, conventional, digital, general-purpose computers are considered stored-program machines, whereas special-purpose computers tend to be wired-program devices.

With these distinctions in mind, let us now turn to a consideration of conventional machines. Conventional computers are all more or less closely related to the type of machine pioneered by John von Neumann and his co-workers and described in Burks et al. 1946. Hence, conventional architecture is often referred to as *von Neumann architecture*. Equating the two is not strictly correct, however, since the prototypical von Neumann machine is a general-purpose, stored-program device whereas I (and others) use the term 'conventional' to include some wired-program and special-purpose machines as well. It remains true, however, that the von Neumann computer is the paradigmatic conventional machine. Thus, it provides a logical starting place for a description of conventional computers.

A von Neumann machine has the following properties:

• It has four principal functional parts: a memory, a control unit, an arithmetic/logic unit, and input-output devices. The control unit and the arithmetic/logic unit together constitute the central processing unit (c.p.u.).

• It is a stored-program computer. Programs and data are both stored in the same memory.

• The memory is large but finite, consisting of a long string of storage locations each of which has a unique *address*. Memory locations can, hence, be accessed directly (*random-access memory*, or "RAM") in order either to read the datum stored at that location or to write a datum at that location. (Some computers also have a memory which can only be read but not written to. This is called *read-only memory*, or "ROM".)

• The function of the control unit is to read and execute instructions from the program stored in memory, either by moving data between memory and a temporary register within the c.p.u. or by activating the arithmetic/ logic unit. The program is executed one instruction at a time by repeating the following *fetch-execute cycle* until the program is completed:

(i) Determine the next instruction in the program.

(ii) Transfer a copy of the instruction to the c.p.u.

(iii) Execute the instruction.

(iv) Return to step i.

• The arithmetic/logic unit is made up of various hard-wired circuits capable of performing the basic arithmetic and logical operations of the machine.

The structure of a von Neumann machine is depicted in figure 3.3.

The architecture of the von Neumann machine gives it a number of important capabilities. First, operations can be performed on variables (variables can simply be treated as addresses where different data can be stored on different occasions). Second, it is capable of running programs with branching operations (operations that alter the sequence in which the instructions are performed). Such branching operations can be either un-

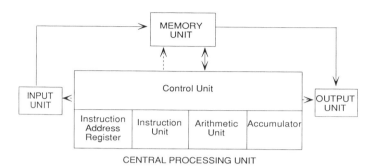

Figure 3.3
The structure of a von Neumann machine. Solid arrows indicate paths of information flow; dashed lines indicate control flow. (From D. U. Wilde, *An Introduction to Computing*, © 1973. Reprinted by permission of Prentice-Hall, Inc.)

conditional or dependent on the fulfillment of some condition. And, finally, a von Neumann machine can use *subroutines* (mini-programs stored in memory that can be "called up" as necessary by a single instruction in the larger program).

The architecture of a von Neumann device, as specified above, can be "virtually" modified by its software[23]—in particular, by programs written in so-called *high-level languages*. This can happen in at least three ways: Its basic instruction set can be extended, its operations can be performed on *data structures* rather than on isolated single data representations, and it can appear to operate in accordance with a very different control structure. When a von Neumann machine is modified in one of these ways, it comes to function as if it were a different kind of machine. This "as-if" machine is called a *virtual machine*.

The basic instruction set of a von Neumann computer picks out those operations the machine can perform on the basis of a single instruction. In the original von Neumann machine, such operations were all hard-wired; today, many are often in somewhat more flexible form called "microcode." The basic instruction set varies from (kind of) computer to (kind of) computer, but the following list is typical of currently existing von Neumann machines:

Arithmetic operations   addition, substraction, multiplication, division, finding the absolute value

Logic operations   AND, OR, EXCLUSIVE OR, and NOT

Data-movement operations   operations that shift data from input devices to memory locations and processing registers, between registers and memory, and to output devices

Comparison operations   operations that ascertain if a number or a piece of binary-coded data is the same as another, less than or equal to another, or greater than or equal to another

Branching operations   operations that alter the sequence in which instructions are performed.

In order for a computer to execute a program stored in memory, the program must be built out of instructions from the machine's basic instruction set. Such programs are said to be written in *machine code*. Machine code may, in some sense, be "understood" by the computer that uses it, but it is extremely intractable from the human user's point of view. It is for that reason that high-level languages like FORTRAN, COBOL, BASIC, LISP, and Pascal were developed. What makes a high-level language usable on a von Neumann computer is that each basic command of the high-level language is equivalent to a subroutine in machine code. However, because such programs are not written in machine code, they cannot be executed directly. Instead, they must be "translated" into machine code by either a *compiler* or an *interpreter*. A compiler works by "translating" the high-level program into machine code before any of the instructions are executed. An interpreter, in contrast, works in a piecemeal way, translating statements in the high-level program one by one as the program is being executed.

At the level of the machine code, a von Neumann machine operates on representations of single items of data, each stored in a distinct and unique storage location. High-level languages typically operate on *data structures* rather than on single data representations. A data structure consists of a set of single data representations, often of a characteristic *type*, structured in a particular way. (See section 5.2 for more detailed discussion.) Any particular high-level language will typically permit only certain sorts of data structures and will include, within its repertoire of basic commands, commands that operate specifically on those permitted structures. For instance, a language that can operate on tree structures would probably include such commands as tree traversal, tree search, tree insertion, and tree deletion.

Control is determining what part of a program is executed when. The control structure of a program made up of von Neumann basic instructions is basically sequential, with the possibility of conditional branches and subroutine calls. Programs written in some high-level languages have a very different control structure. In LISP, for example, each "line" of the program typically consists of a complex function which may take other functions as arguments (and these functions may themselves take other functions as arguments, etc.). At the gross level, when a LISP program is executed, control passes from one line of the program to the next in standard sequential fashion. However, since individual lines consist of complex functions, the control structure at the level of each individual line is quite different.

For example, a single line of a LISP program might consist of an instruction to evaluate the arithmetic expression

$$[(8 - 3) + 6] \times [(1 + 3) - 0].$$

In a more LISPish-looking language, this complex function would look like

TIMES (PLUS (DIFFERENCE (8,3), 6)),

(DIFFERENCE (PLUS (1.3), 0)).

The point is that evaluating the outermost TIMES function requires calling the PLUS and DIFFERENCE functions, and evaluating these requires calling the DIFFERENCE and PLUS functions again. And it is only after the control unit has worked its way "down" to the innermost function can it start working its way back "up" by returning values. This mode of processing is quite different from that of a simple von Neumann machine.[24]

We have seen how von Neumann computers programmed in a high-level language can differ from basic von Neumann machines in three ways: with respect to their basic instruction set, in the fact that they operate on data structures rather than on simple data representations, and with respect to their control structure. Such virtual machines are similar to their poor relations, however, in every other respect. In particular, they continue to be general-purpose, stored-program, serial computers.

If we allow for variation even on these dimensions, we arrive at the notion of a *conventional* computer. More precisely, the points of similarity and difference between a conventional computer and a basic von Neumann machine are as follows: Like a basic von Neumann machine, a conventional computer

has distinct components for memory, processing, and input-output,

has a set of basic operations defined over data representations, and

computes its input-output functions by executing its basic operations in accordance with a program (a set of explicit instructions).

However, unlike a basic von Neumann machine, a conventional computer

can have an enhanced set of basic operations,

can have a non–von Neumann control structure (either because a non–von Neumann control structure is hard-wired or because the computer in question is a virtual machine defined by a high-level language with a non–von Neumann control structure),

can operate on data structures rather than simple data representations,[25]

can be general-purpose or special-purpose,

can have programs that are stored or wired in,

can have multiple memories and processers,

can involve processing that is either strictly serial or partly parallel, and

need not have a separate executive or control unit.[26]

It should be clear that conventional computers satisfy our general definition of a computer (i.e., C2) in a straightforward way. C2 defines a computer as a device capable of automatically accepting, storing, manipulating, and outputting information in virtue of accepting, storing, manipulating, and outputting representations of that information, either directly or indirectly. Conventional computers accomplish these tasks quite directly. Information is accepted by the input unit, stored in memory, manipulated by the processing units, and output by the output unit. The operations of all of these units are accomplished by means of the basic operations of the device, which are defined over a set of data structures. These data structures "carry" the information being processed and, hence, function as representations of that information.[27]

C2 further requires that the information processing of a computer be in accordance with a finite set of rules that are effective and that are, in some sense, in the machine itself. The rules or program governing the operation of a conventional machine are effective because they are built out of the basic instruction set of the virtual machine, and this basic instruction set is, in turn, ultimately reducible to the effective basic instruction set of the computer's machine language (akin to the basic instruction set of a simple von Neumann machine). The rules or program are "in" the machine itself because a conventional machine is either a stored-program machine (in which case the program is stored in memory) or a wired-program machine (in which case the program is hard-wired in the device in a way that cannot be altered by the device itself).

3.4 Connectionist Machines

Since the early 1980s a growing number of cognitive scientists interested in architecturally specific research have become disenchanted with the hypothesis that the cognitive mind/brain is (or is significantly like) a conventional computer and have begun to explore a new hypothesis: that the cognitive mind/brain is (or is significantly like) a connectionist machine. The reasons for this disenchantment and the counterarguments put forth by pro-conventionalists need not concern us here.[28] What does concern us is getting at least a rough idea of what this new hypothesis comes to.

What is a connectionist (or, as it is sometimes called, a "parallel distributed processing") computer? A useful place to start is with a relatively simple kind of massively parallel device that is not fully connectionist in the contemporary sense but which is structurally similar to connectionist machines in many important respects: the "neural net" developed by McCulloch and Pitts (1943).[29]

In section 3.2 I characterized a finite-state automaton (FSA) as a device with inputs, outputs, and internal states whose behavior is governed by a transition function and an output function. A McCulloch-Pitts (M-P) neural net is simply a collection of FSAs of a specific sort linked together in such a way that outputs from one FSA become inputs to another.[30] An M-P computational device can thus be completely described by specifying the properties of its individual "cells" and its "pattern of connectivity." As depicted in figure 3.4, the FSA "cells" of an M-P neural net have the following properties:

Inputs The input to a cell takes the form of a signal carried by one or more input fibers. Each fiber can carry only one pulse at a time; however,

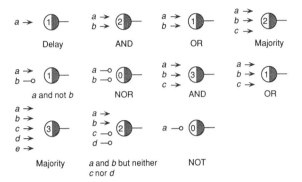

Figure 3.4
Some McCulloch-Pitts cells. Arrowheads represent excitatory fibers; little open circles represent inhibitory fibers. The number inside each cell indicates its firing threshold. These cells were first described in McCulloch and Pitts 1943. (From M. Minsky, *Computation: Finite and Infinite Machines*, © 1967. Reprinted by permission of the author and Prentice-Hall, Inc.)

these pulses may either be excitatory or inhibitory. The net input to a cell is determined by the number and the nature (i.e., excitatory or inhibitory) of the input pulses. More specifically, if there is an inhibitory input pulse, then the net input is 0. If there is no inhibitory pulse, then the net input is the sum of the individual excitatory pulses.

Internal states   Each cell has only two internal states: a state of *firing* and a state of *quiet*. In addition, each cell has a certain threshold of firing which determines whether it fires or not, given a certain input.

Outputs   Each cell has a single output fiber which is capable of carrying a single unit pulse. This output fiber may branch, however, connecting the cell in question to more than one additional cell.

Transition function   Whether a cell is firing or quiet at time $t + 1$ is a function of its net input at time t. If the net input is equal to or exceeds the threshold value, the cell will fire; otherwise, it will be quiet. Note that the internal state of the cell at t is not relevant to its state at $t + 1$.

Output function   The output of a cell at $t + 1$ is a direct consequence of its internal state at $t + 1$. If the state is firing, there will be an output pulse; if the state is quiet, there will not. The output function is, thus, very similar to the transition function. If the net input is equal to or exceeds the

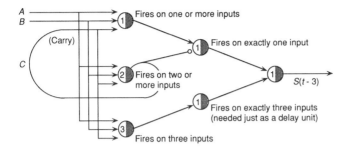

Figure 3.5
Example of a McCulloch-Pitts neural net. This device is a serial binary addition network. (From M. Minsky, *Computation: Finite and Infinite Machines,* © 1967. Reprinted by permission of the author and Prentice-Hall, Inc.)

threshold value, then the cell will generate an output pulse. If the net input is below threshold, there will be no output.

These five points pertain to the properties of individual M-P cells. To describe the neural net, we also need to say how these cells are connected to one another by means of their input and output fibers (see figure 3.5):

Pattern of connectivity In comparison to contemporary connectionist networks, M-P neural nets have patterns of connectivity that are both simple and stable. They are comparatively simple because they are determined solely by which cells are linked to which other cells and whether these connections are excitatory or inhibitory. They are stable because these patterns of connection do not change over time.

The above description of an M-P neural net can easily be elaborated to yield a general characterization of a connectionist network.[31] There are many "subspecies" of connectionist machines which differ in important ways from a computational point of view. The characterization to be provided is general because it purports to articulate what all connectionist machines have in common.

Both McCulloch-Pitts neural nets and connectionist machines consist of basic computing units linked together in networks. Furthermore, describing the behaviors of both sorts of machines involves specifying the computational properties of the units (i.e. their inputs, internal states, outputs, transition function, and output function) and specifying the pattern of

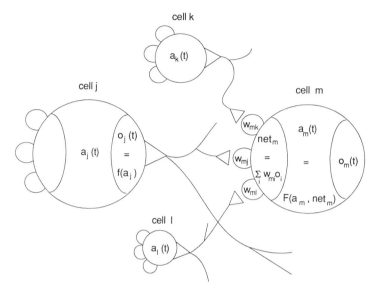

Figure 3.6
A connectionist processing unit. (Adapted from Rumelhart, Hinton, and McClelland 1986. Reprinted by permission of the authors and The MIT Press.)

connectivity among the units. However, there are two important differences. First, all M-P neural nets have cells with the same simple computational properties, whereas connectionist units exhibit (from one device to another) a great variety of computational properties, from the simple to the complex. Second, connectionist machines have an extremely important capacity that M-P neural nets do not have: They can "learn" by modifying their pattern of connectivity.

The computational properties of a connectionist processing unit can be summarized as follows (see figure 3.6):

Inputs   Like the input to an M-P cell, the input to a connectionist processing unit takes the form of a signal carried by one or more input links, each of which is either excitatory or inhibitory. However, in contrast to an M-P fiber, a connectionist link can carry a signal whose value is either digital or continuous (either bounded or unbounded). Links are also associated with *weights* or *strengths*. The *net input* to a unit is thus determined by the number of input signals, the value and the nature (excitatory or inhibitory) of each signal, and the weight of the link. In the simplest case, the net input would be the weighted sum of the individual signal values, with excitatory links corresponding to positive weights and inhibitory links corresponding to negative weights. However, more complex input functions are also possible.

Internal states   M-P cells have only two internal states, a state of firing and a state of quiet. Connectionist units can have, in principle, indefinitely many internal states. In connectionist jargon, these are called the *activation values* of the unit. These values may be either discrete or continuous.

Outputs   Like an M-P cell, a connectionist unit has a single output fiber, which may branch. What this means, in effect, is that, while any unit may connect on the output side to many other units, the output signal being sent to each of these other units is always the same. The values of output signals, like the values of input signals, may be discrete or continuous.

Transition function   The "activation rule" for a connectionist unit is a function that takes as arguments the activation value of the unit and the net input to the unit at t and yields a new activation value for $t + 1$. In contrast to the M-P transition function, the internal state of the cell at t is relevant to its internal state at $t + 1$.

Output function   This function generates a value for the output signal at $t + 1$ on the basis of the unit's activation value at t. The output function of a connectionist unit may be an identity function, a threshold function, or a stochastic function. In the first case, the output value is identical to the activation value; in the second, there is no output unless the activation value reaches a certain minimal threshold; in the third, the output depends probabilistically on the activation value.

Pattern of connectivity   The network of connections among connectionist units is determined not only by which unit connects to which other unit and whether the connections are excitatory or inhibitory but also by "weights" assigned to these connections. Weight information can be neatly summarized in a matrix. For example, figure 3.7 shows a matrix for the connectionist network depicted in figure 3.8.

Another important difference between the pattern of connectivity of connectionist machines and that of M-P neural nets is that the former can change over time whereas the latter is fixed. Such modification is accom-

	u_1	u_2	u_3	u_4	u_5	u_6	u_7	u_8
u_1	0	0	0	0	0	-5	-5	0
u_2	0	0	0	0	+6	+5	0	+6
u_3	0	0	0	0	0	-3	-2	+3
u_4	0	0	0	0	-4	0	0	+1
u_5	+4	0	0	+4	0	0	0	0
u_6	0	0	+6	-1	0	0	0	0
u_7	0	-2	0	+4	0	0	0	0
u_8	-6	+1	0	0	0	0	0	0

Figure 3.7
Matrix for an eight-unit network. (From Rumelhart, Hinton, and McClelland 1986.
Reprinted by permission of the authors and The MIT Press.)

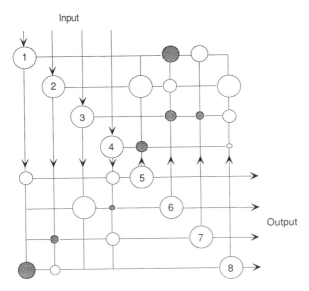

Figure 3.8
A simple eight-unit connectionist network. (Based on the network depicted in Rumelhart,
Hinton, and McClelland 1986. Reprinted by permission of the authors and The MIT Press.)

plished by changing the weights of the connections in a network in accordance with one "learning rule" or another. In some cases, "learning" will simply be a function of the activation value of unit i and the output value of unit j. However, in most current models there is another factor. Unit i is provided with some sort of "teaching" input from outside the system.[32] Thus, according to Rumelhart, Hinton, and McClelland (1986), virtually all learning rules in current connectionist models are variants of the following general rule:

$$\Delta w_{ij} = g(a_i, t_i) \times h(o_j, w_{ij}),$$

where w_{ij} is the weight of the connection between unit i and unit j when i receives input from j. In other words, the change in weight w_{ij} is equal to the product of the values of two functions g and h, where the value of g depends on the activation value of unit i and the value of the teaching input to unit i and where the value of h depends on the output from unit j and the current weight of the connection between units i and j. For example, the so-called *delta rule* looks like

$$\Delta w_{ij} = k(t_i - a_i) \times o_j,$$

where k is a constant. Here all that is important is the output from unit j and the *difference* between the target teaching value and the current activation value of unit i.[33]

The similarities and differences between McCulloch-Pitts neural nets and connectionist networks are summarized in table 3.1.

Let us now see why connectionist devices are computers in the sense of C2.

A computer, according to C2, is a device that processes information in virtue of its processing representations of that information. Thus, to see why (and how) a connectionist machine is a computer we must determine where its representations are to be found.

We have seen that computers can be described at different "levels" of analysis, even within a computational framework. This means, in particular, that at different computational levels different sorts of representations may be involved. This point is nicely illustrated by a von Neumann machine running a high-level language such as LISP. In such a virtual machine, there are two levels of representations: the LISP tree structures of the virtual machine and the machine code of the basic von Neumann machine.

Table 3.1
A comparison of McCulloch-Pitts neural nets and connectionist networks.

M-P neural nets	Connectionist networks
Unit inputs	
1. A cell can have more than one input fiber.	1. A unit can have more than one input connection.
2. Each input fiber is either excitatory or inhibitory.	2. Each input connection is either excitatory or inhibitory.
3. Each fiber carries a signal whose value is either 0 or 1.	3. Input connections can carry signals whose value is discrete or continuous.
4. Fibers do not have weights.	4. Input connections have weights.
5. The net input (net) to a cell is determined by the number and nature of its input signals. If there is an inhibitory pulse, then net = 0; otherwise, net = sum of the excitatory pulses.	5. The net input to a cell is determined by the number, value, and nature of its input signals and the weighting of each connection.
Internal states	
1. Internal states are either firing or quiet.	1. Internal states can have different possible activation values, which may be discrete or continuous.
2. Each cell has a threshold which determines whether it fires or not.	
Unit outputs	
1. Each cell has a single output fiber which may branch.	1. Each cell has a single output fiber, which may branch.
2. Each output fiber carries a signal whose value is 0 or 1.	2. Output signals may be discrete or continuous.
Transition function	
1. If net > threshold at t, then state $(t + 1)$ = firing; otherwise, state $(t + 1)$ = quiet.	1. Activation value $(t + 1)$ = function (activation value (t), total input).
Output function	
1. If net > threshold at t, then output $(t + 1)$ = a single unit pulse; otherwise, there is no output.	1. Output $(t + 1)$ = function (activation value (t)).
	2. This output function may be an identity, a threshold, or a stochastic function.
Pattern of connectivity	
1. The pattern of connectivity is fixed. That is, it cannot be modified as a function of the neural net's "experience."	1. The pattern of connectivity can be modified as a function of "experience."
	2. This modification occurs by altering the weights associated with each connection by means of one or another "learning rule."

Connectionist machines also have representations at different levels of analysis. Let us refer to these simply as "high-level" representations and "low-level" representations. We have seen how the individual units of a connectionist device have inputs and outputs, but we have not yet seen in what sense the device as a whole has inputs and outputs. Typically, certain units in the network serve as input units, certain units serve as output units, and there may or may not be "hidden" units in between. However, it is not the input *signals* to the input units that typically encode the input to the machine as a whole. Rather, when a connectionist machine is used to perform some task, the input to the machine as a whole is encoded by *activation* of certain input units, and the output from the machine is encoded by activation of certain output units. Furthermore, if the device has hidden units and the process from input to output involves other "internal" representations, then the "bearer" of these representations also consists of activation states of the individual units. These connectionist representations are all "high-level" representations.

Connectionist devices also have "low-level" representations, namely the representations involved in the computations carried out by each individual unit. That there are representations involved at this level tends to be disguised by talk about "signals," "pulses," and "values" and by the fact that computation at the unit level is all "number crunching." Nevertheless, it is not numbers themselves that constitute the input to and the output from these mini-computers, nor is it simply something physical. It is representations of numbers—something akin to numerals.

In what sense, then, are connectionist devices computers? There are two possibilities: they are computers with respect to their "low-level" representations or they are computers with respect to their "high-level" representations (or both). Whether connectionist devices are computers in the first sense rests on whether connectionist *units* are computers. If the signals fed into and out of connectionist units are representations, as I have argued above, then such units clearly input and output numerical information in virtue of inputting and outputting representations of that information. Furthermore, such input-output processes are carried out in accordance with a finite set of rules (namely, the transition and output functions) which are effective and which are "in" the machine itself. And since this numerical information is automatically passed from unit to unit, the machine as a whole also inputs and outputs numerical information in virtue of its inputting and outputting representations of that information in

accordance with effective and internal rules. But do these units "manipulate" this information in any meaningful sense? And do they "store" it?

The first question has been disputed by Pylyshyn (1984) and Nelson
(1987). In particular, they are concerned with whether finite-state automata are genuine "symbol processers."[34] Since as we have seen, connectionist units are simply fancied-up finite-state automata, a brief look at the
Pylyshyn-Nelson debate will be useful in answering our question about
connectionist units.

Pylyshyn argues that FSAs don't compute anything. Among his reasons,
according to Nelson, is that FSAs fail to satisfy the *processing requirement*—that is, in comparison to Turing machines, FSAs can only deal with
their inputs unidirectionally; they cannot "vary the occurrences of tokens
in the input (or output), nor do they permute them" (Nelson 1987, p.
404). Nelson replies by pointing out that von Neumann computers have
been shown to be FSAs, and that clearly such computers process symbols
in the required sense.[35] This reply may show that FSAs cannot be dismissed out of hand as a class of computational models relevant to cognitive science (which is the question Nelson cares about), but it is not very
helpful for our purposes. The fact that *some* FSAs (the ones that are
equivalent to von Neumann machines) process symbols does not mean
that all FSAs do. And since the FSAs that constitute the basis of M-P
nets (and are the forerunners of connectionist units) are clearly *not* von
Neumann machines, the aforementioned proof does not counter Pylyshyn's
objection.

In fact, Pylyshyn's point seems well taken when applied to connectionist
units. If the existence of symbol processing—in the sense of some sort of
manipulation that goes beyond the simple inputting and outputting of
symbols—is taken to be a necessary condition for a device's being a
genuine computer (which I accept), then it would appear that connectionist
units are not computers in the full-fledged sense. And if connectionist units
are not computers in the full-fledged sense, then it would follow that, with
respect to their "low-level" representations, connectionist networks are not
either. Similar considerations apply to the requirement of storing representations.[36]

If we focus our attention on the "high-level" representations of a connectionist unit, the picture is more complicated. As it turns out, there are two
sorts of "high-level" representations employed in connectionist modeling.
In both cases, the representation bearer consists of an activation state.

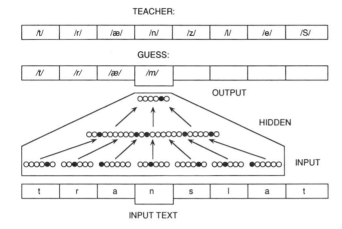

Figure 3.9
The NETtalk network architecture. (From Churchland and Sejnowski 1989. Reprinted by permission of the authors and The MIT Press.)

However, in the one case (called *local* representation) the representation bearer is an activation state of a *single* unit; in the other case (called *distributed* representation) the representation bearer is a *pattern* of activation involving many units, which may be distributed across the network.

Are connectionist networks computers with respect to their "high-level" representations? An example may help us consider this question. Sejnowski and Rosenberg's (1986, 1987, 1988) NETtalk system is capable of "learning" to convert English text into speech sounds. NETtalk is made up of 203 input units, 80 hidden units, and 26 output units (see figure 3.9). The input units consist of seven groups of 29 units each: one locally representing each letter of the alphabet and three locally representing punctuation and word-boundary information. Twenty-one of the 26 output units locally represent different articulatory features; the remaining five locally represent stress and syllable-boundary information. Phonemes, which consist of groups of articulatory features, are thus represented in distributed fashion.

NETtalk inputs text by stepping through the sequence of the words that make up the text with a seven-letter window. The task is to output the phoneme that corresponds to the middle (fourth) letter in the window. The other six letters are, thus, used to supply contextual information which might be relevant in determining the pronunciation of the target letter.

Like all connectionist networks, NETtalk operates in two phases: a learning/training phase and a performance phase. NETtalk begins the learning phase with its weights set in arbitrary fashion. Thus, when it initially receives written text as input, its output is, in effect, phonemic gibberish. Training then consists in adjusting the weights of the network after the presentation of each word as a function of the discrepancy between the actual output and the desired output (i.e., the correct pronunciation). This is done by means of the "back-propagation" learning algorithm introduced by Rumelhart, Hinton, and Williams (1986).

Sejnowski and Rosenberg trained NETtalk on two texts: phonetic transcriptions from informal, continuous speech of a child and 1000 common words from a dictionary. They describe the performance of the system on the informal corpus as follows:

> The distinction between vowels and consonants was made early; however, the network substituted the same vowel for all vowels and the same consonant for all consonants, which resulted in a babbling sound. A second stage occurred when word boundaries [were] recognized, and the output then resembled pseudowords. After just a few passes through the network many of the words were intelligible, and by 10 passes the text was understandable.
>
> Errors in the best guesses were far from random. For example, few errors in a well-trained network were confusions between vowels and consonants: most confusions were between phonemes that were very similar, such as the difference in voicing between the "th" sounds in "thesis" and "these". Some errors were due to inconsistencies in the original training corpus. Nevertheless, the intelligibility of the speech was quite good.   (Sejnowski and Rosenberg 1986, p. 7)

Since the network "learns" by, in effect, programming itself, it is natural to wonder how, in the end, it manages to accomplish its task. In particular, what role do the hidden units play? According to P. S. Churchland and T. J. Sejnowski (1989), this question was addressed by computing the average level of activity across the hidden units for each letter-to-sound correspondence. As it turns out, each letter-to-sound correspondence is represented by a distinct pattern of activity among the hidden units, typically involving about 15 of the 80 hidden units in a state of high activation. Thus, the network's representation of these letter-to-sound correspondences is partially distributed.

With this example in mind, let us now return to our original question: Are connectionist networks computers with respect to their "high-level" representations? I would say the answer is "yes." According to C2, something counts as a computer only if it has three automatic capacities, all of which occur in accordance with a finite, effective, internal set of rules: the capacity to input and output represented information, the capacity to store represented information, and the capacity to manipulate represented information.

Connectionist networks are certainly capable of automatically inputting and outputting information in virtue of their inputting and outputting representations of that information. For example, NETtalk inputs the information that a certain seven-letter string is present in virtue of its locally representing each letter in the string in one of its input units. It outputs information concerning how the letter is to be pronounced by generating a distributed phonemic representation corresponding to the letter in its output units. Once the network has been trained, it produces the output representation automatically, given the input (and, of course, a pattern of connectivity among the units) in accordance with a set of effective, internalized rules (namely, the transition and output functions governing the operation of each individual unit). In contrast to the high-level rules in a conventional machine, these rules are not defined "over" the high-level input representations of the connectionist network. Nevertheless, the process of producing an output when given an input is completely rule-governed in the sense that C2 requires.

What about storage? One of the distinguishing characteristics of connectionist systems, in contrast to conventional machines, is that there is no distinct memory. Memory and processing are handled by the very same set of units. In what sense, then, are representations stored? Since there is nothing analogous to the long-term memory of a conventional machine, representations obviously cannot be stored in the literal sense of being *put* somewhere. However, the information they contain is *implicitly* stored by means of the pattern of weights in the network. For example, once NETtalk has been trained, we can say that it has stored the letter-to-sound correspondence c to the hard-c sound /k/ in the sense that if it is given a c as input, the c-to-/k/ correspondence representation will become activated.

We turn finally to the question of whether connectionist networks can manipulate representations. What exactly does the term 'manipulate' mean in this context? If we think about that paradigm of a computer, the Turing machine, symbol manipulation comes down to the ability to create symbols (write them on some medium, such as a tape), the ability to eliminate them (erase them from the tape), and the ability to move them (which really amounts to eliminating them at one location on the medium and immediately creating them somewhere else).

A connectionist network certainly seems to have the first two abilities. For example, during training, NETtalk is, in effect, altering the network so that it can represent the letter-to-sound correspondences of English. In other words, a whole new set of representations is being created. Furthermore, if we were to retrain the network with a French corpus, these representations of the English letter-to-sound correspondences would be eliminated. Neither the creation nor the elimination occurs during the course of performance, of course, but it is not difficult to imagine a more complex network in which weight alteration, and hence the creation and elimination of symbols, would be part of carrying out a certain computational task. And if this were possible, why not a network that "erased" a representation in one part of the network only to "write" it somewhere else in the network soon thereafter? If these speculations are correct, then there is every reason to believe that connectionist networks can not only input, output, and store symbols but also manipulate them, and, hence, that they are computers in the desired sense.

3.5   The Evolution of Cognitive Science

In his 1987 Presidential Address to the Psychonomic Society, Walter Schneider raises the question of whether the recent "explosive interest" in connectionism represents a Kuhnian paradigm shift in psychology. In this section I would like to briefly consider the analogue of Schneider's question for cognitive science: Does the recent interest in connectionism signal a paradigm shift for cognitive science?

As I have rejected the use of Kuhn's notion of a paradigm as inappropriate for cognitive science, I can hardly endorse the idea that there has been a revolutionary paradigm shift. However, there have clearly been important changes in the field in the last ten or so years, and it would be useful if these changes could be reflected in my metatheoretic characterization. The best way to do this, on my view, is to say that, from its inception in the mid 1950s to the present, the research framework of cognitive science has undergone a certain amount of evolution.

What does it mean to say that a research framework has evolved? Recall the discussion in section 1.1. Strictly speaking, a research framework is a schema for a set of *versions* of a research framework that specifies the unrevisable elements and either leaves the revisable elements blank or specifies them in terms of a range of options. A research framework can evolve when, over time, the revisable "slots" in the schema are filled in different ways. In other words, the evolution of a research framework consists of a temporal series of *instantiations* of versions of the research framework in which there is either no change or a minimal change from one instantiation to the next.

Thus, in order for a research framework to be able to evolve, at least one of its components must consist of a revisable element. Neither component of the computational assumption as we have characterized it thus far (that is, neither C1 nor C2) seems revisable. What, then, has changed? As I suggested at the start of section 3.3, the vagueness of C2 has prompted cognitive scientists interested in architecturally specific research to supplement C1 and C2 with a more detailed hypothesis concerning the computational nature of the mind/brain. What has changed is the nature of that more detailed supplemental assumption.

Roughly speaking, there seem to have been two stages. In the first stage, from the mid 1950s to around 1980, cognitive scientists interested in architecturally specific research assumed that the mind/brain was something like a general-purpose conventional machine. Ironically, this view received its most explicit articulation in 1980 (in Allan Newell's paper "Physical Symbol Systems"), just when important changes were in the offing. To be more precise, in the first stage C1 and C2 were supplemented by something like this:

C1.1 (SUPPLEMENTARY LINKING ASSUMPTION) More specifically, the human mind/brain is a general-purpose, stored-program, conventional computer.

C2.1 (SUPPLEMENTARY SYSTEM ASSUMPTION) A general-purpose, stored-program, conventional computer is ... [as described in section 3.3].

Around 1980, C1.1 started coming under fire. The attacks came from two directions. Some researchers began to feel very unhappy with the general-purpose part of the assumption. This view received its clearest articulation in Fodor's 1983 book *The Modularity of Mind*, where it was suggested that significant portions of the cognitive mind/brain (specifically, the "input systems") are controlled by a set of distinct special-purpose, wired-program, conventional devices rather than being under the control of a single general-purpose, stored-program machine.[37] The other prong of the attack, which came from advocates of connectionism, was the view that the mind/brain is a connectionist device. The upshot was a considerable loosening of the original supplementary linking hypothesis, starting around 1980,[38] in which C1.1 and C2.1 were replaced by the following more eclectic assumptions:

C1.2 (SUPPLEMENTARY LINKING ASSUMPTION)   More specifically, the human mind/brain is either a general-purpose, stored-program, conventional

D1-D3
Q1-Q4
SA1: The Computational Assumption
    C1 (linking assumption): The human, cognitive
    mind/brain is a computational device.
    C2 (system assumption): A computer is a
    device capable of automatically inputting,
    storing, manipulating, and outputting infor-
    mation . . .
SA2
    .
    .
    .

Research Framework of Cognitive Science

D1-D3
Q1-Q4
SA1: Computational Assumption
    C1 (linking assumption)
        C1.1: More specifically, the human
        mind/brain is a general purpose,
        stored program, conventional
        computer . . .
    C2 (system assumption)
        C2.1: A general purpose, stored
        program, conventional computer
        is . . .
SA2
    .
    .
    .

D1-D3
Q1-Q4
SA1: Computational Assumption
    C1 (linking assumption)
        C1.2: More specifically, the human
        mind/brain is either a general
        purpose, stored program,
        conventional computer or a special
        purpose, wired program,
        conventional computer or a
        connectionist computer or some
        combination of these.
    C2 (system assumption)
        C2.2: A general purpose, stored
        program, conventional computer
        is . . .
        A special purpose, wired program,
        conventional computer is . . .
        A connectionist computer is . . .
SA2
    .
    .
    .

Version 1   Version 2

1956   1980   present

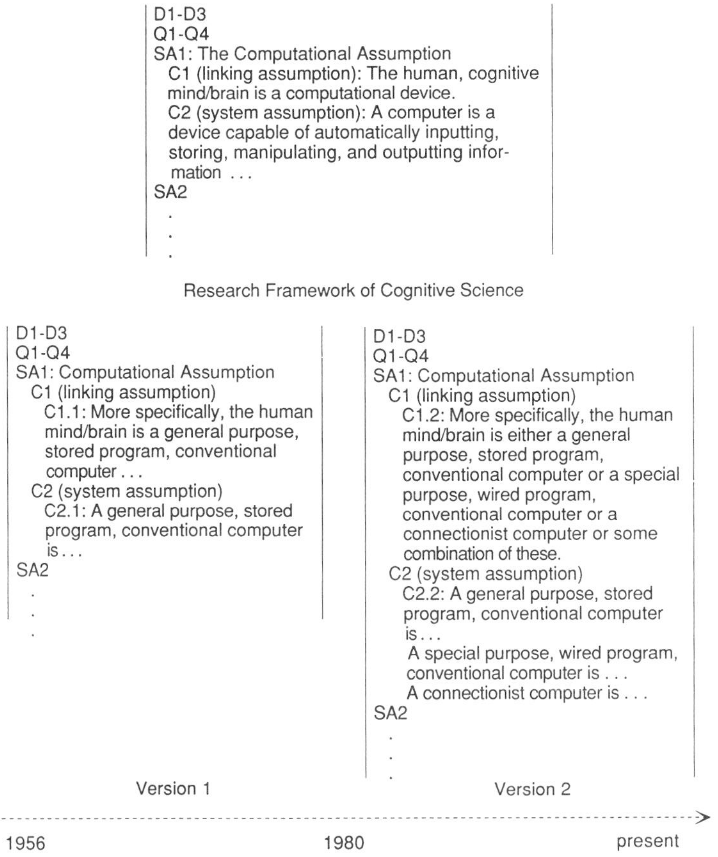

Figure 3.10
The evolution of cognitive science from the mid 1950s to the present.

computer or a special-purpose, wired-program, conventional computer or a connectionist computer, or some combination of these.

C2.2 (SUPPLEMENTARY SYSTEM ASSUMPTION)   A general-purpose, stored-program, conventional computer is ... [as described in section 3.3]. A special-purpose, wired-program, conventional computer is ... [as described in section 3.3]. A connectionist computer is ... [as described in section 3.4].

In sum, the evolution of cognitive science, to date, can be envisioned as in figure 3.10.

4 Representation in General

4.1 The Representational Linking Assumption

The cognitive mind is not only a computational device, according to cognitive science; it is also a representational one (Fodor 1975; Newell and Simon 1976; Pylyshyn 1984; Gardner 1985; Partee, Peters, and Thomason 1985; Putnam 1986; Stillings et al. 1987; Johnson-Laird 1988). Thus, the second major substantive linking assumption of the field is this:

SA2: THE REPRESENTATIONAL ASSUMPTION

R1 (linking assumption) The human cognitive mind/brain is a representational device; hence, the human cognitive capacities consist of a system of representational capacities.

As we saw in the previous chapter, computers are—on the standard conception—devices that process information by processing representations of that information. Fodor (1975, p. 27) therefore seems to be quite correct when he claims that "computation presupposes a medium of computation: a representational system." In other words, the computational assumption seems to *entail* the assumption that the mind has representations (Dietrich 1989).[1] Doesn't this mean, then, that the representational assumption is redundant?

If the representational assumption consisted simply of R1, then the answer would be "yes." However, as we shall see in chapters 5–8, cognitive scientists impose several additional constraints on what human mental representations are like, and some of these are not entailed by the assumption that the mind is a computational device.[2] Thus, a distinct substantive assumption is necessary to capture the commitments of the field.

R1 is a *linking* assumption. That is, it is an assumption that connects the real-world system of human cognitive capacities with the theoretical idea of a representational device. For this assumption to mean anything, therefore, it must be accompanied by a "system" assumption that says what a representational device is.

A rough statement of such an assumption is easy to formulate. It might look like this:

R2 (SYSTEM ASSUMPTION) A representational device is a device that has states or contains within it entities that are representations.

At this point, however, we run into difficulties. What, exactly, is a representation? Clearly, R2 requires some expansion.

In dealing with the analogous question in the case of the computational assumption (i.e., What is a computer?), we discovered two things. First, the cognitive science concept of a computer is borrowed from areas of inquiry that existed before the inception of cognitive science. Second, the concept that best fits the current research commitments and practices of cognitive science (namely, C2) is relatively vague, raising the more specific question of what *kind* of computer the cognitive mind/brain is.

As we shall see shortly, both of these points get echoed in the case of the representational assumption. There is, however, one difference between the two cases that has significant consequences for the present discussion: Whereas the cognitive science concept of a computer derives from a relatively well-developed, widely accepted body of knowledge in mathematics and computer science, the source of the cognitive science concept of representation is far more amorphous. As a result, cognitive science's current theorizing about representation is in far worse shape than its current theorizing about computation.

The source of the current cognitive science concept of representation is amorphous because, insofar as the notion of representation in cognitive science is borrowed, it is borrowed just as much from our unreflective daily experience with representations as from the reflections *about* representation that occurs in other disciplines. And although we are all familiar with various forms of representation in our daily life (words, sentences, pictures, photographs, maps, diagrams, mathematical formulas, etc.), it is far from clear whether we really understand how such representations function as representations. Thus, while such unreflective daily experience may provide us with many helpful insights and intuitions, it does not cut much theoretical ice.

Furthermore, despite the reams upon reams of pages that have been written on specific forms of representation, and on representation in general, there is no explicit, systematic body of knowledge on the subject that is widely accepted. Hence, there is no clear theoretical source for cognitive scientists to borrow from.

These facts about the origins of cognitive science's current concept of representation have the following consequence for my discussion: As in the computational case, it will be extremely useful to discuss current views on the representational nature of the human cognitive capacities against the background of some relevant general theory. In particular, we will gain a more systematic picture of what cognitive scientists think about *mental* representation if we consider it in the context of a view of representation in general. But since cognitive scientists do not share—at least, explicitly—any common view concerning the nature of representation in general, I will need to supply one.

Specifically, I propose to sketch a view of the nature of representation in general that was developed before cognitive science was even a gleam in the eyes of Newell and Simon—the view of Charles Sanders Peirce. Although, as we shall see, Peirce's general theory of representation (otherwise known as his "semiotics") has its weak points, I believe that my rather unorthodox use of Peirce in this context is warranted for two reasons. First, the general outline, if not all the details, of what Peirce has to say about representation (at least, as I reconstruct him) is tacitly assumed by many cognitive scientists. Second, I have found Peirce's theory extremely helpful in introducing some order to the rather messy current concept of mental representation.[3,4]

4.2 Peirce's Triadic Analysis

Peirce's writings on semiotics are fragmented and often obscure; furthermore, they evolved over many years. Since I am looking at Peirce's work not for its own sake but as a vehicle for saying something about mental representation, I will ignore some of the more obscure aspects of his doctrine (such as its basis in a system of metaphysical categories Peirce called "Firstness", "Secondness", and "Thirdness") and will introduce corrections and clarifications where they seem required. I will also, on occasion, suggest a revision of the Peircian terminology.

The fundamental claim Peirce wants to make about representation (or signification—Peirce uses these two terms interchangeably) is that it involves a triadic relation. Something is a sign (or a "representamen", as Peirce sometimes calls it) only if it is a sign *of* an object *with respect to* an "interpretant". He writes, for example:

A sign, or *representamen*, is something which stands to somebody for something in some respect or capacity. It addresses somebody, that is, creates in the mind of that person an equivalent sign, or perhaps a more developed sign. That sign which it creates I call the *interpretant* of the first sign. The sign stands for something, its *object*.   (2.228)

and

I define a Sign as anything which is so determined by something else, called its Object, and so determines an effect upon a person, which effect I call its Interpretant, that the latter is thereby mediately determined by the former. (in Hardwick 1977, pp. 80–81)

Let us consider each of the relata in turn.

The sign   Although something is a sign only if it is involved in a representing relation with an object and an interpretant, we can, of course, consider what kinds of entities, picked out independently of their representational properties, can function as signs. Peirce writes:

Since a sign is not identical with the thing signified, but differs from the latter in some respects, it must plainly have some characters that belong to it in itself, and have nothing to do with its representative function. These I call the *material* qualities of the sign. As examples of such qualities, take in the word "man", its consisting of three letters—in a picture, its being flat and without relief. (5.287)

As the 'man' example makes clear, Peirce is using the word 'material' here in an extremely broad sense. The material qualities of a thing do not necessarily have anything to do with *matter* in the more limited physical sense. In fact, when Peirce taxonomizes signs as they are "in themselves," he distinguishes the following three classes: qualities (by which I think he means properties), actual existent things or events, and general types. All of the following are signs: the particular shade of red of a color swatch (it represents the color of the entire bolt), a portrait of Winston Churchill (it represents Winston Churchill), the word 'dog' (it represents the class of all dogs). The first of these examples is a quality, the second an individual thing, and the third an abstract entity or type. Later writers on semiotics, beginning with Charles W. Morris, coined the term 'sign-bearer' to refer to the sign when it is considered solely in terms of its material qualities. I shall use the term *representation bearer* to pick out representations in terms of their *nonrepresentational* properties.

The object   When Peirce talks about "the" representational object, the definite article is not intended very seriously. A sign may have multiple objects, which for purposes of discussion can be treated as one complex object (2.230). Two kinds of object are particularly important to Peirce:

We have to distinguish the Immediate Object, which is the Object as the Sign itself represents it, and whose Being is thus dependent upon the Representation of it in the Sign, from the Dynamical Object, which is the Reality which by some means contrives to determine the Sign to its Representation. (4.536)

It is a matter of controversy among Peirce scholars precisely what Peirce has in mind by this distinction. The dynamical object (or, as I shall say, the *object itself*, since the object in question is not necessarily dynamical in any ordinary sense of the word) is clearly intended to be any object whatever, whether concrete or abstract, that exists independent of the mind.[5] However, what is the immediate object? The most natural interpretation of what Peirce says is this: A sign does not typically represent an object *tout court*. Rather, it represents that object in a certain way or under a certain *aspect*. That is, it represents the object as having a certain set of properties. The object being represented, considered as a totality independent of mind and of the representation relation, is the object itself. The particular aspect being represented by the sign (or the properties of the object itself in terms of which the sign represents the object itself) is the immediate object. A photograph of my dog Sydney both represents the actual living being, with all her charming and not-so-charming properties, and represents her in a certain way (e.g., how she looks from the front, when viewed at a certain angle, under certain lighting conditions, or lying down on the grass).[6]

Although regarding the immediate object as an aspect of the object itself is the most natural interpretation of what Peirce has to say on the subject, it is not clearly a reading that generalizes to all forms of representation. Most semantic theories of natural language, for example, honor a distinction between two kinds of objects corresponding, roughly, to sense and reference (Frege 1952), or to intension and extension (Carnap 1947), but not all treat sense or intension as something like aspect. Thus, if we are interested in providing Peirce's theory with a high degree of generality, we should leave the precise nature of the immediate object somewhat open-ended. I shall thus assume only the following:

• Whatever the immediate object is ontologically (e.g., an aspect of reality, a set of properties, or an abstract object), it is not mental.

• A particular instance of representation may involve only an immediate object, only an object itself, or both.

• Where it involves both, the immediate object will not be identical to the object itself; however,

• It will be implicated in the representation relation somehow or other; furthermore, it will be implicated in the representation relation in such a way as to bear some sort of close relation to the object itself (it will constitute an aspect of the object itself or "determine" it, for example).

The interpretant   Peirce conceives of the interpretant as a "mental effect" in the mind of the interpreter for whom the sign is a sign. He evidently held two views (early and late) regarding the nature of this mental effect. In his early writings he always speaks of it as a thought (5.287). Later, he distinguishes three kinds of "significate effects": emotional, energetic, and logical. An emotional effect is a feeling produced in the interpreter by the sign. For example, the performance of a piece of concert music is a sign that conveys the composer's musical ideas. "But these usually consist merely in a series of feelings" (5.475). An energetic interpretant is an effort of some kind, either muscular (as in the automatic response to a military command) or mental. Finally, a logical interpretant is either a thought or what Peirce called a "habit-change" (a modification of the interpreter's disposition to behave).[7] Of these three effects, however, the logical is clearly still the most important for Peirce. At one point, he suggests that the emotional and energetic interpretants are relevant only to a "sign in its *broadest* sense" (8.332); at another, he distinguishes between genuine signs and quasi-signs, where the former requires that the interpretant be a thought (5.474). To simplify matters, I will assume that the interpretant of a non-mental representation is always a thought (or a series of thoughts) in the mind of the interpreter. I will discuss Peirce's views on the nature of the interpretant for mental representation in chapter 8.

Let us see where we are. We have seen that Peirce maintains that representation is essentially triadic. That is, he wants to hold that R is a representation only if R is a representation of an object O with respect to an interpretant I. We now have some idea of what the three relata of the sign relation are, on Peirce's view. The next question to be addressed is this: What relation must hold among these three relata for there to be a triadic relation of representation? That is, what is it for a representation R to be a representation of O with respect to an interpretant I?

I shall explore this question by considering, one at a time, the relations between the representation and each of the other two elements. That is, I shall begin by schematizing Peirce's triadic relation as follows:

R is a representation of an object O with respect to an interpretant I (in a subject S) just in case

(i)   R _____ O

and

(ii) R _____ I.

I shall then attempt to fill in the blanks.

Peirce scholars may object at this point that analyzing Peirce's triadic representation relation into two apparently dyadic component relations seriously misrepresents his view, for Peirce holds that the representation relation is not only triadic but *genuinely* triadic—that is, that "its members are bound together by [the relation] in a way that does not consist in any complexus of dyadic relations" (2.274). My response is that in adopting the above analytic strategy as a framework for further exploration I am not making any assumption about the nature of the two subrelations (that is, about how subrelations i and ii will be filled in). In particular, I am not assuming that the subrelation between the representation and the object and that between the representation and the interpretant must be *purely* dyadic relations. Thus, if Peirce is right about the character of his own view, it will turn out that an explication of subrelation i will require reference to the interpretant and an explication of subrelation ii will require reference to the object.[8]

4.3   The Representation-Object Relation

When we say that a sign represents an object for someone, or that it represents an object with respect to some interpretant, it is natural to suppose that it also represents the object, *tout court*—perhaps in some other sense of 'represents'. Thus, one way to fill in the first blank in our schema would be to say simply

(i)   R represents$_o$ O,

where representation$_o$ is a relation that can exist between a representation bearer and an object independent of whether there is an interpreter or an interpretant. (The subscript 'o' stands for 'objective'.) In a way, Peirce does adopt this solution, but he is not content to leave the relation of representing$_o$ as an unanalyzed semantic relation. Thus, he aims to find a relation (or a set of relations, as the case may be) that will "ground" the semantic relation of representation$_o$. In contemporary terms, he is looking for a set of relations *in virtue of which* the relation of representation$_o$ holds. In this section I will survey what Peirce has to say about the different possible kinds of ground a representation can have.

There are, on Peirce's view, only three possible kinds of pure ground: iconic, indexical, and symbolic. An *icon* is a sign that represents its object in virtue of its being similar to the object in some respect (2.282, 3.556). It exhibits or exemplifies some property of its object (1.558, 2.247, 2.255). The properties that underlie the sign's iconic nature are properties it has intrinsically, regardless of whether the object in question exists or not (4.447). Because of this feature of icons, Peirce claims that they cannot represent particular individuals but only general classes of things (e.g., all those things which they in fact resemble and are taken to resemble) (3.434) or possible objects (4.447).

Peirce distinguishes three kinds of icons. Two of these are interesting for our purposes. Icons that are similar to their objects in terms of their "simple qualities" are called *images*; those that represent "the relations ... of the parts of one thing by analogous relations in their own parts" (2.277) are *diagrams*.[9] An example of an image is a square of color on a paint can which represents the color of the paint inside the can by resembling it in hue. An example of a diagram is a map in which the spatial arrangement and the relative lengths of certain lines are analogous to the spatial arrangement and the lengths of routes in a certain part of the country.

The ground of an *index* is supposed to be the existence of an "existential" relation or a real connection between the sign and its object (2.243). Precisely what Peirce takes a "real" connection to be in general is far from clear; however, most of his examples of indices fall into two categories. Either the connection between the index and its object is causal or the connection is spatial or temporal. For example, a rap on a door is, for Peirce, an index of the presence of someone at the door. A weathervane is an index of the direction of the wind. In both cases, the signifying property of the sign is a causal effect of a property of the object being represented. The second class of cases includes such standard indexicals as a pointing finger and a demonstrative pronoun. Here the relation between the sign and the object being represented is not clearly causal (although it may be); however, there is a spatial or temporal relation. The pointing finger represents objects that are in a certain spatial relation to the pointing finger. The word 'now' is an index of the time at which the word is uttered.

Indexical signs differ from icons in at least three respects, according to Peirce. First, the ground of the signification relation is not one of resemblance; second, the objects represented are always "individuals, single units, single collections of units, or single continua" (2.304); third, the relation between sign and object is existential in the sense that the sign-bearer or the representing properties of the sign-bearer could not exist were it not for the existence of the object (5.73).

The third way in which a sign may relate to its object is by virtue of a convention. This is the defining characteristic of the class of signs Peirce calls *symbols*. Any ordinary word, such as 'give', 'bird', or 'marriage', is an example of a symbol. Symbols are abstract entities or types, instantiated by *replicas*—particular utterances or inscriptions (that is, tokens) of the symbol in question. The paradigm case of a symbol, for Peirce, is what the logicians call a "predicate"—a noun, an adjective, or a verb that picks out a class of individuals characterized by some defining property (the class of all birds, for example). For this reason, Peirce frequently declares that the object to which a symbol refers is "of a general nature" (2.249).[10]

Precisely what it is for one thing to be related to another by convention is not clear, but there are indications in the text that, ultimately, Peirce wants to understand this sort of ground psychologically. Specifically, he seems to want to understand it in terms of the psychological processes of interpretation to which a representation typically gives rise.[11] He writes, for example, that "a conventional sign is neither a mass of ink on a piece of paper or any other individual existence, nor is it an image present to consciousness, but is a special habit or rule of interpretation and consists precisely in the fact that certain sorts of ink spots ... will have certain effects on the conduct, mental and bodily, of the interpreter" (4.431). Clearly, if this sort of approach is to work, much more needs to be said about what the relevant "certain effects" are. In particular, for this to succeed as an account of how a sign is conventionally related to a *specific* object, the "certain effects" must somehow have something to do with *that* object.[12]

There is a hint here that, in the final analysis, Peirce is seeking a wholly naturalistic way of grounding representation, that is, a way of grounding representation that does not involve any semantic or intentional properties or relations. Icons and indices are unproblematical in this respect. Thus, the hang-up would appear to be symbols. However, if the conventional, semantic grounding of symbols can ultimately be understood in terms of the intentionality of mental interpretants and these, in turn, ultimately give way to a nonintentional habit change, then a naturalistic account is ensured.[13]

Peirce's distinction among icon, index, and symbol is primarily a distinction among the *possible* relations that can exist between a sign and its object. It is not certain that he believes in the existence of actual signs which are *pure* in the sense of involving only one of these grounds. There is no question, however, that he recognizes the existence of many mixed cases. He realizes, for example, that many iconic signs, such as diagrams, cannot function iconically without a convention indicating what aspects of the sign are to be interpreted as similar to the object (4.418). He also notes that a portrait can be both an icon and an index (2.92). In addition, he recognizes that linguistic indexicals are never purely indexical but necessarily involve some conventional component (4.56).

To summarize: What is Peirce's view of the relation between sign and object? Clearly he does not have a general, univocal view. He does, however, offer us a sketch of a complex disjunctive answer. There are three possible relations of a sign to an object that are relevant to representation: iconic, indexical, and symbolic. These can be combined in various ways. Any actual relation will either be pure or will involve some combination of these pure relations. Let us say that when a sign is related to an object by such a combination it is "related by an appropriate ground." We can then fill in the first condition of our schema as follows:

R is a representation of an object O with respect to an interpretant I (in a subject S) only if (i) R is related to O by some appropriate ground.

4.4   The Representation-Interpretant Relation

As we have seen, Peirce is insistent that something is a representation only if it is a representation with respect to some interpretant I. However, two points about this doctrine remain unclear: What precisely is the ontological status of I? What is it for a representation R to represent with respect to an interpretant I?

By the question of the ontological status of I, I have in mind the following. We have seen that the interpretant of a nonmental representation is a thought in the mind of an *interpreter*. Does Peirce require that the inter-

Table 4.1

	Liberal	Middle-of-the-road (1)	(2)	Conservative
Interpreter	possible	possible	actual	actual
Interpretant	possible	actual	possible	actual

preter be actual or will a possible interpreter do? And if the interpreter has to be actual, does he or she have to be living? Further, what is supposed to be the status of the interpretant mental effect in that interpreter: actual, possible, present? A number of positions seem possible here, ranging from extremely liberal to extremely conservative. We can characterize them roughly as in table 4.1.

As far as I know, Peirce never considers the question of the ontological status of the interpreter. However, there seems to be only one reasonable possibility: The interpreter must be actual, for if we allowed the interpreter to be merely possible then virtually anything would count as a sign, completing undercutting Peirce's triadic requirement. That is, Peirce's insistence that something counts as a representation only if it is interpreted would be so weak as to be virtually meaningless. To see this, imagine a possible interpreter with a vast amount of knowledge of the world. Since almost everything bears some causal or resemblance relation to something, this possible superknower would be able to interpret virtually anything as an icon or index of something else. And this, I take it, would be counter to Peirce's conception of a representation, which is intended to be somewhat restrictive. Virtually anything is a possible representation for Peirce, but only certain things are actual representations. I shall, thus, assume that in order for something to be a representation the interpreter must be actual. Furthermore, I shall assume that the tense of the representational claim is coupled with the temporal status of the interpreter. That is, I shall take it that R *is* (present tense) a representation only if there currently exists an interpreter bearing the right relation to R. However, if a relevant interpreter existed in the past, we can say that R *was* a representation (as in a "dead" language); and if a relevant interpreter will exist in the future, we can say that R *will be* a representation. (Similarly, the modality of the representational claim is coupled with the modal status of the interpreter. Thus, if there is a possible interpreter, then R *could be* a representation.)

Although Peirce does not address the question of the interpreter (to my knowledge), he does have something to say about the ontological status of the interpretant. If we consider our space of possibilities and restrict ourselves to the two options in which the interpreter is actual, we see that we are left with the conservative position and the second middle-of-the-road position. On the conservative position, something counts as a sign only if it is now being interpreted by an actual interpreter. Such a view would have extremely counterintuitive consequences. A token representation such as this word

dog

would be a sign only while someone was reading it. And some things which we would intuitively regard as representations, such as printed words in copies of books that no one has read or will ever read, would, on the conservative view, never count as representations at all.

Fortunately, some passages suggest that this is not Peirce's position. In order for something to be a sign, it is not necessary for it actually to produce an interpretant. Rather, the relation of sign and interpretant must "consist in a *power* of the representamen to determine *some* interpretant to being a representamen of the same object" (1.542). Elsewhere, Peirce draws a distinction between the sign's *actually functioning* as such and its simply *being* a sign: "... no Representamen actually functions as such until it actually determines an Interpretant, yet it becomes a Representamen as soon as it is fully capable of doing this; and its Representative Quality is not necessarily dependent upon its ever actually determining an Interpretant...." (2.275)

We can conclude, I think, that Peirce is opting for our second middle-of-the-road position. Thus, he is suggesting that the second condition of our schema should read (in part, at least) as follows: R is a representation of O with respect to I in S only if (ii) S is currently existing and R has the power (or is capable) of determining an interpretant I in S. Can we unpack this suggestion any further?

To a first approximation, when we say that something X has the power to do or cause A in Y, what we generally mean is that X, Y, and the surrounding environment are capable of satisfying certain conditions C such that the presence of X, conjoined with satisfaction of C, will *in fact* result in A. There is, however, an obvious difficulty with this formulation. Consider the claim that a lit match has the power to burn down a building.

Clearly the building will not in fact burn down unless a host of positive conditions are met: the building must be of a suitably combustible material, oxygen must be present in the air, etc. However, the presence of these positive conditions is not sufficient. What if it began to rain just as the match was lit, or if a strong wind blew, or if the fire department showed up? Even more fantastic, what if the laws governing combustion simply changed and no longer held just as the fire was getting started, so that under the prevailing conditions a lit match caused the building to turn blue rather than to burn? The point is that a *complete* specification of the relevant conditions will include not only positive conditions but also negative ones. The lit match will cause the building to burn only if certain conditions are present (e.g., there is enough oxygen) *and* certain conditions are absent (e.g., the fire department doesn't show up). The problem is that these negative conditions are notoriously difficult, if not impossible, to specify exhaustively.

This situation is usually handled by introducing a *ceteris paribus* clause. We say that X has the power to do or cause A in Y just in case X, Y, and the surrounding environment are capable of satisfying certain conditions C such that the presence of X, conjoined with satisfaction of C, will in fact do or cause A, *ceteris paribus* (other things being equal). Note that the *ceteris paribus* clause does not solve the problem of the negative conditions; it merely acknowledges it.

If we now apply the above explication to the case at hand, we get the following:

R is a representation of O for S only if (ii) R has the power to produce an interpretant I in S (i.e., R and S are jointly capable of satisfying certain conditions of interpretability CI such that the presence of R conjoined with satisfaction of CI will, *ceteris paribus*, result in I).

This formulation is fine as far as it goes, but it would be even more illuminating if we could say something further about the "conditions of interpretability" for representation. Unfortunately, a difficulty arises at this point. Ideally, we would like to specify the conditions of interpretability for the interpretation of *all* forms of representation. It turns out, however, that this is not possible. Although it is fairly easy (as we shall see shortly) to tell a plausible-sounding story concerning what these conditions are with respect to *nonmental* representation, this story does not apply to the interpretation of mental representation. Thus, if we wish to say what it means for *any* representation to have significance for a subject, we must be content with the above formulation, which simply mentions rather than explicates the relevant conditions of interpretability.

Although the conditions of interpretability for nonmental representation do not generalize directly to the mental case, it will be useful for us to have them in mind when we come to consider the problem of interpretation for mental representation in chapter 8. Basically, what is required for a nonmental representation R to produce an interpretant I in an interpreter S is that the representation be *understood* by the interpreter. In particular, as Peirce himself notes, a mental effect counts as an interpretant of a particular sign R only if it involves understanding the sign in such a way that the interpretant is brought into relation to the object of the sign. What is involved in an act of understanding? Although Peirce is not explicit on this point, I believe that we can make sense of it as follows: A sign is related to its object by virtue of some appropriate ground. Understanding a sign requires a "grasp" of its ground—an understanding of what its ground is (at least, roughly)—for only in this way can the interpreter come to have a relation to the object being represented.

For example, suppose I see a photograph. To understand that photograph I must know (in some sense) that there are both a causal relation and a similarity relation between the photograph and its subject, and I must know (in some sense) the respects in which the photograph is a causal effect of and is similar to its subject. If I know all that, then I will be able to form a belief or a thought about the subject of the photograph (that is, who or what the photograph represents)—specifically, that there was such a subject and that this subject looked a certain way at the time the photograph was taken. In other words, by considering the photograph in conjunction with its ground I come to be in a relation to the object it represents.

Such an act of understanding makes demands on both the representation bearer and the interpreter. Roughly speaking, the representation bearer must have properties that suffice to make it understandable, while the interpreter must be capable of doing the requisite understanding. More specific, the representation bearer must have certain perceptible surface characteristics that allow the interpreter to categorize it as a representation that falls under some ground relation. The interpreter must, then, know the relevant ground relation and be able to use it in order to ascertain what object is being represented. In the case of an icon, the interpreter must know the relevant resemblance relations; in the case of an index, he or she must know the relevant causal or spatiotemporal relations; in the case of a symbol, the interpreter must know the relevant conventions.

Thus far we have been focusing on the fact that, in order for a representation R to have significance for S, R must have the power to produce an interpretant in S. We must now consider what it is about the mental effect that is produced that makes it an interpretant of *R*. On Peirce's view, the interpretant of a representation R is an interpretation of *R* because it serves to mediate between the subject and the *representational objects* of R. More specific, the interpretant I must be related to both R and S in such a way that the object of R can make a difference to the internal states and the behavior of S. This comes down to two things: The interpretant I must be *connected* to *O* in some way as a result of the interpretation process, and this connection must be *psychologically efficacious* for S.

The case of nonmental representation, again, is fairly clear. Consider the interpretation of an utterance in a natural language—for example, "It is hot today." The interpretant of such a representation, according to Peirce, is a thought. It is connected to the object of R because either it is itself a representation of that object or it is akin to a metastatement about the representation relation between R and its object.[14] In the first case, the interpretant would simply be the thought that it is hot today; in the second case, it would be the thought that the utterance "It is hot today" means that it is hot today. In both cases, the thought would be connected to the representational object of "It is hot today", namely the proposition that it is hot today. Such an interpretant is psychologically efficiacious for S because it is a thought that consists in (belongs to?) an act of *understanding*, and understanding is precisely the sort of mental state that has subsequent effects on the internal states and the behavior of the system that has it. Having recovered the meaning of the sentence, the interpreter is in a position to go on. For example, if the interpreter believes that the sentence was *asserted* and believes that the speaker was sincere, then he or she may assent, or reply "Let's go to the pool", or do any of a number of things each of which depends in some way on the interpreter's having grasped the representational object of the original sentence.

Unfortunately, as we shall see in chapter 8, none of the details I have just spelled out about how the interpretant of R mediates between the interpreter and the object of R generalize to the case of mental representation. Thus, once again, in order to have a characterization that covers both nonmental and mental representation we must be content with a fairly abstract formulation. I shall make do with the following:

R is a representation of an object O for a subject S only if I is related to both R and S in such a way that, by means of I, the nature of O can make a difference to the internal states and behavior of S.

A full specification of condition ii will then look like this:

R is a representation of an object O for a subject S only if (ii) (a) R has the power to produce an interpretant I in S (i.e., R and S are jointly capable of satisfying certain conditions of interpretability CI such that the presence of R conjoined with satisfaction of CI will, *ceteris paribus*, result in I) and (b) I is related to both R and S in such a way that, by means of I, the nature of O can make a difference to the internal states and behavior of S.

4.5   The Representational System Assumption

In discussing Peirce's theory of representation in general, I have tried to focus on those aspects of his view that will help us understand the cognitive science conception of mental representation. However, since exegesis of Peirce is not a straightforward business, there is the ever-present danger of losing track of the main points. Before concluding this chapter on Peirce, therefore, I would like to briefly rehearse what it is about Peirce's view that I take to be important and relevant.

I have found many aspects of Peirce's view illuminating for understanding the cognitive science conception of mental representation.[15] Here is a rundown of the most salient points:

Peirce's distinction between a representation and a representation bearer

his insistence that something can be a full-blown representation only if it is both grounded and interpreted

his attempt to understand what makes a mental effect an interpretant of some particular representation

his struggle with the problem of interpretation for mental representation[16]

the idea that sign and object are related by two very different sets of relations—semantic relations (such as representing, signifying, referring to, and expressing) and the ground relations in virtue of which those semantic relations hold

his taxonomy of kinds of ground

his apparent interest in ultmately understanding representation in a completely naturalistic way.

Each of these points will reemerge in the following chapters.

Making use of Peirce's theory of representation, let us then fill in our representational system assumption:

R2 (SYSTEM ASSUMPTION) A representational device is a device that has states or contains within it entities that are representations. Any representation will have four aspects essential to its being a representation: it will be realized by a representation bearer, it will represent$_0$ one or more representational objects, its representation$_0$ relations will be grounded somehow, and it will be interpretable by (that is, it will function as a representation *for*) some currently existing interpreter.

5 Mental Representation

Cognitive science assumes that the cognitive mind is a representational—device—that is, a device that has states or that contains entitles that are representations. Let us dub the total collection of these representations the *mental representation system* (MRS).[1] We must now raise the following question: Is the nature of MRS completely a matter of empirical research, or does the research framework of cognitive science make any further assumptions concerning what mental representations are like?

Our Peircian framework allows us to pose this question in a more pointed way. According to Peirce, any form of representation will have four aspects essential to its being a representation: It will be realized by a representation bearer, it will represent$_0$ one or more representational objects, its representation$_0$ relations will be grounded somehow, and it will be interpretable by some presently existing interpreter. Since mental representation is, by assumption, a form of representation, our question can be reformulated thus: Does the research framework of cognitive science make any further assumptions with respect to the representation bearer, the semantics, the ground, or the mode of interpretation of the members of MRS?

I believe that the answer is "yes," and in the next four chapters I will attempt to spell out what these further assumptions are. Before embarking on this task, however, I would like to try to disabuse the reader of a common misconception about mental representation.

5.1 What Mental Representations Are Not

One of the substantive assumptions of the research framework of cognitive science is, as we have seen, that the cognitive mind is a representational device and, hence, is capable of having mental representations. Since the substantive assumptions of a research program constrain what can count as a possible answer to the basic questions of the program, entities posited by such assumptions will play a significant role in the explanatory strategy of the program. Thus, I am clearly claiming that cognitive science is committed to the existence of mental representations as a significant component of its explanatory apparatus.

Many writers about cognitive science take this (often implicitly) to be equivalent to or to entail the fact that cognitive science is committed to the existence of propositional attitudes as a significant component of its explanatory apparatus. In chapter 2 I discussed the view, held by Fodor and others, that the propositional attitudes constitute the domain of cognitive science, and, hence, constitute what cognitive science seeks to explain. What is at issue here is a different (though related) view: that propositional attitudes figure prominently in the conceptual apparatus invoked by cognitive science to do the explaining. I shall call the first the "propositional-attitude explanandum thesis" and the second the "propositional-attitude explanans thesis." It is my view that, strictly, neither thesis is correct.

In my earlier discussion of the role of the propositional attitudes in cognitive science, I quoted a passage from Fodor (1975) in which the propositional-attitude explanandum thesis is clearly expressed. It turns out that that very same passage also expresses the propositional-attitude explanans thesis. Fodor claims that cognitive science provides us with a propositional-attitude psychology in *two* senses. First, propositional attitudes constitute the main subject matter of the theory (the propositional-attitude explanandum thesis). Second, "propositional attitudes are the constructs in terms of which the theory elaborates its typical explanations: much of what the theory explains, it explains by reference to processes in which propositional attitudes are involved" (Fodor 1975, p. 1).

The picture of cognitive science conveyed by the preceding passage has been fairly influential in the philosophical and foundational literature of cognitive science. For example, Pylyshyn (1984) claims that "the basic assumption of cognitive science" is that there are at least three distinct, independent levels at which we can find the explanatory principles of cognitive science: the biological, the functional, and the representational or semantic. Pylyshyn then compares his levels hierarchy to that of Newell (1982, 1990), remarking that Newell calls the third level the "knowledge" level rather than the "representational" level. Pylyshyn (1984, p. 130) rejects Newell's terminology on the following grounds: "the term *knowledge* raises philosophical eyebrows (strictly speaking, it should be called *belief*). By implication, the term *knowledge* also suggests that one is ignoring other representational states, such as goals, as well as such propositional attitudes as fears and hopes.... That is why ... I use the term *representational* or *semantic* for this level...." The import of these remarks seems to be that the level at which we describe the cognitive mind in terms of its representations and representation-governed processes is, for Pylyshyn, the same level at which we describe it in terms of its propositional attitudes.

As a way of getting at what is wrong with the propositional-attitude explanans thesis, it is useful to consider the sort of argument (actually, it is an argument schema) that appears to underlie it:

THE INFERENCE TO PROPOSITIONAL ATTITUDES

(1) Cognitive science is committed to mental representations as a significant component of its explanatory apparatus.

(2) Cognitive science is committed to the view that mental representations bear some intimate relation _____ to the propositional attitudes of folk psychology.

(3) Therefore, cognitive science is committed to the propositional attitudes as a significant component of its explanatory apparatus.

In the current literature of cognitive science there are two views of the relation of mental representations to the propositional attitudes that could, in principle, serve to license the above inference (that is, that could serve to specify the relation in premise 2). The first is based on using 'mental representation' in such a way that propositional attitudes are mental representations by definition. The second posits a theoretical identification of propositional attitudes with mental representations. I shall argue that neither succeeds in making the above inference an acceptable argument.

The first view can be found in Searle 1983. Searle claims that the term 'mental representation' refers to any mental phenomenon with a propositional content and a psychological mode. And since the propositional attitudes are mental phenomena with propositional contents and psychological modes, they are by definition mental representations. However, while defining 'mental representation' in this way makes it true that all propositional attitudes are mental representations, it does not, in itself, make it true that all mental representations are propositional attitudes. Hence, the conclusion of the above inference does not follow, for cognitive science could be committed to mental representations of precisely the sort that are not propositional attitudes.

To surmount this difficulty, let us suppose, not only that 'mental representation' is used in the broad sense of including propositional attitudes, but also that there are no other kinds of mental representations besides the propositional attitudes (either as a matter of contingent fact or by virtue of the meaning of the terms). In other words, let us take the intimate relation of premise 2 to be the extensional equivalence of the terms 'mental representation' and 'propositional attitude'.

Even with this addition, the inference is not justified, for it is simply a fact that when cognitive scientists use the term 'mental representation' they are not using it as extensionally equivalent with 'propositional attitude'. Rather, they are using it to refer to computational entities (data structures in conventional devices) or computational states (nodes or patterns of activation in connectionist devices) with representational properties, hypothesized in the context of a scientific research program.

In a review article on mental representation in memory, Rumelhart and Norman (1988) discuss the various kinds of representations and representational systems currently being entertained in research on memory in cognitive science. These representations and representational systems are broadly categorized into four groups: proposition-based representation systems, analogical representations, procedural representations, and superpositional memory systems. The first group (the largest) is further broken down into semantic feature representations, semantic networks, schemata, and frames. Note that propositional attitudes, as such, are nowhere to be found.

Searle himself comments that there is a difference between his use of the term 'mental representation' and that found in contemporary cognitive psychology and artificial intelligence. For him, a representation "is defined by its content and its mode, not by its formal structure" (Searle 1983, p. 12), where the latter, presumably, is a feature of the kinds of representations posited by cognitive scientists.[2]

There is another important difference. A propositional attitude is individuated by more than just its content; it is also individuated by the attitude involved (believing, hoping, fearing, etc.). That is, two propositional attitudes are not identical unless they involve the same attitude toward the same content. This component is missing from the individuation of mental representations of the cognitive science sort. Mental representations are type individuated by content (and, perhaps, by form). In other words, two token representations that belong to the same type could have very different computational "locations" in the system (e.g., one is in long-term memory, the other is in working memory) or could be "used" in very different ways (e.g., one is the end result of perceptual processing, the other occurs in the context of a reasoning task). There is a direct analogy to public linguistic representations here. Words and sentences are so individuated that they can be used in various ways (spoken, written, heard, stored, transmitted, etc.) without losing their identity. The same point holds about mental representations as cognitive scientists conceive of them. The very same kind of representation can be used computationally in various ways without losing its identity. This is simply not the case with the propositional attitudes, however. We do not *use* our propositional attitudes. Rather, they themselves involve a "use" of, or an attitude toward, a content. If the use changes, the identity of the propositional attitude does too.

The upshot is that, if the above inference schema is fleshed out by using the term 'mental representation' as extensionally equivalent with 'propositional attitude', the resulting argument will be valid but not sound. The conclusion will go through, but the first premise will simply be false. Cognitive scientists are not committed to mental representations in this sense as a significant component of their explanatory apparatus.

The second approach to fleshing out the inference to propositional attitudes is based on a suggestion made by Fodor (1975, 1987). Fodor is quite content (most of the time, at least) to use the term 'mental representation' in its more narrow, information-processing sense. Propositional attitudes are not, therefore, on his view, mental representations by definition. Instead he proposes that the relation between them is, roughly, one of *intertheoretic identification*. Specifically, for any organism O and any (type of) propositional attitude A to a proposition P there will exist a (type of) computational relation CR and a (type of) representation R such that R means that P and O will have (a token of) A just in case O bears CR to (a token of) R.[3] I shall call this the "attitude-representation identification assumption." The second approach to filling in the argument schema is, then, to specify the intimate relation of premise 2 as the relation characterized by the attitude-representation identification assumption.

What happens to the inference to propositional attitudes if premise 2 is understood in this way? Again, there are difficulties. In the first place, although premise 1 is now consistent with current cognitive science practice (cognitive science *is* committed to mental representations in the narrow, information-processing sense as a central component of its explanatory apparatus), the new version of premise 2 is problematic because cognitive science is *not* committed to the existence of such an intertheoretic identification. Cognitive theory might eventually vindicate the propositional attitudes by Fodorian intertheoretic identification or it might not;

this is entirely an empirical matter.[4] Second, even if cognitive science were committed to the sort of intertheoretic identification Fodor envisages, it would still be misleading to say—as Fodor (1975, p. 1) does—that "the propositional attitudes are *the* constructs in terms of which the theory elaborates its typical explanations." Fodor's assumption claims only that each token of a propositional attitude is identical to some token of a computational relation to a representation; it does not claim that each token of a computational relation to a representation is identical to some token of a propositional attitude. In other words, even Fodor allows for the possibility that there exist representations that are not component parts of some propositional attitude.

In a more recent work, Fodor (1987) acknowledges this possibility fully. The mind/brain, on his view, has a cognitive architecture "constituted of *hierarchies* of symbol processors." At the top are states which may well correspond to propositional attitudes, but at the bottom and middle levels "there are bound to be lots of symbol-processing operations that correspond to nothing that *people*—as opposed to their nervous systems—ever do" (p. 23). The point is that the representational states involved in these subpersonal operations may play just as important a role in the explanatory apparatus of cognitive science as the higher-level ones. Hence, it is misleading to say that the propositional attitudes are *the* constructs in terms of which cognitive science elaborates its typical explanations.

The last criticism is admittedly a quibble. But there is an even more important reason why the conclusion of the inference to propositional attitudes does not go through even if we suppose (counterfactually) that cognitive science is committed to the attitude-representation identification assumption. The assumption says something about what the propositional attitudes are. That is, it is concerned with the nature of propositional attitudes as entities in the world. However, what is relevant to explanation is not the nature of the entities themselves but the concepts we use to pick them out. In other words, explanation is intensional (with an 's'). Even if we believe that some object X is identical to some object Y, it does not follow that explanations which trade on the concept of X also trade on the concept of Y. Chemists are committed to H_2O molecules as a component of their explanatory apparatus in the sense that the concept of H_2O plays an important role in chemical explanations. They also believe that H_2O is identical to water in the ordinary sense (barring considerations of impurity). But this does not mean that they are committed to *water* in the ordinary sense as a component of their explanatory apparatus. The ordinary notion of water does not appear anywhere in the explanans of chemical explanations.

The point is illustrated by some recent work in cognitive science. Rapaport (1986) has developed an AI model for representing belief reports expressed in natural language. He is particularly concerned to model a number of the logical properties associated with such reports, such as failure of reference and quasi-indexicality. The model itself takes the form of a certain kind of semantic network, specifically a SNePS network (Shapiro 1979; Shapiro and Rapaport 1987). Rapaport summarizes the principle features of this network thus:

A SNePS network consists of nodes linked by labeled, directed arcs. The nodes and arcs have the following features, among many others:

(S.1) Each constant node represents a unique concept.

(S.2) Each concept represented in the network is represented by a unique node.

(S.3) Arcs represent nonconceptual, binary relations.

(S.4) Deduction rules are propositions, and so are represented by nodes.

What is interesting about Rapaport's work, for present purposes, is that, while he is primarily modeling the semantics of *reports* about the beliefs of others, he takes the semantic representation of these reports to constitute a representation of what the system itself believes as a result of receiving these reports. In particular, he claims that "*nondominated* nodes—that is, nodes with no arcs pointing to them—represent *beliefs of the system*" (Rapaport 1986, p. 393). For example, suppose the system is given the English belief report "John believes that Lucy is sweet" as input. This sentence is then translated (by the system) into a semantic-network representation that (presumably) captures the meaning of the input sentence. At this point, Rapaport makes the further assumption that the system comes to believe what it has been "told." Hence, the semantic-network representation that constitutes the end result of the "understanding" process also becomes a representation of the system's resulting belief (that John believes that Lucy is sweet). This representation can then be operated on in various ways in order to reflect how the system might "reason" on the basis of its beliefs.

Whether any of this works theoretically or empirically is, of course, an open question. For present purposes, the point is only this: Rapaport's research fits quite nicely with the program envisaged by Fodor. Rapaport is interested in giving an account of what beliefs are. Furthermore, he is trying to do this by describing the sort of computational relation and the sort of representation which satisfy the attitude-representation identification assumption for beliefs. In the context of his model, the sort of representation implicated in belief consists in nondominated nodes of the SNePs network. The computational relation is defined by the role these representations play in the translation and inference programs used by the model. In view of all this, it is quite natural to attribute to Rapaport the sort of commitment expressed by premise 2 of the inference to propositional attitudes. That is, it seems reasonable to assume that Rapaport himself, if not the entire cognitive science community, is committed to the existence of a Fodorian intertheoretic identity for beliefs. However (and this is the moral of the story), although this might be the case, Rapaport is not committed to using the concept of belief *in its ordinary sense* as part of his explanatory apparatus. Beliefs may be identical with nondominated nodes in SNePS networks, but only the latter appear in the model.

5.2   The Representation Bearer

Let us now turn to the task of characterizing the cognitive science conception of a mental representation in terms of its four Peircian components: representation bearer, semantics, ground, and interpretant.

Of the four components, the cognitive science conception of the representation bearer of a mental representation is the clearest and, at a general level, the least controversial.[5] It can be formulated thus:

R2.1   The representation bearer of a mental representation is a computational structure or state in the mind/brain, considered purely formally.[6]

Recall that when Peirce talks about the nonrepresentational or "material" properties of a representation, he does not restrict himself to material properties in the usual sense of physicochemical properties. He is perfectly happy to consider the "matter" of a word to be the letters of which it is composed. This point is important in the case of mental representation, for while cognitive scientists tend to be physicalists of a sort (and, hence, to regard all mental representations to be ultimately physicochemical) the representation bearer of a mental representation is more usefully thought of as a computational entity rather than as a physicochemical or even as a neurophysiological entity.

Can we be more specific about what sorts of formal computational structures or processes "bear" or "realize" our mental representations? It turns out that further specification is possible only relative to an assumption concerning the nature of the mental computational architecture; and since cognitive science is not committed to the computational architecture of the mind being one way or another, such specification is inappropriate at the level of the substantive assumptions of the field. We can, however, give some examples of the kinds of hypotheses with respect to the representation bearers of our mental representations cognitive scientists have entertained in the course of their theoretical and empirical work.

As we have seen, two kinds of architectural speculations currently dominate theorizing in the field: that the cognitive mind is a conventional machine and that it is a connectionist machine. I shall, therefore, consider what the representation bearers of our mental representations would be if the mind were conventional, on the one hand, or connectionist, on the other.

When cognitive scientists speculate that the mind is a conventional computer, they invariably imagine it to be a high-level device capable of manipulating complex data structures. It is these complex data structures, construed purely formally, that constitute the representation bearers of our mental representations on the conventional approach. I shall first consider what a data structure is, in general, and then examine a specific example of a data-structure hypothesis in cognitive science.[7]

A data structure is an orderly arrangement of component data representations, usually of some specified type. In the simplest case, the component data representations are themselves unstructured. That is, they consist simply of well-formed expressions. A particular programming language will usually include certain standard or predefined primitive unstructured types. Standard predefined types include Integer (consisting of numerals which designate integers), Character (consisting of the letters of the alphabet, numerals, and assorted punctuation marks), and Boolean (consisting of the values: 'true' and 'false'). In addition to these, the programmer can introduce new, primitive unstructured types by enumeration by means of so-called declaration statements. For example, within a suitable programming language, a declaration statement might look something like this:

type Shape = (rectangle, square, ellipse, circle).

This says that the set consisting of the expressions 'rectangle', 'square', 'ellipse', and 'circle' are to be considered a primitive, unstructured data type called 'Shape'.

Data structures fall into two important classes: *fundamental* data structures, which are fixed in size, and *dynamic* data structures, which can vary in size during computation. Let us first consider two of the most common kinds of fundamental data structures, the *array* and the *record*.

An *array* is an *n*-dimensional arrangement of individual data representations all of which belong to the same type. An *array type* can be defined in terms of the base type of the components and an index specifying the number of dimensions and the number of components:

type T = array[I] of T_o .

Thus, for example, we might define an array called "Shaperow" consisting of five values drawn from our defined type Shape:

type Shaperow = array[1 .. 5] of Shape

An *instance* of Shaperow might, then, look like this[8]:

Square	Square	Circle	Square	Ellipse
1	2	3	4	5

The constituents of array types may themselves be structured. An array whose constitutents are also arrays is called a *matrix*. For example,

type ShapeX = array[1 .. 3] of Shaperow

defines an array consisting of three five-element arrays—that is, a 5 × 3 matrix whose components are values from the type Shape.

A *record* is an *n*-dimensional data structure whose components may be of multiple types. It is defined by specifying the type that corresponds to each "slot" of the record, in order:

type T = record $s_1: T_1$
$\qquad\qquad\quad s_2: T_2$
$\qquad\qquad\quad \cdots$
$\qquad\qquad\quad s_n: T_n$
$\qquad$ end .

This says that the first slot will be filled with a value belonging to type T_1, the second slot with a value from type T_2, etc. Thus, a record for containing information about dates might be defined thus:

Date = **record**   Day: 1 .. 31;
$\qquad\qquad\qquad$ Month: 1 .. 12;
$\qquad\qquad\qquad$ Year: 1 .. 2000
$\qquad\quad$ end .

This declaration indicates that any record of the type Date will consist of three components. The first will be drawn from the type Day, whose values are the integer numerals from 1 to 31; the second will be drawn from the type Month, whose values are the integer numerals from 1 to 12; and the third will be drawn from the type Year, whose values consist of the integer numerals from 1 to 2000. A particular instance of this type of record—one corresponding to the date January 3, 1991—would look like this:

3   1   1991

Within a computer, the ordering relations of a data structure can be instantiated either via the physical configuration of the cells in memory or via what are called *pointers*. To illustrate the notion of a pointer, imagine a set of numbered cards, each of which contains an English word plus the number of some other card. In such a format, the English sentence 'John went to the store' might be expressed as

card 1	card 2	card 3	card 4	card 5
JOHN	TO	STORE	WENT	THE
4	5	end	2	3

where card 1 is designated as the initial card. Since the notion of a *next element* is here represented explicitly rather than by physical adjacency or some other physical relation in the medium, it should be obvious that this format allows for considerable freedom in how elements can be connected. Thus, in addition to simple arrays, matrices, and records, pointers make it easy to define such structures as *trees* (in which every nonterminal element points to at least two other elements but no element can receive pointers from more than one element) and *graphs* (in which any element can point to any number of other elements and any element can receive pointers from any number of other elements) (Wilde 1973).

Pointers not only allow for greater freedom in structuring; they also make possible data structures of unspecified cardinality. To get an idea of how this works, consider the simplest type of dynamic structure, the *linear list*. A linear list consists of a set of elements each of which is linked to its successor by means of a pointer. Each element has three components: an identifying key, the pointer to its successor, and the representation of whatever contentful information is contained in the list. In other words, each element is a record which we can specify thus:

type T = record Key: Integer;

        Next: $>$T;

        Content: T_o

   end

where 'T_o' is the base type of the contentful information and '$>$T' is a type whose values are pointers to data structures of type T. Note that this definition is recursive: that is, in defining what type T comes to, it refers to type T in the definiens. It is precisely this property of linear lists that allows them to be of unspecified length. Similar (but, obviously, more complicated) definitions can be given of tree structures and graphs.

Kosslyn's work on mental imagery provides us with a nice illustration of theorizing about mental representations as data structures.[9] According to Kosslyn (1980), a cognitive theory ought to describe the brain in terms of two sorts of functional capacities: structures and processes. With respect to the structure side, "one must specify the nature of the data-structures that can occur in memory and the nature of the internal media that support these data-structures" (p. 117).

Data structures, on Kosslyn's view, should be specified in terms of their format, their organization, and their content. Media should be specified in terms of their "formatting" and accessibility. Before looking at the bearers associated with the three kinds of representations Kosslyn posits in his theory of imagery, let us examine these basic distinctions. I shall first indicate what Kosslyn has to say on the matter, and then provide my own reconstruction in terms of the above discussion of data structures.

Kosslyn (1981, p. 47) writes:

Data structures   Data structures are the information-bearing representations in any processing system. They can be specified by reference to three properties, their *format, content,* and *organization.* The format is determined by (a) the nature of the "marks" used in the representation (such as ink, magnetic fluxes, or sound waves) and (b) the way these marks are interpreted (the mark A could be taken as a token of a letter of the alphabet or a picture of a particular pattern). The format specifies whether a representation is composed of primitive elements and relations and, if so, specifies their nature. The content is the information stored in a given data structure. Any given content can be represented using any number of formats.... The organization is the way the elementary representations can be combined. The format of a representation constrains the possible organizations but does not determine them. For example, propositional representations can be ordered into various kinds of lists and networks.

Media   A medium does not carry information in its own right. Rather, a medium is a structure that supports particular kinds of data structures. This page, a TV screen, and even the air are media—supporting ink, glowing phosphor and sound patterns, respectively. Media can be specified by reference to their *formatting* and *accessibility.* The formatting places restrictions on what sorts of data structures can be supported by a medium. A short-term store, for example, might have five "slots" that take "verbal chunks"—but not visual images or abstract propositions. The accessibility characteristics dictate how processes can access data structures within a medium. The slots of a short-term store, for example, might be accessible only in a given sequence.

Of the various properties Kosslyn attributes to data structures and their media, only some are relevant for present purposes (that is, with respect to the question of what constitutes the *bearers* of our representations). Two of the properties are clearly irrelevant. What Kosslyn calls the "content" of a data structure corresponds to Peirce's representational object, and what he calls the "accessibility" of the medium will play a role when we consider the nature of the Peircian interpretant. Thus, we are left with the format and organization of the data structures and the formatting of the medium.

Kosslyn's treatment of these three properties is slightly misleading. Though it is true that the terms 'format' and 'medium' may include reference to physical properties when used in noncomputational contexts (for example, the format of a book may include the kind of paper it is printed on), this is not the case when we speak of the data structures in a computer.

How a computational representation is *realized* physically has nothing to do with its format or medium in the computationally relevant sense. Kosslyn probably would not disagree; note that when he gives an example of formatting in a medium he talks about a short-term store with five "slots" designed to take only "verbal chunks."

Let me now offer the following reconstruction of Kosslyn's distinction in terms of my general discussion of data structures. Recall that an important feature of data structures is their *type*. Thus, given the defined, unstructured type Shape,

type Shape = (rectangle, square, ellipse, circle),

we define the structured type ShapeX like this:

type ShapeX = array[1 .. 5, 1 .. 3] of Shape.

This type can then be instantiated in various alternative ways, with the various instances distinguished by which of the various Shape values ('rectangle', 'square', etc.) are placed in the "slots" of the 5 × 3 matrix. I take it that when Kosslyn talks about the *medium* of a representation, he is talking about its type in the above sense (with, perhaps, the added constraint that a medium be a type of data structure that is fairly abstractly defined). A medium, thus, has two aspects: (a) the data types (which, themselves, may be unstructured or structured) used as its *components*, and (b) how these component data types are *structured* (that is, as a matrix, a linear list, a tree, etc.). These two aspects, taken together, constitute what Kosslyn calls the "formatting" of the medium. Note, however, that it is quite natural to keep these two aspects distinct and, hence, to apply the format/organization distinction to media as well as to data structures (in Kosslyn's sense). If we do this, then the format of the medium corresponds to (a) above, and its organization corresponds to (b).

An *instance* of a given structured data type corresponds to what Kosslyn calls a "data structure." This is not yet a token, in the sense of a spatio-temporal particular, for there may be many tokens of the data structure type ShapeX instantiated with a particular set of values. Such instances also have format and organization, of course, and the format and organization of any given instance will be constrained by the format and organization of the type to which it belongs. As Kosslyn says, "the formatting places restrictions on what sorts of data structures can be supported by a medium." If the format of ShapeX includes only data representations of the unstructured type Shape, then this medium (= type) can only support data structures (= instances) with 'rectangle', 'square', etc. as their basic components. Furthermore, any instance of ShapeX must be a 3 × 5 matrix.

As we know from chapter 1, Kosslyn believes that three kinds of representations are involved in our capacity to image: a surface representation, which underlies our experience of having an image and which thus represents how the imaged object appears in a quasi-pictorial format; literal encodings, stored in long-term memory, which contain the information necessary for generating the surface representation; and propositional encodings, which represent factual information associated with each imageable object. What kinds of data structures and media, specified solely in terms of their format and organization, are associated with each kind of representation?

The surface representation   Surface representations depict the appearances of objects from a "viewer-centered" point of view. Their semantics are such that parts of the representation represent parts of the imaged object. The medium of the surface representation is called "the visual buffer." It has the following properties:

• Its components are individual "local regions" capable of either being activated or not (there is no representation of color); in the model, this is simulated by "cells" each of which represents a spatial point on the surface of the imaged object.

• These "local regions" are structured in a coordinate space; in the model, this is simulated by organizing the individual cells into an array.

• This space has a limited extent and a specific shape (probably, roughly circular).

• The visual buffer has a limited resolution; thus, the array has a "grain."

• The resolution is sharpest near the center of the medium and more degraded toward the periphery.

• Any given region of the visual buffer can be activated only for a short period of time without being renewed.

All the above things are true of the medium or the visual buffer. The data structures of the surface representation simply correspond to particular patterns of activation in this medium.

The literal encodings   The literal encodings contain the information necessary for generating the surface representations. There are literal encodings for whole objects (such as a car) and for their parts (such as a tire). The literal encodings for a whole object represents only its global shape. In the model, shape information is stored in the form of polar coordinates, indicating which cells in the array must to be filled. The literal encodings for any given imageable object are organized as follows: each unit is structured as a linear list, and each list is prefaced with the name of an imageable object or part followed by the polar coordinates for that object or part. The data structures of the literal encodings are, again, simply instantiations of such (types of) lists for a particular imageable object.

The propositional encodings   The propositional encodings represent various facts about the imageable object. In Kosslyn's model these include what the object's parts are, where these parts are located relative to the global shape of the object, how big the object is relative to a single standard (such as human body size), what the superordinate category of the object is, and so on. These facts are represented in a sentence-like way and organized in terms of a list which is stored in long-term memory. The medium of the propositional encodings simply consists in the types of data structures appropriate for containing all this factual information. The data structures themselves will, of course, just be instantiations of these general types.

Thus far we have been discussing what the representation bearer of our mental representations would be like if the mind/brain were a conventional computational device. Let us now turn to the analogous question with respect to the connectionist machines.

In chapter 3 we saw that there are two kinds of high-level representations in current connectionist models: local representations and distributed representations. The representation bearer of a local representation consists of a single node's being activated. The representation bearer of a distributed representation consists of a set of nodes' being activated. In the NETtalk example discussed above, we found that articulatory features were locally represented, whereas phonemes (which consist of groups of articulatory features) were represented in distributed fashion.

Let us consider two more examples.

(1) McClelland, Rumelhart, and Hinton (1986) describe a network that represents information about the members of two gangs. Specifically, this

network stores the name of each gang member, which gang he belongs to (the Jets or the Sharks), how old he is (20s, 30s, or 40s), how much education he has completed (junior high, senior high, or college), what his marital status is (single, married, or divorced), and what his occupation in the gang is (pusher, burglar, or bookie). Each piece of information is represented locally. There is an "instance unit" for each individual gang member and one unit for each of the above properties. The instance unit for each gang member is then linked by mutually excitatory connections to each of the units whose activation represents one of this person's properties. See figures 5.1 and 5.2.

(2) Smolensky (1987) gives an example of a distributed representation of the concept *cup with coffee* which is similar to NETtalk's representation of a phoneme. The concept of a cup with coffee is analyzed into a set of microfeatures such as + upright container, + hot liquid, and + porcelain curved surface, each of which is locally represented. The representation bearer of the concept as a whole then consists of activation of the set of

Name	Gang	Age	Edu	Mar	Occupation
Art	Jets	40's	J.H.	Sing.	Pusher
Al	Jets	30's	J.H.	Mar.	Burglar
Sam	Jets	20's	COL.	Sing.	Bookie
Clyde	Jets	40's	J.H.	Sing.	Bookie
Mike	Jets	30's	J.H.	Sing.	Bookie
Jim	Jets	20's	J.H.	Div.	Burglar
Greg	Jets	20's	H.S.	Mar.	Pusher
John	Jets	20's	J.H.	Mar.	Burglar
Doug	Jets	30's	H.S.	Sing.	Bookie
Lance	Jets	20's	J.H.	Mar.	Burglar
George	Jets	20's	J.H.	Div.	Burglar
Pete	Jets	20's	H.S.	Sing.	Bookie
Fred	Jets	20's	H.S.	Sing.	Pusher
Gene	Jets	20's	COL.	Sing.	Pusher
Ralph	Jets	30's	J.H.	Sing.	Pusher
Phil	Sharks	30's	COL.	Mar.	Pusher
Ike	Sharks	30's	J.H.	Sing.	Bookie
Nick	Sharks	30's	H.S.	Sing.	Pusher
Don	Sharks	30's	COL.	Mar.	Burglar
Ned	Sharks	30's	COL.	Mar.	Bookie
Karl	Sharks	40's	H.S.	Mar.	Bookie
Ken	Sharks	20's	H.S.	Sing.	Burglar
Earl	Sharks	40's	H.S.	Mar.	Burglar
Rick	Sharks	30's	H.S.	Div.	Burglar
Ol	Sharks	30's	COL.	Mar.	Pusher
Neal	Sharks	30's	H.S.	Sing.	Bookie
Dave	Sharks	30's	H.S.	Div.	Pusher

Figure 5.1
Characteristics of members of two gangs, the Jets and the Sharks. (From McClelland 1981. Reprinted by permission of the author.)

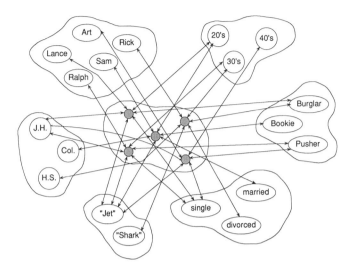

Figure 5.2
A network representing information about the some of the gang members described in
figure 5.1. (From McClelland 1981. Reprinted with corrections by permission of the author.)

units which locally "bear" the representations of the relevant microfeatures. See figure 5.3.

It should be evident that connectionist representations—at least, as they
are conceived in current models—are, formally, far simpler than data
structures. From a formal point of view, there is just not that much to say
about them. In fact, some have argued that they are, in principle, too
simple to account for certain key features of cognition. In the rest of
this section, I will briefly consider the controversy surrounding this claim.

One of the attractive features of the conventional view of mental representations as data structures is that data structures are *structured*. In
particular, complex data structures exhibit what is known as "constituent
structure": they have parts that are also representation bearers (and, hence,
parts that have content), and these parts are formally related to one
another in such a way that the "arrangement" typically has semantic
consequences.

Many cognitive scientists, including some noted connectionists, take
being structured in this way to be an important or even a necessary
property of the mental representations underlying cognition. For example,

Units	Microfeatures
●	upright container
●	hot liquid
○	glass contacting wood
●	burnt odor
●	brown liquid contacting porcelain
●	porcelain curved surface
○	oblong silver object
●	finger-sized handle
●	brown liquid with curved sides and bottom

Figure 5.3
Representation of *cup with coffee* in terms of microfeatures. (From Smolensky 1987.
Reprinted by permission of the author and *The Southern Journal of Philosophy*.)

the connectionists Hinton, McClelland, and Rumelhart (1986, p. 104) allude to "the major insights from the field of artificial intelligence concerning the importance of structure in representations and processes", and the conventionalists Fodor and Pylyshyn (1988) have recently mounted an argument (accepted by the connectionist Smolensky [1987]) that constituent structure is necessary if MRS is to account for the productivity and the systematicity of our cognitive capacities.

Let us look at the Fodor-Pylyshyn argument in more detail. Consider, first, productivity. As was discussed in chapter 2 above, the human cognitive capacities are productive in the sense that once a capacity has been mastered it can be exercised in a practically unlimited number of novel ways. For example, since I can see, I can see a practically unlimited number of things I have never seen before, and since I am a speaker of the English language, I can understand a practically unlimited number of novel English sentences. How are these things possible? If representations underlie the intentionality of the human capacities, then it would seem that we must posit that the capacity to form a practically unlimited number of representations "underlies" the practically unlimited number of novel applications of seeing, understanding, reasoning, and so forth of which humans are capable. Since Chomsky (1965, 1968), the standard way to view the practical limitlessness of this representational capacity is as the interaction of an "unbounded competence with resource constraints" (Fodor and Pylyshyn 1988, p. 34), where the unbounded competence in question is the in-principle capacity of MRS to generate an infinite number of representations and where the resource constraints in question are processing limitations such as the size of memory. However, such infinite expressive power can only be obtained by finite means by recursively *building up* complex representations out of simpler components. But the existence of such a recursive mechanism, in turn, entails that at least some representations of MRS have constituent structure.

The systematicity of the human cognitive capacities amounts to the fact that the subcapacities that constitute those larger capacities are typically mastered in "clumps" that are systematically related. The clearest examples of this phenomenon come from the domain of language acquisition. The child at the two-word stage who can say 'my kitty' and who knows the words 'truck' and 'baby' will typically also be able to say 'my truck', 'my baby', and 'baby kitty'. Children learning to use negation begin by putting the negative word (in this case, 'no') at the beginning of the expression to be negated. Thus, a child who says 'no eat' will also typically say such things as 'no sit down' and 'no Mommy go' (Foss and Hakes 1978). See table 5.1 for a list of common utterances typically found in the early multiword stage.

According to Fodor and Pylyshyn, an analogous sort of systematicity exists in thought. A working assumption of psycholinguistics is that anything that is uttered will first be mentally represented. Thus, the child who says 'my kitty' and 'my truck' will first be representing these sentences in MRS. What accounts for the "clumping" of the utterance capacities? On Fodor and Pylyshyn's view, the only plausible explanation is that the representations in question are made up of representational *parts* in a structured relation, and a person who has a repertoire of certain representational parts and the ability to handle certain sorts of structures will typically be able to construct all the propositional representations that have the right structures and are composed of those parts. But, clearly, this explanation entails that there are representations with constituent structure.

I find the above arguments very persuasive. However, since they are not demonstrative, and since Fodor and Pylyshyn ultimately use these arguments to support the very controversial conclusion that the human cognitive architecture cannot be connectionist, I suspect that there may well be a

Table 5.1
Common types of utterances typically found in the multiword stage. (Adapted from Foss and Hakes 1978 by permission of the first author and Prentice-Hall, Inc.)

Semantic character	Forms	Examples
1. Nomination (naming, noticing)	here it there's + Noun this see that hi	there book that car see doggie hi spoon
2. Possession	Noun + Noun Pronoun	my stool baby book Mommy sock
3. Attribution	Adjective + Noun	pretty boat party hat big step
	Noun + Adjective Pronoun	carriage broken that dirty Mommy tired
4. Plurality	Quantifier + Noun	two cup all cars
5. Actor-Action	Noun + Verb	Bambi go Mommy push (Kathryn) airplane by
	Noun + Noun	Mommy (wash) jacket Lois (play) baby record
	Verb + Noun	pick glove pull hat helping Mommy
6. Location a. object location	Noun + Prep P	sweater chair lady home baby room
b. action toward location	Verb + Prep P	sat wall walk street
7. Requests and Imperatives	Verb + Noun	want milk gimme ball
	more + Noun 'nother	more nut 'nother milk
8. Negation a. nonexistence	Neg + Noun Verb Adjective	allgone milk no hot nomore light any more play
b. rejection	Neg + Verb Noun	no dirty soap no meat no go outside
c. denial	Neg + Noun Verb Adjective	no morning (it was afternoon) no Daddy hungry no truck
9. Questions a. requests and imperatives	Same word order as statements and imperatives; signaled only by rising intonation	
b. information requests	Fixed forms with wh-	What dat? What (NP) do? Where (NP) go?

significant number of cognitive scientists who will want to halt the march toward anti-connectionism at this point. For these reasons, I propose not to include the claim that some representations of MRS have constituent structure as an assumption of cognitive science's research framework *per se*. (Instead I will mark it as an assumption whose status is currently open to question.) However, I will raise the following question: If Fodor and Pylyshyn are right and structured representations are needed in order to account for the productivity and systematicity of the human cognitive capacities, does the connectionist computational framework have the resources to support such representations?

As I have just indicated, according to Fodor and Pylyshyn (1988) the answer is clear. Connectionist representations, as currently conceived, simply do not, and cannot, have constituent structure. Why not? Their argument can be reconstructed as follows. Within the connectionist framework, there are only a fixed number of resources that one can employ to endow connectionist representations with structure: one can exploit the fact that connectionist representations can be distributed, one can explicitly encode the role played by the parts of a representation, and one can assign a representational function to the connections between nodes.[10] But none of these will do, according to Fodor and Pylyshyn. Hence, connectionist representations cannot have constituent structure. Let us examine this argument in more detail.

Distributed representations, typically, have two characteristics: the representation bearer of the representation is distributed (that is, it consists of activation of a set of nodes rather than activation of a single node), and the concept being represented has a microfeature analysis. Fodor and Pylyshyn argue against the possibility of introducing structure by using distributed representations by pointing out that neither of these characteristics necessarily leads to constituent structure. On the one hand, a representation can have a representation bearer that is distributed and still be structurally primitive. For example, simply imagine that the representation bearer of the concept *cup* is distributed without there being any local representation of microfeatures. On the other hand, the representational object of a representation can have a microfeature analysis and still be structurally primitive. For example, imagine that we can analyze the meaning of 'cup' in terms of some set of microfeatures but that in the network used to represent the concept *cup* this concept is represented locally. Fodor and Pylyshyn (1988, pp. 21–22) write:

A moment's consideration will make it clear ... that even on the assumption that concepts are distributed over microfeatures, '+ has-a-handle' is not a constituent of CUP in anything like the sense that 'Mary' (the word) is a constituent of (the sentence) 'John loves Mary'. In the former case, "constituency" is being (mis)used to refer to a semantic relation between predicates; roughly, the idea is that macro-level predicates like CUP are defined by sets of microfeatures like 'has-a-handle', so that it's some sort of semantic truth that CUP applies to a subset of what 'has-a-handle' applies to. Notice that while the extensions of these predicates are in a set/subset relation, the predicates themselves are not in any sort of part-to-whole relation. The expression 'has-a-handle' isn't *part of* the expression CUP any more than the English phrase 'is an unmarried man' is part of the English phrase 'is a bachelor'.

Fodor and Pylyshyn are certainly right that the existence of a micro-feature analysis of the concept *cup* does not entail that a distributed representation of *cup* will have constituent structure, but on my view their argument misses a crucial point. The point is that, typically, the representational objects of distributed representations not only *have* a microfeature analysis, they are also explicitly represented *in terms of* the designated microfeatures. Let us use angle brackets to designate representations in MRS in a way that reveals both their content and their structure (in other words, as an analogue of the quote convention for natural language). Then, in example 2, the representation of the concept *cup with coffee* is not written (in connectionese) as ⟨cup with coffee⟩; it is written as ⟨ + upright container, + hot liquid, + porcelain curved surface, + burnt odor, + brown liquid contacting porcelain, + porcelain curved surface. + finger-sized handle, + brown liquid with curved sides and bottom.⟩ Hence, contrary to Fodor and Pylyshyn's claim, ⟨ + finger-sized handle⟩ is formally a part of this representation.[11]

Does this fact mean that Fodor and Pylyshyn are simply wrong and that connectionist representations have constituent structure after all? The debate becomes somewhat confused at this point because of a lack of consistency in the use of the term 'constituent structure'. Earlier I suggested that a representation bearer (representation) with constituent structure has two properties: (a) it has parts that are also representation bearers (representations) and, hence, have representational content, and (b) these parts are "arranged" in a certain way that, typically, has semantic consequences. The confusion stems from the fact that, although Fodor and Pylyshyn clearly are interested in constituent structure in this strong sense, they occasionally give the impression that property a alone will do. ("You have constituent structure when (and only when) the parts of semantically evaluable entities are themselves semantically evaluable." [Fodor and Pylyshyn 1988, p. 19]) Let us call property a the "weak sense" of constituent structure. The point is, of course, that my argument shows only that distributed, microfeature representations have constituent structure in the weak sense. There is no evidence that they have constituent structure in the sense of both property a and property b.

In fact, Fodor and Pylyshyn introduce other arguments that indicate that distributed, microfeature representations do not exhibit property b. The reason is that the part-whole relationship within a distributed, microfeature representation is something like the relationship of set membership. The activation state of each individual node is a member of the set of activation states of the relevant collection of nodes. But members of a set, *qua* members of a set, are not ordered. The only relation they bear to one another is the relation of belonging to the same set.

That set membership provides too weak a notion of constituent structure can be seen by considering example 1. Although that example was presented as an example of a network with local representation, it seems clear that it is intended to represent not only individuals and properties but also propositions. That is, it is intended to represent such propositions as that Art is a Jet and a pusher and that Ike is a Shark and a bookie. But does it succeed in doing this? There are two problems, as Fodor and Pylyshyn point out. Suppose that the only nodes that are activated are the nodes ⟨Art⟩, ⟨is a Jet⟩, ⟨is a pusher⟩, ⟨Ike⟩, ⟨is a Shark⟩, and ⟨is a bookie⟩.

The first problem is that, on the assumption that there is nothing to determine constituent structure besides the relationship of set membership, the system cannot pick out just the intended propositions, for it is representing not only the propositions that Art is a Jet and a pusher and that Ike is a Shark and a bookie but also the propositions that Art is a Shark. that Art is a bookie, that Ike is a Jet, that Ike is a pusher, and so on for all the permutations and combinations (including conjunctive propositions) of the activated concepts.

The second problem requires an elaboration of the example. Suppose that we add to the various unary properties a node for the relational property of hating, and suppose that this node is activated along with the nodes mentioned previously. Then another sort of underdetermination is introduced. Even if we could solve the first problem and determine which concepts were supposed to be grouped together as propositions, we are still left with the possibility of *within-group* ambiguity. For example, suppose the only activated nodes are the nodes ⟨Art⟩, ⟨Ike⟩, and ⟨hates⟩. Then this state of affairs still does not determine whether the proposition being represented is that Art hates Ike or that Ike hates Art. The bottom line is that the fact that connectionist representations can be distributed is not sufficient to introduce constituent structure in the desired strong sense.

Hinton (1981) and Hinton, McClelland, and Rumelhart (1986) suggest that the second difficulty might be solved by explicitly representing not only the parts of a proposition but also the roles played by those parts within the proposition as a whole. In other words, if we want to represent the proposition that Art hates Ike rather than that Ike hates Art, we need to represent Art as ⟨Art-subject⟩ rather than simply as ⟨Art⟩ and we need to represent ⟨Ike⟩ as ⟨Ike-obJect⟩ rather than simply as ⟨Ike⟩. If we do this, activation of the nodes ⟨Art-subject⟩, ⟨hates⟩, and ⟨Ike-object⟩ will unambiguously represent the proposition that Art hates Ike.

But, as Fodor and Pylyshyn note, this solution still does not introduce enough structure. It may solve the problem of introducing structure within the set of concepts which make up a single proposition but it fails to solve the problem of determining how to individuate the propositions within a set of activated nodes intended to represent more than one proposition. For example, suppose the following nodes are activated: ⟨Art-subject⟩, ⟨Fred-subject⟩, ⟨Ike-object⟩, ⟨Neal-object⟩, and ⟨hates⟩. Then is this supposed to represent that Art hates Ike and Fred hates Neal, or that Art hates Neal and Fred hates Ike?

Of course, all is still not lost. One might disambiguate the above situation by making the representation of the hate relation more specific. That is, one might introduce one node for Art-subject-hates-Ike-object, one node for Art-subject-hates-Neal-object, one node for Fred-subject-hates-Ike-object, and one node for Fred-subject-hates-Neal-object. Then when one wanted to represent that Art hates Ike and Fred hates Neal, one would activate only the first and the fourth of these nodes rather than the second and the third.

But, as Fodor and Pylyshyn (1988, p. 24) so aptly put it, this proposal "requires rather a lot of microfeatures [i.e. nodes]" (roughly, a number of the order of magnitude of the sentences of a natural language), and it completely undercuts the strategy of representing complex objects (such as propositions) combinatorially in terms of their parts. We are, thus, left with the third alternative: capturing structure by exploiting the connections among connectionist nodes.

In discussing the problem of representing constituent structure in connectionist networks, Hinton, McClelland, and Rumelhart (1986, p. 105) implicitly suggest that the problem does not exist for local representation, for in the localist scheme "a whole is a node that is linked by labeled arcs to the nodes for its parts." But is this, in fact, the case? Can exploiting the connections among connectionist nodes serve to introduce constituent structure even where representation is local?

Obviously, if we are thinking of connectionist networks as models of the mind/brain, simply labeling a connection will not do the trick, just as labeling a node 'cup' does not, *ipso facto*, endow the activation of that node with the content *cup*. Both the syntactic and the semantic features of connectionist representations must be *grounded* (in Peirce's sense) in real properties and relations of the networks themselves.[12] Thus, we must ask whether there is any real property of the network that would warrant interpreting (and, consequently, labeling) some internode connection as a structural connection. This question has received no explicit attention in the connectionist literature, to my knowledge; however, reconsideration of example 1 reveals that, implicitly, internode connections are being put to structural use. The distributed-representation strategy for solving the problem of constituent structure failed in the case of example 1 because it provided no way of identifying which nodes were supposed to count as the representation bearer of a single propositional representation. But clearly there is something in the model that is supposed to serve this function: the fact that the "instance unit" representing each individual gang member is linked by mutually excitatory connections to all the units for the gang member's properties. In other words, under the intended interpretation, the model is supposed to be representing the propositions that Art is a Jet and that Ike is a Shark rather than that Art is a Shark and Ike is a Jet. How does it do this? Presumably, by the fact that the link between the instance node ⟨Art⟩ and the node ⟨is a Jet⟩ is mutually excitatory while the link between the instance node ⟨Art⟩ and the node ⟨is a Shark⟩ is inhibitory (or, at least. extreme weak) while the links between the instance node ⟨Ike⟩ and the nodes ⟨Jet⟩ and ⟨Shark⟩ are just the opposite.

Fodor and Pylyshyn (1988, p. 18) discuss the possibility of using the connections between nodes to endow a representation with structure and simply dismiss it out of hand:

... although graphs can sustain an interpretation as specifying the logical syntax of a complex mental representation, this interpretation is inappropriate for graphs of Connectionist networks. Connectionist graphs are not structural descriptions of mental representations; they're specifications of causal relations. All that a Connectionist can mean by a graph of the form X → Y is: *states of node X causally affect states of node Y.* In particular, the graph can't mean *X is a constituent of Y* or *X is grammatically related to Y* etc., since these sorts of relations are, in general, not defined for the kinds of mental representations that Connectionists recognize.

This argument does not seem very convincing. In fact, it seems downright question-begging. The reason Fodor and Pylyshyn give to support the claim that internode connections can't be interpreted as structural connections is that this sort of relation is not defined for connectionist representations. But the whole point of the proposal is, precisely, to "define" this sort of relation in terms of internode connections.

Fodor and Pylyshyn's position becomes even more puzzling when one notes that they are perfectly sanguine about the idea of using a connectionist network to *implement* a conventional architecture. Thus, they clearly do believe that resources exist within a connectionist computational framework to create representations with constituent structure (such as data structures). But, supposedly, to create structured representations in this way would not be to create structured representations of the sort connectionists are after, although what the difference is remains far from clear.

To claim that Fodor and Pylyshyn's argument is unconvincing is not, of course, to claim that the proposal to create structure by means of internode connections is without problems. In the first place, even if we grant that internode connections can function as structural connections, there must be something *in the system* to distinguish those internode connections that are to count as structural connections from those that are not. Presumably this will have to do with the kinds of computational consequences that the connections have, but how this might go is anybody's guess. Second, since connections, on this proposal, must function to define processes as well as to define structure. I suspect that their availability for the latter will be limited. If that is the case, then the internode-connection strategy for supplying structure may well have to be supplemented with something like the second strategy discussed above. That is, two things would be needed to represent a proposition: the nature of the connections among representational units would serve to *individuate* propositional representations (that is, to distinguish the proposition that Art is a Jet from the proposition that Ike is a Jet), and the use of nodes to represent a combination of role and content (e.g., Art-subject) would provide the necessary *intra*-propositional structure (and, hence, distinguish the proposition that Art hates Ike from the proposition that Ike hates Art). Finally, even if the above proposal could be made to work, it would work in a straightforward way only for local representation. Whether there is any reasonable way of making use of internode connections to structure the relations among distributed propositional representations remains a major question. (I take it that an unreasonable way would be to designate a single node to function as a sort of proxy for each node cluster involved in a distributed representation. Using single-node proxies in this way would permit the introduction of structural relations between distributed representations, but it would also lead us back to the problem of too many nodes. In particular, if we tried to handle the problem of propositional connections—and, or, if-then, and so on—in this way, we would end up with the untenable consequence of a single node for every proposition.)

It should be clear that there is no easy answer to the question of how to endow connectionist representations with constituent structure. There may even be no answer, as Fodor and Pylyshyn suggest. However, largely because of a gut aversion to transcendental arguments concerning scientific matters, I am reluctant to draw such a pessimistic conclusion at this stage of the game. Constituent structure may pose a problem for connectionist networks, but I am not yet convinced that it is a hopeless problem.[13] Scientific imagination often has a way of overriding philosophical skepticism.

5.3 The Semantics of Mental Representation

On the Peircian view of representation, representations represent an object partly in virtue of representing$_o$ it, where representation$_o$ is an objective semantic relation that can hold between a representation bearer and a representational object independent of whether that relation is significant for an interpreter. In this section, we will consider whether cognitive science imposes any constraints on what the mental representation system can represent$_o$. First, however, two terminological points must be made.

Thus far, in talking about the semantic properties of representations, I have used a rather restricted vocabulary. In particular, I have talked

almost exclusively of "representing$_o$," and of "representational objects."
The reader may have guessed, however, that—despite the fact that the
vocabulary was restricted—the intended meaning of this vocabulary was
quite unrestricted. To say that a given representation R "represents$_o$" some
object O was, and is, intended simply as a shorthand way of saying that R
bears one of many possible semantic relations to O. Depending on the
nature of O, it might express$_o$ O, refer$_o$ to O, describe$_o$ O, be true of$_o$ O,
have the content$_o$ O, etc.[14] Likewise, to talk of a "representational object"
was, and is, shorthand for whatever it is that representations bear semantic
relations to. These might be objects, properties, or states of affairs in the
world, Fregean senses, contents, intensions, extensions, character, truth
values, truth conditions, functions from possible worlds to truth values,
etc. In the contemporary philosophical literature, the term 'content' is
sometimes used in the same way that I have used the term 'representational
object'—that is, to refer to any and all of the above kinds of "meanings".[15]
In contrast, sometimes it is used in a narrower sense as akin to intension
or Fregean sense and in contrast to extension or character. In what follows, I will adopt the broader use. Thus, in talking about the semantics
of MRS, I will talk sometimes about a representation representing$_o$ an
object and sometimes about a representation having content$_o$. It should be
understood, however, that neither way of talking is intended to carry much
theoretical baggage (at least, from the point of view of semantic theory).[16]

The second terminological point is this. As we discovered through our
study of Peirce's theory of representation, there are *two* sorts of relations
that can exist between a representation and its object or content: *semantic*
relations of representing$_o$ (or referring$_o$, expressing$_o$, etc.) and *ground* relations in virtue of which these semantic relations are supposed to hold.
There is an unfortunate tendency in the literature to refer to theories of
both sorts of relations as "semantic" theories. Thus, for example, the study
of natural language includes Fregean semantics, Tarskian semantics, possible-world semantics, and conceptual-role semantics. But whereas the first
three study the way natural language maps onto meanings or objects in the
world, the last attempts to give an account of in virtue of what the semantic
relations documented by semantic theories of the first kind hold.

A similar ambiguity can be found in the realm of mental representations.
The structure-content relations of MRS have yet to be studied seriously,
but when they are studied this study will undoubtedly be called a "semantics" of MRS. However, there are also, at present, numerous other

"semantic" investigations that address a quite different problem—not what the structure-content relations of MRS *are*, but how they are *determined*. I have in mind "conceptual role semantics" (Harman 1982; Loar 1982; Loewer 1982; Block 1986), "correlational semantics" (McLaughlin 1987), "information-based semantics" (Fodor 1988), and "interpretational semantics" (Cummins 1989).

I object to the practice of using the term 'semantics' in this dual way on the grounds that it promotes a conflation between two aspects of representation that should be distinguished. Thus, in what follows, when the term 'semantics' is being used to refer to a theory it will be used only for theories that describe the relations between representation bearers and contents of a given representational system. (I shall also, following standard practice, occasionally use it to refer to the semantic relations themselves.) In contrast, I will call a theory of the ground of these relations a "theory of content determination" (TCD). On my usage, a genuine semantics for MRS would stand with respect to MRS as truth-conditional semantics, Fregean semantics, and possible-world semantics stand with respect to natural language. That is, it would be a theory, framed in some metalanguage (such as English), that assigns to each representation bearer of MRS some content or representational object. It would not tell us *why* or *in virtue of what* these structure-content mappings exist; it would simply describe them, using the resources of the metatheory. In contrast, a TCD would tell us these things. It would take a semantics for MRS (or some fragment thereof) as its *starting point*[17] and then give us an account, in more or less detail, of where the posited structure-content mappings come from.[18]

The question of what a person represents$_0$ when he or she executes a certain cognitive capacity is an empirical question to be answered by the usual empirical means; hence, the precise nature of these answers is not our concern here. What *is* our concern is whether the substantive assumptions of the research framework of cognitive science impose any constraints on what can count as a possible answer to such questions. More precisely, does the representational assumption carry with it any specific assumptions about what can or cannot function as even a *possible* object of a mental representation? This question is difficult to answer. While *individual* claims about what we represent$_0$ are made all the time in the cognitive science literature, we do not know enough about MRS (and, particularly, about its formal properties) to theorize about its semantics as a system.[19]

Thus, there is virtually no descriptive evidence on the basis of which to make any claims. There are, however, some normative grounds. Therefore, in what follows I will offer some suggestions regarding assumptions about the semantics of MRS which, if they are not already commitments of cognitive science, ought to be, on my view.

Roughly speaking, the normative argument is this: In view of the domain and the basic questions of cognitive science and the explanatory strategy it has adopted, the semantic assumptions to be discussed are, in a sense, *required* if the explanatory strategy is to succeed. Let me spell out this argument in more detail. The domain of cognitive science consists of the human cognitive capacities. Pretheoretically conceived, these capacities have a number of important properties. In particular, they are intentional, evaluable, coherent, reliable, and productive. The basic questions of the field concern these capacities. Cognitive scientists want to know precisely what these capacities are, in virtue of what mental resources we have them, how we exercise them, and how they interact.

The fundamental explanatory strategy of cognitive science, as I shall discuss in greater detail in chapter 11, consists in assuming that the cognitive mind is both a computational and a representational device and seeking to answer its basic questions in terms of that assumption. Two aspects of that strategy are relevant for present purposes. First, when cognitive science seeks to answer its basic questions, it is, in part, seeking to explain the intentionality, evaluability, coherence, etc. of our cognitive capacities. Second, it seeks to explain these properties of cognition, in part, by means of the representational assumption. Note, however, that this strategy can be successful only if representations have the sort of properties that allow us to account for this intentionality, evaluability, coherence, etc. The semantic assumptions to be articulated specify those required properties.

There is another compelling reason for thinking that cognitive science ought to embrace these assumptions at the present time (although I am not sure that this reason speaks to their foundational status). One of the capacities cognitive science wants to account for is the human capacity to understand language. The current conception of the end state of this capacity among psycholinguists is that to understand a sentence of some natural language is to recover and represent the meaning of that sentence. If this is what sentence understanding is, then MRS must be able to represent everything that sentences of natural language can mean. That is, the semantics of MRS must be at least as rich as the semantics of natural language. The assumptions to be discussed then follow from certain theoretical assumptions embraced by most semantic theories of natural language.[20]

R2.2(a)[n]   Mental representations are semantically *selective.*

According to Lloyd (1987, p. 27), "representations employ their powers of aboutness selectively, picking out *proper objects* (to borrow a phrase from Dretske 1981)." There may be many objects and situations related to a representation, but an individual representation picks out only a small number of these as what it represents. In general, cognitive science seeks to account for the intentionality of the propositional attitudes involved in our cognitive capacities by positing mental representations with semantic properties. The specificity of those semantic properties is required, precisely, because the propositional attitudes themselves are relatively content-specific.

R2.2(b)[n]   Mental representations are semantically *diverse.*

Mental representations, as a class, possess many different kinds of representational objects. On different occasions and with different representation bearers, we can represent concrete objects, sets, properties, events, and states of affairs in this world; objects, sets, properties, events, and states of affairs in possible and fictional worlds; and abstract objects such as universals or numbers: This assumption again follows from the fact that one of the theoretical functions of mental representations is to account for the intentionality of cognition. Insofar as we can think and speak about all these things, they must be representable$_0$ by the members of MRS.

R2.2(c)[n]   Mental representations are *semantically complex.*

Mental representations not only have many different kinds of representational objects as a group; most individual representations also have more than one representational object. Precisely what these representational objects are like is, of course, a matter for research, but the semantic complexity of both our propositional attitudes and the expressions of natural language seem to require a similar complexity in MRS. Propositional attitudes specify conditions of satisfaction in two senses: as a requirement and as a thing required. Similarly, according to most semantic theories in linguistics, most expressions of natural language have both an intension (sense) and an extension (referent). For example, in possible-world semantics the intension of a sentence is a function from possible worlds to truth values whereas its extension is a truth value. The intension of a one-place predicate is a function from possible worlds to sets, whereas its extension is a set of individuals in this world. And the intension of a noun phrase is a function from possible worlds to individuals, whereas its extension is null or an individual in this world.[21]

In current psychological research in cognitive science, semantic complexity manifests itself primarily as a distinction between a representation's representing$_o$ a Peircian "object itself" and a representation's representing$_a$ an aspect of that object. Consider, for example, the psycholinguistic view of how we perceive and understand written text. According to Garnham (1985) there are six processing stages, each of which issues in a characteristic representation. (Whether these stages occur serially or in parallel, and to what extent they operate autonomously, is a matter of controversy.)

Stage 1: Low-level perceptual processing results in a representation of the lines and curves of the written text, and possibly also in a representation of the overall shapes of the words.

Stage 2: The process of word recognition results in the identification of the words that make up the text—in other words, it results in a representation of what the words are.

Stage 3: The process of parsing results in a representation of sentence structure.

Stage 4: The process of semantic interpretation results in a representation of the linguistic meaning of each sentence—that is, a representation of the range of situations that the sentence in question could describe.

Stage 5: The process of model construction results in a representation of what particular situation in the real or imaginary world a particular text is, or is most probably, about.

Stage 6: The process of pragmatic interpretation results in a representation of the *point* of the text—that is, its intended message.

At first blush it would appear that we are dealing here with six distinct kinds of representations, each with a distinct representational object. In an important sense this is true. But note that the above representations have something important in common. If we consider their content within the context of a single act of text understanding, they will all be representations of the *same* text. The representation of stage 1 is a representation of this text as a set of lines, curves, and shapes; the representation of stage 2 is a representation of the very same text in terms of its lexical components; the representation of stage 3 is a representation of the very same text in terms of its sentence structure; and so on. In other words, in each case, the Peircian object itself is the same. What varies is the immediate object or aspect under which the object itself is represented.

I would like to suggest that the same sort of duality is true of virtually every other kind of mental representation currently under empirical and theoretical consideration.[22] Here are some examples drawn from nonperceptual areas of cognition:

• A *script* (Schank and Abelson 1977) is a representation of a frequently occurring sequence of events, usually of a social nature, such as going to a restaurant or going to a doctor. However, it represents such a social event (the object itself) in a particular way: in terms of the sequence of the subevents that typically constitute it (the aspect), with special attention to optional and mandatory features of this sequence.

• A *mental model* (Johnson-Laird 1983) is a representation of an actual or conceivable state of affairs (the object itself) in terms of the entities that figure in that state of affairs and the relations that hold of them (the aspect).

• According to Smith and Medin (1981), there are currently three competing hypotheses regarding the representation of concepts: the classical view, the probabilistic view, and the exemplar view. On the classical view, a concept (the object itself) is represented by means of a description of the set of features that are necessary and sufficient for something to count as an instance of that concept (the aspect). On one version (the featural version) of the probabilistic view, a concept is represented by a description of a set of features that are salient and have a substantial probability of occurring in instances of the concept. On the exemplar view, a concept is represented by a description of some of its exemplars (either instances or subsets). For each of these kinds of conceptual representation, the object itself is a concept. However, each view advocates a different way of representing concepts.[23]

R2.2(d)[n]   Mental representations are semantically *evaluable.*

Insofar as mental representations are sentence-like, they may be true or false; insofar as they are term-like, they may be nonvacuous or vacuous; insofar as they are picture-like. they may be accurate or inaccurate. If mental representations did not have this property, it would be impossible for them to account for the fact that our cognitive capacities can be both correctly and incorrectly exercised. Correct exercise of an input capacity amounts to the fact that the intentional end state specifies conditions of satisfaction satisfied by the beginning state. Conversely, correct exercise of an output capacity amounts to the fact that the intentional beginning state specifies conditions of satisfaction satisfied by the end state. Thus, if intentional states are to be the result of having certain mental representations, mental representations must also be the sort of things that have conditions of satisfaction that can be satisfied or not. That is, they must be evaluable.

Another assumption that should be mentioned is probably too controversial to include on our official list of assumptions. This is the claim that the semantics of MRS is compositional. A representational system is compositional insofar as the content of its complex representations is determined by the content and arrangement of its constituents. The claim is controversial because it presupposes that mental representations have structure. As was noted in section 5.2, this is a claim that some connectionists might want to reject.

The argument for compositionality is very strong. Like the argument for constituent structure, it is based on the productivity and the systematicity of the human cognitive capacities. In fact, the two arguments really go hand in hand. At the present time, the only plausible explanation for productivity and systematicity is that the representations of MRS exhibit constituent structure. But constituent structure without compositional semantics can't do the job it is supposed to do, for novel exercises of our capacities typically involve novel *content* (relative to our experience), such as when we understand a sentence we have never understood before, and systematically related subcapacities (such as the capacities to utter 'More milk' and 'More cookie') are typically semantically related. But these semantic aspects of productivity and systematicity cannot be explained simply by positing the existence of constituent structure. They require, in addition, that the constituents of a representational "expression" contribute systematically to the content of the representation as a whole. Hence the need for compositionality.

6 Current Approaches to Content Determination

Theories in cognitive science seek to explain the human cognitive capacities by, among other things, positing mental representations (that is, entities or states with semantic properties). For the most part, cognitive scientists interested in actually figuring out how we perceive visual scenes or understand sentences or answer questions have been so concerned with ascertaining *what* we represent, and what formal and computational properties these representations have, that little attention has been devoted to the question of where the posited semantic properties come from. The notion of mental representation has, in other words, been treated as a primitive.

The question has refused to go away, however, and in recent years a number of people have begun to find it increasingly troubling. According to Fodor (1985b, p. 115), doing one's science this way (that is, without trying to answer the question of what makes a mental representation *represent*) is "like living on credit cards. Comes the end of the month, somebody has to pay the bill. Sooner or later we're going to have to say what it is that flows when information does." Or, as Fodor puts it in an earlier passage (p. 109), "we are in the position of having a representational theory of the mind without having a theory of mental representation. This is not a stable position; something has to be done."

The bill has yet to be paid. But a growing number of cognitive scientists are beginning to scout around for where the funds might come from. As a consequence, there has been a spate of efforts to develop what I call a theory of content determination (TCD) for the human mental representation system (MRS)—that is, a theory of the ground of MRS in a Peircian sense.

Before continuing, let me remind the reader about what a TCD is not. First, a TCD should not, on my view, be considered a *semantics* of MRS. As I mentioned in the previous chapter, I will use the term 'semantics' to refer only to theories that attempt to map the structure-content relations of a representational system. In contrast, a TCD is a theory about what *determines* those structure-content mappings. Second, a TCD is not, strictly speaking, a complete theory of what makes a mental representation a mental *representation*. This is because, following Peirce, I have adopted the view that for something to be a representation, in the full-blooded sense, it must have both content and significance. To mark the distinction between merely having content and being a representation (with significance), I introduced (in chapter 4) the distinction between representation$_0$ and representation. A representation$_0$ is a state or entity with objective content; a representation is a representation$_0$ with significance for an interpreter. The point is that most current theories of content determination are primarily theories of mental representation$_0$ rather than theories of mental representation. That is, they purport to tell us what grounds the semantic properties of MRS without telling us how these semantic properties become available for the individual cognizer[1] (although, as we shall see, on at least one proposal, if a representation is grounded, it *ipso facto* has significance for the cognizer). I will address the question of significance in chapter 8.

My principle concern in this book is with the foundations of cognitive science rather than with its current theories. Thus, in the case of content determination I am interested not so much in the details of current TCD research as in its general direction. In particular, I will try to address two fundamental questions:

(1) When TCD researchers attempt to develop a theory of the ground of MRS, what kind of thing (ontologically and logically) do they take a ground to be?

(2) Do they impose any substantive (as opposed to logical) constraints on what can count as an adequate ground for MRS?

Question 1 will be discussed in section 6.1; question 2 will be taken up in chapter 7. These more foundational questions constitute my principle concern. However, it turns out that answers to both question 1 and question 2 become more intelligible if they are supplemented with some working knowledge of current efforts to develop a TCD. Such working knowledge provides us with examples of the sort of thing alluded to in the answer to question 1 and a subject for the constraints discussed in the answer to question 2. Since current TCD research is not widely known outside of philosophy, I will briefly survey current efforts to develop a theory of content determination for MRS in sections 6.2–6.6.

6.1 Grounding Mental Content

By stipulation, a TCD is a proposed answer to the question: In virtue of what do our mental representations have the semantic properties they apparently have? Let us call this "the content-determination question."

Inspired by Peirce, we have decided that answers to this question will refer to the *ground* of MRS. That is, roughly speaking, they will have the following form: Mental representations have their semantic properties by virtue of having such-and-such a ground. But this is, of course, mere terminological stipulation. The interesting question is: What is it for something to be a ground?

Peirce is not very helpful on this point. Although he insists that representations must be grounded to count as representations and he provides us with a taxonomy of kinds of ground (iconic, indexical, and symbolic), he has nothing to say about what makes something a ground of a representation. His conception appears to have been completely intuitive. Can we do any better?

I believe we can. Current TCD researchers introduce greater specificity in two ways. First, they typically attempt to cash out the notion of a ground in terms of the notion of *supervenience*. And, second, they implicitly distinguish between the task of grounding the semantic properties of MRS *as a whole* and the task of grounding theoretically interesting *individual* properties of MRS one by one. Let us begin by getting clear on these two points.

The ground of the mental representation system, according to current TCDs, consists of a set of properties or relations that *determine* the semantic properties in question. What does it mean to say that one kind of thing X determines another kind of thing Y? The consensus among philosophers in recent years is that the relation of determination should be understood as the converse of another relation: that of *supervenience*. In other words, we can say that Y determines X just in case X supervenes on Y. Unfortunately, while everyone agrees that determination should be defined in terms of supervenience, there is as yet no consensus as to precisely what supervenience comes to, even for the purposes of cognitive science. A number of different supervenience relations are under discussion, and content-determination theorists have tended not to pick and choose among them.[2] For present purposes, I shall rely on a notion of supervenience that has come to be known as "strong supervenience."

Kim (1984), the chief proponent of strong supervenience, defines the relation as follows:

Let A and B be two nonempty families of properties. Call A "the supervenient family" and B "the supervenience base family." Then A strongly supervenes on B

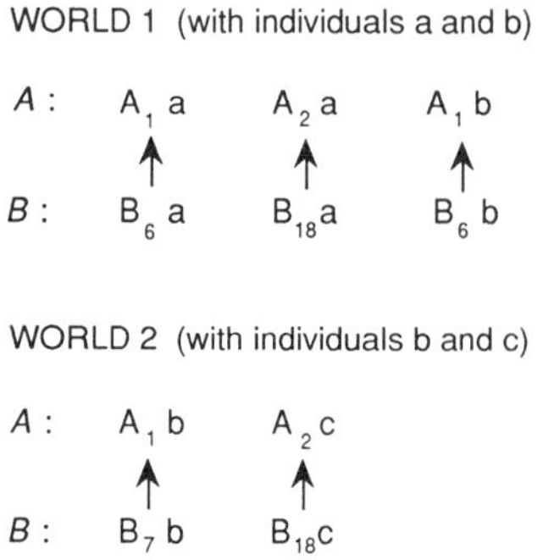

WORLD 1 (with individuals a and b)

A : A_1 a A_2 a A_1 b

B : B_6 a B_{18}a B_6 b

WORLD 2 (with individuals b and c)

A : A_1 b A_2 c

B : B_7 b B_{18}c

Figure 6.1
Graphic representation of a supervenience relation between two families of properties. In this example there are only two possible worlds, WORLD 1 and WORLD 2, and the supervenient family A includes only two basic properties, A_1 and A_2. The arrow means that the state of affairs referred to below the arrow is nomologically sufficient for the state of affairs referred to above the arrow.

just in case, necessarily, for each x and each property A_i in A, if x has A_i, then there is a property B_j in B such that x has B_j, and necessarily if any y has B_j, it has A_i.[3]

Note that the term 'property' here is intended to include not only singular properties but also relations of any number of relata.

Figure 6.1 is an attempt to depict strong supervenience graphically. Note that strong supervenience allows for what has come to be known as "multiple realizability." This is because for any given A_i within the supervenient family A, there can be two or more independent B properties from the base family B which serve as the supervenience base properties of A_i. For example, in figure 6.1, A_1 is associated with both B_6 (in world 1) and B_7 (in world 2). Note, however, that, in *every* possible world, if an individual is A_1, then there is *some* associated B property. This is the force of the outermost necessity operator. The innermost necessity operator says further that *if* some particular B property is associated with A_1 in some possible world, it is nomologically sufficient for A_1 (that is, in *every* possible world, whenever *that* B property occurs, the associated A property occurs). Thus, in figure 6.1, whenever B_{18} occurs (in both world 1 and world 2), it is associated with A_2.

Strictly, strong supervenience is a relation that holds between families of properties. However, it will be convenient to have a name for the relation that holds between the specific A and B properties just in case strong supervenience holds between their respective families. Let us say, then, that if A strongly supervenes on B, then property A_i *individually supervenes on* property B_j (or property B_j *individually determines* property A_i) just in case A_i and B_j are members of A and B, respectively, B_j is correlated with A_i in some world, and B_j is nomologically sufficient for A_i.

I have talked rather loosely of *the* ground for MRS. However, explicating the notion of a ground in terms of supervenience makes it clear that there are really two sorts of things a TCD might be concerned with. First, it might seek to identify the *general* class of properties and relations—for example, causal relations to the environment or similarity relations—that determine content for MRS taken as a whole. Or, second, it might seek to identify, for each theoretically motivated semantic property of MRS, which *specific* property or relation within the general class of relevant supervenient base properties individually determines that semantic property. I shall refer to these, respectively, as the *general ground* for MRS and the *individual ground* of the particular semantic property in question.

It appears, then, that current theories of content determination make the following assumptions about what it is to be a ground for MRS:

A *general ground* for MRS consists of a set of properties G such that G constitutes a strong supervenience base for the semantic properties of MRS.

An *individual ground* for some specific semantic property S_i of MRS will be that member of G upon which S_i individually supervenes.

These characterizations are useful in specifying the metaphysical terrain in which to locate the notions of general and individual ground, but several additional qualifications are required to capture the two notions more precisely.

The first qualification stems from the logical characteristics of nomological sufficiency. The difficulty is this: Recall that if strong supervenience holds between an A family and a B family, then the B property associated with any given A property is nomologically sufficient for that A property. That is, necessarily, if any y has that B property, it will have the associated A property. Imagine now that we have established that some A_i individually supervenes on B_j. Consider now the property that consists of B_j conjoined with some totally irrelevant property D. It will be the case that if B_j is nomologically sufficient for A_i, then B_j and D will also be nomologically sufficient for A_i. But a supervenience base family filled with such conjoint properties is not precisely what we want for a theory of content determination. The solution, of course, is to insist that the supervenience base family be a *minimal* one. In particular, no property in the A family should individually supervene on a conjoint property in the B family that includes as one of its conjuncts a property on which that A property also individually supervenes.[4]

Thus far, I have been exceedingly vague about the nature of the *supervenient* family of interest. To a large extent such vagueness is inevitable until we have a semantics for MRS in hand. However, a few points can be made at present.

Roughly speaking, the supervenient family of interest consists of all the various semantic properties associated with MRS. Let us call this family "MRS-SEMPROP". The main point to note is that, although MRS-SEMPROP consists of semantic properties, fixing the semantics for MRS may not completely fix what semantic properties will be in MRS-SEMPROP. Since MRS-SEMPROP is the family of properties to be grounded in our theory of content determination, it must distinguish properties in all cases where content-determination distinctions exist. But these theoretically motivated "bottom-up" distinctions may correspond to only one way of parsing the semantics into semantic properties, or they may even introduce nonsemantic elements into the membership of MRS-SEMPROP.

Suppose the semantics we develop for MRS (or, at least, for the more language-like portion of MRS) turns out to be Fregean in character. Then for each type of expression in MRS there will exist both a sense and a referent. For example, suppose that MRS included expressions that functioned like singular terms, predicates, and sentences. Then our semantics might make the general assignments shown in table 6.1.

Table 6.1

	Sense	Referent
Singular term	Individual concept	Individuals
Predicate	Property or relation	Sets of individuals
Sentence	Proposition	Truth values

There are at least two ways in which this sort of semantics might be mapped onto MRS-SEMPROP. According to the first way, MRS-SEMPROP would only include two semantic relations: the relation of expressing, which holds between a representation and its sense, and the relation of referring, which holds between a representation and its referent. The distinctions between *kinds* of senses or *kinds* of referents would not be directly reflected in MRS-SEMPROP, although, of course, it would still be the case that whenever a singular term expressed something it would express an individual concept and whenever a predicate referred to something it would refer to a set of individuals, and so on. According to the second way of mapping this semantics onto MRS-SEMPROP, these relata distinctions would be explicitly preserved. Thus, there would be six semantic relations included in MRS-SEMPROP: expressing an individual concept, expressing a property or a relation, expressing a proposition, referring to an individual, referring to a set of individuals, and referring to a truth value.

Which way is the right way would depend on how the story of content determination turned out. On the first way, all forms of expressing, whether they involve an individual concept, a property, or a proposition, would be determined by the same supervenience base relation or relations (in the case of multiple realization). In contrast, on the second way, the point of preserving the distinction between expressing an individual concept and expressing a property would be that each of these semantic relations would be determined differently.

Another reason that fixing the semantics of MRS might not fix the membership of MRS-SEMPROP is that the latter will almost certainly have to incorporate some nonsemantic distinctions. For example, a nonsemantic parameter that will clearly have to be reflected in MRS-SEMPROP concerns the nature of the representations bearing the semantic relations in question. It seems intuitively clear that two very different kinds of representations (say, a mental representation and a sentence of English) can express the same content—for example, that Sydney is hungry—and yet be determined by very different supervenient base properties. Thus, we must pick out the semantic properties of interest (that is, those in MRS-SEMPROP) in a way that makes their *mental*-representational nature explicit. For example, we might pick them out like this: expressing a proposition in a mental-representation way, referring to an individual in a mental-representation way, and so forth.

An analogous point may hold even if we restrict ourselves to mental-content properties. That is, it may well be true that two token mental representations could share the same content and yet have that content determined by the instantiation of a different supervenience base property. For instance, a representation underlying the visual experience of there being a red square on the table in front of me might have its content determined by a different base property than a representation with the same content stored in long-term memory. In other words, content determination might be sensitive to something like the computational "location" of the representation.

Summing up these various points, let me propose the following schema for generating properties that might belong to MRS-SEMPROP:

r bears semantic relation _____ to _____ kind of object o in a _____ kind of mental-representation way,

where 'r' ranges over representations and 'o' ranges over semantic values (that is, over whatever entities a representation can bear a semantic relation to). Substituting for the blanks, we get the following properties which might be included in MRS-SEMPROP: r expresses the property o in a perceptual mental representation way, r refers to an individual o in a long-term memory mental representation way, r expresses a proposition in an "intention" mental representation way, and so on.

We are finally in a position to explicate our intuitive notion of the ground for MRS more precisely. Let us assume that the supervenient class, MRS-SEMPROP, is specified by the above schema. Then the definitions of the general ground and the individual ground of MRS will read as follows:

A *general ground* for MRS consists of a set of properties G such that G constitutes a minimal strong supervenience base for MRS-SEMPROP.

An *individual ground* for some specific semantic property S_i belonging to the set MRS-SEMPROP will be that member of the general ground for MRS upon which S_i individually supervenes.

At the start of this section, I suggested that TCDs answer the question of content determination by identifying a ground for MRS. Until now we have been taking this suggestion at face value and directing our efforts toward getting a clearer picture of what such a ground is. The final point

I would like to make here concerns the accuracy of the suggestion itself. The point is that, although it is perfectly correct that TCDs attempt to answer the content-determination question by identifying a ground for MRS, we may well want to have more.[5] *What* more we may want can best be seen by reflecting on how we would respond if the sought-after identification simply materialized one day on our doorstep. Would we be satisfied? There are at least two reasons we might not be. First, the sought-after ground description might not even be comprehensible. The supervenience base properties cited might simply be too complex to be intelligible. Second, even if it were comprehensible, it might still leave us completely in the dark as to how the content of MRS was determined. Though we would now know by *what* it was determined, we might not understand at all *why* the supervenience base family in question was doing this determining. In other words, we would lack an *explanation* of why or in virtue of what the identified ground was doing its work. Whether it will be possible to develop TCDs that are comprehensible and that include such explanations (indeed, whether it will be possible to develop TCDs at all) remains a question only future research can answer.

Now that we are tolerably clear on what sort of thing (logically speaking) TCD researchers take the ground of MRS to be, we are in a position to survey some current proposals as to the nature of this ground. The efforts I will consider constitute a diverse group. Some of the proposals have been explicitly developed as theories of content determination for MRS; others are intended as theories of content determination for the propositional attitudes and, thus, require a certain amount of reconstruction for our purposes. Some proposals seem to be premised on a rather naive conception of the problem and are intended to hold, without further elaboration or modification, for all forms of mental representation. Others are more sophisticated efforts put forward as the first step of a multiphase research program designed to take on the problem of content determination for MRS-SEMPROP by a strategy of incremental conquest. In what follows, I will concentrate primarily on elucidating the main idea of each of the proposals with no critical comment. As a consequence, for some proposals my treatment will be somewhat oversimplified. However, since my purpose here is merely to provide an idea of the kind of theories that are currently being entertained, a rough-and-ready treatment will suffice. It should also be noted that, at the present time, none of the approaches to be discussed has come up with an adequate TCD for MRS.

That is, none can currently provide a satisfactory account of all the properties attributed to mental representations in section 5.3.

With these remarks in mind, let us now turn to surveying current TCD proposals. The various approaches can be taxonomized as follows:

the structural isomorphism approach

the functional role approach

the causal historical approach

the indicator approach

the biological function approach.

One fascinating point that will emerge from my survey is that most of the options currently being entertained were anticipated by Peirce in his trifold taxonomy of grounds for representation in general. Recall that Peirce hypothesized the existence of three fundamental kinds of pure ground: iconic, indexical, and symbolic (i.e. conventional). As we shall see in chapter 7, the existence of a conventional ground is ruled out at the outset because of cognitive science's commitment to naturalism. Thus, on Peirce's taxonomy, we are left with two possibilities: the existence of an iconic ground and the existence of an indexical ground. As it turns out, precisely one or the other of these two options is at the heart of most of the current approaches to the content-determination question.[6] In particular, the structural isomorphism and functional role approaches are basically iconic whereas the causal historical and indicator approaches are basically indexical. The biological function approach resists easy classification, although in some sense its proposed ground contains both iconic and indexical elements.

6.2   The Structural Isomorphism Approach

The view that mental representations represent$_0$ in virtue of resembling their representational objects was popular with many of the British Empiricist philosophers and has a close affinity with Wittgenstein's (1961) "picture theory of meaning." Palmer (1978) put forth an information-processing version of this view. Palmer's theory of content determination has been accepted by a number of psychologists (Roitblatt 1982; Lachman and Lachman 1982; Rumelhart and Norman 1988; McGuiness 1986; Freyd

1987), but it has been subject to very little critical discussion[7] and it has, by and large, remained outside the current debate in philosophy.

Palmer approaches the problem of content determination for cognitive representation by putting forward a theory of representation$_0$ in general.[8] The basic idea is that a representation is "some sort of model of the thing (or things) it represents" (Palmer 1978, p. 262). We can think of it metaphorically as a *representing world* standing in the representation relation to a *represented world*. More precisely, the representing world represents aspects of the represented world by means of aspects of itself. Thus, in order to specify a representation completely, one must, according to Palmer (p. 262), state "(1) what the represented world is; (2) what the representing world is: (3) what aspects of the represented world are being modeled; (4) what aspects of the representing world are doing the modeling; and (5) what are the correspondences between the two worlds."

Palmer attempts to make the idea of an aspect of a thing more precise by talking about the objects and relations that constitute that thing. He thus takes his inspiration from model theory (Tarski 1954) and views both the represented world and the representing world as, ultimately, relational systems—that is, as sets of constituent objects and sets of relations defined over these objects (with properties treated as one-place relations). Let us call the set of relations being represented "D" (for "representeD") and the set of relations doing the representing "G" (for "representinG"). Note that D and G do not necessarily exhaust the relations making up the represented world and the representing world, respectively. They simply pick out those aspects of the worlds that are relevant to the representation relation. The core idea of Palmer's TCD, as depicted in figure 6.2, is, then, this:

PALMER'S STRUCTURAL ISOMORPHISM VIEW   A representation bearer RB represents$_0$ a representational object O under some aspect D if there exists a set G of relations which constitute RB and a set D of relations which constitute O such that G is isomorphic to D.[9]

Figure 6.2 illustrates how several different representing worlds can represent$_0$ the same represented world, in this sense, despite their superficial dissimilarities.

I have expressed Palmer's view (and will express all the other TCDs I consider) in the form of a sufficiency claim between two propositions, viz. 'A representation bearer RB represents$_0$ an object O if _____'. How-

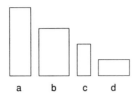

The Represented World
(represented relation: taller than)

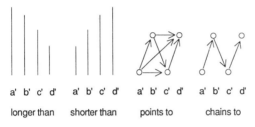

a' b' c' d'   a' b' c' d'   a' b' c' d'   a' b' c' d'

longer than   shorter than   points to   chains to

Possible Representing Worlds

Figure 6.2
Different "representing worlds" which represent$_0$ the same "represented world." The
relations longer than, shorter than, points to, and chains to in the lower diagrams are all
isomorphic to the relations taller than in the upper diagram. (Adapted from Palmer 1978
with permission of the author and Lawrence Erlbaum Associates.)

ever, I intend that this be taken as shorthand for a supervenience claim.
Thus, strictly, any TCD expressed in the form 'P if Q' should be read like
this: "The family of properties picked out by the expression that appears
before the 'if' supervenes on the family of properties picked out by the
expression that appears after the 'if'." In this case, the supervenience claim
comes down to the claim that the supervenient family consisting of the
relation of a representation bearer RB's representing an object O supervenes on the supervenience base family consisting of the relation of RB's
being structurally isomorphic to O.

It may be helpful to look at the relation of isomorphism more carefully.
Any n-ary relation can be thought of *extensionally* as simply a set of
n-tuples of elements. Thus, the relation *father of* defined on members of my
immediate family consists of the following ordered pairs: {(Wolf, Barbara),
(Peter, Jeffrey), (Jeffrey, David), (Michael, Alisa)}, where the first member
of each pair is the father of the second member. According to Goodman

(1951, p. 14), a relation R is isomorphic to a relation S if and only if R (that is, the set of n-tuples of elements that constitutes R construed extensionally) can be obtained by consistently replacing the elements of S. Consistent replacement here requires that each element from S be replaced by one and only one element from R and that different elements in S always be replaced by different elements in R.[10] Thus, for example, the relation

$$\{(a,b), (c,d), (d,e), (f,g)\}$$

is isomorphic to the relation *father of* because we can obtain the former from the latter by consistent replacement of its elements.

Note that in the case at hand we are dealing not with a single relation in the representing world and the represented world, respectively, but with a *set* of such relations. Goodman's definition is easily extended to this more complex situation, however. We need simply say that the set of relations G is isomorphic to the set of relations D if and only if for each relation g in G there exists a relation d in D such that g is isomorphic to d in the above sense and each of these isomorphisms is based on a plan of replacement which is not only internally consistent but also consistent with each of the other replacement plans being utilized. In other words, what is demanded is isomorphism *of the whole* (Goodman 1951, pp. 18–21). Figure 6.3 illustrates just such a relation. The representing world RGW is isomorphic to the represented world RDW because there exists a single, consistent plan of replacement that makes each relation that constitutes RGW isomorphic to some relation constituting RDW.

6.3   The Functional Role Approach

Functional-role TCDs have close ties, both historically and logically, with a philosophical position known as "functionalism." They also constitute a form of resemblance TCD, although this point is not always recognized.

Functionalism is a *metaphysical* doctrine concerning the nature of mind which holds that some types of mental states—either ordinary mental states, such as believings and desirings, or psychological states of the sort posited by a scientific psychology—are, essentially, states definable in terms of all or some of their causal or computational relations to inputs, outputs, and other mental states.[11] Characterizing a state in terms of such causal or computational relations is said to be charactering it with respect to its *functional role*.[12]

Representing World RGW

    constituent objects: a, b, c

    relations (G):

aP	P: {a}
aRb	R: {(a,b),(b,c)}
bRc	S: {(a,b,c)}
aSb,c	

Represented World RDW

    constituent objects: e,f.g

    relations (D):

eM	M:{e}
eNf	N: {(e,f), (f,g)}
fNg	O: {(e,f,g)}
eOf,g	

Plan of Replacement: e > a, b > f, c > g

Figure 6.3
Abstract example of one world representing$_0$ another by means of "isomorphism of the whole." For each relation constituting RGW there is a relation constituting RDW to which it is isomorphic in accordance with a single plan of replacement. '>' means 'is replaced by'.

As in functionalism, functional-role TDCs assign a key theoretical place to the idea of functional role. However, in contrast with functionalism, the object of the game is not to *define* some or all mental states; rather, the aim of theorizing is to *ground* the semantic properties that make up MRS-SEMPROP. Roughly speaking, functional-role TDCs attempt to do this in terms of the functional roles of the representation bearers having the semantic properties in question.

Note, however, that it is not just functional role that is supposed to do the trick. The key idea is, rather, that a representation bearer RB represents an object O because the functional role of RB "mirrors" the role of O in some other domain of objects. The structural isomorphism approach makes use of an isomorphism between the structure of a representation bearer and the structure of the representational object. The functional role approach also relies on the existence of an isomorphism. However, in contrast with the structural isomorphism approach, the isomorphism in question is between sets of relations that hold *among* the relevant represen-tation bearers and representational objects, respectively, rather than between sets of relations that *constitute* the individual representation bearers and objects.

There are two reasonably clear versions of the functional role approach in the literature. It is useful to contrast them in terms of what each has to say concerning the following four parameters: (a) the nature of the represented objects, (b) the nature of the relations among the represented objects, (c) the nature of the representing objects, and (d) the nature of the relations among the representing objects.

The first version is the "conceptual role" approach of Field (1977, 1978), McGinn (1982), Loar (1982), Harman (1982), Block (1986, 1987), and Schiffer (1987).[13] Here is how the above five parameters are specified: (a) The focus of the conceptual role approach is on propositions, although on some views one finds vague suggestions concerning how propositional components, such as concepts, might be grounded once propositions are grounded (see, for example, Block 1986, p. 628; Schiffer 1987, p. 92). (b) The relevant relations among these propositions are logical relations, such as entailment. (c) The representing objects are, of course, representation bearers in MRS with propositional content. (d) The relevant relations among the representing objects are the functional roles of the propositional representation bearers involved in reasoning and inference, including whatever unconscious inferential processes might be involved in perception and in bringing about action (Block 1986).

Under the above specification of (a)–(d), the content-determination story is, then, as follows: Propositions are related to one another in complex ways by logical relations. For example, any proposition with the logical form (p & q) will be entailed by a proposition of the form

(r & (if r then (p & q)))

and will entail a proposition of the form (p). We can thus think of any particular proposition, such as the proposition that Sydney wants to go outside, as having a *logical role* relative to the total space of propositions and their logical interconnections. Now suppose we are trying to figure out what determines the fact that a given token representation bearer has the propositional content that Sydney wants to go outside. A conceptual-role TCD says that the content of this representation bearer is determined by the conceptual role associated with the representation type of which it is an instance. Why is that? Answer: because there exists an *isomorphism* between the network of causal relations that define the conceptual role of

LOGICAL SPACE

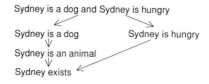

Sydney is a dog and Sydney is hungry

Sydney is a dog   Sydney is hungry

Sydney is an animal

Sydney exists

(Here 'X $\rightarrow$ Y' means X entails Y, where X and Y are
propositions representable by the subject.)

COMPUTATIONAL SPACE

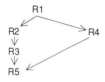

R1

R2

R3

R5   R4

(Here 'R1 $\rightarrow$ R2' means R1 normally results in R2 during
processes of inference, where R1 and R2 are representational
states.)

Figure 6.4
Relation of isomorphism between a logical network of propositions and a computational
network of representational states.

the representation that p (under some appropriate idealization) and the
network of logical relations that define the logical role of p. Furthermore—and this is the key—the mapping from propositions to representations that yields this isomorphism pairs p with the representation that p.
See figure 6.4.[14]

The view can be summarized as follows:

THE CONCEPTUAL ROLE VIEW   A representation bearer RB represents$_0$ a
proposition P if RB belongs to a causal network of representation bearers,
RBNet, P belongs to a logical network of propositions, PNet, and there
exists an isomorphism between RBNet and PNet such that RB maps
onto P.

A slightly different version of the functional role approach is that of
Cummins (1989). Cummins' proposal, which he calls "interpretational semantics," abstracts away from conceptual role theory's emphasis on prop-

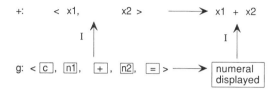

Figure 6.5
A computational function (g) of a calculator interpreted as the addition function ($+$). The boxed symbols 'c', 'n1', '$+$', 'n2', and '$=$' refer to button pressings (clear, first numeral, plus, second numeral, and equals, respectively). 'x1' and 'x2' are variables ranging over numbers, and I is the interpretation function. (After Cummins 1989, with permission of the author and The MIT Press.)

ositions and inference to put the focus on functions in general. The basic idea is that computational processes in the mind/brain can be viewed as *satisfying* certain formal, computational functions (point d) whose domain and range are representation bearers (point c). However, these computational functions are isomorphic to certain other (usually nonformal) functions (point b),[15] such as the plus function, whose domain and range are representational objects, such as numbers (point a). Roughly speaking, then, interpretational semantics says this:

CUMMINS' INTERPRETATIONAL VIEW   A representation bearer RB represents$_0$ an object O if RB is an argument or value of some computational function g, O is an argument or value of some other function h, and there exists a structure-preserving interpretation function I from g to h that pairs RB with O.[16]

In figure 6.5, for example, a computational function g whose arguments are button pressings (clear, first numeral, plus, second numeral, equals) and whose value is a numeral on the display maps onto the addition function $+$ by means of an intepretation I. Interpretation I assigns no value to clear, plus, or equals (these are treated by the device as instructions rather than representations of data) but maps the first numeral button pressing onto the number x_1 and the second numeral button pressing onto the number x_2. The numeral displayed is then mapped by I onto the sum of x_1 and x_2.

A similar view, although expressed in a different vocabulary, is that of Newell (1990), who describes what I have called the "other" function h as a "transformation" from one external situation to another and the compu-

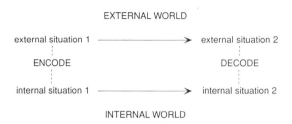

Figure 6.6
Representation of part of the external world by part of the internal world.

tational function g as a transformation from one internal situation to another. And instead of Cummins' "interpretation function," we now have "encoding" and "decoding" between the external and internal situations. (See figure 6.6.) However, the content-determination story is essentially the same. Newell (1990, p. 59) writes:

> The original external situation is *encoded* into an internal situation. The external transformation is also *encoded* into an internal transformation. Then the internal transformation is *applied* to the internal situation to obtain a new internal situation. Finally. the new internal situation is *decoded* to an external situation. Suppose that the resulting external situation is the same as the situation produced by the external transformation. Then the internal system—the encoding process, the internal situation, the internal transformation, and the decoding process—has successfully been used as a representation of the external situation.

The matter can be put more succinctly: For representation to occur, according to Newell, the encode-apply-decode path in question must satisfy the "representation law"

$$\text{decode}[\text{encode}(T)(\text{encode}(X))] = T(X),$$

where X is the original external situation and T is the external transformation.

6.4   The Causal Historical Approach

In the late 1960s, several prominent philosophers argued that referring expressions in natural language, such as proper names and natural-kind terms, attach to the world not by means of any implicit description associated with the referring expression but rather by means of causal links to the objects and phenomena being referred to (Kripke 1972; Putnam 1975c). Theories of this sort were called "causal theories of reference."

The third TCD we shall consider, proposed by Devitt (1981) and described in Devitt and Sterelny 1987 and in Sterelny 1990 (where it is called a "Kripkean causal theory"), was developed in the context of elaborating on and defending such a causal theory of reference for "designational expressions" (e.g., proper names, demonstratives, pronouns, and definite descriptions). Although Devitt is primarily concerned with sketching a TCD for natural language, his work is of interest to us because, on his view, natural-language designation and MRS designation are inextricably intertwined. Thus, in working out his views on how certain expressions of natural language designate, Devitt makes some interesting suggestions regarding how mental representations might designate.

The basic idea is this:

DEVITT'S CAUSAL HISTORICAL VIEW   A token designational expression RB designates a representational object O if there is a certain sort of causal chain, which Devitt calls a "d-chain" ('d' for 'designating'), connecting RB with O. Such d-chains are made up of three sorts of links: groundings, abilities to designate, and reference borrowings.

The *grounding* of a mental representation bearer RB in an object O consists of an episode in which a person perceives O and, as a consequence, comes to have a "grounding thought"—that is, a thought (or a propositional representation, from the cognitivist perspective)[17] which includes RB and which would typically be expressed in public language as a demonstrative. Suppose, for example, you see my dog Sydney for the first time and this act of perception results in the propositional representation ⟨This dog is panting⟩, which contains as a distinct representational component the representation ⟨this dog⟩. (Recall that I am using angle brackets to refer to expressions in MRS in a way that exhibits their surface structure. Thus, '⟨This dog is panting⟩' refers to a representation in MRS that has a surface structure similar to that of the English sentence 'This dog is panting' and expresses the proposition that this dog is panting.) Such a thought would constitute a grounding thought, according to Devitt, for the representation ⟨this dog⟩. Devitt calls representations that can be grounded in this way "demonstrative representations."

D-chains can be extended via "identity beliefs." Such extension can happen either directly or indirectly. If, for example, your meeting with

Sydney leads you to form the identity belief ⟨This dog is Sydney⟩, then this belief extends the d-chain underlying ⟨this dog⟩ to ⟨Sydney⟩. ⟨Sydney⟩ is thereby grounded in Sydney and, hence, comes to represent Sydney.

Indirect extension of a perceptual grounding simply carries this process one step further. Once a person's MRS contains nondemonstrative representations that have been grounded by direct extension of a perceptual grounding, the causal chain can be further extended by linking other representations with the grounded nondemonstrative representation by means of additional identity beliefs. Thus, once ⟨Sydney⟩ is in your mental repertoire and has become grounded, it can be used to ground other representations by means of identity beliefs of the form ⟨Sydney is the F⟩.[18]

When a person comes to have token representations representing some object O in virtue of being grounded in O (either perceptually or by means of identity beliefs), he or she acquires the ability "in thought" to designate O. According to Devitt (1981, p. 132), for a person to have such an ability associated with a physical type (in our terms, a type of representation bearer) "is for him to have a set of thoughts including tokens which are grounded in the object and which dispose him to use the type."

Such designating abilities can be passed from one person to another by means of *reference borrowing*. It is here that public language enters the picture. Reference borrowing enables a person to ground a representation in an object by his or her perceiving, not the object itself, but another person's act of *designating* that object. Public language is required as a mediating link because acts of mental designation cannot be observed directly. Thus, what a person A can observe is that person B exercises his ability to designate O with some natural-language expression E. If A then comes to have a mental representation R associated with E, R inherits the d-chain that grounds E in O. Suppose you have never laid eyes on my dog Sydney but you hear me talk about her and, as a result, you form the representation ⟨Sydney⟩. Then this representation will also be grounded in Sydney. The reason is that it is connected by a d-chain to the public-language expression 'Sydney', which in turn is causally connected to the representation ⟨Sydney⟩ in me, which at some time was perceptually grounded in Sydney. Figure 6.7 illustrates the contrast between such mediated d-chains and the unmediated d-chains discussed above.

There is a potential circularity here, of course. Devitt wants to account for public-language designation, ultimately, in terms of MRS designation

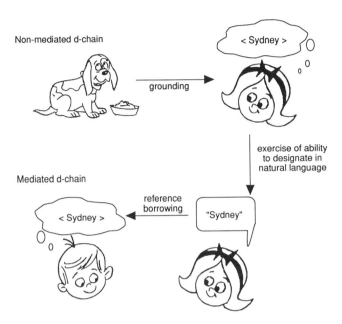

Figure 6.7
Two ways a mental representation can be connected to its representational object by a
d-chain.

(*very* roughly, conventional meaning reduces to speaker's meaning, which
reduces to propositional attitudes, which reduce to representations), and,
as we see here, his explanation of MRS designation, in turn, invokes
public-language designation. He fully acknowledges this problem, however, and he attempts to avoid it by turning the potential circle into "more
like a spiral" (p. 85). The spiral goes like this: Our first thoughts, as a species
and as individuals, were very primitive representations which acquired
their meaning via unmediated d-chains. Utterances with speaker's meaning were developed on the basis of these representations, and in time
the desire for communication led to a system of conventional meaning.
Once established, however, this system of conventional meaning served to
enrich individual mental representations (via mediated d-chains, as described above), which expanded the individual capacity for speaker meaning and reinforced the patterns of conventional meaning in the linguistic
community.

6.5   The Indicator Approach

As in the causal historical approach, indicator theories of content determination regard causal relations to the environment as the key to solving the problem of content determination. However, the indicator approach differs from the causal historical approach in putting the emphasis on counterfactual, rather than historical, relations between a representation and what it represents. Roughly speaking, the idea is that a representation has the content it has in virtue of its counterfactual causal or probabilistic relations to the part of the world that the representation represents. Versions of such theories have recently been proposed by Dretske (1981, 1986a, 1986b), Fodor (1987, 1991), Harnad (1990), Lloyd (1987, 1989), Stalnaker (1984), and Stampe (1977).

Like proponents of the causal historical approach, indicator theorists have attempted to tackle the problem of content determination for MRS by focusing attention initially on a "target" set of representations to which the core idea seems applicable in a relatively straightforward way. The assumption is that, once the theory for this target set is in place, other, more problematic kinds of representations can eventually be dealt with.

The initial target set has been delimited in three ways, although not all indicator theorists adopt all three of these delimitations: restriction to veridical representations, restriction to representations of simple *de re* subject-predicate form (representations which assert of an object O that it is F), and restriction to representations that underlie sensation or perception.

How does the indicator approach attempt to handle this target set of representations? Because there are currently many variations on the indicator theme and each indicator theorist formulates his or her core idea slightly differently, any general answer to this question (that is, one that purports to be true of all the recent indicator proposals) runs the risk of either misrepresenting some proposal or being so nonspecific as to be quite uninformative. Since neither consequence is very attractive, I propose to opt for greater detail at the cost of some loss of generality and focus on one specific indicator theory as an exemplar of the entire class.

The specific indicator theory I will describe is due to Fodor (1987, 1991). I choose this proposal rather than one of the others not because I think it is more successful than any other version (I don't—they all have shortcomings). but because it has received a fair amount of attention among philosophers of psychology and because it is relatively straightforward.[19]

I have suggested that MRS-SEMPROP might include a number of semantic properties—properties such as expressing a proposition, expressing a property or relation, referring to a truth value, and referring to a set of individuals, all of which must be dealt with by an adequate TCD. Most of the TCD approaches I have discussed thus far have been concerned with grounding the semantic property of representing (usually in the sense of referring to or designating) an object. Fodor's theory shifts the emphasis from referring to an object to expressing a property. That is, he is interested in developing a TCD for how the *predicates* of MRS—predicates like ⟨horse⟩, ⟨cow⟩, and even ⟨proton⟩—express the properties they do.

Fodor approaches the problem of developing an indicator TCD by first articulating a crude version of the sort of theory he is after and then attempting to respond to the obvious difficulties posed by the crude version. His "Crude Causal Theory" looks like this:

A representation bearer RB's having some nonsemantic property G (say, being a data structure of a certain sort) expresses the property F in a subject S if (1) F instantiations cause G instantiations in S and (2) only F instantiations cause G instantiations in S.

Thus, according to this theory, a representation bearer expresses the property of being a horse (that is, is a token of the representation ⟨horse⟩) if instantiations of the property horse cause tokenings of ⟨horse⟩ representations (that is, if a horse were present it would cause the tokening of a ⟨horse⟩ representation) and if only instantiations of the property horse cause tokening of ⟨horse⟩s (that is, only horses are such that if one were present it would cause the tokening of ⟨horse⟩).

There are two problems with the Crude Causal Theory, according to Fodor: Clause 1 is false and clause 2 is false. Suppose we are interested in the following question: In virtue of what do representations of the type ⟨horse⟩, tokened in me, express the property of being a horse? The first problem is that there are lots and lots of horses (millions upon millions, in fact) whose presence in this world does not and would not cause the tokening of ⟨horse⟩ in me, located as I am in one particular place. Does this mean that tokenings of ⟨horse⟩ in me cannot express the property of being a horse? Surely not, for if we insisted on maintaining clause 1 as a condition for RB's expressing the property F my conceptual repertoire would be minuscule. In fact, my representational system could express only properties whose instantiations I had some sort of privileged access to. Clearly, this will not do.

The obvious response to the first problem, and the one Fodor adopts, is this: Of course, not *all* property instantiations are relevant to the content of a specific subject's representations. The presence of horses in China is not relevant to *my* tokening of ⟨horse⟩ here in the United States; what matters is only the presence of horses in my *immediate* environment, and this only when my body and brain are in a condition suitable for being causally affected by that presence.

This is clearly the right tack to take, but there are difficulties. To be satisfactory, the set of relevant property instantiations must be restricted in a way that is purely naturalistic—that is, without resort to semantic or intentional notions. Satisfying such a naturalistic constraint may be fairly straightforward for a low-level "phenomenal" concept like *red*, but it becomes much less straightforward for a middle-size object concept like *horse* and positively tortuous for a scientific-theoretical concept like *proton*. According to Fodor, humans are psychologically so constructed that if an "intact organism" sees red under psychophysically optimal circumstances, he or she will think 'there's red' (that is, will token ⟨red⟩ in his or her "thought box").[20,21] The situation with respect to ⟨horse⟩ is supposedly more complex because the causal chain between forming a representation of the *appearance* of a horse and perceptually recognizing a horse *as a horse* (that is, invoking the representation ⟨horse⟩) is longer and is, on most accounts, said to involve things such as "inference" and "knowledge" which fly in the face of the naturalistic constraint. And, of course, the situation with respect to ⟨proton⟩ is even worse. Protons themselves are not directly observable (hence, they don't cause representations of appearances of protons); rather, there are circumstances under which protons have observable physical effects (on photographic plates, in cloud chambers, and so on. These physical effects can cause representations of their appearances which, in turn, can cause tokenings of ⟨proton⟩. But mediating the latter causal link will be not only perceptual recognition of the physical effects, with its attendant *ordinary* inferences and background knowledge, but also all the "expert" inferences and background knowledge required to connect observable evidence of the presence of protons with the conclusion that there are protons present.

Nevertheless, Fodor remains optimistic that the task of characterizing what he calls the "psychophysically optimal" conditions under which instantiations of F cause tokenings of F-concepts in naturalistic terms can be accomplished. Psychophysics is already in the business of telling us under what conditions an instantiation of an F causes a representation of the *appearance* of an F, and the hope is that cognitive psychology will eventually give us a purely *mechanical* story that specifies the conditions under which a representation of the appearance of an F will cause a tokening of the concept of F (that is, under which a representation of the appearance of a horse will cause the tokening of ⟨horse⟩ and a representation of the appearance of physical effects of a proton will cause the tokening of ⟨proton⟩). These conditions will, no doubt, involve inferences and background knowledge, but Fodor's point is that, if the mind/brain is an information-processing system, these conditions will also be describable in purely formal terms, and the latter sort of description will suffice from the point of view of content determination.

Let us turn now to the second problem facing Fodor's Crude Causal Theory: It is not the case that *only* F instantiations cause G instantiations (only horses cause ⟨horse⟩ representations); sometimes cows do, and sometimes they are caused simply by other thoughts. Such non-F causings raise havoc for the Crude Causal Theory because, unless they are somehow ruled out as "wild" and hence irrelevant to content determination, the theory cannot assign the proper contents.

Suppose I represent the cow in front of me as a horse. That is, faced with my neighbor's cow, I produce the representation ⟨horse⟩. Now, of course, this tokening of ⟨horse⟩ is a case of *mis*-representation. However, it counts as a case of misrepresentation only if the content of my representation, in fact, expresses the property of being a horse rather than the property of being a cow. What makes it have equine content rather than bovine content? The Crude Causal Theory doesn't have an answer. It tells us that ⟨horse⟩ *would* express the property of being a horse if ⟨horse⟩ representations reliably covaried with horses. But, of course, we are supposing that this reliable covariation has broken down. In fact, under the current supposition, what ⟨horse⟩ reliably covaries with is not the property of being a horse but the property of being either a horse or a cow. But if the representation in question has this *disjunctive* content, then my tokening of ⟨horse⟩ in the presence of my neighbor's cow doesn't count as a case of misrepresentation at all!

A similar situation exists for representations of ⟨horse⟩ that are caused by other thoughts. Given that the representation ⟨horse⟩ is sometimes caused by the representation ⟨rodeo⟩, how is it that ⟨horse⟩ expresses only the property of being a horse and not the disjunctive property of being a horse or being a ⟨rodeo⟩ representation? Thus, we are faced with what Fodor (1984, 1987, 1991) has termed "the disjunction problem." If clause 2 of the Crude Causal Theory is true, then all our representations will have radically disjunctive content and misrepresentation will be impossible. Since, presumably, neither of these consequences holds in the world, clause 2 must go, at least in its crude form.

A number of suggestions have been made in the recent philosophical literature as to how to handle the disjunction problem.[22] Fodor (1987, 1990a) surveys the principal candidates and opts for what he calls the "asymmetrical dependence" approach. The idea is this: To solve the disjunction problem, we need to be able to distinguish between tokenings that contribute to determining the content of a given representational expression and tokenings that don't (i.e., those that are "wild"). Fodor (1987) attempts to develop a way of making this distinction by trading on what he takes to be the asymmetrical dependence of irrelevant or "wild" tokenings on relevant ones. That is, he proposes to distinguish the irrelevant tokenings by noting that they are always *dependent* on relevant tokenings in a way that relevant tokenings are not dependent on irrelevant ones.

What kind of dependence does Fodor have in mind? This question is answered in two stages. First, Fodor gives us an intuitive but nonnaturalistic characterization of the dependence relation in question; then he attempts to cash in this initial characterization in purely causal terms.

Consider again my tokening of ⟨horse⟩ when confronted with my neighbor's cow. Intuitively—and semantically—the asymmetrical dependence Fodor wishes to exploit is exemplified by the following:

A person S misrepresents (is misrepresenting, has misrepresented, will misrepresent) a cow as a horse by tokening ⟨horse⟩ only if S can represent a horse as a horse by tokening ⟨horse⟩. However, it is not the case that S can represent a horse as a horse by tokening ⟨horse⟩ only if S is misrepresenting, has misrepresented, or will misrepresent a cow as a horse by tokening ⟨horse⟩.[23]

A characterization of asymmetrical dependence of this sort will not do, however, because insofar as it uses the notions of representing and misrepresenting it is not entirely naturalistic. Fodor thus offers us the following necessary and sufficient conditions for "wildness", which dispense with semantics in favor of causation:

Z-caused $\langle @ \# \$ \rangle$ tokenings are "wild" or irrelevant (because $\langle @ \# \$ \rangle$ expresses the property of being an X, where X is not identical to Z and does not contain Z as a disjunct) if and only if

(1) Xs cause $\langle @ \# \$ \rangle$s.
(2) If it were not true that Xs cause $\langle @ \# \$ \rangle$s, then Zs would not cause $\langle @ \# \$ \rangle$s. (This is logically equivalent to: Zs would cause $\langle @ \# \$ \rangle$s only if Xs caused $\langle @ \# \$ \rangle$s.)
(3) If it were not true that Zs cause $\langle @ \# \$ \rangle$s, then Xs could still cause $\langle @ \# \$ \rangle$s. (This is logically equivalent to: it is not the case that Xs would cause $\langle @ \# \$ \rangle$s only if Zs caused $\langle @ \# \$ \rangle$s.)[24]

We can now sum up Fodor's "slightly less crude" causal theory as follows:

FODOR'S INDICATOR VIEW   A representation bearer RB's having some non-semantic property G (say, being a data structure of a certain sort) expresses the property F in a subject S if (1) all F instantiations cause G instantiations in S when F instantiations are causally responsible for psychophysical traces to which S stands in a psychophysically optimal relation and (2) if non-F instantiations cause G instantiations then they are "wild" (that is, their doing so is asymmetrically dependent upon F instantiations' causing G instantiations).[25,26]

6.6   The Biological Function Approach

According to Millikan (1984, 1986, 1989a, 1989b, forthcoming), the key to grasping the ground of mental representation is to view it as a biological phenomenon. What does this come to on Millikan's account? Basically, it comes to the fact that we must understand mental representation in terms of three closely interrelated notion: *proper function, normal explanation,* and *normal condition.*

Millikan claims that all biological phenomena, including organisms, systems, and the states and activities of such organisms and systems, exhibit *proper functions*, where the paradigm of a proper function is a capacity that *historically* contributed to the survival and proliferation of the ancestors of the phenomenon in question. Millikan takes the historical dimension of proper functions very seriously. In particular, the fact that the proper functions of a biological phenomenon are determined by history means that they do not always correspond with the *current* capacities of that phenomenon. A defective heart may not be capable of pumping blood, but pumping blood is its proper function nevertheless. Conversely, something can have capacities that are identical to the capacities of a biological system capable of performing some proper function, but if these capacities have the wrong history the thing will not have the proper function in question and, consequently, will not fall under the appropriate biological category. Thus, Millikan (1984, p. 93) claims that a molecular duplicate of me that simply materialized one day by cosmic accident would not have a heart or a kidney or a brain.

Millikan distinguishes many different subspecies of proper functions. For the purposes of this somewhat simplified rendering of her view, I will mention only two of these: relational proper functions and adapted proper functions. A relational proper function is a proper function "to do or to produce something that bears a specific relation to something else" (Millikan 1984, p. 39). For example, a chameleon has within it a mechanism whose relational proper function is to change the chameleon's skin color so that it matches the chameleon's immediate environment.

The relations referred to by relational proper functions usually involve two variables. Thus, the relational proper function of the chameleon's skin-changing mechanism is to produce X so that it bears the relation same-color-as to Y, where X ranges over skin color and Y ranges over the color of the nether environment. If we fix the value of Y, then we get what Millikan calls an "adapted proper function": a relational function *adapted to* some particular *adaptor* (namely, the value of Y). In the chameleon case, if we fix Y as brown, then it will be an adapted proper function of the chameleon's skin-changing mechanism to produce a skin color that is the same color as brown.

Not only do biological phenomena have proper functions; there is also a biologically proper or normal way for these functions to be performed, and there are biological normal conditions under which a proper function can be performed in the normal way. Millikan usually expresses the idea of a biologically normal way for performing a proper function in terms of the idea of a "normal explanation."[27] Thus, she will typically put the point this way: Associated with each proper function is a normal explanation for the performance of this function that explains the performance of that function, "telling how it was (typically) historically performed on those (perhaps rare) occasions when it was properly performed" (1989a, p. 284)—that is, when it was performed in a way that contributed to the survival and proliferation of the relevant biological group.

Such normal explanations may be more or less proximate. Suppose we are trying to provide a normal explanation for the performance of function F in system S. All normal explanations would include information about the structure of S, the conditions under which F has historically been performed ("these conditions being uniform over as large a number of historical cases as possible" [Millikan 1984, p. 33]), and natural laws mediating between this structure, these conditions, and actual performance of F. A more proximate explanation would be the *least detailed* such explanation possible. In particular, it would simply mention the conditions under which the function was performed without describing "the historically most usual origins" of those conditions. In contrast, a less proximate explanation would include all the information included in a more proximate explanation but would also mention the historically most usual origins of the normal conditions (Millikan 1984, p. 33).

How are the above biological notions brought to bear in grounding MRS-SEMPROP, on Millikan's view? The first point to note is that, according to Millikan, if we are interested in the problem of content determination, there is nothing particularly distinctive about mental representations *qua* mental. There are certainly different kinds of signs (in roughly, the Peircian sense) which get their content in correspondingly different ways, but the point is that the class of mental representations does not, *by itself*, correspond to one of those kinds. Rather, if we classify signs in accordance with how their content is determined, mental representations belong to a type of sign Millikan calls the "intentional icon", which also includes public-language expressions and animal communication signals such as the dances of bees, the tail splashes of beavers, and the mating dances of stickleback.[28] The question thus becomes: How is the content of intentional icons grounded?

Before we can answer that question, we need to say more about intentional icons, as Millikan conceives them. Intentional icons have a number of important properties:

• They are "articulate." I take it that what this means is that intentional icons have constituent structure and a compositional semantics, in something like the sense discussed in chapter 5 above. More specifically, according to Millikan, any intentional icon must contain at least one significant variant aspect and one significant invariant aspect; hence, any intentional icon will belong to a *family* of related intentional icons which share the invariant aspects but vary in their variant aspects along some specified dimension. The semantics of this family of intentional icons will then be described by a "mapping relation" (in the mathematical sense) that pairs these variant and invariant aspects (and, consequently, also the intentional icons themselves) with aspects of the world in a systematic way. The systematicity comes to this: If we start with some particular intentional icon with its own specification of the variant aspects, and we then "transform" some of these variant aspects by substituting other variants, this transformation will correspond to a transformation in the aspects of the world to which the variant aspects are paired by the relation.

An example of a family of articulate intentional icons is the dance performed by "scouter" bees to inform "gatherer" bees of the locations of new sources of nectar. According to von Frisch (1967), one aspect of this dance—its having form—signals the distance of the nectar from the hive. What is invariant is that scouter bees perform a dance in the hive that has some form or other. However, this form parameter can be specified in various ways; it can be a figure-eight, a sickle, or a circle (see figure 6.8). Each of these specific forms represents a specific range of distances. For example, in some bees (not all bees dance the same "dialect" of honeybee language), a figure-eight represents more than 60 feet, a sickle shape represents between 60 feet and 20 feet, and a circle represents less than 20 feet. Thus, these specific forms are variant aspects of any given dance.

Another aspect of these dances is that two of the three forms—the sickle dance and the figure-eight dance—indicate not only distance but also direction. Consider the figure-eight dance as depicted in figure 6.8. This dance is also called the "tail-wagging dance," because as bees traverse the "waist" of the figure-eight they make a certain tail-wagging motion. It turns out that the orientation of the tail-wagging portion of the dance

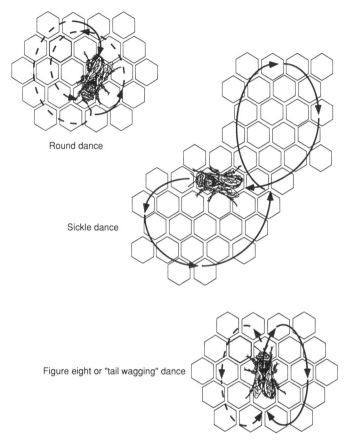

Round dance

Sickle dance

Figure eight or "tail wagging" dance

Figure 6.8
The three basic forms of bee dances.

relative to the surface of the earth represents the direction of the food source. Specifically, the angle between the tail-wagging movement in the hive and an imaginary vertical line is identical to the angle between the food source and the sun, relative to the hive.

• Intentional icons always mediate between two cooperating devices or mechanisms: a producer device and an interpreter or consumer device. Each of these components has proper functions that refer to the other component. One proper function of the producer device is to produce intentional icons for the interpreter device to respond to, and one proper function of the interpreter device is to respond to intentional icons produced by the producer device. In addition, these components are "designed" to fit one another so that the presence and cooperation of one component is a normal condition for the proper performance of each of the others.

• There are two fundamental classes of intentional icons: indicative intentional icons and imperative intentional icons. An indicative intentional icon, like an indicative sentence, makes a statement about some world affair O. In contrast, an imperative intentional icon, like an imperative sentence, expresses a command or a request—something like *bring it about that O*. Although there are important similarities in how the contents of all intentional icons are grounded, there are also significant differences between the respective grounds of indicative and imperative icons. Specifically, while the contents of all intentional icons are determined primarily by proper functions of the relevant *interpreter* device, the role these functions play in the ground for imperative and indicative icons is somewhat different.

Suppose we are given a family of intentional icons (including both indicative and imperative intentional icons), an associated interpreter device, and an associated semantics (i.e. a mapping relation M systematically pairing the intentional icons of the family, and their variant and invariant aspects, with various contents). How is the relation M grounded, according to Millikan?

Any given family of intentional icons will normally be associated with numerous different *sets* of world affairs. For example, bee dances occur midpoint in a causal chain (see figure 6.9) from conditions in the environment (nectar's being present somewhere outside the hive) through neurophysiological mechanisms in the scouter bees (scouter bees' perceiving the nectar), through behavior in the scouter bees (scouter bees' flying home and dancing in the hive), to neurophysiological mechanisms in the gatherer bees (gatherer bees' perceiving the dance), to patterns of behavior in the gatherer bees (gatherer bees' flying off toward the nectar, locating the nectar, and flying home with the nectar), to new conditions in the environment (nectar's being present in the hive). Thus, there will normally be a systematic association between different bee dances and *many* different types of states of affairs located at various points in the causal chain. For example, there will be distinct mapping relations from bee dances onto nectar locations, from bee dances onto neurophysiological mechanisms in scouter bees, from bee dances onto scouter bee's behavior, and so on.

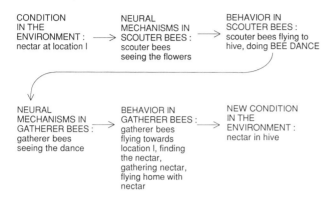

Figure 6.9
Causal chain in which bee dances occur.

Because of this plurality of normal mapping relations, Millikan cannot simply derive the semantics of the intentional icon family (namely, identify *the* mapping relation M that defines the semantics) from consideration of what this family is normally associated with in the world. There are just too many systematic associations (i.e., mapping relations). Thus, some additional constraint is required.

It is at this point that the proper functions of the interpreter device enter the picture. Roughly speaking, the semantic mapping relation for a family of indicative intentional icons will be that real-world mapping relation whose values constitute a *normal condition* of the relevant interpreter device performing its proper functions. And the semantic mapping relation for a family of imperative intentional icons will that real-world mapping relation it is a proper function of the interpreter device *to produce*. More precisely:

MILLIKAN'S BIOLOGICAL FUNCTION VIEW   Suppose that (1) there exists a family of intentional icons *RB* one of whose members is RB, and a set of world affairs *O*, one of whose members is O; (2) there exists a normal mapping relation M between *RB* and *O* which pairs RB with O; and (3) among the proper functions of the interpreter device for *RB* are various relational proper functions adapted to the members of *RB*, including some adapted relational proper functions adapted to RB. Then RB represents$_o$ world affairs O if, for each member rb of *RB* and each member o of *O* paired with rb, it is a normal condition, according to the most proximate normal explanation, of the interpreter of *RB* performing some of its proper functions (including its rb-adapted relational proper functions) that rb is paired with o—and, hence, if it is a normal condition, according to the most proximate normal explanation, of the interpreter of RB performing some of its proper functions, including its RB-adapted relational proper functions, that RB is paired with O. RB represents$_o$ the command *bring it about that O* if, for each member rb of *RB* and each member o of *O* paired with rb, it is an adapted relational proper function of the interpreter of rb, relative to rb, to bring it about that o, and o is the last member of the series of world affairs rb is supposed to map onto and to produce—and, hence, if it is an adapted relational proper function of the interpreter of RB, relative to RB, to bring it about that O, and O is the last member of the series of world affairs RB is supposed to map onto and to produce.[29]

In view of the abstract and technical character of the above formulations, a closer look at the bee-dance example may be helpful. In Millikan's terminology, a dialect of bee dances at-times-in-places constitutes a family of intentional icons, the scouter bees constitute the producer device, and the gatherer bees constitute the interpreter device.

Bee dances at-times-in-places are both imperative and indicative intentional icons. Suppose that, on some occasion, the scouter bees return to their hive and perform bee dance 23, which involves a figure-eight movement with tall-waggling at some specific angle. Suppose further that, *among other things*, performances of dance 23 at time t in a hive h are associated with nectar at t 120 feet to the north of h. *If* it is an adapted relational proper function of gatherer bees, relative to performances of bee dance 23 at t in hive h, to find nectar at t 120 feet to the north of h, then *the nectar is 120 feet to the north of h at t* will be the indicative content of bee dance 23 performed at t in hive h. This is because the most proximate normal explanation for how the gatherer bees carry out this proper function is that perception of bee dance 23 at t in h triggers in the gatherer bees a certain flight pattern which results in the bees' flying 120 feet to the north of h at t. And a normal condition of the gatherer bees' actually finding the nectar 120 feet to the north of h at t in this way is that bee dance 23 performed in h at t is the dance that *in fact* corresponds to the nectar's being in that location at that time. Performance of bee dance 23 at t in h will also have the imperative content *bring it about that the nectar that exists at t 120 feet to the north of h is gathered.* This is because, as we have seen, it is an adapted relational proper function of the gatherer bees, relative to performances of bee dance 23, to bring it about that nectar 120 feet to the north of h is gathered, and presumably the state of affairs of this nectar's being gathered is the last member of the series of world affairs that performance of dance 23 is supposed to map onto and to produce.

7 Constraints on a Theory of Content Determination

The aim of a theory of content determination for the mental representation system is to provide an account of what grounds the semantic properties of our mental representations. In the last chapter I developed a more or less formal characterization of what such a ground is in terms of the notion of strong supervenience. In this chapter, I will raise the question of whether cognitive science imposes, or ought to impose, any additional substantive constraints on the nature of such a ground.

There are three constraints whose status in cognitive science is under discussion: Naturalism, Internalism, and Methodological Individualism*. I will look at each of these constraints in turn, focusing on the arguments that have been presented for and against considering each as a commitment of cognitive science. In the end, I will fully endorse only Naturalism as a commitment of cognitive science. However, it will turn out that the probative situation with respect to Internalism and Methodological Individualism* is quite different. Both are violated by some current TCD research; however, the strength of the normative case for each differs considerably. Internalism, in my opinion, doesn't have a leg to stand on, whereas there are normative arguments with considerable *prima facie* plausibility both for and against Methodological Individualism*. This suggests that the question of the latter's inclusion in the research framework of cognitive science deserves more consideration.

An assumption can be included as part of our reconstruction of cognitive science for one of two reasons: because there is good reason to believe that it *in fact* constitutes a commitment on the part of the cognitive science community (indicated by means of a simple alphanumeric symbol, e.g. 'R2'—the unmarked case, as it were), or because there is good reason why it *should* (on rational grounds) constitute such a commitment, even though it currently doesn't (indicated by following the alphanumeric symbol with the superscript n, e.g. 'R2^n'). These two possible bases for inclusion in the research framework of cognitive science become particularly important in the present context, as the arguments presented for and against the various suggested ground constraints include both *descriptive* arguments (that is, arguments that rely, more or less directly, on appeals to current practice or thinking in cognitive science) and *normative* arguments (arguments that claim that endorsement or rejection of one or another of the constraints follows *logically* from some other commitment that cognitive science has, and that hence should be endorsed by any rational agent).

7.1   Naturalism

The first candidate constraint I shall consider is relatively uncontroversial in cognitive science circles. It looks like this:

NATURALISM   An acceptable ground for MRS will consist exclusively of properties that are naturalistic, i.e., that are neither semantic nor intentional.

Inclusion of the naturalistic constraint in my reconstruction of the research framework of cognitive science is supported by both descriptive and normative arguments. Consider first the descriptive argument:

THE DESCRIPTIVE ARGUMENT FOR NATURALISM

(1) Although most research in cognitive science is *neutral* on the question of content determination, where the question has been specifically addressed (that is, in TCD research) the naturalistic constraint has been unanimously honored. In particular, all the current major working hypotheses about the nature of the ground for MRS are clearly intended to satisfy the constraint.

(2) The best explanation of this fact is that insofar as TCD theorists take themselves to be cognitive scientists they are committed to Naturalism.

(3) Therefore, cognitive science is committed to Naturalism.

The evidence for the first premise is threefold. In the first place, to a very large extent, current TCD proposals actually *do* satisfy the constraint. In chapter 6 I surveyed five current approaches to the problem of content determination, each of which seeks to ground the content of MRS in a different family of properties. Roughly speaking, the stuctural isomorphism approach looks to an isomorphic mapping between the formal structure of the representation bearer and the object represented. The functional role approach looks to an isomorphic mapping between the causal role of the representation bearer and the logical role of the object represented. Both the causal historical approach and the indicator approach focus on causal relations to the environment. The biological function approach looks either to the proper function of a representation or to the normal conditions under which that function can be performed, where both 'proper function' and 'normal conditions' are unpacked in terms of evolutionary history. The point is that each of these families of properties is, fundamentally, naturalistic.

I say "fundamentally naturalistic" because TCD theorists, in figuring out exactly how the content of MRS is determined by the proposed supervenience base, occasionally stray into non-naturalistic territory. However, when such lapses have been noted, criticism adverting to them has been taken to constitute a very serious objection to the theory in question.[1]

There is one additional piece of evidence that current TCDs are intended to be naturalistic: Many TCD theorists have testified in no uncertain terms that satisfaction of the naturalistic constraint is one of the aims of their enterprise. For example, here are two quotes on the subject[2]:

The entire project can be viewed as an exercise in naturalism.... Can you bake a mental cake using only physical yeast and flour? The argument is that you can. Given the sort of information described in Part I, something that most reflective materialists should be willing to give, we have all the ingredients necessary for understanding the nature and function of our cognitive attitudes, all that is necessary for understanding how purely physical systems could occupy states having a content (meaning) characteristic of knowledge and belief.   (Dretske 1981, p. xi)

Here are the ground rules. I want a *naturalized* theory of meaning; a theory that articulates, in non-semantic and non-intentional terms, sufficient conditions for one bit of the world to be *about* (to express, represent, or be true of another bit.   (Fodor 1987, p. 98)

I have argued that current TCD work is clearly intended to satisfy the naturalistic constraint. This widespread endorsement is, no doubt, due to the fact that commitment to Naturalism is supported by a very compelling normative case. This normative case rests on two requirements that cognitive scientists impose on any satisfactory TCD for MRS: that the proposed account of content determination not be question-begging and that the proposed account be consistent with the precepts of physicalism.

The relevance of these considerations to the endorsement of Naturalism is widely recognized. What I think has not been widely recognized is that neither consideration alone will do the trick. The strongest available normative case for Naturalism requires both. To see why, let us see what happens when one attempts to build a case on only one of these requirements. I shall begin trying to develop an argument based on cognitive science's commitment to physicalism.

Like most scientists, cognitive scientists tend to have strongly physicalistic ontological intuitions. That is, they believe that, ultimately, everything is in some sense physical (Schiffer 1987, p. 10: Fodor 1987, p. 97). Given this belief, one might try to argue that, since acceptance of a TCD that violates the naturalistic constraint constitutes endorsement of a theory whose ontology is not in accord with these basic, physicalistic, ontological intuitions, cognitive scientists ought to accept the naturalistic constraint on pain of inconsistency. Let us call this "the naturalistic argument from physicalism."

The above argument is on the right track, but unfortunately things aren't quite so simple. On current conceptions of the sense in which it is reasonable to claim that everything is physical (Post 1987; Poland, forthcoming) there turns out to be a way of having one's physicalism and rejecting Naturalism too.

To understand why this is so we need to understand, roughly, what contemporary physicalists mean when they claim that everything is physical. Current conceptions of physicalism make three assumptions:

• Roughly speaking, nature is organized in a hierarchy of ontological levels (e.g., the physical, the chemical, the biological, the psychological, and the social) which are such that any given level of the hierarchy will (for the most part) supervene on the level immediately below.[3]

• The lowest level of the hierarchy consists of the entities and properties of physics.

• Supervenience is a transitive relation.

Thus, physicalism, in its current manifestation, claims that everything is physical in the sense that everything ultimately supervenes on the physical.

In view of the above conception of physicalism, the Normative Argument from Physicalism will get cashed out like this:

THE NORMATIVE ARGUMENT FROM PHYSICALISM

(1) Cognitive science is committed to physicalism.

(2) Physicalism claims that everything ultimately supervenes on the physical.

(3) The physical is naturalistic.

(4) Hence, cognitive science is committed to the view that MRS-SEMPROP ultimately supervenes on the naturalistic.

(5) Suppose cognitive science were to reject Naturalism.

(6) Then, cognitive science would be committed to the view that MRS-SEMPROP does not supervene on the naturalistic and that it does.

(7) But this cannot be. Therefore, cognitive science ought to accept Naturalism.

On the surface this argument sounds persuasive, but on close inspection a difficulty emerges. Physicalism, as applied to MRS-SEMPROP, claims that MRS-SEMPROP *ultimately* supervenes on the physical and hence on the naturalistic; however, Naturalism is a claim about the *immediate* supervenience base of MRS-SEMPROP. And, of course, it is possible for the immediate supervenience base of MRS-SEMPROP to be non-naturalistic even though MRS-SEMPROP ultimately supervenes on the physical. We need simply imagine that the determination of the non-naturalistic by the naturalistic occurs somewhere else in the hierarchy of supervenience relations than at the point at which the ground of MRS determines MRS-SEMPROP. That is, the immediate supervenience base of MRS might still be intentional or semantic while, at the same time, itself ultimately supervening on the physical. Hence, stated correctly, line 6 does not really involve a contradiction, and the above argument for Naturalism does not go through.

Thus far we have been considering the kind of argument that can be built on the requirement that any satisfactory theory of content determination must be consistent with physicalism, and we have seen that considerations of physicalism alone will not do the trick. Consider now what happens when we try to develop an argument based on the other requirement, viz. that any satisfactory TCD cannot be question-begging.

THE NORMATIVE ARGUMENT FROM CIRCULARITY

(1) Suppose cognitive science developed a TCD that did not honor the naturalistic constraint.

(2) Then it would be answering the question of content determination by reference to a ground that includes semantic or intentional properties.

(3) But this would be to explain content in terms of content. Hence, the account would beg the question.

(4) Hence, on pain of circularity, the naturalistic constraint ought to be adopted.[4]

Although basically sound, this argument, like the previous one, has a loophole. Careful rendition requires that we distinguish three cases: (a) where the proposed ground includes semantic properties of mental representations, (b) where the proposed ground includes intentional properties of propositional attitudes, and (c) where the proposed ground includes semantic properties of natural language. The circle in case a requires no intermediate links and, thus, is obvious and unproblematic. To get a circle in case b requires the additional assumption that propositional attitudes have their intentional properties in virtue of the semantic properties of representations. Although this assumption may be controversial for some people, it constitutes a working assumption for most cognitive scientists; hence, I will regard case b as also unproblematic in this context.

The real difficulty lies with case c and, in particular, with the question of where the semantic properties of natural language come from. Either one adopts something like the Gricean program of "reducing" the semantics of natural language to the intentionality of propositional attitudes or one does not.[5] If we do, then again we have our circle, though this time with two intermediate links (the semantics of natural language is "reduced" to the intentionality of propositional attitudes, and the latter is "reduced" to the semantics of MRS). However, if one does not buy into something like the Gricean program—and, in particular, if one treats natural-language semantic facts as "irreducible"—then no circle is forthcoming. In other words, a TCD that violates the naturalistic constraint by invoking non-Gricean semantic properties of natural language could not, strictly speaking, be charged with begging the question. Thus, we are again left with an argument that doesn't quite work.

Of course, the failure of these two arguments to be demonstrative does not mean that there is no good reason for adopting the naturalistic constraint. Most of what we take to be good reasons are not demonstrative. In addition, if the two arguments are combined, the normative case for Naturalism is strengthened considerably.

Consider the second argument again. The loophole in the Normative Argument from Circularity is the possibility of treating natural-language semantic properties as not reducible to either intentional properties or MRS semantic properties. However, suppose that we now invoke, as an additional premise, the doctrine of physicalism. Since everything supervenes on the physical, it will follow that the semantic properties of natural language also supervene on the physical. How? Only three possibilities have ever been entertained: the semantic properties of natural language ultimately supervene on the physical because they immediately supervene on (i) the intentional properties of speakers-hearers, or on (ii) the nonintentional behavioral properties of speaker-hearers, or on (iii) some combination of the two. But option ii seems highly implausible, at least from a cognitivist perspective. Hence, if the semantic properties of natural language ultimately supervene on the physical, it must be because either option i or option iii is true. That is, it must be because something like the Gricean program is correct. But if this is the case, then the option of there being natural language semantic properties that are not reducible to intentional properties is not available. As a consequence, there is no loophole, and the Argument from Circularity (in augmented form) works after all.

7.2 The Descriptive Case against Internalism

Naturalism imposes a constraint on the ground for MRS, but it is a relatively liberal one. The next constraint I shall consider is much more restrictive. In order to formulate this constraint, I need to define several terms. We have seen that any proposed ground for MRS-SEMPROP consists of a family of properties and relations. In the discussion that follows I shall occasionally refer to such properties and relations as *factors*. These factors fall into two rather natural and mutually exclusive groups. On the one hand, there are *internal* factors. These are properties and relations of objects or states that are completely "in the head." Both the structural isomorphism approach and the functional role approach (the purer version, not the two-factor version) include only internal factors in their theories. On the other hand, there are *external* factors. These are relations between objects and states in the head and objects and states outside the head (in the environment). The causal historical, indicator, and biological function approaches all include external factors in their theories.

Given this terminology, we can now formulate the constraint we are interested in:

INTERNALISM   An acceptable ground for MRS will consist exclusively of naturalistic factors that are internal.[6]

This particular claim, or claims very similar to it, has gone by various names in the philosophical literature. I have in mind Putnam's (1975c) and Fodor's (1981a) "methodological solipsism" (but not Fodor's [1987] "methodological individualism"), Stich's (1983) "principle of autonomy," and Burge's (1979, 1986a) "individualism."

Does cognitive science accept (or ought it to accept) Internalism? The dialectical picture is somewhat more complicated here than in the case of Naturalism. Again, I will consider two sets of arguments, one descriptive and one normative. This time, however, the descriptive and normative arguments will not be in agreement. The descriptive arguments will point to the conclusion that cognitive science is not currently committed to Internalism, whereas the force of the normative arguments will be that it should be. I will end up endorsing only the conclusion of the descriptive arguments. However, as it turns out, I will not endorse all of the descriptive arguments themselves. In particular, I will take issue with the mode of argumentation (but not with the conclusions) of a widely discussed descriptive argument found in Burge's (1986a) paper "Individualism and Psychology" (henceforth I&P).

Before looking at Burge's arguments in detail, we must understand their place in the larger context of Burge's recent philosophical concerns. In a series of recent papers, Burge (1979, 1982a, 1982b, 1986a, 1986b) has mounted an extended and multi-pronged attack on the doctrine of individualism (the view that "the mental natures of all a person's or animal's mental states and events are such that there is no necessary or deep individuative relation between the individual's being in states of those kinds and the nature of the individual's physical or social environments") (I&P, p. 4). Two features of the arguments published before I&P are important for our purposes: they focus exclusively on individualism with respect to propositional-attitude attributions, they rely heavily on a series of thought experiments patterned after the Twin Earth thought experiment designed by Putnam (1975c) to show that "meaning ain't in the head."

The I&P discussion is motivated by two convictions on Burge's part: the recognition that any conclusions drawn from the earlier arguments concerning our ordinary propositional attitudes are not automatically applicable to the sorts of mental representations posited by cognitive science and the belief that, nevertheless, his original conclusions *do* apply to mental representations. Burge, thus, intends his I&P arguments to counter "a common reaction" to his original conclusions, viz. to "concede their force, but to try to limit their effect" by denying their applicability to the problem of content determination for MRS (as opposed to our ordinary attitudes).

The first I&P argument I shall consider appears relatively early in the paper.

SIMPLE THOUGHT EXPERIMENT ARGUMENT   "Since the relevant parts of psychology frequently use attributions of intentional states that are subject to our thought experiments, the language actually used in psychology is not purely individualistic.... For ordinary understanding of the truth conditions, or individuation conditions, of the relevant attributions suffices to verify the thought experiments."   (p. 9)

In other words, according to Burge the matter is quite straightforward: the pre-I&P thought experiments apply to the representational attributions of cognitive science just as they do to the propositional attributions of folk psychology. Therefore, cognitive science is not committed to Internalism.

Let us look at the Simple Thought Experiment Argument more carefully. It will be helpful, to begin with, to have one of the thought experiments clearly in mind. Burge's thought experiments all have three components: an imagined actual situation, an imagined counterfactual situation, and an interpretation of these. The experiment most relevant for present purposes goes like this:

Imagined actual situation   Consider a person A who thinks that aluminum is a light metal used in sailboat masts. We assume that A can pick out instances of aluminum and knows many familiar general facts about aluminum. A is, however, ignorant of aluminum's chemical structure and microproperties.

Imagined counterfactual situation   Now we can imagine a counterfactual case in which A's body has the same history considered in isolation of his or her physical environment but in which there are significant environmental differences from the actual situation. A's counterfactual environment lacks aluminum and has in its place a similar-looking light metal, which we can call "twalum."

Interpretation   In the actual situation A has thoughts about aluminum, but in the counterfactual situation he does not.[7]

Burge claims that this thought experiment "applies" to the MRS case. What precisely does this mean? Let us distinguish the *experimental procedure* of the thought experiment (namely, the imagining of the actual and counterfactual situation) from its *results*, or what Burge calls the *interpre-*

tation. And let us distinguish both of these from any *conclusion* we might want to draw on the basis of the results, such as the conclusion that common sense is not committed to Internalism. Let me then suggest that the above thought experiment—which I shall refer to as TE—applies to cognitive science just in case the following conditions hold:

(1) It is possible to devise another thought experiment with the same experimental procedure as TE except for the fact that Actual and Counterfactual A have representations rather than propositional attitudes.

(2) If this new procedure were carried out with cognitive scientists, we would get results (an interpretation) analogous to those in TE—namely, cognitive scientists would judge that the contents of the representations in the actual and counterfactual situations are different.

(3) These results are relevant to the issue under consideration, namely whether cognitive science is committed to Internalism.

I shall call the new thought experiment generated by applying TE to cognitive science in senses (1)–(3) "the representational version of TE."

I want to raise the question of whether Burge's thought experiment does indeed apply to cognitive science in the sense specified by conditions 1–3. But before I do so, let us be clear as to why a representational version of TE would show cognitive science not to be committed to Internalism: It would show this because it, in effect, provides a counterexample to the claim that the ground of the MRS consists exclusively of internal factors.

Here's how. Assume for the moment that MRS-SEMPROP (i.e., the set of semantic properties of MRS to be grounded in a theory of content determination) strongly supervenes on some set I of internal factors of persons having mental representations. Then, corresponding to the property of having a representation expressing the content that aluminum is a light metal used in sailboat masts (call it C_a), there will be some internal property or relation (call it I_a) that is nomologically sufficient for C_a. Now, in Burge's thought experiment, Actual A is internally identical to Counterfactual A. Thus, given that Actual A has the property I_a, it follows by virtue of their internal identity that Counterfactual A will also have that property. But if Counterfactual A has the property I_a, then by the supervenience assumption he or she will also have the property C_a. In other words, by the supervenience assumption and the assumptions of the thought experiment, Counterfactual A will share with Actual A the representation that aluminum is a light metal used in sailboat masts. However, if we accept the interpretation part of Burge's thought experiment, then the representational contents of Actual A and Counterfactual A are not the same. Actual A is having "aluminum representations" but Counterfactual A is not. Hence, the supervenience claim must be false.

Let us now return to the question of whether Burge's thought experiment applies to cognitive science, as he assumes. It seems to me clear that it doesn't, at least in the sense of conditions 1–3. Suppose that it is possible to devise a representational version of TE—that is, that condition 1 is satisfied. Then what about conditions 2 and 3? If the experimental procedure of this new thought experiment were carried out with cognitive scientists, would we get results analogous to those in TE? And would such results even be relevant to whether cognitive science is committed to Internalism?

Prima facie, there is no reason to think that condition 2 is true. Burge has conducted no polls of cognitive scientists, and it is doubtful that he would even want to claim that his own intuitions on the matter are the intuitions of a single but highly representative member of the cognitive science community in the way that a linguist claims that his or her linguistic intuitions are representative of all speakers of the linguist's language. How, then, can Burge claim to know what judgment a cognitive scientist would typically make regarding the contents of A's representations in the imagined situation? I think his reasoning is as follows:

THE DISCOURSE SIMILARITY ARGUMENT

(a) The experimental results in the thought experiments (either TE or the representational version of TE) constitute a judgement regarding what the contents of A's mental states are in the two hypothetical situations and, hence, also a judgement regarding whether they are the same or different.

(b) In both thought experiments, this judgement is based on the nature of the relevant mentalistic *discourse*. In TE the comparative content judgement is based on our ordinary mentalistic discourse; in the representational version of TE it is based on the theoretical discourse of cognitive science.

(c) In principle, there are certainly differences between the theoretical discourse of cognitive science and the mentalistic discourse of common sense.[8]

(d) However, there are no sound reasons to believe that these differences include differences regarding the individuation of a person's contentful states.[9]

(e) Hence, interpretations made on the basis of knowledge of our ordinary mentalistic discourse will coincide with interpretations made on the basis of the theoretical discourse of cognitive science.

(f) And, hence, also, the intuitions of a speaker of ordinary English, such as Burge, will be a reliable indicator of the intuitions of cognitive scientists versed in the theoretical discourse of cognitive science.

The above argument is problematic, on my view. But to see where the problem lies will take a bit of digging. The key to understanding its problematic nature lies in raising the question of *why* Burge might take (b) and (d) to be true.

Consider again the original thought experiment. To make TE more clearly relevant to the truth of Internalism, let us assume that the negative conclusion to be drawn from TE is construed as a thesis about the *ground* of our propositional-attitude states.[10] Furthermore, let us assume that the point of the original thought experiment is to reveal certain *implicit* assumptions regarding the nature of this ground—assumptions which constitute part of our folk psychology.

Now, why, on Burge's picture, does TE have such revelatory powers? Folk psychology is a nebulous and ill-defined beast. Burge seems to think, as do many people, that our folk-psychological assumptions are *embodied* somehow in our ordinary-language practices (specifically, in the ordinary-language practices that have to do with our mental states) and that, as a consequence, reflection on these practices will reveal what our folk psychology is committed to. The interpretation Burge advocates for the original thought experiment stems from the fact that, on his view, our ordinary propositional-attitude *ascriptions* are not individualistic. That is, he takes it that Actual A and Counterfactual A do not have the same thoughts because a speaker of English would not *say* that they do.

Furthermore, Burge offers us an account of why our ordinary attribution practices are non-individualistic in this way. The account goes roughly like this: Once a person has developed a certain level of competence in a language, we typically interpret his or her utterances against the standard set by the conventions of the language being used, even when the individual in question exhibits imperfect knowledge of the phenomenon being referred to (for example, doesn't know the fundamental nature of aluminum). The same communal standard also applies to our propositional-attitude attributions, presumably because the most specific source of evidence for what propositional attitudes a person has consists of his or her reports about those attitudes. Thus, according to Burge (1979, p. 114), "the expressions the subject uses sometimes provide the content of his mental states or events even though he only partially understands, or even misunderstands, some of them."

Why is this communal standard invoked? Here is Burge on that point:

The key to our attribution of mental contents in the face of incomplete mastery or misunderstanding lies largely in social functions associated with maintaining and applying the standard. In broad outline, the social advantages of the "special weight" [i.e. weighting propositional-attitude attributions in the direction of the communal standard] are apparent. Symbolic expressions are the overwhelmingly dominant source of detailed information about what people think, intend, and so forth. Such detail is essential not only to much explanation and prediction, but also to fulfilling many of our cooperative enterprises and to relying on one another for second-hand information. Words interpreted in conventionally established ways are familiar, palpable, and public. They are common coin, a relatively stable currency. These features are crucial to achieving the ends of mentalistic attribution just cited. They are also critical in maximizing interpersonal comparability. And they yield a bias toward taking others at their word and avoiding *ad hoc* interpretation, once overall agreement in usage and commitment to communal standards can be assumed. (Burge 1979, p. 116)

It should be clear that there is far more to Burge's argument than his thought experiments. He also offers us a picture of how our intuitions in the thought experiments come about. I have summarized this picture in figure 7.1.

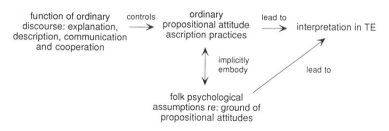

Figure 7.1
Burge's view of the source of intuitions in Twin Earth thought experiments.

We now have some understanding of how, on Burge's view, comparative content judgment in TE is based on the nature of ordinary mentalistic discourse. What about the scientific case? That is, how, on Burge's view, is our interpretation in the representational version of TE supposed to be based on theoretical discourse? We have little textual evidence to go on, but it seems fair to assume that Burge regards the relations among theory, discourse, and intuition in the scientific case to be roughly analogous to the ordinary case—at least, analogous enough that the assumption that the interpretations of both thought experiments are based on the nature of the relevant mentalistic discourse becomes true. For example, it seems reasonable to assume that Burge would say that our comparative content judgement in the representational version of TE is based on the theoretical discourse of cognitive science because that discourse reflects our theoretical commitments regarding the ground of MRS and it is precisely the latter that the thought experiment is attempting to tap.

Thus far we have considered why Burge might take assumption b to be true. Let us now turn to a consideration of assumption d—the claim that, although there may well be important differences between ordinary and theoretical discourse about the mental, they do not differ significantly with respect to their individuation practices. Why does Burge believe assumption d? Again, he doesn't really say. But let me offer the following hypothetical reason, which, if nothing else, allows (d) to provide support for (f), the conclusion that the intuitions of a speaker of ordinary English will be a reliable indicator of the intuitions of cognitive scientists versed in their theoretical discourse. The hypothetical reason for this is that the theoretical discourse of cognitive science has evolved and continues to evolve out of our ordinary mentalistic discourse by a process of refinement. For present purposes, the precise nature of this refinement is irrelevant. The important point to note is that the process of transformation is, essentially, a conservative one in the sense that it is governed by the conservative principle of keeping everything the same until there is some good scientific reason to change it. In particular, according to the reasoning I am attributing to Burge, the transformation of ordinary to theoretical discourse preserves the assumptions about the ground of our contentful states sanctioned by folk psychology until there is good scientific reason to change or reject them.

If one accepts this view of the relation between ordinary and theoretical discourse and if one holds, as Burge apparently does, that there is no good reason to change our ordinary individuation practices, then point f seems ensured—the intuitions of a speaker of ordinary English can be used as a reliable indicator of the intuitions of a theoretically fluent cognitive scientist with respect to the individuation of our contentful states. It is for this reason that he can say, in putting forth the Simple Thought Experiment Argument, that "the language actually used in psychology is not purely individualistic … for ordinary understanding of the truth conditions, or individuation conditions, of the relevant attributions suffices to verify the thought experiments."

What is wrong with all this? A lot. In the first place, although there may be a sense in which comparative content judgments in the representational version of TE are based on the theoretical discourse of cognitive science (that is, a sense in which point b is true), there is also a sense in which point b is extremely misleading. If we try to spell out the interrelations among theory, discourse, and intuition in the scientific case, we get a picture that is subtly but significantly different from the one previously sketched.

There are at least two important differences. In the first place, the function of theoretical discourse in cognitive science is primarily concerned with explanation and prediction. Thus, the pull toward communal standardization, which Burge ascribes to ordinary mentalistic attributions, is by and large absent. Second, in contrast to folk psychology, theory in cognitive science is explicit rather than implicit. As a consequence, the relation between representational ascriptions in cognitive science and the TCD they express is quite different from the relation between ordinary mentalistic ascriptions and the folk-psychological assumptions they embody. In the ordinary case, the ascriptions in some sense determine the assumptions. In the scientific case, the ascriptions are, or should be, a reflection of the theory. Thus, we get a very different picture (figure 7.2) of what underlies the comparative content judgments of a cognitive scientist in the representational version of TE.

The contrast between figures 7.1 and 7.2 suggests that the story about the transformation of ordinary to theoretical discourse speculatively attributed to Burge is also problematic. Adopting a conservative principle of preserving the individuation practices of ordinary discourse, unless there is reason to change them, is simply not good scientific practice. Clearly, we have no choice but to start our scientific investigation with ordinary mentalistic discourse. But since, ultimately, individuation is to be decided

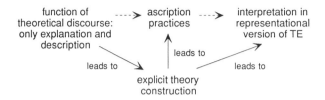

Figure 7.2
Alternative view of the source of a cognitive scientist's comparative content judgments in representational versions of Twin Earth thought experiments.

by our scientific TCD, it is best to begin by clearing the decks as much as possible. At a minimum, the stance we take toward the assumptions that ordinary discourse embodies should be one of polite skepticism rather than total acceptance. In other words, the operative principle should be to question the assumptions about the ground of contentful states sanctioned by folk psychology until we are in a position to replace them with a scientifically warranted TCD.

My corrected picture of the scientific theory-discourse-intuition interrelationship, in combination with my more radical transformation hypothesis, has a number of implications with respect to the Simple Thought Experiment Argument. In the first place, while it is still possible to maintain that point d (that there are no sound reasons to suppose that commonsense and cognitive science discourse differ with respect to the individuation of content) and point e (that the interpretations in the two thought experiments will coincide) are true, they are true in a sense that provides no support for point f (that the intuitions of a speaker of ordinary English will be a reliable indicator of the intuitions of cognitive scientists versed in the theoretical discourse of cognitive science). One might claim, for example, that the stance adopted by both ordinary and theoretical discourse on the matter of individuation just happens to be the same, even though the reasons for this stance are in each case different. This would make (d) and (e) true. However, while such a position would allow (d) and (e) to be true, it would provide no support at all for (f) in the intended sense. Since the individuation practices of folk psychology and cognitive science just happen to be the same, we cannot count on the intuitions of a speaker of ordinary discourse unless we already know about the congruence in stances. But if we know about the congruence, then the ordinary intuitions are of no value. The bottom line is that if we are interested in getting at the commitments of someone literate in the theoretical discourse of cognitive science, we must go straight to the appropriate source. A mere speaker of English will not do. Thus, it is simply not the case, as Burge asserts, that ordinary understanding of the individuation conditions of the relevant attributions will suffice to verify the thought experiments.

In fact, only scientific understanding will do. But simple literacy in the theoretical discourse of cognitive science is not sufficient either, for the intuitions of a cognitive scientist in the representational version of TE are relevant only insofar as they reflect theoretical knowledge of the nature of content determination for MRS.

We are now ready for some punch lines.

PUNCH LINE 1   The Simple Thought Experiment fails because TE does not apply to cognitive science. Why not? Because if a representational version of TE were presented to cognitive scientists capable of producing relevant intuitions, then the experimental results would be completely agnostic, for the judgement would be that we don't know what the content of Actual A's and Counterfactual A's representations are because we don't at present have a warranted and accepted theory of how the content of MRS is determined.

Punch line 1 presupposes that the same/difference judgment evoked by the representational version of TE is a judgement about the content of the representations in question. There is, however, an alternative intuition one might solicit. Instead of asking one's informants whether they judge that the content is, in fact, the same or different, one might ask them which of the two possibilities they would entertain. In other words, one might use the thought experiment to expose what sort of TCDs a cognitive scientist would seriously *consider*, as opposed to what sort of TCD he or she in fact *accepts*.

PUNCH LINE 2   Used in the first way (that is, as a tool for revealing assumptions regarding how content is, in fact. determined), the thought experiments are incapable of providing us with evidence relevant to the endorsement question. Cognitive scientists simply don't know how content is determined. In contrast, used in the second way (that is, as a tool for revealing assumptions as to how content might be determined), they can provide such evidence. However, even in this case their usefulness is limited, for intuitions as to whether the representational content of Actual

A and Counterfactual A might be the same or different are relevant only insofar as they reflect the kinds of TCDs that cognitive science would seriously entertain. And there is a far more direct source of evidence regarding the latter: the kinds of TCDs currently under investigation. In other words, I would endorse the following argument:

THE DESCRIPTIVE ARGUMENT AGAINST INTERNALISM

(1) Several current approaches in cognitive science to the problem of content determination for MRS do not honor the constraint of Internalism. These include the causal historical approach, the indicator approach, and the biological function approach.

(2) Therefore, cognitive science is not committed to Internalism.

Let us see where we are. The issue before us is whether cognitive science in fact endorses or ought to endorse Internalism as a constraint on the general ground for MRS. At the moment we are considering only descriptive arguments relevant to endorsement; thus, we are interested in arguments whose conclusion is that cognitive science does or does not, at present, endorse Internalism. After considerable reflection, we have concluded that Burge's Simple Thought Experiment Argument cannot decide the issue. However, in coming to understand why that argument cannot speak to the question of descriptive endorsement, we have gained insight into what the relevant considerations are. Specifically, it has become clear that one of the best ways to find out whether cognitive science is currently committed to Internalism is to consult current attempts within cognitive science to develop a theory of content determination for MRS. And if we do this, the answer to the question of descriptive endorsement becomes obvious: Cognitive science is not currently committed to Internalism for the simple reason that TCDs which violate this constraint—the causal historical approach, the indicator approach, and the biological function approach—are currently under serious consideration by cognitive scientists.

I take the Descriptive Argument against Internalism to be decisive on the question of whether cognitive science is committed to Internalism. However, just for the record, I would like to make a few comments about Burge's second argument in I&P, which is designed to support the same conclusion.

In some respects, Burge's second argument is very similar to my Descriptive Argument against Internalism. Like my argument, Burge's argument rests on pointing to certain instances of current practice in cognitive science that violate Internalism as the basis for claiming that cognitive science is not, in fact, committed to the constraint. The principal difference between his argument and mine is that Burge rests his case on a particular instance of cognitive science theorizing, namely David Marr's work on early vision, whereas I trade on the existence of certain approaches to the problem of content determination. In broadest outline, Burge's argument goes like this:

BURGE'S DESCRIPTIVE ARGUMENT AGAINST INTERNALISM

(1) Marr's theory of vision "treats intentional states non-individualistically" (p. 26).

(2) Marr's theory is a paradigmatic example of theorizing in cognitive science.

(3) Therefore, cognitive science is not committed to Internalism.

So far the argument seems straightforward enough. However, when we take a closer look at how Burge supports his first premise, controversy emerges.

After providing us with a fairly detailed description of Marr's theory, Burge summarizes his argument for premise 1 as follows:

BURGE'S MARR ARGUMENT

(1) The theory is intentional.

(2) The intentional primitives of the theory and the information they carry are individuated by reference to contingently existing physical items or conditions by which they are normally caused and to which they normally apply.

(3) Thus, if these physical conditions (and, possibly, attendant physical laws) were regularly different, the information conveyed to the subject and the intentional content of his or her visual representations would be different.

(4) It is not incoherent to conceive of relevantly different physical conditions and perhaps relevantly different (say, optical) laws regularly causing the same non-intentionally, individualistically individuated physical regu-

larities in the subject's eyes and nervous system. It is enough if the differences are small; they need not be wholesale.

(5) In such a case (by point 3), the individual's visual representations would carry different information and have different representational content, though the person's whole non-intentional physical history (at least up to a certain time) might remain the same.

(6) If some perceptual states are identified in the theory in terms of their informational or intentional content, it follows that individualism is not true for the theory of vision (Burge 1986a, p. 34).

On the basis of the textual evidence he cites, Burge's case seems, *prima facie*, to be a strong one. Where, then, do the disagreements lie? Issue has been taken with two points in Burge's argument. Egan (1991, p. 202) has argued that step 1 is simply false. Marr's theory is "not demonstrably intentional," and that hence "any argument to the effect that the theory is non-individualistic is a non-starter." Segal (1989) has challenged steps 2 and 3. He does not believe that Marr is committed to a non-individualistic mode of individuating representational states, and he holds that there is a way of interpreting Marr that is better justified than Burge's way. In accordance with this better-justified way, Marr would assign the same contents to internally identical subjects located in different physical environments.

Since I take it that we already have in hand a decisive argument for believing that cognitive science is not committed to Internalism (namely, the Descriptive Argument against Internalism), I will not take the time here to evaluate the challenges raised by Egan and Segal. I would, however, like to make a few observations about the controversy.

The first is that the mere existence of serious controversy over what Marr's theory says on the question of individuation shows that Marr's words do not speak for themselves—at least, not about the issue in question. And this makes perfect sense. After all, Marr was not a philosopher; his theory was not designed to address philosophical questions about content determination or individuation. Thus, there is every reason to expect that either he would have had no views on these matters at all or that the views he did have would not have been articulated in sufficient detail to distinguish between various philosophical positions. But if Marr's words do not speak for themselves, then whether or not Marr's theory individuates representational states non-individualistically is a matter of interpretation. The problem with this consequence is that interpretative arguments are notoriously tenuous from an epistemic point of view.

My second observation concerns Burge's strategy of argumentation. Burge claims that although his Twin Earth thought experiments "will not carry over simply to early human vision" (p. 26), the "abstract schema" which those thought experiments articulate does apply. While it is not completely clear what Burge means by "the abstract schema" of his thought experiments, it is evident that the strategy of argumentation employed in Burge's Marr Argument is similar to that of the thought experiments. Points 1–6 of Burge's Marr argument allow us to construct a counterexample to Internalism of the standard twin sort: a twin case in which Actual A and Counterfactual A are internally identical yet have representations with different contents, yielding the conclusion that content cannot be grounded in internal factors alone. Note, however, that there is an important difference between this case and the representational version of TE, namely, in the *source* of the claim that the twins' contents is different. In the standard thought experiment, the source of this claim is an intuitive judgment, as we have seen. In contrast, in the above case the source of the claim is an incipient TCD which Burge attributes to Marr: that a representation R represents$_0$ an object O if Os cause Rs under normal conditions. This fact makes Burge's second I&P argument far stronger than the Simple Thought Experiment Argument, on my view. However, it also suggests that the twin counterexample strategy is unnecessary, for if Marr is committed to an incipient TCD and that TCD grounds the content of perceptual representations in causal relations to the environment (a claim whose truth I am not taking a stand on) then Marr is, *ipso facto*, not committed to Internalism. End of story. Construction of a twin-style counterexample is completely superfluous.

7.3 A Normative Case for Internalism

Thus far, the focus of attention in this chapter has been on two descriptive arguments given by Burge (1986a) *against* the claim that cognitive science is committed to Internalism. In the process of discussing the first of these arguments, I developed a third argument—the Descriptive Argument against Internalism—which I take to be decisive and which concurs with Burge's conclusion.

Of course, this is not the end of the matter. The Internalist is still free to mount a normative case in favor of the claim that cognitive science *ought* to be committed to Internalism, even if at present it is not. Burge considers and rejects two such arguments. Since I am largely in agreement with what Burge has to say about these arguments, I will consider only the one that has received the most attention.[11]

Stich (1983, p. 164) aims to defend a principle that is closely related to the constraint of Internalism:

THE PRINCIPLE OF AUTONOMY   The states and processes that are relevant to cognitive science are those that supervene on the current, internal, physical state of the organism.[12]

Stich wants to defend this principle because he believes it will aid his case for the Syntactic Theory of Mind—the view that cognitive science can accomplish its explanatory goals by regarding the mind as a purely syntactic engine. For present purposes, however, I would like to divorce Stich's defense of the principle of Autonomy from his commitment to the Syntactic Theory of Mind. It should be clear that if one does happen to assume that representations exist, *contra* Stich and as cognitive science undoubtedly does, then this assumption conjoined with the Principle of Autonomy entails Internalism. Hence my interest in Stich's argument.

Stich attempts to defend the Principle of Autonomy by what he calls "the replacement argument." His initial version goes like this:

STICH'S NORMATIVE ARGUMENT FOR INTERNALISM (ORIGINAL VERSION)

(1) "Suppose that someone were to succeed in building an exact physical replica of me—a living human body whose current internal physical states at a given moment were identical to mine at that moment. And suppose further that while fast asleep I am kidnapped and replaced by the replica." (Stich 1983, p. 165)

(2) Since I and my replica are physically identical, we will behave identically in all circumstances.

(3) Cognitive science is the science that aspires to explain behavior.

(4) Thus, any states, processes, or properties not shared by me and my identically behaving replica must surely be irrelevant to cognitive science.

(5) Therefore, cognitive science ought to endorse the Principle of Autonomy.

(6) Therefore, cognitive science ought to endorse Internalism.

This argument contains "an important kernel of truth," but as it stands it "plainly will not do" (Stich 1983, p. 166). Premise 2 is simply false. On a broad, commonsense conception of behavior, there are behaviors that Stich and his replica would not share. For example, only Stich could sell his car (although, of course, his replica could go through the motions of doing so). To remedy this problem, Stich introduces the notion of an "autonomous behavioral description"—a description which is such that "if it applies to an organism in a given setting, then it would also apply to any replica of the organism in that setting" (p. 167). He then replaces premises 2 and 3 in the original version of his argument with two new premises which refer to behavior that falls under an autonomous behavioral description (let us call this "autonomous behavior") rather than behavior *tout court*. We thus get the following:

STICH'S NORMATIVE ARGUMENT FOR INTERNALISM (VERSION 2)

(1) (Replacement experiment)

(2′) Since I and my replica are physically identical, all of our autonomous behavior will be identical, where autonomous behavior is behavior shared by me and my replica in any given setting.

(3′) Cognitive science is the science that aspires to explain autonomous behavior (and only autonomous behavior).

(4) Thus, any states or processes or properties not shared by me and my identically behaving replica must surely be irrelevant to cognitive science.

(5) Therefore, cognitive science ought to endorse the Principle of Autonomy.

(6) Therefore, cognitive science ought to endorse Internalism.

How does version 2 of the Replacement Argument fare? Stich clearly believes that things are now OK. Since the validity of the argument is never in doubt for him, and the change from 'behavior' to 'autonomous behavior' renders premise 2′ true (in fact, trivially true), Stich now takes it that the burden of the argument is placed on premise 3′. He therefore proceeds to mount a second, supplementary argument in support of premise 3′.

I shall consider premise 3′ shortly. Before doing so, however, I would like to raise a question concerning Stich's assessment of the status of version 2 of his argument. Barring, for the moment, considerations pertaining to the truth of premise 3', is the argument in as good a shape as Stich assumes?

I think not. The flaws are reparable and hence not extremely damaging to Stich, but they are interesting and thus worth considering. There are two problems. To get at what these problems are it is useful to compare Stich's replacement thought experiment with the "experimental procedure" of the thought experiments of Burge and Putnam. How are they similar and how are they different? They are similar because in all three cases we imagine that there are two physically identical protagonists, each in a slightly different situation. However, they differ in what factors get varied in the two different situations.[13]

The first problem with Stich's modified argument is that the variation introduced by imagining that Stich's replica *replaces* Stich (rather than that it lives on Twin Earth, or that it is Stich himself in a counterfactual situation) is insufficient for his purposes. Let us call any property or state of affairs that does not supervene on the internal, physical state of an organism a *non-internal* factor. Replacement won't do for Stich's purposes because, while it varies some non-internal factors, it doesn't vary them all. In particular, while the histories of the two individuals are clearly different (hence the force of the car-sale example), their physical, linguistic, social, and cultural environment remains the same. This affects the argument because it impedes the inference from step 4 to the conclusion: If Stich and his replica continue to share the non-internal factors of physical, linguistic, social, and cultural environment, then these will not be ruled out as "irrelevant" in step 4. And then, of course, step 4 will not entail the conclusion that cognitive science ought to adopt the Principle of Autonomy, which countenances no non-internal factors at all.

The second problem (relative to Stich's argumentative aims) is similar. In defining the notion of an "autonomous behavioral description," Stich says that it is a description of behavior which satisfies the following condition: "If it applies to an organism in a given setting, then it would also apply to any replica of the organism in that setting." But what does Stich mean by a "setting"? If the setting includes the physical (or worse, linguistic, social, or cultural) environment, then Stich's notion of autonomous behavior is, again, much too broad for his purposes, for if autonomous behavior need be the same only when the physical, linguistic, social, and cultural environments are the same, but could (presumably) differ otherwise, then very little is ruled out as irrelevant to cognitive science, and again step 4 will not until the conclusion.

It is quite evident, I think, why Stich relativizes autonomous behavior to setting. He needs some way of matching the bit of behavior that he manifests (in the thought experiment) with the analogous bit that his replica manifests. Thus, if setting is conceived of as something like the input to the two individuals, then if their input is shared, and they are physically identical, presumably their output (i.e., their autonomous behavior) will be shared. In contrast, if setting is not controlled for, then we might end up comparing Stich and his replica under different input conditions. And if their inputs differ, their peripheral outputs will quite likely differ.

Stich thus needs a way of matching the analogous bits of behavior for the two individuals in his thought experiment. But there are better ways to do this than via the nebulous (and hence, for Stich, problematic) notion of setting. One way is to make the notion of setting more precise and more internalist by relativizing the notion of autonomous behavior to either the "peripheral" or the "internal" inputs of the system. If we do this, then the relevant behaviors of Stich and his replica can be paired for purposes of identifying the autonomous behaviors, but we will not have strayed outside the confines of the organism's skin to the realm of non-internal factors.

Let us now consider what Stich's argument would look like if the above two problems were taken care of. Solving the first problem requires combining Stich's replacement procedure with Putnam's Twin Earth procedure. (Replacement is necessary to vary history, and Twin Earth is necessary to vary the physical, linguistic, social, and cultural environment.) Solving the second problem requires changing the definition of 'autonomous behavior'.

STICH'S NORMATIVE ARGUMENT FOR INTERNALISM (VERSION 3)

(1') Imagine a possible world W2 which is identical to this world in every respect until January 1, 1983, when a number of strange things happen. On W2 a philosophy professor named 'Stephen Stich' is kidnapped in the dead of night and replaced with an exact replica. In addition, the physical, linguistic, social, and cultural environment in which Stich lives on W2 undergoes a number of subtle but significant changes. For example, the microstructures of certain metals change, and certain words in the language undergo subtle changes in meaning.[14] Despite these changes, the peripheral stimulation of Stich on W2 continues to parallel exactly the peripheral stimulation of Stich in this world.

(2″) Since Stich in this world and his replica on W2 are physically identical, and since their history of peripheral stimulation is identical, their autonomous behavior at any given moment in time will be identical, where autonomous behavior is the behavior that is necessarily shared by an individual and his or her replica under the same peripheral stimulation.

(3′) Cognitive science is the science that aspires to explain autonomous behavior (and only autonomous behavior).

(4′) Thus, any states, processes, or properties not shared by Stich in this world and his replica in W2 must surely be irrelevant to cognitive science.

(5) Therefore, cognitive science ought to endorse the Principle of Autonomy.

(6) Therefore, cognitive science ought to endorse Internalism.

Although the above argument still relies on a number of missing premises, these are sufficiently unproblematic that we can now turn our attention to the argument's soundness. In particular, we can consider the truth of the notorious premise 3′, upon which the burden of the argument can now legitimately be placed.

Is it the case, as Stich asserts, that cognitive science aspires to explain nothing but autonomous behavior? On the basis of the discussion in chapter 2 above, the answer is clearly "no." The explanandum of cognitive science is not exclusively autonomous behavior for the simple reason that most of the time it is not behavior at all, autonomous or otherwise. Rather, the basic aim of cognitive science is to explain the human cognitive capacities—what they are, how they are exercised, in virtue of what we have them, and how they interact. Of course, as I pointed out above, the explanandum of cognitive science is sometimes behavior in the sense that cognitive science sometimes attempts to explain *exercises* of one or other of the cognitive capacities, and sometimes (in the case of output capacities such as speech production) those exercises involve behavior. But the aim of cognitive science is certainly not to explain *nothing but* behavior, for every cognitive capacity has an input component and some capacities have output components that are nonbehavioral (that is, purely internal).

This answer is not entirely satisfying, however. Although correct, it is too quick. One might argue that the real issue raised by Stich's argument is not whether the explanandum of cognitive science consists of behavior or of capacities, but whether the explanandum (whatever it is) is autonomous in some sense.

One way to respond to this objection is to reject Stich's exclusive focus on behavior and attempt to reformulate his argument in terms of the cognitive capacities. Such a reformulation will take care of both kinds of explananda mentioned above (the cognitive capacities *per se* and certain kinds of behavior), because any instance of behavior that cognitive scientists are interested in explaining will be an instance of an *exercise* of some cognitive capacity. In other words, we might consider the argument (version 4) that results from replacing points 2″ and 3′, respectively, with the following:

(2‴) Since Stich in this world and his replica in W2 are physically identical, and since their history of peripheral stimulation is identical from the time of the replacement, the autonomous cognitive capacities they exercise at any given moment after the replacement will be identical, where an autonomous capacity is one whose exercise is necessarily shared by replicas under the same peripheral stimulation.

(3″) Cognitive science is the science that aspires to explain autonomous cognitive capacities (and only such capacities).

What, then, about this new version and its reformulated third premise? Burge's (1986a) response to Stich's argument can be read as putting forth the following two reasons for rejecting premise 3″: First, the "molar abilities and activities" (e.g. capacities) that cognitive science appears to be about involve propositional attitudes, but "the propositional attitudes attributed do not seem to be fully individuable in individualistic terms" (p. 12). Second, cognitive science "seems to be partly about relations between people ... and their environment. It is hard to see how to provide a natural description of a theory of vision, for example, as a science of behavior. The point of the theory is to figure out how people do what they obviously succeed in doing—how they see objects in their environment.... In my view, these relations help motivate non-individualistic principles of individuation." (pp. 12–13)

On my view, Burge's reasoning here is almost exactly right. I say "almost" because I disagree with him on two relatively minor yet significant points.

The first point of dispute concerns the nature of cognitive science's explanandum. In resting his anti-autonomy case partly on what the propositional attitudes are like, Burge is clearly assuming that cognitive science seeks to explain the cognitive capacities as they are ordinarily construed. And there is certainly a sense in which this assumption is correct. However, although I agree with Burge that cognitive science seeks to explain our ordinary cognitive capacities, I do not think that these capacities exhaust the explanandum of cognitive science. As Stich (1983, pp. 166–167) points out, the cognitive scientist, like every scientist, "must select or formulate an appropriate descriptive language for his explananda. And the formulation of such a vocabulary will be a fundamental part of psychological theory construction." As a consequence, cognitive science, like all sciences, has two "levels" of explananda. There is the explanandum (i.e., the domain and basic questions) that constitutes the original motivation for the enterprise, and then there is the explanandum (i.e., a reconceptualized domain and a revised set of basic questions) that constitutes the immediate focus of attention for empirical and theoretical research.

Our ordinary cognitive capacities constitute the original explanandum for cognitive science. The revised explanandum, as we shall see in chapter 9, consists of these ordinary cognitive capacities reconceptualized as what I shall call *broad* information-processing capacities.[15] More specifically, these capacities are reconceptualized as involving some or all of the events depicted in figure 7.3. I say "some or all" because some capacities will involve only the first half of this chain, from the distal stimulus to a representational state; some will involve only the second half, from a representational state to a motor movement with certain characteristic environmental consequences; and some will involve only the middle, from a representational state to a representational state. Note, however, that *every* cognitive capacity will involve a representational state.

Now, I take it that it is the revised explanandum of cognitive science (and, hence, information-processing capacities of the above sort), rather

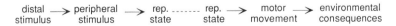

Figure 7.3
Sequence of events underlying the class of broad information capacities. Input capacities begin with a distal stimulus and end with a representational state. Output capacities begin with a representational state and end with environmental consequences. Input-output capacities encompass the entire sequence.

than the original explanandum, that is pertinent to Stich's Replacement Argument, for the notion of "relevance" in premise 4 is connected with the question of what theoretical entitles are needed to answer the questions cognitive science wants to answer. (That is, if a theoretical state, process, or property is not needed, it will be considered irrelevant; if it is needed, it will be considered relevant.) But the questions cognitivist theories seek to answer *directly* are questions that concern the revised, not the original explanandum (although, in directly answering the revised basic questions, cognitive scientists take themselves to be *indirectly* answering the original basic questions.)

If this point about the explanandum is granted, then the question of whether the explanandum of cognitive science is autonomous becomes easy to answer. It is not autonomous, for two reasons. First, information-processing capacities involve representational states, and insofar as the content of these states may be grounded in ways that are not invariant between Stich and his replica we cannot assume that the capacities themselves are autonomous. Second, insofar as some information-processing capacities make reference to *distal* stimuli or motor movements coupled with characteristic *environmental* consequences the class as a whole will not be autonomous.

It should be obvious that these two reasons correspond very closely to Burge's two reasons for rejecting premise 3″. However, the differences between my reasons and Burge's should now also be clear. In the first place, I reject Burge's implicit assumption that the explanandum of cognitive science is exhausted by the cognitive capacities as ordinarily construed. Second, I do not believe that premise 3″ is false because the representations implicated in our information-processing capacities are clearly grounded in non-internalist factors. Rather, I want to say that, on the basis of what we currently know (which is not much), these representations *may* be so grounded. (They would be non-internalistically grounded if, for example, one or another of the causal historical, indicator, and biological function approaches were to pan out.) We simply don't know enough to say one way or the other at this point. Note, however, that I am more in accord with Burge with respect to the second reason. I take it that, insofar as the revised explanandum of cognitive science consists of information-processing capacities that reach out into the environment, this explanandum will not be autonomous, for the nature of any given input or output capacity will be partly determined by the nature of the environment. Hence, the capacities exercised by Stich and his replica at any given moment will not necessarily be the same.

It is time to sum up. I have been considering Stich's "replacement argument" because that argument, if sound and if coupled with a commitment to representations, would constitute a normative argument for Internalism. Stich's own formulation of the argument (my version 2) was found wanting because the experimental procedure of replacement invoked in the argument does not adequately control for all relevant non-individualistic factors. To remedy this problem, I formulated another version of the argument (version 3), which combines the replacement procedure with Putnam's Twin Earth procedure. I then proceeded to consider the crux of this new version of the argument: premise 3', which asserts that cognitive science is the science that aspires to explain only autonomous behavior. Premise 3' was dismissed on the grounds that the explanandum of cognitive science includes much more than behavior, autonomous or otherwise. But, recognizing that this fact constitutes a somewhat shallow reason for dismissing premise 3', I developed a fourth version of the argument, which contained a new third premise (premise 3") formulated in terms of autonomous cognitive capacities rather than autonomous behavior. Finally, with Stich's Normative Argument for Internalism reconstructed in its strongest possible form, I rejected premise 3" on two grounds: because information-processing capacities involve representational states and representational states may be determined in part by externalist factors, and because the class of broad information-processing capacities includes input capacities and output capacities, both of which reach out into the subject's environment. I conclude, therefore, that premise 3" is false and that, as a consequence, Stich's argument will not do as a normative argument for Internalism.

7.4   Methodological Individualism*

In comparison to Naturalism, Internalism is somewhat prohibitive—too prohibitive, it seems. On the other hand, Naturalism alone, insofar as it allows the ground of MRS-SEMPROP to consist of *any* naturalistic properties and relations, is extremely tolerant. The question we will consider in this section is whether, from the point of view of cognitive science, Naturalism is *too* tolerant—whether, in other words, cognitive science does or ought to endorse a constraint more restrictive than Naturalism but less restrictive than Internalism.

The tolerance of Naturalism can be brought out by reflecting on the theories of content determination it permits. For example, it permits a theory that treats two representations as distinct in contents simply because they have different histories. Our roster of current approaches to the problem of content determination, in fact, includes two such TCDs: Devitt's causal historical approach and Millikan's biological function approach. Naturalism also permits a theory that treats two representations as content-distinct simply because they belong to individuals who live in different language communities. To my knowledge, no one has actually tried to work out a detailed theory of this sort; however, the idea of treating mere membership in a linguistic community as a content-determining factor has been endorsed by many philosophers on the basis of another of Burge's twin-type thought experiments.

Because this second sort of TCD seems particularly outlandish from a cognitivist perspective, let me elaborate on it for a moment. Following the form used in section 7.2, we can summarize Burge's thought experiment thus:

Imagined actual situation   Consider a person A who lives in an English-speaking community in which the word 'arthritis' means what it standardly does. A is generally intelligent and speaks English. In addition, his behavior is such that we would normally attribute to him all sorts of true beliefs identified by content clauses containing 'arthritis' in oblique occurrence. We would also, however, attribute to him the false belief that he has arthritis in his thigh.

Imagined counterfactual situation   Counterfactual A is identical to actual A in all non-intentional, internal respects. However, he lives in a language community that speaks English* rather than English, where English* differs from English only in that 'arthritis' refers to a disease that can occur not only in the joints but also in the thighs.

Interpretation   In the actual situation. A has thoughts about arthritis; in the counterfactual situation he does not. One way to describe the thoughts of Counterfactual A would be to say that he has the concept *tharthritis* rather than *arthritis*.

This is the thought experiment as Burge (1979) presents it. I shall call it "the original version of TE'." To make the original version of TE' speak to our concerns, we must make two alterations: we must construct a representational version of TE' and we must introduce the following modification. Imagine that Actual A and Counterfactual A are identical not only with respect to all internal factors but also with respect to all external factors with the exception of membership in the relevant linguistic communities. In particular, both A and Counterfactual A exhibit the same immediate causal relations to their respective environments. The first modification is necessary for the usual reason that we are concerned with the mental representation system rather than the propositional attitudes. The second is necessary because Burge presumably wants to maintain that it is *simply* membership in the respective language communities that leads to the interpretative judgment of different contents in the original version of TE'. Thus, the thought experiment must be set up so that every other nonlinguistic external factor is controlled for.

The conclusion of the representational version of TE' is, then, that the external relation of belonging to such-and-such a language community counts as a factor in determining the ground of MRS-SEMPROP even when every other internal and external factor is controlled for. Let us call this "the language community determination thesis." My reason for discussing this conclusion is not that I think cognitive scientists have to worry about the conclusion's being *true* on the basis of the representational version of TE'. Since (as I have indicated above) I don't think the twin-type thought-experiment methodology is relevant to cognitive science, I obviously do not think that cognitive scientists need worry about conclusions that issue from that methodology. Rather, the point is that (a) at this juncture in the book the research framework of cognitive science is committed to nothing stronger than Naturalism, (b) Naturalism is consistent with the language community determination thesis, and (c) the language community determination thesis is a *very wild claim*! Or, at least, it has struck some philosophers (most notably, Jerry Fodor) as such. And it strikes me as such. How *could* certain subtle features of the linguistic practices of persons around you influence the content of your mental representations when those features do not directly impinge on you in any way?

What is wild about Burge's position is not that it claims that the language spoken around you affects the contents of your mental representations. Of course that is true. We probably acquire most of the concepts we acquire through the mediation of public language. What is radical about Burge's view is that it claims that public language affects MRS-SEMPROP without the mediation of *any other external or internal factor.*

To rule out the excesses of endorsing Naturalism alone, Fodor (1987, 1991) has proposed and tried to defend a sort of intermediate position between Naturalism and Internalism. This intermediate position derives from a view that Fodor (1987) calls "Methodological Individualism." Methodological Individualism (not to be confused with Burgean "Individualism") is the doctrine that psychological states, at least to the extent that they are implicated in causal explanation, are individuated with respect to their causal powers—that is, they count as type-identical just in case they have the same causal powers, and as type-different just in case they have different causal powers. If we apply the doctrine of Methodological Individualism to the question of what can count as an acceptable ground for MRS-SEMPROP, we get the following, which I shall call "Methodological Individualism*."

METHODOLOGICAL INDIVIDUALISM*   An acceptable ground for MRS will consist of either internal or external naturalistic factors so long as such factors satisfy the following restriction: if two token representations are ground-distinct, and if this difference in ground results in a difference in content, these representations must also differ in their causal powers to produce relevant effects across nomologically possible contexts.[16]

To fully understand this constraint, we must get clear on a number of questions concerning causal powers; in addition, we must understand what the restrictions to "relevant" effects and "nomologically possible contexts" come to and why Fodor introduces these restrictions. We will then ask our two familiar questions about the commitments of cognitive science: the descriptive question (Is cognitive science, in fact, committed to Methodological Individualism*?) and the normative question (Ought cognitive science to be committed to Methodological Individualism*?).

What is it for something to *have* causal powers? As a first pass, to say that something has causal powers is to say that it has the *capacity* to cause one or more effects. What does that mean? I think Fodor would say something like this: X has the capacity to cause an effect (say, Y's having a certain effect property EP) if and only if X has some causal property CP such that there are nomologically possible conditions C under which X's having CP conjoined with the presence of C *would* cause Y to have EP.

Now, if a thing *has* causal powers, what *are* the causal powers of that thing? Suppose that X has three distinct causal capacities: the capacity to cause Y's having EP1, the capacity to cause Z's having EP2, and the capacity to cause W's having EP3. Then it is natural to say that X's causal powers simply are X's capacities (in this case, three) to cause certain individual effects. (We often, of course, combine various individual effects into higher-order types of effects and talk about the capacity to cause that higher-order type of effect, but the above will do for present purposes.) Finally, under what conditions will two things differ in their causal powers? The identification of causal powers with causal capacities suggests that two things X and Y will differ in their causal powers only if X and Y differ in their capacities to cause one or more individual effects—that is, only if X has a capacity to cause an effect that capacity Y does not share (or vice versa).

The above seems to clarify matters considerably. Why, then, does Fodor feel it necessary to introduce the restriction to relevant effects and the restriction to effects across nomologically possible contexts? And what do those restrictions come to? The first question is somewhat misleading because it suggests that Fodor believes it makes sense to talk about causal powers (capacities) that do not honor the above two restrictions. My sense is that this is not the way Fodor thinks about the matter, however. Rather, I take his view to be that the causal powers of a thing only (and *ipso facto*) concern relevant effects, and that they always (and *ipso facto*) concern effects across nomologically possible contexts. But since the restriction to relevant effects, at least, is controversial, I have formulated the constraint of Methodological Individualism* so as to make both features explicit. When such explicitness becomes too cumbersome I will refer to causal powers with these two features as "strict" causal powers.

Suppose someone were to argue that in Burge's TE case the twins' representations have different causal powers (capacities) because when the representations lead to can-picking-up behavior, Actual A's representation always causes him to pick up an aluminum can whereas Counterfactual A's representation always causes him to pick up a twalum can. This is precisely the sort of difference that ought not to count, according to Fodor, for we are interested not in what the causal consequences of the twins' representations actually are but in what they could (or would) be under all the various possible circumstances. (Recall that X has the capacity to cause an effect if X has some causal property such that there are *nomologically possible* conditions under which X's having that causal property conjoined with the presence of those conditions would cause that effect.) Thus, to ascertain what their causal powers (capacities) are, we must subject the twins to a counterfactual investigation. In particular, we must ask the following counterfactual questions: If we were to transport Actual A to the twalum environment, what would he pick up there? If we were to transport Counterfactual A to the aluminum environment, what would he pick up there? Fodor's point is that specifying the causal powers of a thing requires us to inquire about the causal effects of that thing's causal properties (strictly: of that thing's having the causal properties it has) in all *nomologically possible contexts*. And if we make such a counterfactual inquiry in the above twin case, we see that, with regard to can-picking-up behavior at least, the nomologically possible causal effects of the representation ⟨aluminum⟩ in the twins are the same. There are nomologically possible conditions under which both Actual A's and Counterfactual A's ⟨aluminum⟩ representations would lead to aluminum-can-picking-up behavior and there are (other) nomologically possible conditions under which both Actual A's and Counterfactual A's ⟨aluminum⟩ representations would lead to twalum-can-picking-up behavior. Hence, in this respect at least, the twins' representations have the same causal powers.

Consider now the restriction to relevant causal effects. We have seen that the causal powers of a thing depend on its capacities to produce individual effects. The causal effects of a representation can include immediate computational and neural effects "in the head," muscular and skeletal movements, behavioral effects, and consequences of these behavioral effects on the environment. What motivates Fodor's restriction to relevant effects is that behavior can be described in multiple ways. In particular, behavior can be described intentionally—that is, in terms of the contents of the mental states that give rise to it. Now suppose one is a Burgean and believes that the contents of a person's mental representations are, in part at least, determined by the nature of the physical and linguistic environment in which that person lives. Such a Burgean might argue as follows: Methodological Individualism* *does* permit TCDs that assign the twins different mental contents in the thought experiments TE and TE′, because the environmental and linguistic differences that determine these different mental contents also make the behavioral effects of these mental contents different. Thus, for example, when Actual A entertains the representation ⟨I want an aluminum can⟩, expressing the proposition that Actual A wants an aluminum can, this representation will typically give rise to aluminum-can-seeking behavior, whereas when Counterfactual A entertains the representation ⟨I want an aluminum can⟩, expressing the proposition that Counterfactual A wants a twalum can, this representation will typically give rise to twalum-can-seeking behavior.[17] The twins' representations thus have different causal effects; hence, they have different causal powers; hence, content determination by historical and linguistic external factors satisfies the constraint of Methodological Individualism*.

Fodor's insistence on relevant causal effects is designed to undercut precisely such an argument. In other words, his intuition is that the twins' representations have the same causal powers because they have the same relevant effects. However, since this intuition is not shared by all parties to the discussion, Fodor has devoted considerable effort in his recent writings to clarifying and defending it.

A useful place to start in getting a handle on this effort is with what Fodor (1991) calls "schema S." (See figure 7.4.) Fodor describes the schema thus:

Suppose we have a pair of causes C1, C2, together with their respective effects E1, E2. Assume that:

C1 differs from C2 in that C1 has cause property CP1 where C2 has cause property CP2.

E1 differs from E2 in that E1 has effect property EP1 and E2 has effect property EP2.

The difference between C1 and C2 is responsible for the difference between E1 and E2 in the sense that, if C1 had had CP2 rather than CP1, then E1 would have EP2 rather than EP1; and if C2 had had CP1 rather than CP2, E2 would have had EP1 rather than EP2.   (1991, p. 9)

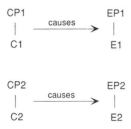

Figure 7.4
Graphic depiction of Fodor's (1991) "schema S."

With this schema, the question then is: When is the difference between C1's having CP1 and C2's having CP2 a difference of causal power in virtue of the difference between E1's having EP1 and E2's having EP2? Or, put somewhat differently: If it is only a difference in relevant effects that makes for a difference in causal powers, when is the difference between E1's having EP1 and E2's having EP2 a difference in relevant effects?

As I read him, Fodor has suggested three answers to this question, two in his 1987 book and one in his 1991 paper. Each takes the form of presenting only *necessary* conditions in response to the question of when a difference in effects constitutes a difference in causal powers. That is, the three suggestions all take the following form:

The difference between C1's having CP1 and C2's having CP2 counts as a difference in the causal powers of C1 and C2 in virtue of the difference between E1's having EP1 and E2's having EP2 only if....

I shall henceforth abbreviate this as "the difference between C1 and C2 in schema S counts as a difference in causal powers only if...." Since Fodor's 1991 paper ignores one of the suggestions in his 1987 book and contains remarks that are inconsistent with the book, I will focus only on his most recent answer.[18]

To defend his suggestions, Fodor first develops a number of imaginary cases which satisfy schema S and about which we are supposed to have clear intuitions regarding whether the difference in effects makes a difference to the causal powers of C1 and C2. He then develops a principle that accounts for these clear intuitions and argues that the principle is justified *because* it accounts for these clear intuitions.[19]

Consider the following case:

I have before me this genu-u-ine United States ten cent piece. It has precisely two stable configurations; call them 'heads' and 'tails'.... I define 'is an H-particle at t' so that it's satisfied by a particle at t iff my dime is heads-up at t. Correspondingly, I define 'is a T-particle at t' so that it's satisfied by a particle at t iff my dime is tails-up at t. By facing my dime heads-up, I now bring it about that every particle in the universe is an H-particle ... thus! And then, by reversing my dime, I change every particle in the universe into a T-particle ... thus!   (Fodor 1987, p. 33)

Now suppose that Fodor tosses his dime here on Earth at time t and it lands heads-up. And suppose that in some other possible world Fodor tosses his dime at the same time but it lands tails-up. We then have an instance of schema S (see figure 7.5). Do the two coin tosses have different

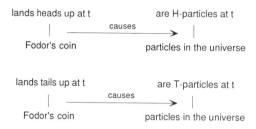

Figure 7.5
Fodor's (1987, 1991) case of H and T particles. The particles of the universe become H particles if and only if Fodor's coin lands heads up; they become T particles if and only if Fodor's coin lands tails up. Although H and T particles differ, our intuition is supposed to be that this difference is not relevant to there being a difference in the causal powers of Fodor's coin.

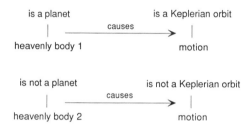

Figure 7.6
Fodor's (1991) planet case. Here our intuition is supposed to be that the difference in effects is relevant to there being a difference in the causal powers of heavenly body 1 and heavenly body 2.

causal powers in virtue of causing the particles in the two possible worlds to become H and T particles, respectively? Fodor has, and we are supposed to have, a clear negative intuition: that, in this respect at least, the two coin tosses do not differ in causal powers. (The coin tosses may, and probably do, have different causal powers in virtue of causing other effects.)

In contrast, here is an instantiation of schema S (see figure 7.6) in which Fodor has, and we are supposed to have, the intuition that the effects *are* relevant to the causal powers of C1 and C2:

Suppose there are two molecularly identical chunks of rock, one of which is a planet and the other of which isn't. These chunks of rock have different effects. One has a Keplerian orbit and the other doesn't.

To account for these and other similar intuitions, Fodor (1991) makes the following suggestion:

Causal Powers Difference Condition (CPDC)   The difference between C1 and C2 in schema S counts as a difference in causal powers if and only if C1 and C2 differ in their capacities to cause relevant individual effects. The difference between E1's being EP1 and E2's being EP2 counts as a difference in relevant effects only if it constitutes a difference in effects *tout court* and the relations between CP1 and EP1, on the one hand, and CP2 and EP2, on the other, are *non-conceptual*, that is, only if these relations are neither conceptually necessary nor mediated by a conceptually necessary relation.[20]

Thus, being an H particle does not count as a relevant effect property with respect to the causal powers of Fodor's coin toss because the relation between Fodor's coin toss being heads-up and particles becoming H particles is conceptually necessary. In contrast, having a Keplerian orbit does count as a relevant effect property with respect to the causal powers of some planet because the relation between being a planet and having a Keplerian orbit is not conceptually necessary.[21]

Recall that the point of restricting causal powers to only relevant effects is to prevent someone from arguing that the twins' representations in TE and TE′ have different causal powers, and hence that Methodological Individualism* permits TCDs that claim that representational content is partly determined by historical and linguistic external factors. It is thus important to note that CPDC handles the twin cases in the way Fodor wants. When intentional behavior is described intentionally, it is often described in terms of the needs, wants, and intentions that produce it. Hence, for example, when a want gives rise to seeking behavior, there will typically be a conceptual connection between the content of that want and the content of that seeking behavior. Since the cognitivist attempts to account for the contents of our needs, wants, and intentions in terms of the contents of certain representational states (namely, representations playing need, want, and intention functional roles), this conceptual connection is preserved. Consequently, it will be conceptually necessary that if the representation ⟨I want an aluminum can⟩ (expressing the proposition that the thinker wants an aluminum can) gives rise to appropriate can-seeking behavior, then the effect will be the behavior of seeking aluminum (as opposed to twalum) cans. Similarly, it will be conceptually necessary that if the twin's representation ⟨I need to take my arthritis medicine⟩ (expressing the proposition that he needs to take arthritis medicine) leads to appropriate medicine-seeking behavior, the effect will be the behavior of seeking arthritis medicine rather than tharthritis medicine. Hence, according to CPDC, such differences in the effects of the twins' representations will not count in assessing the causal powers of those representations.

It should now be apparent what Methodological Individualism* says. I turn next to the question of whether it should be included in my characterization of the research framework of cognitive science.

Methodological Individualism* is clearly not honored by current TCD research in cognitive science. To see this, we need only carry out the following test: Consider two persons, Person 1 and Person 2, each of whom is entertaining a representation. These persons can be conceived of as actual and counterfactual twins or as distinct persons in this world—it doesn't matter. Call the representation bearers associated with the representations entertained by these persons RB_1 and RB_2 respectively. Now consider some theory of content determination T and ask the following question:

According to T, is it possible for RB_1 and RB_2 to be different in their individual ground, where this difference results in a difference in content, and yet have the same causal powers to produce relevant effects across nomologically possible contexts?

If the answer is "yes," then T violates Methodological Individualism*. If the answer is "no," then T satisfies Methodological Individualism*.

If we apply this test to the TCDs discussed in chapter 6, we find that the test is clearly violated in a number of cases. The point is probably obvious in the case of the causal historical approach and in the case of the biological function approach. Surprisingly, it is also true for the functional role approach, for the following reason: On the functional role approach, if two representations differ in their ground, they will differ in their functional roles within the subject; however, the functional roles of two representations can differ even if their strict causal powers are the same, for functional role depends not only on the possible causal *consequences* of the two representations but also on their causal *histories* (what caused them).[22]

We can thus formulate the following argument against Methodological Individualism*:

THE DESCRIPTIVE ARGUMENT AGAINST METHODOLOGICAL INDIVIDUALISM*

(1) Most current approaches to the problem of content determination for MRS violate the constraint of Methodological Individualism*.

(2) Therefore, cognitive science is not currently committed to Methodological Individualism*.

Of course, this descriptive argument is not the end of the story for Methodological Individualism*, for the now familiar reason that an advocate of the constraint can always resort to normative considerations to make his or her case. And this is, in fact, what Fodor (1987) does. In particular, he argues for inclusion of the constraint in the research framework of cognitive science by appealing to the aims of science and to the nature of scientific explanation in general. His argument can be reconstructed as follows:

FODOR'S NORMATIVE ARGUMENT FOR METHODOLOGICAL INDIVIDUALISM* (VERSION 1)

(1) Cognitive science is sometimes in the business of giving causal explanations by appeal to mental representations.

(2) Causal explanations require that the states and processes appealed to be type-individuated in terms of their strict causal powers.

(3) Hence, when giving such causal explanations, cognitive science ought to type-individuate mental representations in terms of their strict causal powers.

(4) One way to type-individuate mental representations is in terms of their content.

(5) Therefore, when giving causal explanations, cognitive science ought to type-individuate mental representations as described by their contents in terms of their strict causal powers.

(6) The content of a representation supervenes on its individual ground.

(7) Therefore, cognitive science ought to honor the constraint of Methodological Individualism*.

There are at least two difficulties with this argument, one of which can be easily repaired. I shall proceed by first fixing what can be easily fixed and then focusing on the less tractable problem. Before switching into critical mode, however. let me clarify why premises 5 and 6 are supposed to (and do) entail premise 7.

If premise 6 is true, then it follows that, so long as no content is multiply grounded, two representations that differ in their grounds will differ in their contents. If premise 5 is true, then when giving causal explanations cognitive science ought to be committed to the fact that if two representations differ in their contents they will differ in their causal powers. It follows that, when giving causal explanations, cognitive scientists ought to be committed to the fact that if two representations differ in their grounds and no content is multiply grounded they will differ in their causal powers. But this is just the constraint of Methodological Individualism*.

Where, now, do the difficulties lie? In the first place, compliance with premise 3 does not require compliance with premise 5; hence, it is possible to avoid the conclusion of the argument. There are at least two theoretically significant ways to type-individuate mental representations: in terms of their formal, computational properties (that is, as representation bearers) and in terms of their contents (and grounds). Type-individuation in terms of former *is*, by and large, type-individuation in terms of strict causal powers—at least in terms of strict causal powers that matter to cognitive science. Thus, one can accept the claim that cognitive science ought to type-individuate mental representations in terms of their strict causal powers without being forced to accept Methodological Individualism*.

It is instructive to contemplate what Fodor's response to this criticism would be. "Wait a minute!" he would say. "The fact that you can wiggle out of the conclusion in this way only shows that you have misunderstood my argument. We want to be able to make sense of the fact that mental representations have causal effects *in virtue of their content*. But this means that cognitive science must type-individuate mental representations in terms of their strict causal powers not only when mental representations are described formally but also when they are described semantically."

The response suggests that version 1 does not quite capture the essence of Fodor's argument. In particular, it looks as if what he really wants to argue is something like this:

FODOR'S NORMATIVE ARGUMENT FOR METHODOLOGICAL INDIVIDUALISM* (VERSION 2)

(1) Cognitive science is sometimes in the business of giving causal explanations by appeal to the *contents* of mental representations.

(2) Causal explanations require that the states and processes appealed to be type-individuated in terms of their strict causal powers.

(3) Hence, when giving such causal explanations, cognitive science ought to type-individuate mental representations in terms of their strict causal powers even when these representations are described by content.

(4) The content of a representation supervenes on its individual ground.

(5) Therefore, cognitive science ought to honor the constraint of Methodological Individualism*.

In short, according to Fodor. the only way to make sense of genuinely mental causation is to embrace Methodological Individualism*.

Version 2 represents what I take to be the strongest (in the sense of most charitable) possible reconstruction of Fodor's normative argument for Methodological Individualism*. Yet, a serious difficulty still remains that prevents the argument from making a successful case for its conclusion. This difficulty concerns the acceptability of premise 2.

Fodor (1987, p. 34) takes premise 2 to be true for the reason that "giving such explanations essentially involves projecting and confirming causal generalizations. And causal generalizations subsume the things they apply to in virtue of the causal properties of the things they apply to." However, this line of support for premise 2 is not convincing as it stands, for philosophers are by no means agreed on the nature of causal explanation and, in particular, on whether causal explanations require appeal to causal generalizations.

Davidson (1980) is a prominent supporter of the view that such generalizations are not necessary as components of causal explanations. Instead, he claims, "one way we can explain an event is by placing it in the context of its cause; cause and effect form the sort of pattern that explains the event, in a sense of 'explain' that we understand as well as any" (p. 10). That is, on Davidson's view, we can explain the occurrence of event E by simply pointing to its cause C. But this does not require citing a causal generalization, or even describing the explanandum and explanans events using the predicates that figure in such a causal generalization. Events are non-abstract particulars with multiple properties, and causality is an extensional relation that holds between events no matter how they are described. It is, of course, true that if two events are related as cause and effect, there must *be* a law that covers the case. But the point is that this law need not be *cited* in describing such a causal relation. And since one way to explain the occurrence of an event is simply to describe the causal relations in which it figures as effect, citing the relevant causal law is not necessary for purposes of explanation. Davidson (1980, p. 17) puts the point this way:

The most primitive explanation of an event gives its cause; more elaborate explanations may tell more of the story, or defend the singular causal claim by producing a relevant law or by giving reasons for believing such exists. But it is an error to think no explanation has been given until a law has been produced. Linked with these errors is the idea that singular causal statements necessarily indicate, by the concepts they employ, the concepts that will occur in the entailed law.

The implication of Davidson's view for Fodor's premise 2 is this: If Davidson is right about the nature of causal explanation, then we can appeal to the causal role of mental representations in giving such explanations *under any description whatsoever*. In particular, we do not need to type-individuate them in terms of their strict causal powers in order for the appeal to have explanatory force. Thus, given Davidson's view, premise 2 is false.[23]

Since I have not presented an argument in favor of Davidson's view, I cannot claim to have shown that premise 2 is, in fact, false. However, I do claim to have shown that it is controversial. And given that it is controversial and that Fodor provides very little support in its favor, I conclude that he has not succeeded in making a normative case for Methodological Individualism*.

As we have just seen, Fodor attempts to develop a normative case for including Methodological Individualism* in the research framework of cognitive science on the basis of general considerations concerning scientific explanation. Another (and, arguably, a better) way to approach the problem of weighing the pros and cons of the constraint is to focus on purely local considerations. That is, one might ask: What are the implications for explanation *in cognitive science* if Methodological Individualism* is or is not included within the framework of cognitive science? Before closing this section, I would like to provide a little food for thought along these lines.

The question of whether or not cognitive science ought to accept Methodological Individualism* appears to generate a dilemma, for it appears that certain assumptions dear to the heart of at least some cognitive scientists will be violated whether the constraint is accepted or rejected. Thus, it is not at all clear how the field ought to proceed.

The favored assumptions being violated are different in each case. Consider, first, the consequences of rejecting the constraint. If one adopts the

Peircian conception of representation, as I have suggested one ought to do, then x is a representation only if x has content and the content of x is significant for some currently existing interpreter. In the next chapter I will argue that, on the cognitivist approach, the significance of a mental representation for some subject S is ultimately determined by the set of computational processes and non-intentional behaviors that can result from the presence of that representation in S in conjunction with other possible representations. But if significance is determined in this way, then two representations cannot *differ* in their significance unless they differ computationally and behaviorally (in a non-intentional sense). Hence, they cannot differ in their significance unless they differ in their strict causal powers.

Assume, now, that we have two representations, R_1 and R_2, with different contents, where the content of each is determined in a way that violates the constraint of Methodological Individualism*. Then, although R_1 and R_2 differ in their grounds, these ground differences will not affect the causal powers of R_1 and R_2. R_1 and R_2 will have the same causal powers. In view of what I have just said about significance, the result will be that although the two representations differ in content these content differences will not be significant for the respective subjects of these representations. In short, it appears that if cognitive science permits representational grounds that violate the constraint of Methodological Individualism*, it will thereby be allowing for the possibility of representations with *insignificant content*.

That settles it, you might say. We clearly don't want insignificant content; hence, cognitive science should accept the constraint of Methodological Individualism*. Unfortunately, things are not so simple. It turns out that if cognitive science accepts the constraint, and if it also accepts a highly favored theory of reference for natural language, then the field will be faced with an equally undesirable outcome: There will be terms of natural language whose meaning we will not be able to grasp. The argument goes as follows.

On the causal theory of reference proposed by Kripke (1972) and Putnam (1975c), natural-kind terms such as 'aluminum' acquire their meaning by an act of pointing—for example "by 'aluminum' I mean any stuff like *this*, where what constitutes "stuff like this" may not be known at the time the term acquires its meaning and is a matter to be ultimately decided by science. The meaning of a natural-kind term will thus be tied to the world in which the term acquires its meaning. For example, here on

Earth 'aluminum' will refer to aluminum, whereas in a world just like Earth except for the fact that it has twalum (which looks similar but is atomically different) instead of aluminum, 'aluminum' will refer to twalum. Furthermore, if we buy into something like a possible-world semantics for natural language, then 'aluminum' here on Earth will have the intension "refers to aluminum in every possible world" and 'aluminum' on twalum-earth will have the intension "refers to twalum in every possible world."

Suppose now that we accept the standard cognitivist view of natural-language understanding. Then when a person understands a natural-kind term, he or she will form a mental representation of the meaning of that term. For the sake of discussion, let us refer to those representations of meaning as '⟨aluminum (aluminum)⟩' and '⟨aluminum (twalum)⟩', respectively. Suppose further that the contents of our mental representations can be grounded only in ways that respect the constraint of Methodological Individualism*. Then the representational grounds of ⟨aluminum (aluminum)⟩ and ⟨aluminum (twalum)⟩ will consist of either internal or external properties and relations that affect the strict causal powers of the representations in question.

Now consider our friends A and Counterfactual A, who live on Earth and Twalum-Earth, respectively, and who are ignorant of aluminum's and twalum's chemical structures and microproperties. If cognitive science accepts the causal theory of reference, the standard psycholinguistic story about natural-language understanding, *and* the constraint of Methodological Individualism*, then it will not have the resources to distinguish between how A represents the meaning of 'aluminum' here on Earth and how Counterfactual A represents the meaning of 'aluminum' on Twalum-Earth. For under the restriction to relevant effects the causal powers of ⟨aluminum (aluminum)⟩ and ⟨aluminum (twalum)⟩ will be the same; hence, by Methodological Individualism* their grounds will be the same. But if their grounds are the same, then their contents will be the same and neither A nor Counterfactual A will be able to represent the full meaning of 'aluminum' as it is used in their respective natural languages. In short, cognitive science will be stuck with the consequence of *ungraspable natural-language meaning*.

Since the logical path from acceptance or denial of Methodological Individualism* to one or other of the undesirable conclusions is mediated by various intermediate assumptions, one obvious way to escape the above dilemma is to deny one of the intermediate assumptions. But which one? All seem *prima facie* plausible, at least from a cognitivist perspective.[24]

A more creative escape route can be found in Fodor 1987. We might call it the having-your-cake-and-eating-it-too approach. The above dilemma is generated, in part, by the implicit assumption that the content of MRS is grounded in a way that either respects or fails to respect the constraint of Methodological Individualism*, but not both. But what if MRS has *two* kinds of content, as Fodor (1987) suggests: one whose ground respects the constraint and one whose ground does not respect the constraint? After all, Methodological Individualism* seems to make the most sense when applied to mental representations being invoked in causal explanations. But we might want to appeal to the contents of mental representations for other reasons. In any case, if there are these two kinds of content, then the first kind (Fodor's "narrow content") can be determined in a way that makes it fully significant, and the second kind ("broad content") can be determined in a way that allows for the representation of natural-kind-term meaning.[25] And, as a consequence, we will get everything we want.

Or so it would seem. But, on closer inspection, it is not so clear that we can have our cake and eat it too. According to our original dilemma, cognitive science is stuck either with insignificant mental content or with ungraspable natural language meaning. Fodor's two-tiered theory of mental content seems initially appealing because it offers us two kinds of content, one of which will serve each of the functions we are interested in. But, unfortunately, this doesn't solve the problem. Although the function of representing natural-kind-term meaning is handled so long as there is *some* aspect of the ground (and some aspect or part of content) that is anchored to the world, the function of significance is not so easily satisfied. Surely we want *all* forms of MRS content to be significant. In particular, if the representation of natural-kind meaning is to account for a subject's "understanding" of natural-kind terms, surely the representations invoked to do the job must be significant for the subject. But this is precisely where things break down on the Fodorian scheme. On Fodor's view of content, although the narrow contents of a subject's representations are fully significant, the broad contents are not. Hence, we are still left with one of our undesirable consequences—insignificant content.

Representations, including mental representations, have semantic properties in virtue of bearing some "ground" relation to their contents. In this chapter and the previous chapter, we have been considering whether cognitive science imposes any constraints on what can count as the ground of MRS-SEMPROP. To answer this question, we discussed what it means, formally, for a set of properties to constitute a ground, reviewed a number of prominent theories of content determination, and carefully assessed three proposed substantive constraints. For all that effort, our results (at least, our non-negative results) are extremely modest. They can be summed up as follows:

R2.3 (THE GROUND)   The ground of a mental representation is a property or relation that determines the representation's having the object (or content) it has.

(a) This ground is *naturalistic* (that is, nonsemantic and non-intentional).

?(b) This ground may consist of either internal or external factors. However, any such factor must satisfy the following restriction: If two token representations have different grounds and this ground difference determines a difference in content, then they must also differ in their causal powers to produce relevant effects across nomologically possible contexts.

8 Significance

On the Peircian general theory of representation we have adopted, something counts as a representation only if it has significance—that is, only if it has the power to produce an appropriate interpretant. We must now ask the following question: What kind of thing is the interpretant of a mental representation? In this chapter I shall try to articulate what I take to be cognitive science's answer to this question. First, however, I shall consider Peirce's response, for it turns out that Peirce, in struggling to come to grips with the problem of how representations can be significant for the subjects that have them, anticipated many of the key moves now being discussed by cognitive scientists.

8.1 Peirce's View

According to Peirce, a representation of any sort is significant for a person only if it has the power to produce a particular kind of mental effect in the mind of that person. Peirce calls this effect the "interpretant" of the representation. What distinguishes mental effects that are interpretants from those that are not is, roughly, this: A mental effect produced by a representation R in a subject S is an interpretant of R if it serves to mediate between S and the content or referent of R. More specifically, the interpretant must be related to both R and the subject S in such a way that the content or referent of R can make a difference to either the internal states or the behavior of S. This comes down to two things: the interpretant must be *connected to* the content or referent in some appropriate way as a result of the interpretation process, and the interpretant must be *psychologically efficacious* for S in an appropriate way (in other words, it must be able to make a difference to either the internal states or the external behavior of S in ways that depend on the content or referent of R).

Let us see how this works in the case of a nonmental representation. Suppose you gaze out the window and utter "It is snowing outside." This linguistic representation has significance for me, according to Peirce, because it gives rise to a certain kind of thought in my mind. This thought counts as an interpretant because it is both connected to the content of the utterance and psychologically efficacious for me in the appropriate ways. It is connected to the content of the utterance because the content of the thought includes the content of the utterance. (Either it is simply the thought that it is snowing outside or it is a more complex meta-level though* that the utterance "It is snowing outside" means that it is snowing outside—it is not clear which option Peirce had in mind.) It is psychologically efficacious for me in the appropriate ways because it is a thought that consists in or belongs to an act of *understanding*, and understanding is precisely the sort of mental state that has subsequent (and relevant) effects on my internal states and external behavior. That is, my understanding the utterance "It is snowing outside" can lead to other thoughts (for example, that I had better wear my boots when I go outside) and also to actions (such as my actually putting my boots on). This, in essence, is what makes a nonmental representation significant, according to Peirce. But what about mental representations? Here things get a bit more problematic, as Peirce himself realized.

Peirce believed—just as contemporary cognitive scientists do—that all thinking involves representations (6.338). But since something is a representation only if it has an interpretant, he—like cognitive science—was faced with the question of what interprets a mental representation. The most obvious possible answer to this question is that mental representations are interpreted in the same way as nonmental representations. But Peirce recognized that this obvious possible answer was highly problematic, in that since nonmental representations are interpreted by thoughts (in the mind of the interpreter) this view would lead to an infinite regress. The initial mental representation would be significant only if it had an interpretant, but that interpretant itself would involve a representation and, thus, would itself have to have an interpretant, which itself would involve a representation, and so on.

Such a regress is problematic, according to Peirce, because "if the series is broken off, the Sign, in so far, falls short of the perfect significant character" (2.92). This assessment seems far too rosy. If representation necessarily requires an interpretant and if interpretation is a black-or-white affair (that is, does not admit of degrees), then if the series is broken off *none* of the members of the series will be a genuine representation, for none will have a genuine interpretant. The last member of the series—call it R_n—will not be a genuine representation, since it will not be followed by anything and, hence, it will not have an interpretant. But if R_n. is not a representation, it will not be able to serve as the interpretant of R_{n-1} (since all interpretants are representations, on the view we are considering). As a consequence, R_{n-1} will not be a genuine representation either, and so on back up the line to the initial putative representation.

For ease of discussion, let me now distinguish two problems: the "regress problem" and "the significance problem." The regress problem is a problem in the sense of a troublesome fact, namely the fact that when we apply the account of significance that is natural for nonmental representation to the case of mental representation we get an infinite regress. The significance problem, in contrast, is a problem in the sense of a task whose adequate execution requires that certain constraints be met. In this case, it is the task of providing an account of the significance of mental representation in a way that avoids the regress problem. The first problem is, thus, to be avoided; the second is to be solved.

Peirce appears to have considered several alternative solutions to the significance problem during the course of his writings on sign interpretation. Two are of interest to us because they anticipate ideas to be found in the current literature of cognitive science.[1]

The first Peircian solution retains the representational character of the interpretant but tries to disarm it. The suggestion is that a putative representation need not be interpreted by an *actual* interpretant in order to be a genuine representation; a *potential* interpretant will suffice. More precisely, as Peirce puts it, the relation of sign and interpretant consists in "a *power* of the representamen to determine *some* interpretant to being a representamen of the same object" (1.542). Let us call this the "potential-interpretant solution." On this view, there is still an infinite series of representations. However, the regress is supposedly no longer vicious, because it consists primarily of potential rather than actual interpretants.

Whereas the potential-interpretant solution attempts to take the sting out of the regress of interpretants, the second solution Peirce entertained halts it altogether by proposing a new kind of interpretant which need not, itself, be interpreted. Recall that the infinite regress is generated in the first place when one assumes that the interpretant of a mental representation, like the interpretant of a nonmental representation, is a state involving another representation. Clearly, one way to avoid the regress is to find something that can function as an interpretant but which is not, itself, also representational and therefore in need of interpretation. In proposing his second solution, Peirce argues that there is only one possible viable candidate: "a modification of a person's tendencies toward action," or a "*habit-change*" (5.476). On this view, a mental representation is interpreted in virtue of producing a change in the subject's mental life which, in turn, changes his or her disposition to act. What kinds of changes? Peirce does not spell this out, but presumably not just any old changes will do. Rather, the modifications must be in the person's tendencies to act in ways *dependent on the content of the representation*, for only such modifications will make a representation of some object O not only a representation *for* the subject but also a representation *of O* for the subject. Thus, if I come to have a perceptual representation of my dog Sydney standing in the kitchen looking hungry, this representation will be interpreted, according to Peirce's second solution, by the following interpretant: a modification in my disposition to act in ways relevant to Sydney's being hungry. Precisely *how* my disposition to act will change in Sydney-relevant ways will depend, of course, on other aspects of my mental life—specifically, on what other representational states I am in (or, in folk psychological terms, what Sydney-relevant beliefs, attitudes, desires, etc. I have). But the mere fact that this disposition does change somehow or other in ways dependent on Sydney's actually standing in the kitchen looking hungry will suffice to interpret the representation in question.

Note that Peirce does not take the view that all mental representations must *immediately* be interpreted by a modification in our tendency to *external* action. Some mental representations may well be interpreted by interpretants that are themselves representational. Alternatively, the action that is modified may itself be a *mental* action, involving further mental representations. It is just that *ultimately* the regress must be halted by interpreting some representations in terms of a habit change, where the action in question is nonmental. As Peirce put it: "I do not deny that a concept, proposition, or argument may be a logical interpretant. I only insist that it cannot be the final logical interpretant for the reason that it is itself a sign of that very kind that has itself a logical interpretant. The habit alone, which though it may be a sign in some other way, is not a sign in that way in which that sign of which it is the logical interpretant is the sign." (5.491)

The three aspects of Peirce's treatment of the significance problem I have been discussing can be summarized as follows:

• his recognition that, if the interpretants of mental representations are the same kind of thing as the interpretants of non-mental representations, a regress will result

• his attempt to undercut (though not to eliminate) the regress by making it a regress of potential rather than actual interpretants ("solution 1")

• his attempt to eliminate the regress altogether by proposing that the interpretant of a mental representation is ultimately a habit change rather than another representational state ("solution 2").

8.2   The Regress Problem in Cognitive Science

Close analogues to all three of these aspects of Peirce's work can be found in the contemporary literature of cognitive science. Consider first the regress problem. Both Dennett (1978a) and Cummins (1983) worry about how a mental representation constitutes a representation for the subject that has it, and both recognize that a regress will result if the interpretant of a mental representation is taken to be either another representation or a representational state (which involves a representation). However, these treatments of the regress problem differ from each other in two important respects. First, although both predicate their discussion on the assumption that the interpretant of a mental representation is itself either a representation or a representational state, they have different conceptions of what this interpreting representation or representational state is like; hence, the generated regress takes somewhat different forms in the two cases. Second, Dennett and Cummins opt for quite different solutions to the problem. In effect, Cummins attempts to solve the problem by means of Peirce's potential-interpretant view, while Dennett embraces the solution which he (rightly) claims has been adopted by the cognitive science community, a solution very much akin to Peirce's "habit-change" hypothesis.

Dennett has probably done more than any other cognitive science philosopher to emphasize the important role interpretation plays in mental representation. As he puts it: "Nothing is intrinsically a representation of anything; something is a representation only *for* or *to* someone" (Dennett 1978a, pp. 101, 122). Here is Dennett's version of the regress argument, an argument which he claims "has bedeviled philosophers and psychologists for over two hundred years":

First, the only psychology that could possibly succeed in explaining the complexities of human activity must posit internal representations ... *second*, nothing is intrinsically a representation of anything; something is a representation only *for* or *to* someone; any representation or system of representations thus requires at least one *user* or *interpreter* of the representation who is external to it. Any such interpreter must have a variety of psychological or intentional traits ... : it must be capable of a variety of *comprehension*, and must have beliefs and goals (so it can *use* the representation to *inform* itself and thus assist it in achieving its goals). Such an interpreter is then a sort of homunculus.

Therefore, psychology *without* homunculi is impossible. But psychology *with* homunculi is doomed to circularity or infinite regress, so psychology is impossible. (Dennett 1978b, pp. 121–122)

As in the case of Peirce's treatment of the regress problem, what produces the regress in Dennett's version is the assumption that the interpretant of a mental representation is a representational state and, hence, involves a mental representation. The particular form the regress takes in Dennett's "homuncular version" is due to the fact that the interpretant is specifically conceived of as an act of *understanding* located in the "mind" of a homunculus (an interpreter internal to the subject but not identical with the subject). And, since on the cognitivist approach such an act of understanding will involve at least one representation, and this second representation must itself be interpreted, we get a regress of mental representations in smaller and smaller homunculi, each located in the "mind" of the homunculus (or person) before it (him or her) in the series.

The regress in Cummins' (1983) discussion of the interpretation of MRS takes a quite different form. Like Dennett, Cummins recognizes that cognitive science must account for the fact that mental representations are interpreted by the system that has them. However, according to Cummins, the research program of cognitive science has focused its explanatory energies on formulating hypotheses in information-processing terms, including representational hypotheses, without attempting to provide such an account. Cummins thus takes it upon himself to offer some suggestions as to how such an account might go.

If I understand Cummins correctly, the core of his idea comes to this: An information-processing representation R_1 becomes a representation *for* the subject S only if S is capable of representing in another representation, R_2, the semantics of R_1. In other words, Cummins takes the view that in order to be explanatorily adequate an information-processing representation must not only be provided with content by means of a ground, it must also have an interpretant in the system that has it. And this interpretant will be another representation—specifically, a representation of the semantics of the first representation.

Let us now consider how this kind of interpretant leads to its own form of regress. To represent the semantics of R_1, R_2 must express something like the proposition that R_1 represents O, where 'O' is replaced by whatever it is that the semantics of R_1 assigns to R_1 as its representational object. Just to make things more concrete, imagine that the mental representation system is something like the predicate calculus with an English vocabulary and that R_1 represents my favorite representational object, my dog Sydney. From a theoretical perspective, we might describe this situation thus:

$R_1 = \langle \text{Sydney} \rangle$.

(The representation R_1 is thus like a constant or a proper name.) Then R_2 might represent the proposition that R_1 represents Sydney like this:

$R_2 = \langle R_1 \text{ REPRESENTS Sydney} \rangle$.

In order to do its job properly, R_2 must be a genuine, full-blooded *representation*, not just a representation$_0$. This is because if it is to be able to function as an interpretant, it must be suitably related to both the representational object of R_1 and the system for which R_1 is a representation. In other words, it must not only represent$_0$ the fact that R_1 represents Sydney; it must also have its own significance for the system that has it.[2]

The big question is: What makes R_2 a representation for S? Cummins would have to say that R_2 is a representation for S because S is capable of representing (in another propositional state, R_3) the semantics of R_2—in other words, because S is capable of having a representation (again, with significance for S) of the form

$R_3 = \langle R_2 \text{ REPRESENTS (that } R_1 \text{ REPRESENTS Sydney)} \rangle$.

But what makes R_3 a representation for S? The story should now be familiar. The state R_3 will be a representation for S only if S is capable of having a *another* representation, of the form

$R_4 = \langle R_3 \text{ REPRESENTS (that } R_2 \text{ REPRESENTS (that } R_1$
$\qquad\qquad\qquad\qquad\qquad\qquad \text{REPRESENTS Sydney} \rangle$.

Clearly, we have a regress on our hands.

8.3 An Inadequate Solution

Cummins (1983, p. 114) acknowledges the problem quite cheerfully but thinks it does not pose any serious difficulties:

... a system powerful enough to represent the semantics of sigma [e.g., R_1] in sigma' [e.g., R_2] might be powerful enough to represent the semantics of sigma' as well (in sigma" [e.g., R_3]). Again, it seems that possession of a recipe—a general capacity—for representing the semantics of any arbitrary state demonstrates the system's "understanding" of its semantics as well as possession of the actual representations. Indeed, since the latter is evidently impossible, it is hard to see how one could ask for more than such a general capacity.

In advocating that the interpretant of a mental representation is itself a representation of a sort, Cummins is clearly stuck with the regress. Since he cannot avoid it, he is forced to disarm it in some way. His proposed solution, like Peirce's first solution, is to make it a regress of potential rather than actual interpretants.

There are two reasons why I think the potential-interpretant solution will not work for Cummins' interpretants.

First, if the representational objects of the representations in question are represented in such a way as to reveal their internal structure, then, as we ascend the hierarchy, the requisite representation bearers will get longer and longer until they exceed the limitations of the medium. Certainly, if the mental representation system is anything like our examples above, we will soon run out of available memory. This fact is relevant because making the regress a regress of potential interpretants does not mean that we can simply forget about the actualization of higher members of the hierarchy. If these interpretants are genuinely potential, it has to be the case that the system could in fact realize them if required (at least, one at a time). And this is precisely what it seems the system could not do, after a point. Perhaps there is some clever way of surmounting this difficulty. However, if there is not, it would appear that the finitude of the medium of our mental representations will render even Cummins' potential hierarchy impossible. And if there is a limit beyond which the hierarchy cannot be generated, then, just as in Peirce's version, none of the representations in the hierarchy will constitute a representation for the system that has it.

A similar though slightly different argument holds for Dennett's homuncular-style interpretants. Let Q_1 be the representation in need of interpretation. Then the first homuncular state interpreting Q_1 will be a state of understanding that Q_1 represents O. By hypothesis, this will involve some computational relation to a representation Q_2 whose object will be the proposition that Q_1 represents O. Q_2 will itself have to be understood by a smaller homunculus, and the representation Q_3 involved in this second act of homuncular understanding will be a representation of the proposition that Q_2 represents that Q_1 represents O, and so on. Thus, just as in Cummins' version, if the representations represent the propositions in question in something like canonical form, the representation bearers will get longer and longer, and again the medium will eventually be taxed beyond its limits, halting even a regress of potential representations. In the homuncular case, in fact, these limits will probably make themselves felt much sooner, because as the representation bearers get longer and longer the mind/brains of the homunculi will, of necessity, get smaller and smaller! Clearly, things cannot go on this way indefinitely.

The second difficulty with Cummins' attempted solution does not manifest itself in either Peirce's or Dennett's version. Recall that, on the Peircian account, the function of the interpretant is to mediate between the subject S and the object O of the initial representation in such a way that the nature of O can make a difference to the internal states and the external behavior of S. This involves establishing a connection between S and O and, somehow, making that connection psychologically efficacious with respect to S. This is handled in both the Peirce version and the Dennett version by positing an interpretant that is a representational *state* rather than simply a representation—specifically, a state of understanding. If we construe such an act of understanding as involving two components, (1) a relation U between the subject and another representation Q_1 and (2) the representation Q_1 itself, then each component has a necessary job to perform in satisfying the function of an interpretant. What establishes a connection between S and O is that some "part" of the interpretant representation Q_1 *represents$_o$* O. In the above example, if Q_2 has the form

$\langle Q_1$ represents $O \rangle$,

the connection between S and O is established by the component $\langle O \rangle$. In other words, the function of connecting S and O is performed by component 2, the interpretant representation itself. However, what is responsible for the fact that Q_2 makes a difference to the mental life and the external behavior of S is component 1, specifically the fact that the relation between S and Q_2 is a relation in virtue of which S—in folk psychological terms— *understands* Q_1. Understanding is precisely the kind of state that allows the content of one's understanding to influence the rest of one's mental life and external behavior. Of course, the U relation is treated as primitive, and is, hence, completely mysterious. Nevertheless, it does succeed in making both Peirce's and Dennett's interpretants psychologically efficacious.

This aspect of the interpretant is entirely missing from Cummins' account. His putatively interpreting representations (e.g., R_2 and up) satisfy the connection function but are completely inefficacious psychologically. A Cummins-style interpretant can do nothing but refer to the representation being interpreted; there is nothing about it, on Cummins' account, that allows it to do the job an interpretant is supposed to do (that is, to mediate in a psychologically effective way between the object of the representation and the system that has that representation).

8.4 Cognitive Science's Solution

How does cognitive science handle the problem of significance for mental representations? There seems to be something like a relatively official, widely endorsed position on the question—a position which is very similar to Peirce's second (habit-change) solution and which stems quite naturally from the cognitivist commitment to the assumption that the cognitive mind is not only a representational device but also a computational one. Here are two expressions of this position from the recent literature of cognitive science, one from Dennett's (1978) discussion of the regress problem and the other from Rumelhart and Norman's (1988) review paper on representation in memory.

Dennett (1978a, p. 102) puts the point this way:

In a computer, a command to dig goes straight to the shovel, as it were, eliminating the comprehending and obeying middleman. Not *straight* to the shovel, of course, for a lot of sophisticated switching is required to get the right command going to the right tools, and for some purposes it is illuminating to treat parts of this switching machinery as analogous to the displaced shovellers, subcontractors and contractors. The beauty of it all, and its importance for psychology, is precisely that it promises to solve Hume's problem [i.e., the regress problem] by giving us a model of vehicles of representation that function without exempt agents for whom they are ploys.

In the introduction to their paper reviewing current conceptions of representation in memory, Rumelhart and Norman (1988) make the point that anything that is represented can be represented in multiple ways. For example, the relation of being taller than can be represented by means of a propositional representation such as 'TALLERTHAN (A,B)', by line length in a diagram, or by a numerical value.[3] This example is followed by the following remarks:

> There is ... one more important aspect of a representational system that must be considered: the processes that operate upon the representations.... Note that the representations within the representing world did not carry their meaning without the assistance of some process that could make use of and interpret the representational structures. Thus, if height is to be represented by line length, there must exist some process capable of comparing line lengths. If height is to be represented by numbers, then there must be some processes that can operate upon those numbers according to the appropriate rules of mathematics and the rules established by the choice of representation. Similarly, the representational system established by the use of formulas from the predicate calculus requires interpretation and evaluation. In all these cases, the processes that evaluate and interpret the representations are as important as the representations themselves.   (p. 517)[4]

Roughly speaking, what both Dennett (1978) and Rumelhart and Norman (1988) are suggesting is that, from a cognitivist perspective, the interpretant of a mental representation consists of the set of computational processes contingent upon entertaining that representation. As we might expect, to get a more detailed understanding of this suggestion requires that we consider the conventional and connectionist cases separately.

In describing the computational operations of conventional computers, it is useful to distinguish between what Newell (1980) calls a *process* and the *behavior of a process*. By a "process" Newell means a *type* of computational operation or a series of computational operations of the sort specified by an algorithm. Processes of this sort are typically defined over variable inputs. Since, ultimately, I will be using the term 'process' in a broader sense, let me refer to such Newellian processes as *determinable processes*.

Determinable processes are defined over variable inputs; thus, they can be executed in many different ways, depending on how those variables are specified. In the case of a simple program, this might simply mean that different items would be stored and manipulated. In a more complex program with a conditional branching structure, the operations themselves might be different in nature. It is these different modes of execution that Newell has in mind by the "behavior of a process." To clearly distinguish such behaviors from external behaviors, I shall talk about *execution behaviors of a process*.

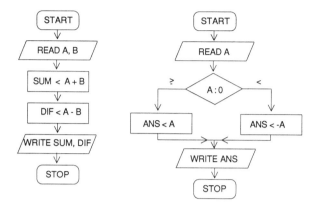

Figure 8.1
Flow charts for two simple mathematical algorithms. The program on the left adds and substracts two numbers, A and B. The program on the right finds the absolute value of a given number, A. (From Wilde 1973. Reprinted by permission of Prentice-Hall, Inc.)

Consider, for example, the simple addition and subtraction program in figure 8.1. The determinable process in this case is simply the sequence of operations depicted by the flow chart, where the numbers to be added and substracted are represented by two variables, A and B. An execution behavior of this determinable process consists in the very same sequence of operations defined over particular numbers rather than variables. Note that we are not yet dealing with a sequence of spatiotemporal events, for a given execution behavior of a process can be instantiated at many different times and in many different places.

The branching case is also shown in figure 8.1. Executing the algorithm for finding the absolute value of a single number results in two kinds of variation: variation in the specific numbers being stored and manipulated (as in the addition and substraction algorithm) and variation in the specific operations being performed. This is because if the input is greater than or equal to 0 the program places the number itself in the storage area labeled 'ANS', whereas if the input is less than 0 the program places the negation of the number in ANS.

We can now formulate cognitive science's position on the nature of the interpretant for a mental representation in a conventional machine:

THE CONVENTIONAL SIGNIFICANCE THESIS   If the mind were a conventional computational device, the interpretant of a mental representation R would consist in the set of all possible execution behaviors of the various determinable processes defined for R, given the presence of R in the appropriate computational location (for example, working memory) and the presence of any other, relevant, supplemental representations.

Let us see what this solution of the significance problem comes to in a particular case. As my example, I will again explore certain aspects of Stephen Kosslyn's model of how humans create and manipulate mental images. Recall that Kosslyn posits three kinds of representational structures (surface matrices, literal encodings, and propositional encodings) and a host of processes defined over these representations (including processes that generate the surface display from the deep representations and processes that can interpret and transform the surface display once it is generated). The processes posited by Kosslyn's theory are our concern at present. Consider, for example, the operation FIND. According to table 1.1, FIND takes as its input the name of a sought part (and, presumably, some already-generated surface matrix) and yields as its output either ⟨LOCATE⟩ and the Cartesian coordinates of the part on the image or ⟨NOT LOCATE⟩. With respect to Newell's distinction, FIND is being described here as a determinable process rather than as an execution behavior of a process. However, specific execution behaviors of FIND can easily be generated by simply supplying the determinable process with particular types of input. Thus, if we were to supply FIND with a surface matrix of my car viewed from the side and facing left and with ⟨HAT⟩ as the name of the sought-after part, it would do its thing and produce the output ⟨NOT LOCATE⟩. If we were to supply it with the same surface matrix but the name of the sought-after part ⟨TIRE⟩, it would produce the output ⟨LOCATE⟩ plus the Cartesian coordinates corresponding to the locations of the tires on the image. Each of these distinct executions of the operation counts as a distinct behavior of the determinable process FIND.

Within any given conventional computational system, there are a finite number of determinable processes defined for any given kind of representation. For example, in Kosslyn's model FIND, PUT, RESOLUTION, REGENERATE, LOOKFOR, SCAN, ZOOM, PAN, and ROTATE are all defined over surface matrices, whereas PICTURE and IMAGE are not. Any *particular* kind of surface matrix, such as the surface representation of my car viewed from the side and facing left, will obviously have the power to produce only specific sorts of execution behaviors in these various determinable processes.

Note, however, that many of the determinable processes defined for a given representation R may require the presence of other data representations in addition to R in order for the determinable process to be executed. For example, although FIND is defined for surface matrices, it cannot be executed (and result in a behavior of the process FIND) unless it also has as an input the name of a sought-after part.

It should now be clear what the distinction between determinable process and execution behavior comes to in Kosslyn's model. What functions as the interpretant for, say, a surface representation of my car? According to the conventional significance thesis, the interpretant of a Kosslyn-style surface representation of my car in Kosslyn's model consists of the set of all possible execution behaviors of the various determinable processes defined for that representation (namely FIND, PUT, RESOLUTION, REGENERATE, LOOKFOR, SCAN, ZOOM, PAN, and ROTATE), given all the possible combinations of that representation and any relevant supplemental data representations. Thus, for example, the subset of execution behaviors for FIND will include the execution of FIND given the surface representation of my car plus ⟨TIRE⟩, the execution of FIND given the surface representation of my car plus ⟨HAT⟩, the execution of FIND given the surface representation of my car plus ⟨STEERING WHEEL⟩, and so on.

Conventional computational devices make use of two broad classes of representations: data representations and process (or program) representations. In discussing the conventional conception of the interpretant, I have thus far mentioned only data representations. It should be pointed out, however, that the conventional significance thesis applies to process representations as well. In other words, we can use it to generate an interpretation not only for the data representations that the process FIND operates on (such as the surface representation of my car) but also for the representation ⟨FIND⟩ itself. In this case, we must ask not what representations the determinable process FIND is defined for, but what determinable processes are defined for it.

In a conventional general-purpose device, these processes will be, first and foremost, the determinable processes performed by the control unit when it executes a program: reading an instruction from memory, determining the location in memory of any data specified by that instruction, executing the instruction, and writing the result into the desired memory location. Let us call these "READ", "LOCATE", "EXECUTE", and "WRITE", respectively. Clearly, these processes will give rise to different execution behaviors, given different process representations (plus any other appropriate, supplemental representations) as input. In particular, when the expression ⟨FIND⟩ is operated on by each of these processes, a distinct set of execution behaviors will result. The execution behaviors that result from running READ, LOCATE, EXECUTE, and WRITE (and any other processes defined on ⟨FIND⟩) with ⟨FIND⟩ as *input* (plus any other appropriate, supplemental representations) constitute the interpretant of ⟨FIND⟩, according to the conventional significance thesis. Note that this view is only a slight elaboration of the standard notion of interpretation in computer science, which according to Newell (1980, p. 158) is "the act of accepting as input an expression that designates a process and then performing that process."

Thus far I have been talking about what the interpretant of a mental representation would be if the mind were a conventional machine. What about the connectionist case?

Unfortunately, because conventional and connectionist machines compute differently, there is no direct analogue of the conventional significance thesis. The chief difficulty is that, as connectionist networks are standardly described, the distinction between a determinable process and the execution behaviors of that process does not apply. Nor does it make sense to talk about processes "defined for" a representation. Nevertheless, entertaining a representation in a connectionist network clearly has computational consequences which play the same sort "interpreting" role in these networks as do the execution behaviors associated with a representation in a conventional machine. Thus, to understand what a connectionist interpretant is, we must get clear on the nature of these "interpreting" computational consequences.

As was discussed in sections 3.4 and 5.2, entertaining a representation in a connectionist network is computationally realized by the activation of a node or a pattern of nodes. I shall begin by considering the simpler case of local representation. Suppose that in a particular network, CN, entertaining representation R is computationally realized by activation of node N. Then associated with this activation will be various possible computational consequences whose precise nature will depend on the computational

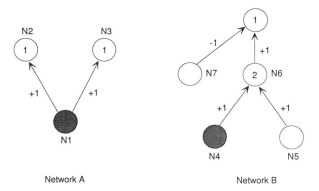

Figure 8.2
Two simple connectionist networks. In Network A the computational consequences of N1's
activation are causally dependent solely on that activation. In contrast, some of the
computational consequences of N4's activation require activation of other nodes as well.

characteristics of the network CN (that is, its pattern of connectivity and
the transition and output functions of all of its nodes) and on what other
nodes are activated.

Consider, for example, network A in figure 8.2. Suppose that entertaining representation R is identical with N_1's being activated to threshold.
Entertaining R will then have the following computational consequences:
A signal will be sent from N_1 to N_2, N_2 will be activated, a signal will be
sent from N_1 to N_3, and N_3 will be activated. Note that in this case the
computational consequences of N_1's activation are causally dependent
solely on that activation.

Network B depicts a slightly more complicated case. Here, suppose that
entertaining representation R is identical with N_4's being activated to
threshold. Then some of the computational consequences of N_4's activation require not only activation of N_4 but also activation (or lack of
activation) of other nodes. In particular, whereas activation of N_4 alone
will cause a signal to travel from N_4 to N_6, N_6 will not be activated unless
it also receives a signal from N_5. Furthermore, once N_6 has been activated
and a signal has been sent from N_6 to N_8, N_8 will not be activated unless
N_7 is dormant.

On the basis of these two examples, we can now say what it means for
something to be a possible computational consequence of entertaining a
local representation in a connectionist network. In general, the computa-

tional consequences of concern are signals' traversing along a link and nodes' being activated. In view of this restriction, the question of interest is this: When is a signal's traversal or a node's activation a computational consequence of some particular node's activation? Let me propose the following:

Given a node N in a network CN, a signal traversal or node activation X is a *possible computational consequence of N's activation in CN* just in case there exists some pattern of activity in CN such that activation of N given that pattern of activity will result in X.

Thus far we have been considering only local representation, but a moment's reflection will reveal that if we take N to range over sets of nodes as well as over single nodes the definition works just as well. Let us therefore revise the definition by substituting "set of nodes" for "node" in the initial clause. The connectionist version of the significance thesis can then be formulated as follows.

THE CONNECTIONIST SIGNIFICANCE THESIS   If the cognitive mind/brain were a connectionist network, the interpretant of a mental representation R would consist in the set of possible computational consequences of activation of the node or set of nodes that computationally realizes entertaining R.

We now have some understanding of both conventional and connectionist interpretants. Is there a way of formulating a significance thesis that will cover both cases? To do so we need a set of generic terms that will cover both the conventional and the connectionist cases. We have already used one such term: the expression 'entertaining a representation', which is intended to apply to both the tokening of a data structure in some active memory buffer and the activation of a representational node or set of nodes. What we need, in addition, is a counterpart term that will cover both the execution behaviors of a process defined for a given representation in a conventional computer and the possible computational consequences of activation of a representational node in a connectionist network. Let me suggest the term *determinate computational process*. The generalized significance thesis will then read as follows:

R2.4 (THE INTERPRETANT)   Mental representations are significant for the person in whose mind they "reside." The interpretant of a mental representation R for some subject S consists of the set of all possible determinate computational processes contingent upon entertaining R in S.

We should now be tolerably clear as to what the cognitivist solution to the significance problem is. The next question to be raised is this: Is the cognitivist solution satisfactory? I shall divide this question into two sub-questions: Can an interpretant of a cognitivist sort do what an interpretant is supposed to do? Does the cognitivist solution to the significance problem really avoid the regress problem?

To be an interpretant I of a representation R, something must (a) be producible by R and (b) be related to both the system S and R in such a way that by means of I the object or content of R can make a difference to the internal states or the external behavior of S. Clearly, the set of possible determinate computational processes contingent upon entertaining R satisfies condition a, for there exist "conditions of interpretation" the satisfaction of which are sufficient for any of the processes in the set to occur. In the case of a conventional machine, the conditions of interpretation are that R and any other necessary supplemental representations be input into each of the processes defined on R. In the case of a connectionist network, the conditions of interpretation are that the node or nodes that realize R's being entertained are activated and any other relevant nodes are either activated or not activated, depending upon what is required to cause the relevant signal traversal or node activation. Hence, I is producible by R in the relevant sense.

Satisfaction of condition b is somewhat less straightforward, for it requires both (i) that I be appropriately connected to the referent or content of R and (ii) that I be psychologically efficacious for S in an appropriate way. Since I, on the cognitivist view, is a *set* (of possible determinate computational processes), satisfaction of condition b comes down to this: (i') that each member of I be somehow connected to the referent or content of R and (ii') that each member of I be psychological efficacious for S in the sense that it can make a difference to either the internal states or the external behavior of S in an appropriate way.

Solutions to the significance problem that retain the representational character of the interpretant (as Peirce's first solution and Cummins' solution do) tend to run into difficulty primarily with condition ii, for either they avoid addressing the problem of psychological efficacy (by resting content with an inert interpreting representation) or they try to ensure psychological efficacy by fiat (by positing that the interpretant is a state of understanding). The situation is exactly reversed in the case of the more "procedural" cognitivist solution. Psychological efficacy is the name of the game: the interpretant can, obviously, make a difference to the internal states and the external behavior of S, because the interpretant consists of a set of possible determinate computational processes in S, and actualization of any of these possible determinate computational processes either involves or gives rise to a change in the internal states and external behavior of S.

But what is it about the possible determinate computational processes that connects them, in any way, with the referent or the content of R? The answer to this question was suggested in my discussion of Peirce's habit-change solution. The possible determinate computational processes associated with R are connected with the referent or content of R because, in some sense, they *depend* on that referent or content.[5]

Thus, consider again a Kosslyn-style surface representation of my car. This is a representation of my actual car as it looks from the side facing left. One of the execution behaviors associated with this representation is the result of executing the process FIND in conjunction with the name of the sought-after part ⟨TIRE⟩. The process will be executed in such a way that the result is ⟨LOCATE⟩ plus the Cartesian coordinates of the locations of the tire images on the car image. This execution behavior depends on the referent of the representation (namely, my actual car and how it, in fact, looks when viewed from the side facing left), because there *are* tires visible when my car is viewed from the side and they are located in places analogous to the locations specified for the image. If the execution of this process were to result in the output ⟨NOT LOCATE⟩ or the output ⟨LOCATE⟩ with Cartesian coordinates corresponding to the location of the steering wheel on my actual car, the execution behavior in question would not depend on the nature of the referent of the representation.

What makes the possible determinate computational processes associated with a representation R depend on the referent or content of R in this way? The design of the system, of course. In the case of an ordinary computer, this design is imposed by the rationality of the designer. In the case of a biological system, such as the human mind/brain, it is imposed, first, by the evolutionary necessity of acting in ways that suit the objective nature of the environment, and, second, by the feedback processes built into the process of learning (Simon 1981a, 1981b).

Prima facie, then, the cognitivist solution seems to fare quite well. The possible determinate computational processes contingent upon R in S are producible by R, connected to the content of R in an appropriate way, and psychologically efficacious for S in an appropriate way. Unfortunately, all is not yet smooth sailing. Construing the interpretant as a set of possible determinate computational processes *seems* to be a way of avoiding positing another representation as an interpretant, yet in a complex system many if not most of the possible determinate computational processes for any given representation will themselves involve other representations. As Dennett says, the command to dig does not really go straight to the shovel. When FIND outputs ⟨LOCATE⟩ or ⟨NOT LOCATE⟩, it is quite obviously outputting representations.

Does this mean that we are again faced with a regress? I think not, but the question is a difficult one. Here are my current thoughts on the matter.

Let us call the potentially troublesome representations the *interpretant representations* of R. I am not convinced that the interpretant representations of R must be fully significant representations (rather than representations$_0$) to play their part in the interpretant of R, for it seems that, even though many of the possible determinate computational processes that interpret a given representation R do involve other representations, their interpretive function *does not rest on this fact*. All that is required for these possible determinate computational processes to function as an interpretant is that R has the power to produce them, that they be connected to the referent or content of R in virtue of depending on that referent or content, and that they be psychologically efficacious in an appropriate way; and all these functions can be accomplished without the interpretant representations, being representations in the full sense of the word. It seems to suffice, in fact, for the possible determinate computational processes to involve representations$_0$ rather than full-blooded, Peircian representations. But, of course, if representations$_0$ will do, there is no regress problem. And even if it is necessary that interpretant representations be fully significant, the regress might still be avoided in most cases. Here again Peirce was on the right track with his habit-change solution. Recall that, on Peirce's view, the interpretant of a mental representation consists of a modification of a person's tendencies toward action as a result of the presence of the representation. However, the dispositional change that constitutes the interpretant of any given mental representation need not always be a change in the subject's disposition to act externally; dispositional changes with respect to mental action also count. However, if the regress is to be halted, some representations must be interpreted by changes in the subject's disposition to external action. To revert to Dennett's metaphor: eventually we must get to the shovel if a regress of inner homunculi is to be avoided.

The analogue in the case of the cognitivist solution is that it is perfectly fine for the possible determinate computational processes of many of our representations to themselves involve representations so long as, eventually, *some* of the processes of *some* of the representations issue in non-intentional, external outputs. Actually, that statement is not quite strong enough. Rather, what is required to avoid a regress of interpreting representations is that every full-blooded representation must be connected by some computational path—a path that can involve as many steps as you please—to some representation whose interpretant (i.e., possible determinate computational processes) can issue directly in a non-intentional, external behavior. What one cannot have, in other words, are full-blooded representations defined solely for processes that function exclusively in self-contained computational loops. In such a loop, every representation would be associated with possible determinate computational processes that involved other representations.

I tentatively conclude, then, that the cognitivist solution can handle the regress problem, and that (in that respect, at least) it is a satisfactory solution to the problem of the significance of mental representations.[6]

One final note to allay a possible confusion. The cognitivist solution to the problem of significance is roughly similar to a functional-role theory of content determination. Does this mean that, despite the pains I have taken to distinguish them, significance is nothing but content after all? Of course not. The *property* of R's having a certain content is clearly distinct from the *property* of R's content's having significance for S. What is the same (or roughly the same) if one adopts a functional-role TCD is the supervenience base of each of these properties. That is, if one adopts a functional-role TCD, then what grounds R's content will, as a matter of fact, overlap with what determines R's having significance for S. More specifically, if we distinguish between the backward-looking aspects of R's functional role (the computational processes leading up to tokenings of R) and the forward-looking aspects (the computational processes that issue from tokenings of R), then what determines the significance of R will be roughly equivalent to the forward-looking aspect of R's functional role. As a consequence, if R has content, it will *ipso facto* have significance for S (Loewer 1982).

This consequence does not, of course, follow for most of the other TCDs. For example, on a causal historical view or an indicator view, it is quite possible for a representation R to have content without having any significance for S. This is because R's content is determined solely by R's backward-looking relations, whereas R's significance for S is determined by R's forward-looking relations, and clearly the one can exist without the other.[7] The same is true on the structural isomorphism view, for there the content of R is determined by the intrinsic structure of R's representation bearer and a representation bearer with intrinsic structure can exist without being associated with any possible determinate computational processes.

9 The Methodological Assumptions

The end of the road is almost in sight. My goal has been to reconstruct the research framework of cognitive science by articulating the four components of that framework: the domain-specifying assumptions, the basic questions, the substantive assumptions, and the methodological assumptions. Thus far, I have dealt with the first three of these components; in this chapter I will consider the fourth. Before doing so, however, I must clarify what I call the "explanatory strategy" of cognitive science, namely how the substantive assumptions are brought to bear to answer the basic questions of the field. I will do this in section 9.1. In the remaining sections I will lay out a number of methodological assumptions that guide or ought to guide research in cognitive science. Most of these are relatively straightforward and will require little elaboration. These unproblematic assumptions are collected in section 9.2. Three more controversial assumptions will be discussed in sections 9.3 and 9.4.

9.1 The Explanatory Strategy of Cognitive Science

Cognitive science seeks to explain the human cognitive capacities by reconceptualizing them as a system of computational and representational capacities. That is the force of the linking assumptions C1 and R1. I have been using the term 'information processing capacity' to refer to a capacity that is both computational and representational. Thus, C1 and R1 together amount to this:

CLA (THE COMBINED LINKING ASSUMPTION)   The human cognitive capacities consist, to a large extent, of a system of information-processing capacities.

Why the qualification "to a large extent"? Basic ordinary cognitive capacities (see section 2.2) come in three varieties: input capacities, output capacities, and purely mental capacities. An important feature of both input and output capacities is that they reach out into the world. Input capacities begin with an ordinary object or state that is perceived; output capacities end with the action that is intended. In contrast, information-processing capacities of the sort referred to in the combined linking assumption (or what I shall refer to as "*narrow* information processing capacities") are purely mental, involving a transformation from one mental representation to another. Because of this difference in scope, the identification between ordinary input and output capacities, on the one hand, and

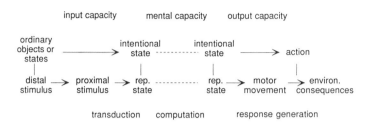

ORDINARY COGNITIVE CAPACITIES

Figure 9.1
How the human cognitive capacities, as ordinarily construed, map onto the human
information-processing capacities.

narrow information-processing capacities, on the other hand, can, at most,
be partial.

If ordinary cognitive capacities are not information-processing capacities *tout court*, then what aspect or component of an ordinary capacity do
cognitive scientists take to be an information-processing capacity? A detailed answer to this question for each individual cognitive capacity can
come only from empirical inquiry. In general, and roughly speaking, however, cognitive scientists seem to assume the mapping depicted in figure 9.1.
I have coined the term 'broad information-processing capacity' to refer
to the extended input-output sequences in which narrow information-
processing capacities are embedded. Thus, a broad, input information-
processing capacity takes as input a distal physical stimulus and yields
as output a representational state, whereas a broad, output information-
processing capacity takes as input a representational state and yields as
output a motor movement with certain characteristic environmental consequences. The view, then, is that ordinary input and output capacities are
identified with *broad* input or output information-processing capacities,
respectively. Such broad capacities consist of three components: an environmental component, a peripheral component (transduction or response
generation), and a narrow information-processing component. The narrow information-processing component maps onto the portion of the
ordinary input and output capacity whose exercise occurs "in the head,"
minus a little bit.[1] This little bit, which is not isolated by common sense,

corresponds to sensory transduction on the input side and to motor-movement generation on the output side.

The combined linking assumption is the cornerstone of the explanatory strategy of cognitive science. Cognitive scientists are interested in explaining the human cognitive capacities. The explanatory strategy they have adopted to arrive at the desired explanations is, in broad outline, as follows:

THE EXPLANATORY STRATEGY OF COGNITIVE SCIENCE   To explain any cognitive capacity C:

(1) Redescribe C as a broad information-processing capacity.

(2) Attempt to explain this broad-information processing capacity by the following steps:

(a) Analyze it into environmental, peripheral, and narrow information-processing components (as in figure 9.1).

(b) Presuppose or borrow accounts of the environmental and peripheral components of the capacity.

(c) Attempt to develop an empirically well supported explanation of the relevant narrow information-processing capacity.

I have described the explanandum as simply a cognitive capacity C. In fact, however, as the reader should by now be well aware, I take the explanandum of cognitive science to be far more specific than that. Explananda, on my view, are not simply things or states of affairs, but questions about these things or states of affairs. Different sorts of questions can be asked about the human cognitive capacities, and these questions can focus on different sorts of properties of these capacities. As we saw in chapter 2, cognitive scientists pursuing the subsidiary research program of ANTCOG are interested in answering four types of basic questions (Q1–Q4) about each of the cognitive capacities. Furthermore, they are interested in answering these questions with an eye to explaining five basic general properties of these capacities: that they are intentional, pragmatically evaluable, coherent, reliable, and productive. How does the explanatory strategy outlined above accommodate these further facts about the explanandum of cognitive science?

According to the explanatory strategy, cognitive scientists seek to explain our ordinary cognitive capacities by reconceptualizing them, in part, as narrow information-processing capacities. Since explaining a capacity

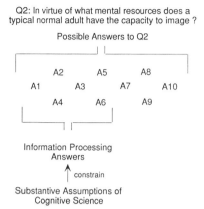

Q2: In virtue of what mental resources does a
typical normal adult have the capacity to image ?

Possible Answers to Q2

Information Processing
Answers

constrain

Substantive Assumptions of
Cognitive Science

Figure 9.2
The substantive assumptions of cognitive science constrain the set of possible answers to
the basic questions of the field to information-processing answers.

C, for the cognitive scientist, amounts to answering the basic questions
about C, the reconceptualization results in the transformation of the original basic questions about C into four *revised basic questions* about the
narrow information-processing capacity corresponding to C. Another way
to put the point is this: Cognitive scientists begin with a desire to answer
the original basic questions about each of the cognitive capacities. The
framework they have adopted, however, constrains the way in which these
questions can be answered. In particular, it constrains the set of possible answers to those formulated in information-processing terms. Since a
question is individuated by its possible answer set, the constrained possible
answer sets, in effect, pick out a new set of questions—namely, the revised
basic questions. See figure 9.2.

To make the point more concrete, consider each of the original basic
questions. The first basic question is this:

Q1   For the normal, typical adult, what precisely is the human capacity
to _____ ?

If the cognitive capacity in question is to be understood, in part, as
a narrow information-processing capacity, then Q1 is transformed into
a question about the nature of the underlying narrow information-
processing capacity. Any narrow information-processing capacity can be
precisely defined in terms of a function (in the mathematical sense) from

representations to representations. The revised basic question corresponding to Q1 can, consequently, be framed as follows:

Q1′ For the normal, typical adult, what precisely is the narrow information-processing function that underlies the ordinary capacity to _____?

Q1′ can be answered either by outlining what Marr (1982) calls a "computation theory" of the capacity (that is, by describing the relevant narrow information-processing function solely in terms of the *content* of the implicated representations) or by describing the function as a mapping from one kind of representational structure to another (where formal features of the implicated representations are also alluded to). An example of the latter can be found in Kosslyn's research. In Kosslyn's model of mental imagery, the ordinary human capacity to image is reconceived as a narrow information-processing capacity to generate a quasi-pictorial matrix representation in a surface buffer on the basis of two sorts of representations in long-term memory: literal encodings consisting of lists specifying which cells should be filled in the surface matrix and propositional representations encoding facts about the object to be imaged.

Once the ordinary capacity is reconceived in information-processing terms, the three remaining questions can be transformed into questions about the underlying narrow information-processing function. For example, Q2 becomes Q2′.

Q2 In virtue of what does a normal, typical adult have the capacity to _____ (such that it is intentional, pragmatically evaluable, coherent, reliable, and productive)?

Q2′ When a normal, typical adult has the capacity to _____, in virtue of what computational and representational resources is he or she able to compute the associated narrow information-processing function (such that the ordinary capacity is intentional, pragmatically evaluable, coherent, reliable, and productive)?

Q2 calls for a description of the mental resources in virtue of which a person has the capacity in question, but the nature of these resources is left unspecified. The substantive assumptions of cognitive science tell us, in broad terms, what sorts of resources are relevant (viz., the resources of a computational and representational device). The precise nature of these resources will, of course, vary depending on whether one takes a conventional or a connectionist approach. Kosslyn, who adopts a conventional approach, answers the Q2' question about imaging by specifying the types of representations and the types of computational operations that, on his view, underlie the capacity (see figure 1.4 and table 1.1). In contrast, a connectionist would answer Q2' by describing the underlying connectionist network both as a formal device and in terms of its representational properties.

Whereas Q2 is a request for a description of the mental resources underlying the capacity in question, Q3 seeks a dynamic account of how a person *exercises* the capacity using those resources. But, again, as in the case of Q2, the exact nature of this dynamic account is left unspecified. Within the cognitive science framework, this question gets transformed into a request for a description of the computational processes that take place when the narrow information-processing function is computed. That is, Q3 becomes Q3'.

Q3   How does a normal typical adult typically exercise his or her capacity to _____?

Q3'   When a normal, typical adult typically exercises his or her capacity to _____, how is the associated narrow information-processing function computed?

The sorts of computational processes that are invoked again depend on whether a conventional or a connectionist approach has been adopted. A conventional response to Q3' takes the form of a flow chart or a program (Newell, Shaw, and Simon 1958; Cummins 1977). The flow charts describing Kosslyn's hypotheses as to how surface images are generated from deep representations and how images are searched to determine whether the object being imaged has a named part (figures 1.5 and 1.6) provide us with a nice set of examples.

Because of their highly parallel nature, connectionist models do not as readily lend themselves to blow-by-blow computational commentaries. In fact, Bechtel (1987, p. 19) speculates that "a potential consequence of the development of connectionist models is that in psychology we may ... need to forgo the mechanistic, decompositional approach, and accept mathematical, statistical explanations of the emergence at a higher level of a phenomenon which is not built up piecemeal from operations at the next lower level." Bechtel may well be right. However, it should be noted that connectionists have begun to develop representational techniques for tracking the changing levels of activation within a connectionist network over time (see figure 9.3). Obviously, such graphic representations do not tell us exactly how the capacity in question is being exercised with respect to every computational detail, but they do provide us with dynamic information about at least one of the key parameters, namely the levels of activation of the nodes in the network.

Explanations of the sort provided by answers to questions Q2′ and Q3′ have been discussed by numerous philosophers, including Fodor (1968b), Dennett (1975), Haugeland (1978, 1985), and Lycan (1981, 1987), although the distinction between a static and a dynamic description of the underlying subcapacities has not always been recognized. The ambiguity is particularly evident in Cummins 1983, where such explanations are categorized as "systematic interpretive functional analyses" (p. 28 ff.). An explanation counts as a functional analysis, on Cummins' view, if it consists in "analyzing a disposition into a number of less problematic dispositions such that programmed manifestation of these analyzing dispositions amounts to a manifestation of the analyzed disposition" (p. 28). It is "systematic" (the term is borrowed from Haugeland 1978) if the explanatory force of the functional analysis rests largely on the fact that the analyzing dispositions interact; it is "interpretive" if the analyzing dispositions are specified semantically. As such, a functional analysis corresponds to answers to question Q2′; it is a static description of the subcapacities (often associated with components of the system) that make up the larger capacity to be explained. This reading is also supported by Cummins' examples: a schematic diagram in electronics and a biological explanation of the capacities of an entire organism in terms of the capacities of its "systems." On the other hand, Cummins also says that a functional analysis can be expressed as a program or as a flow chart—a claim that associates functional analyses with answers to Q3′.

We come now to our final question transformation. The original basic question, Q4, is transformed by the combined linking assumption into Q4′.

Q4   How does the capacity to _____ of the normal, typical adult interact with the rest of his or her cognitive capacities?

Q4′   How does the information-processing capacity associated with the capacity to _____ of the normal, typical adult interact with the rest of his or her information processing capacities?

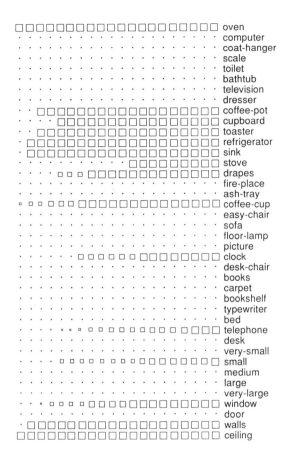

Figure 9.3
Diagram showing the changing levels of activation during a run of a network whose nodes
represent properties of rooms. The network outputs a room schema based on a small set of
room discriptors (indicated in the rightmost column). Each square in the diagram
corresponds to activation in a single node at a moment in the run. The size of the square
corresponds to the degree of activation. The sequence of squares in each row, going from
left to right, indicates the changing levels of activation during the run in the node
corresponding to that row. (From Rumelhart, Smolensky, McClelland, and Hinton 1986.
Reprinted by permission of the authors and The MIT Press.)

9.2   The Study of Cognition

Both Kuhn (1970a) and Laudan (1977) suggest that the framework of shared commitments of a research community includes a methodological component. The Kuhnian "rules" include both "a multitude of commitments to preferred types of instrumentation and to the ways in which accepted instruments may legitimately be employed" (p. 40) and commitments regarding "the fundamental aims and the fundamental methods of science" (p. 42). A Laudanian research tradition includes "the appropriate methods to be used for investigating the problems and constructing the theories" in the domain of the research tradition (p. 80), including methodological principles concerning "experimental technique, modes of theoretical testing and evaluation, and the like" (p. 79).

I agree with Kuhn and Laudan that a framework of shared commitments typically contains a methodological component. Furthermore, I am quite prepared to accept the claim that often the methodological assumptions of a research framework concern what *specific* methods (instruments, experimental techniques, modes of theoretical testing and evaluation, etc.) are appropriate for conducting research within that framework. In fact, many of the methodological assumptions associated with the subdisciplines of cognitive science (cognitive psychology, linguistics, artificial intelligence, etc.) are probably of that sort. However, because cognitive science itself is an umbrella field encompassing these various methodologically distinct subdisciplines, *its* methodological assumptions have a more general character.

Precisely what this general character amounts to is difficult to say. A survey of the various assumptions that seem appropriate to include under the methodological component of ANTCOG reveal something like this: Each of the assumptions either grounds or specifies further one or another aspect of the ANTCOG research framework. I will discuss eleven assumptions. Three of these concern the domain of cognitive science, grounding the exclusive focus on individual human cognition. Two concern the basic questions of ANTCOG, articulating the presupposition of those questions that it makes sense to talk about and study a "normal, typical" adult. The remainder have to do with the cognitivist "approach." One simply defends the explanatory strategy of the field; the rest articulate features of the approach that go beyond the explanatory strategy—its scientific and multidisciplinary character and its relation to the neurosciences.

To simplify the task of reconstruction, I have, where necessary, focused on the subsidiary research framework of ANTCOG rather than on the research framework of cognitive science as a whole. However, since (as we have seen) ANTCOG is embedded within cognitive science, many of its assumptions are inherited from its parent framework. As a consequence, despite the restriction to ANTCOG, many of the assumptions examined in the previous chapters have, in fact, been assumptions shared by all the subsidiary research frameworks of cognitive science. A similar situation exists with respect to the methodological assumptions of ANTCOG. Most of the assumptions I will describe turn out to be assumptions of cognitive science as a whole. In fact, of the ten assumptions to be articulated, only two (M4 and M5) pertain solely to ANTCOG.

Nature consists of a vast complex of entities, properties, and regularities that interact in a multitude of ways. In choosing some aspect of nature for study, science must inevitably abstract that aspect from its context and its natural interactions. That such abstraction occurs in uncontroversial; however, does it result in a domain that is self-contained enough to support significant theorizing? As George Miller so nicely puts it in the Overview to the Sloan Foundation's State of the Art Report (Walker 1978, p. vi): "To factor a complicated problem into proper subproblems, look for things that interact strongly with each other, but only weakly with everything else."

The first two methodological assumptions, M1 and M2, claim that cognitive science's focus on individual cognition—individual as opposed to social, and cognitive as opposed to noncognitive—is warranted in this sense.[2]

M1   Human cognition can be successfully studied by focusing exclusively on the individual cognizer and his or her place in the natural environment. The influence of society or culture on individual cognition can always be explained by appealing to the fact that this influence is mediated through individual perception and representation.

M2   The human cognitive capacities are sufficiently autonomous from other aspects of mind (such as affect and personality) that, to a large extent, they can be successfully studied in isolation.

M1 and M2 assert that it is acceptable to study individual cognition in isolation from social context and other aspects of mind (at least, up to a point). A similar "divide and conquer" assumption, M3, exists for the individual cognitive capacities themselves (Osherson and Lasnik 1990, p. xvi).

M3   There exists a partitioning of cognition in general into individual cognitive capacities such that each of these individual capacities can, to a large extent, be successfully studied in isolation from each of the others.

Precisely which partitioning is the best one is, of course, an empirical question. At the present time, cognitive scientists make use of two sorts of partitions which cross-cut one another. The first involves individuation by kind of process. Roughly speaking, there are input processes (perception), internal processes (reasoning, memory, imaging), and output processes (intentional action). In contrast to this purely functional way of carving up cognition, a growing number of cognitive scientists believe that many of the human cognitive capacities are *domain-specific* (Keil 1981). The claim is most often made for language. The view is then that the perception, memory, and production of language simply cannot be assimilated to perception, memory, and production in general. A similar situation may exist for face recognition, ontological knowledge, numerical reasoning, and other capacities.

What distinguishes the subsidiary research program of ANTCOG from other subsidiary research programs of cognitive science is that it investigates normal, typical adult cognition. That there are adults who cognize (perceive, remember, speak, etc.) is, clearly, beyond dispute. However, that it makes sense to posit a "normal" and (especially) a "typical" adult cognizer is not so obvious. M4 and M5 make these assumptions explicit, thereby providing a foundation for the basic questions of ANTCOG.

M4   Although there is considerable variation in how adult human beings exercise their cognitive capacities, it is meaningful to distinguish, at least roughly, between "normal" and "abnormal" cognition.

M5   Although there is considerable variation in how adult human beings exercise their cognitive capacities, adults are sufficiently alike when they cognize that it is meaningful to talk about a "typical" adult cognizer and possible to arrive at generalizations about cognition that hold (at least approximately) for all normal adults.

As we saw in section 9.1, the explanatory strategy of cognitive science involves the reconceptualization of ordinary human cognitive capacities as broad information-processing capacities. The next assumption explicitly defends this strategy.

M6   The explanatory strategy of cognitive science is sound. In particular, answers to the original basic questions can, to a large extent, be obtained by answering their narrow information-processing counterparts (i.e., the revised basic questions).

M6 is not simply an item of faith. Belief in it is based on the combined force of two convictions: that satisfactory, empirically well-supported answers to the original basic questions can be obtained by identifying ordinary cognitive capacities with broad information-processing capacities, and that the bulk of the explanatory burden falls on the narrow information-processing component. The first conviction is further supported by the belief that for each of the basic general properties of our ordinary cognitive capacities (with the exception of reliability) there is an information-processing property (or a set of information-processing properties) that plausibly realizes, and consequently explains, the ordinary property at the information-processing level.

Let us explore this last point in more detail by considering each of the properties in turn.

Our ordinary cognitive capacities are *intentional*—that is, they involve intentional states. On the cognitivist view, this property corresponds to the fact that narrow information-processing capacities involve transformations of representations. Thus, the contentfulness of our ordinary capacities is said to be realized by the contentfulness of the representations implicated in the narrow information-processing capacities underlying those ordinary capacities.

Our ordinary capacities are *pragmatically evaluable*—that is, they can be exercised with varying degrees of success. This property corresponds to the fact that broad information-processing capacities can also fail to be correctly exercised. Failure can occur in all three components of the broad information-processing capacity (the environmental component, the transducer component, and the computational component). In all three cases, however, failure depends on the fact that the input representations or the output representations of the associated narrow information-processing capacity are themselves evaluable and, hence, can either "correspond" or fail to correspond with the opposite end of the process—that is, with the output and the input, respectively. (More on this correspondence shortly.) If we locate the failure in the computational component, then another way to put the point is this: The processes that compute the input-output function that defines the narrow information-processing capacity (according to a Marr-style computation theory) can always fail to compute properly. The mind/brain might be working normally but may be employing a heuristic algorithm that gets things right more often than not but, under certain conditions, gets things wrong. Or there may be physiological reasons (lack of sleep, inebriation, brain disorder) why the computational apparatus itself fails to work properly.

Our ordinary cognitive capacities are *coherent*. Coherence comes in two forms, depending on whether we are dealing with an input/output capacity or a purely mental capacity (see section 2.2). Ordinary input and output capacities are coherent in the sense that, when they are exercised correctly, they exhibit a "satisfaction" relation between their beginning and end states. The capacity to perceive, when exercised successfully, brings it about that the conditions of satisfaction of the perceptual experience are, in fact, satisfied by the perceptible state of affairs in the world that led, causally, to the experience. The capacity to act intentionally, when exercised successfully, brings it about that the conditions of satisfaction of the intention are, in fact, satisfied by the ensuing action. If we ignore the fact that the mapping from an ordinary capacity to an information-processing capacity sometimes involves reconceptualization of the endpoints of the capacities as well as of its mentalistic processes (that is, instead of ordinary objects and states there are physical objects and states, and instead of actions there are motor movements with environmental consequences),[3] then the satisfaction relation exhibited by ordinary cognitive input and output capacities is mirrored by a satisfaction relation at the information-processing level. Representational states, insofar as they have content, also have conditions of satisfaction. Hence, the broad information-processing capacity to perceive, when exercised successfully, brings it about that the conditions of satisfaction of the final perceptual representation are, in fact, satisfied by the perceptible state of affairs in the world. And the broad information-processing capacity to act intentionally, when exercised successfully, brings it about that the conditions of satisfaction of the intention representation are, in fact, satisfied by the ensuing behavior.

According to the analysis provided in section 2.2, the coherence of any purely mental, ordinary cognitive capacity that can be deliberately exercised lies both in a satisfaction relation of the sort exhibited by output capacities and in a relation of "true closure." For example, the ordinary human capacity to imagine can be analyzed as follows.

Beginning state: X intends (that X imagines (what the front of X's house
                                                                                                looks))

End state: X imagines (that the front of X's house looks like
                                                                                        such-and-such)

The coherence of satisfaction manifests itself in the fact that the intention of the beginning state is satisfied by the end state. The coherence of true closure manifests itself in the fact that the gap in content of the beginning state is filled in the end state. Analogues to both kinds of coherence can be found in the associated information-processing capacity. Corresponding to the ordinary state of intending there will be a representation in the "intention box" with the content

(Generate a representation in the "image box" that depicts what the front
                                                                                  of X's house looks like),[4]

and corresponding to the ordinary end state of imagining will be a representation in the "image" box depicting the content

(the front of X's house looks like such-and-such),

with some appropriate properties filled in for the "such and such." The transformation from one representational state to the other exhibits coherence of the satisfaction sort because the conditions of satisfaction specified by the content of the initial representation in the "intention box" are satisfied by the presence of a final representation of how X's house looks in X's "image box." It exhibits coherence of the closure sort because the content gap of the initial representation is filled by the content of the final representation.

Our ordinary cognitive capacities are *productive*—that is, once mastered, they can be manifested in a practically unlimited number of novel ways. Of the four ordinary cognitive properties we are currently considering, this is the only one whose information-processing account is controversial. Productivity can easily be handled on the assumption that the mind/brain is a conventional computer. However, it is far from clear what to say on a connectionist view.

The conventional story is this: The productivity of our ordinary cognitive capacities results from the fact that the mental representations computed over when exercising the corresponding narrow information-processing capacities are recursively generable. This means that in principle (bracketing resource constraints) there are an infinite number of representations available to the mental apparatus, and that in practice there is certainly always a novel representation available (relative to the system) for exercising a given capacity in a novel way. Thus, for example, suppose a person sees something he or she has never seen before. On a conventional information-processing account, the novelty of the perceptual experience would stem from the novelty of the perceptual representation resulting from computing the person's vision algorithm. And the possibility of such a novel perceptual representation would stem from the fact that perceptual representations are complex representations built recursively out of simpler representations.

All of this is controversial from a connectionist perspective because, as was noted in section 5.2, it requires representations to have constituent structure. As things now stand in connectionist theorizing, it is not clear how or even whether connectionist representations can have such constituent structure. Thus, there are three options for the connectionist: to figure out how connectionist representations can have constituent structure, to develop a computational account of productivity that doesn't require representations with constituent structure, and to deny that our ordinary cognitive capacities really are productive.

I have been discussing the cognitivist belief that for each of the basic general properties of our ordinary cognitive capacities, with the exception of reliability, there is an information-processing property (or a set of information-processing properties) that plausibly realizes that property at the information-processing level. Reliability is excluded for the obvious reason that, in the case of input and output capacities, it requires a certain "fit" with the environment, and this fit is clearly not something that can be captured by information-processing properties alone. Note, however, that the reliability of our cognitive capacities does presuppose that they are pragmatically evaluable, and the latter property, as we have just seen, is one that cognitive scientists believe can be realized in information-processing terms.

The cognitivist approach to the study of the cognitive mind/brain is largely determined by the fact that cognitive scientists seek to explain cognition in information-processing terms, but there are other important features to the approach. For one thing, cognitive scientists clearly situate themselves within the scientific enterprise as a whole. The field is not called "cognitive *science*" for nothing. In addition, the field is founded on the premise that an adequate understanding of the human cognitive capacities will require the conceptual and methodological resources of a number of distinct fields (Gardner 1985, p. 43). We thus get the following:

M7   In choosing among alternative hypothesized answers to the basic questions of the research framework, one should invoke the usual canons of scientific methodology. That is, ultimately, answers to the basic questions should be justified on empirical grounds.

M8   A complete theory of human cognition will not be possible without a substantial contribution from each of the subdisciplines of cognitive science.

In reconstructing the research framework of cognitive science, I have been at pains to isolate what I take to be common coin among cognitive scientists, whatever their primary disciplinary allegiance. However, once such a common framework has been developed, it is fairly easy to describe, at least in rough terms, what the characteristic contribution of each of the subdisciplines is. I have summarized these subdisciplinary task descriptions in table 9.1. They bring out quite clearly, I think, what lies behind the emphasis on a multidisciplineary approach.

9.3   The Role of Neuroscience

It is often said that cognitive science involves a number of "levels of description." For our purposes, the most important levels are the folk-psychology level, the information-processing level, and the neural level. It is also usually assumed that these levels are the products of (respectively) common sense, the non-neural cognitive sciences, and the neurosciences. This correspondence is somewhat problematic, as we shall see; however, for the moment, let us not worry about it.[5]

Cognitive science seeks to understand the cognitive mind/brain as an information-processing device. But a mind/brain is, after all, also a brain,

Table 9.1
Characteristic contributions of the major subdisciplines of cognitive science to the ANTCOG research program.

Psychology
• Provides empirical answers to Q1'; e.g., enhances our understanding of the nature and the limits of each of our cognitive capacities.
• By answering Q1', imposes empirical constraints on what can count as an adequate answer to the other basic questions.
• Formulates possible answers (hypotheses, models) to Q2', Q3', and Q4', and devises experiments for testing these possible answers.

Linguistics
• Provides a theory of ideal capacity (a competence model) for language comprehension and production.
• Puts forward hypotheses regarding the representational part of Q2' for language comprehension and production.

Computer Science
• Develops hypotheses concerning the nature of the representation bearers for MRS.
• Formulates computationally detailed possible answers to Q2', Q3', and Q4'.
• Develops general constraints on computability.

Philosophy
• Articulates the foundations of the field.
• Explores questions concerning the adequacy of the cognitive science research program.
• Contributes toward developing a theory of content determination for the system of mental representation posited in cognitivist theories.
• Helps to develop theories of ideal capacity (competence models) for reasoning (deductive and inductive logic, probability theory, decision theory, epistemology, philosophy of science) and language use (formal semantics, philosophy of language).

Neuroscience
• Studies what happens when our cognitive capacities are exercised abnormally due to neural lesion.
• Studies the realization of our capacities in the brain.
• Helps to develop answers to Q2', Q3', and Q4' on the basis of the two preceding items by, at a minimum, generating constraints on acceptable answers to those questions.

and there is an entire field—neuroscience—whose job it is to study the brain. So what is the relation of neuroscience to cognitive science? Are they engaged in competing research programs, both trying to understand the same phenomena in different terms, or are they partners in a common enterprise? A complete specification of the "approach" of cognitive science clearly requires a clarification of the relationship between cognitive science and neuroscience.

Before we look at the assumptions that bear on this relationship, one preliminary point is in order regarding the above three levels of description. Identifying the folk-psychology level, the information-processing level, and the neural level as levels of description for cognitive science does not preclude there being sublevels within any of these levels. I am not claiming that these are the only levels of importance in cognitive science; I am simply claiming that they are the most useful levels for our purposes. Within the information-processing level, one might distinguish between a semantic and a syntactic level (Pylyshyn 1984) (or, in Newell's [1986] terminology, a "knowledge" level and a "symbolic" level) or among different computational levels. One prominent view of the relation between conventional and connectionist theorizing is, in fact, that they are complementary rather than competitive, with the latter simply representing a finer-grained computational description than the former (Smolensky 1988). In addition, within the neural level one might distinguish a host of sublevels: the membrane, the cell, the circuit, and perhaps others (P. S. Churchland 1986; P. S. Churchland and T. J. Sejnowski 1989).

The most influential proposal regarding levels of description for cognitive science is due to Marr (1982), who distinguishes three levels: computation theory, representation and algorithm, and implementation. Computation theory characterizes the performance of a device as a mapping from one kind of information to another, the level of representation and algorithm describes the representational structures and computational processes that allow the device to compute the function specified by the computation theory, and the implementation level describes how the algorithm and the representation are realized physically. Marr's distinctions easily fit with mine. Computation theory and representation and algorithm are simply two modes of description within my level 2—in fact, they correspond to possible answers to my questions Q1' and Q3', respectively. And his implementation level is simply a generalization of my neural level.

What, then, does (or ought) cognitive science assume about the relation of the non-neural cognitive sciences to neuroscience, or about the relation of the information-processing level to the neural level? There are three issues: (1) In constructing information-processing theories of the mind/brain, should one take findings from neuroscience into account? (2) If so, when? And how should they be utilized? (That is, should research proceed in a "top-down," a "bottom-up," or a "co-evolutionary" fashion?) (3) What is the explanatory status of information-processing descriptions of the mind/brain with respect to neural descriptions? Will the latter ever replace the former as explanations of our cognitive capacities, or are information-processing descriptions theoretically ineliminable? I will discuss issues 1 and 2 in this section and issue 3 in the next.

There seems to be some difference of opinion within the cognitive science community regarding issue 1. Some cognitive scientists believe that information-processing theories of cognition need not be constrained by the findings of neuroscience; others, in contrast, take constraint relations between the non-neural cognitive sciences and neuroscience to be extremely important for developing an adequate theory of cognition. I shall call the first the "isolationist" stance (following P. S. Churchland 1986) and the second the "constraint" stance.

The following two statements are fairly typical of the isolationist stance:

The task of a psychologist trying to understand human cognition is analogous to that of a man trying to discover how a computer has been programmed. In particular, if the program seems to store and reuse information, he would like to know by what "routines" or "procedures" this is done. Given this purpose he will not care much whether his particular computer stores information in magnetic cores or in thin films; he wants to understand the program, not the hardware. By the same token, it would not help the psychologist to know that memory is carried by RNA as opposed to some other medium. He wants to understand its utilization, not its incarnation.   (Neisser 1967, p. 6)

[W]hat we are really interested in, as Aristotle saw, is form and not matter. *What is our intellectual form?* is the question, not what the matter is. And whatever our substance might be, soulstuff, or matter or Swiss cheese, is not going to place any interesting first order restrictions on the answer to this question.   (Putnam 1975, p. 302)

In contrast to these statements, most recent texts that purport to give an overview of cognitive science adopt the constraint stance, suggesting that the findings of neuroscience *are* (ultimately, at least) relevant to theory construction in cognitive science. Neuroscience is generally recognized as one of the subfields of cognitive science (Walker 1978; Gardner 1985; Stillings et al. 1987), and its job, at a minimum, is taken to be that of providing an account of how the representations and computational processes posited by information-processing theories are realized. As Walker (1978, p. 11) puts it, "the scientific analysis cannot be considered complete until its biological foundations are understood." Furthermore, it is held that the specific nature of this brain realization imposes *constraints* on an adequate information-processing theory, in the sense that no proposed theory can ultimately be regarded as acceptable unless it comports with what neuroscience tells us about the brain.

In view of the difference of opinion expressed above, it is worth scouting for any relevant normative arguments. As it turns out, there are several.

The first argument I shall consider has been widely discussed in the philosophical literature and is often read as having negative methodological consequences for the role of neuroscience in cognitive science. This is the so-called "argument from *multiple realizability*" (Fodor 1975; Pylyshyn 1984; P. S. Churchland 1986; P. M. Churchland 1990). The argument goes like this: Information-processing theories are *functional* theories. Since any function can, in principle, be realized by vastly different kinds of stuff, information processing theories are likewise multiply realizable (Haugeland 1985; Simon 1981a; Block 1983). In particular, the very same information processes can be instantiated in mechanical stuff or in biological stuff. But since all these different kinds of stuff can exhibit the same representational structures and computational processes, knowing how any particular system (or class of systems) is realized cannot be essential to understanding those structures and processes. Therefore, in constructing information-processing theories of cognition, cognitive scientists can safely ignore the findings of neuroscience.

How convincing is this argument? In particular, if the claim of multiple realizability is unproblematic, does an isolationist methodological moral follow, or is it even rendered reasonable? Neither, I think. Granted, cognitive scientists are interested in developing theories that are functional in character.[6] And granted, any function can, in principle, be multiply realized. Nevertheless, the information processing functions cognitive scientists are interested in, if they exist at all, are, *in fact*, realized by brain stuff, not by silicon chips or Swiss cheese. And the specific nature of this realization (not just that it is neural, but its specific anatomy and physiology) cannot help but place constraints on how the mind/brain works on a functional level. A moment's reflection makes this point patently obvious. If our brains were the size of a pea, we obviously would not have all the cognitive capacities that we have. If there was no connection between the eyes and the cortex, we would not be able to see. If a horde of little gremlins invaded Earth one night and radically rewired all our brains, our mental life would certainly change in dramatic and fantastic ways. Hence, an isolationist conclusion simply does not follow from the fact of multiple realizability. One way to see this point is to note that side by side with the multiplicity of possible realizations there exists another multiplicity that is at least equally important: given the sorts of evidence that psychology and linguistics make available, there are many *different* information-processing stories to be told. The point is that not all these stories may mesh with how the brain is constructed. Thus, if we are after the correct story, it is foolish to ignore the findings of neuroscience.[7]

As presented above, the multiple-realizability argument goes nowhere, methodologically speaking. There is, however, another form of the argument, espoused by Fodor (1981b), that gets closer to the mark. Fodor seeks to undermine the supposition of a constraint relation between the non-neural cognitive sciences and neuroscience by pointing out that not only are information-processing structures and processes multiply realizable in general, but their realization in neural stuff might itself take a multiplicity of forms. As he says, "there are no firm data for any but the grossest correspondence between types of psychological states and types of neurological states, and it is entirely possible that the nervous system of higher organisms characteristically achieves a given psychological end by a wide variety of neurological means" (Fodor 1981b, p. 135). If the neurological means in question are truly "wide" (going beyond the principled differences one sees between individuals of different developmental ages, or between left-handed and right-handed individuals), then this sort of multiple realization would indeed lend fuel to the isolationist position.[8] Note, however, that human information processing would still be constrained by the nature of the brain; it would just be extremely difficult to discover what those constraints were.

But Fodor's form of the argument is also unpersuasive. The fact that multiple neural realization is "entirely *possible*" clearly carries no weight whatsoever. What is relevant is whether it is actual. Since the extreme sort of neural multiple realization envisioned by Fodor is not entailed by multiple realizability *per se* (as he would be the first to admit),[9] the question becomes: What does the empirical evidence look like? As the above quote makes clear, Fodor focuses on the fact that only "the grossest correspondence between types of psychological states and types of neurological states" is supported by firm data. His argument thus proceeds in two steps.

FODOR'S ARGUMENT FOR ISOLATIONISM

(1) There are firm data for only gross psychoneural correlations.

(2) Therefore, it is likely that there is multiple neural realizability.

(3) Therefore, cognitive science should adopt an isolationist stance.

Both steps—from premise 1 to premise 2 and from premise 2 to premise 3—are questionable. Consider the first step. One difficulty is that the evidential situation referred to by premise 1 is underdescribed. The fact that there are no firm data for the existence of detailed psychoneural correlations is consistent with two epistemic states of affairs: (a) there are firm data that there are *no* such detailed correlations; (b) there are no firm data either for or against the existence of such correlations. I very much suspect the situation is (b). But then another question becomes relevant. If one is interested in inferring from the absence of data concerning detailed psychoneural correlations to the absence of the correlations themselves, it is relevant to ask about the nature of the search for those correlations. In particular, has the search for detailed correlations been thorough enough and technologically sophisticated enough to warrant concluding that no detailed correlations will be forthcoming as a result of future research? On the basis of my own knowledge of brain research (which is, admittedly, limited), it seems to me *extremely* premature in the present state of play to draw from the present evidence any conclusions about the absence of detailed psychoneural correlations. Neuropsychologists have only recently begun to appreciate that the attribution of functions to parts of the brain cannot occur in a seat-of-the-pants way but must proceed in concert with sophisticated scientific psychological theorizing (Von Eckardt Klein 1978b). Furthermore, there are a whole host of fancy research techniques that have become available in recent years (electroencephalograph recording, event-related-potential recording, computerized axial tomography, cerebral blood flow studies, positron-emission tomography, and nuclear magnetic resonance imaging—see P. S. Churchland 1986, pp. 201–221, for a description) whose research potential has only begun to be tapped. In sum, premise 1 seems to me to provide very weak support for premise 2.

There is another reason for being unpersuaded by Fodor's argument, and it concerns the inference from premise 2 to premise 3. Even if cognitive functions *are* multiply realized in human brains, neuroscience may still be able to provide important evidence about the nature of human information processing. Two sorts of findings come to mind. When neuropsychological techniques are used to provide evidence for functional localization, they are, at the same time, providing evidence of the *existence* of a certain psychological function. If the best explanation for a patient's pattern of behavior is the hypothesis that there is selective impairment in a particular component or subcapacity posited by an information-processing theory of some cognitive capacity, then that pattern of behavior is evidence for the existence of that component or subcapacity in normal individuals. As I noted in section 1.2, arguments of this kind have been advanced to support Kosslyn's positing of distinct components for image generation (Farah, Levine, and Calvanio 1988; Farah, Gazzaniga, Holtzman, and Kosslyn 1985), long-term visual memory, and image inspection (Farah 1984).[10] The point is that making inferences of this sort in no way depends on the realization of function's being uniform from one person to another. As long as the psychological functions being realized are assumed to be uniform (a point which Fodor does not doubt), this sort of inference is available.

Another class of findings whose utility is independent of the degree of multiple neural realizability consists of findings that concern the nature of our basic neural machinery. These sorts of considerations have become especially important for cognitive scientists interested in developing connectionist models, since one of the virtues of these models is supposed to be their greater biological plausibility. It is striking that the recently published two-volume compendium *Parallel Distributed Processing: Explorations in the Microstructure of Cognition* (Rumelhart et al. 1986; McClelland et al. 1986) devotes an entire part (six chapters) to biological mechanisms, including a chapter by Crick and Asanuma describing, in effect, what every connectionist should know about the anatomy and physiology of the cerebral cortex and a chapter by Sejnowski describing what is not known but connectionists would like to know about the brain.

The neural constraint most mentioned in this context is the "100-step rule." Many cognitive tasks, such as visual recognition, take only 500 milliseconds to complete. Based on neurophysiological evidence concerning conduction velocities and synaptic delays in neurons, Feldman and Ballard (1982) estimate that such tasks involve only 100 computational steps. This fact is then used to argue against conventional computational models of cognition, which require far more than 100 steps to do anything remotely sophisticated.

Other possible constraints have been noted as well. Feldman (1989, p. 70) suggests that the following facts are relevant to developing a theory of the neural representation of conceptual knowledge:

... the relatively small number of neurons (about 10^{11}, or 100 billion), the large number of connections between neurons (about 10^4 per unit), the low rate of information transfer. It may seem that 10^{11} is not a small number; however, in 10^6 input fibers from each eye a computer scientist immediately detects a major constraint. For example, dedicating one unit to test for a possible line between any pair of points in the retina would take $(10^6)^2$ neurons—more than there are. The information rate between individual neurons at a firing rate of 100 spikes per second is about five bits, enough to encode one letter of the alphabet. (If complex messages are conveyed, it is not by individual neurons.) ... There are also constraints on plasticity that are pertinent. The major findings are that the growth of new fibers in adults is much too slow and constrained to account for learning and that there is no generation of new neurons.

Another issue of concern to biology-minded connectionists is whether the nervous system has the resources to underwrite the backward propagation involved in the "learning" phase of most connectionist models (Nadel et al. 1989).

I have been looking at what is wrong with the multiple-realizability argument as an argument for adopting an isolationist methodology for cognitive science. In the process, however, a positive argument for the importance of neuroscientific constraints has emerged. The argument can be summarized thus: If cognitive scientists restrict themselves to using psychological data gathered from normal subjects to support their information-processing hypotheses, those hypotheses will be seriously underconstrained. On general methodological grounds, therefore, it is important for cognitive scientists to seek other sources of data, if that is at all possible. The neurosciences provide an obvious answer to the underconstraint problem. It has been argued, however, that this answer is illusory—that, despite their promise, neuroscientific findings cannot help to constrain information-processing theories of cognition. None of the proposed arguments are very compelling. The mere fact that information-processing functions are multiply realizable does not mean that a particular class of systems realized in a particular kind of stuff is not constrained by the structure and organization of that stuff. The fact that thus far only gross psychoneural correlations have been discovered does not mean that there are no detailed correlations to be had. Furthermore, even if detailed correlations are not forthcoming, there are still ways neuroscience can constrain the construction of information-processing models. Thus, none of the skeptical arguments carry much weight, and the obvious answer to the underconstraint problem remains just that—the obvious answer.

The existence of the two kinds of evidence pointed to above, neuropsychological findings and general low-level findings about the structure and functioning of brain cells, also serves to undercut another skeptical position against the constraint stance: the one P. S. Churchland (1980a) labeled "boggled skepticism." The boggled skeptic argues that the brain is so complicated and doing neuroscience is so hard that we will never, as a matter of fact, be able discover anything about the brain that could serve to constrain information-processing models, even if such information is not barred to us in principle. I suspect that the argument is based on a failure to appreciate the wide variety of findings that neuroscience is capable of serving up. If one imagines that the only kinds of constraints that are likely to be useful will derive from detailed psychoneural correlations, and if one believes that these will be impossible to trace out even if they exist, then boggled skepticism seems to be warranted. But, as we have just seen, even if such detailed psychoneural correlations are never forthcoming, there are still neuroscientific findings that cognitive science can benefit from.

I shall take it, then, that cognitive scientists should adopt the following methodological assumption:

$M9^n$ Information-processing answers to the basic questions of cognitive science are constrained by the findings of neuroscience.

Even if it is agreed that findings from neuroscience are relevant to developing information-processing theories of human cognition, *when* they are relevant remains an open question. There are three main options.

OPTION 1   Adopt a "top-down" approach—that is, develop information-processing answers to the basic questions of cognitive science by initially considering only findings that pertain to the functioning of the "whole" subject (based either on ordinary reflection and observation or on psychological experimentation) and only subsequently after an adequate theory has been constructed and tested, determine how the posited information-processing structures and processes are realized in the brain by considering findings from the neurosciences.

OPTION 2   Adopt a "bottom-up" approach, that is, develop information-processing answers to the basic questions of cognitive science by starting with findings from the neurosciences and working up to an information-processing description.

OPTION 3   Adopt a "co-evolutionary" approach—that is, develop information-processing answers to the basic questions of cognitive science by using both psychological and neuroscientific findings in whatever order seems the most theoretically fruitful. As a consequence, allow theoretical notions in the non-neural cognitive sciences to be influenced by neuroscience and allow theoretical notions in neuroscience to be influenced by the non-neural cognitive sciences.[11]

P. S. Churchland (1980a) suggests that a significant element within the cognitive science community is committed to the top-down approach and that this approach is naturally associated with functionalist theories of mind. Though I think she tends to see endorsements of the top-down option where they do not really exist,[12] there is no question that it has found a few prominent spokesmen. Here, for example, are a few revealing quotes:

The task of psychology is to explain human perception, learning, cognition, and so forth in terms that will ultimately unite psychological theory to physiology in one way or another, and there are two broad strategies one could adopt: a *bottom-up* strategy ... or a *top-down* strategy ... It is commonplace that both endeavors could and should proceed simultaneously, but there is now abundant evidence that the bottom-up strategy in psychology is unlikely to prove very fruitful. (Dennett 1978b, p. 110)

Why not just open up the black box and see what is going on? There are more problems with this approach than just the ethical. First of all, the brain is a notoriously difficult object to inspect. Second, the terms in which brain processes and structures are described do not make direct contact with the issues that concern the cognitive psychologist.... A knowledge of the circuitry of the computer is of little use in determining how it executes a program. Obviously, one would be foolish to claim that physiological data will never be of use to the cognitive psychologist. However, one would be equally foolish to expect that physiological data will help decide current issues about internal structure and process. (Anderson 1976, p. 14)

Nevertheless, despite the existence of a number of prominent top-downers, my sense is that there is currently, and has always been, significant support for co-evolution. For example, the introduction to the Sloan Foundation's State-of-the-Art Report, written in 1978, includes the following statement:

The connection between neuroscience and cognitive science, moreover, cannot be a one way street.... The topics discussed below emphasize the interdependence of theories of brain and theories of behavior and illustrate end products induced by collaborative work on each.   (Walker 1978, pp. 13–14)

A similar point is made in *An Invitation to Cognitive Science*, a three-volume introduction to contemporary cognitive science. After describing Marr's three levels of analysis, the editors write:

It is crucial for understanding contemporary cognitive science to see that the different levels of analysis are connected, in the sense that facts and principles discovered at one level contribute to analyses at other levels....
   The organization of these volumes has been greatly influenced by this approach. Each part includes chapters that focus on distinct levels of analysis: implementation, representation/algorithm, and computation. Where possible information about theories at one level is brought to bear on theories at another.   (Osherson and Lasnik 1990, p. xviii)[13]

The argument just given in support of M9 goes a considerable distance toward adjudicating the above dispute. In particular, it provides the basis for arguing against the top-down option. We have seen that there are findings from the neurosciences—concerning, for example, the cognitive failures exhibited by neurologically impaired patients and the nature of our basic neural machinery—that are unquestionably evidentially relevant to the construction of information-processing theories of cognition. The point now is that there is no reason to wait to make use of these findings until cognitive scientists have developed an information-processing theory that accommodates all the available psychological data from normal subjects. Such findings can be just as informative as reaction-time data or error data. Why put valuable information on hold? In contrast, there is good reason *not* to wait: Knowing something about the brain now may help us avoid costly and time-consuming theoretical garden paths.

We are thus left with the bottom-up option and the co-evolutionary option. But no one could seriously advocate the former. Good answers to Q2 and Q3, at the neural level, can only be developed against the background of answers to Q1, and the latter has generally been considered the province of the non-neural cognitive sciences. That is, neuroscientists cannot hope to explain in virtue of what (neural structures and processes) a person has a certain capacity, or how he or she exercises that capacity, unless they know fairly precisely what the capacity *is*, and determining the latter is not the sort of job that a neuroscientist *qua* neuroscientist typically undertakes. Furthermore, as I shall argue shortly, there are good reasons to believe that any satisfactory *explanation* of our cognitive capacities must be an explanation in computational and representational terms. This fact in itself does not rule out a bottom-up approach, since, as P. S. Churchland (1986) has convincingly argued, some neuroscientists are just as much in the business of developing computational/ representational accounts of cognition as workers in psychology and artificial intelligence are.[14] But if neuroscientists are going to venture into computational and representational territory, it would be foolish of them not to make use of the results of previous and concurrent explorations by their non-neural cognitive science brethren. I conclude, therefore, that the only reasonable strategy is a co-evolutionary one:

M10^n The optimal research strategy for developing an adequate theory of the cognitive mind/brain is to adopt a co-evolutionary approach—that is, to develop information-processing answers to the basic questions of cognitive science on the basis of empirical findings from both the non-neural cognitive sciences and the neurosciences.

9.4   Explanatory Ineliminability

We come now to the final issue concerning the relation of the information-processing level to the neural level: What is the explanatory status of information-processing accounts of the mind/brain relative to neural accounts? In particular, are there features of cognition of interest to cognitive science that an information-processing theory can, in principle, explain that a neural theory can't? This is a question that has been hotly debated by philosophers ever since the logical positivists became interested in the "unity of science." But since it is not a question with much practical methodological import, there does not seem to be much opinion about it among the rest of the cognitive science community. I shall, thus, treat the question solely in the normative mode.

   The position I shall defend is, roughly speaking, that from the standpoint of cognitive science information-processing accounts are explanatorily ineliminable—in other words, there *are* questions about cognition of central interest to cognitive science that can be answered at the information-processing level but not at the neural level. My defense of this point rests, however, on the view that the neural level includes only *low-level*—and, in particular, nonrepresentational and noncomputational—descriptions of brain cells, their interconnections, and their activities. If, in contrast, one defines the neural level as *any* mode of description issuing from the field of neuroscience, then (insofar as neuroscientists develop their own representational and computational hypotheses) the point will not apply. This is because what matters to explanatory status is not what the disciplinary source of the explanations is but what the explanations are like. In particular, what matters, if cognitive science is to achieve its explanatory aims, is that it retain explanations couched in representational and computational terms.

The point to be defended—let us call it the "information processing ineliminability thesis"—has been argued by Fodor (1981c), Pylyshyn (1984), Schiffer (1981), Field (1978), and Loar (1980, 1981). As I am framing the issue, it does not have any obvious direct opponents, although it may have an indirect one. P. S. Churchland (1986), the best candidate for a direct opponent, is, in fact, primarily concerned to oppose related (but not identical) ineliminability theses, suggested by the discussions of Fodor and Pylyshyn, concerning folk psychology and certain conventional computational modes of theorizing ("the sentential paradigm"), and to oppose unjustified assumptions about the theoretical limitations of neuroscience (pp. 376–399)—neither of which I want to support. Furthermore, she explicitly acknowledges that if the Pylyshyn-Fodor arguments are taken "as arguments for the view that cognitive psychology is worth pursuing and is a necessary, indispensable part of the enterprise of coming to understand how the mind-brain works," they are "fair enough," and she has "no quarrel" with them (p. 380).

Stich (1983), who considers the arguments of Pylyshyn, Fodor, and Schiffer at considerable length in his book, is also not a direct opponent, for the simple reason that he sets up the options differently. He would probably agree that some form of high-level functional account (in contrast with a low-level neural account) is ineliminable. However, he would disagree that this high-level account must be an information-processing account in my sense. Rather, he wants to defend the view that all that is necessary is a formal, syntactic description, and that *representations* are eliminable. (I believe that the arguments I will give in support of the information processing ineliminability thesis also tell against Stich's position, but since that point that is somewhat orthogonal to the focus of the present discussion I will not pursue it here.)

The arguments for the information processing ineliminability thesis in the literature trade on the fact that cognition is intentional, the fact that information-processing functions are multiply realizable, the fact that eliminating the information-processing level would rule out the possibility of capturing certain important generalizations about the mind/brain, and the fact that cognitive science is interested in explaining the reliability of cognition. I believe that, stated correctly, all these considerations contribute to the case for the information processing ineliminability thesis. However, because few advocates of information processing ineliminability share my conception of the explanandum of cognitive science or my belief in the importance of distinguishing the folk-psychological and information-processing levels, I do not always approve of how the arguments have been formulated. I shall, therefore, present what I take to be the best case for the thesis in my own terms, mentioning the various reasons given by others where they fit in.

The linchpin of Fodor's (1981c) and Pylyshyn's (1984) case for information processing ineliminability is that the information-processing level is necessary in order to capture certain important generalizations about cognition. It seems to me that this is to put the cart before the horse. If the issue concerns the explanatory importance of one or another level of description of the mind/brain, then the starting point of the debate must be what cognitive science is trying to explain. Whether a level of description can or cannot capture certain generalizations is neither here nor there unless those generalizations are explanatorily relevant.

Let us begin, then, with the explanandum of cognitive science (or, at least, ANTCOG). My view, at this point, should be boringiy evident. The explanatory aim of cognitive science is to answer questions Q1–Q4 about the various human cognitive capacities. Moreover, answering those questions in a satisfactory way requires providing an account of certain features of those capacities, namely that they are intentional, coherent, pragmatically evaluable, productive, and reliable. In section 9.1 I described the general strategy adopted by cognitive scientists to handle each of these features. The case for information processing ineliminability, therefore, turns on whether the neural level of description also has the resources for providing such explanations. Although I am the first to admit that what counts as explaining something (or, on my view, answering questions of certain sorts) is exceedingly murky, I think it is intuitively quite clear that any attempt to account for the basic general features of cognition in low-level neural terms is doomed to failure. Whatever it is that explanations do for us, cognitively speaking, low-level neural descriptions simply don't have what it takes.

To see why, let us consider Q1 as applied to image generation. From the ordinary point of view, image generation begins with an intention to image an object of a certain sort in a certain way (say, in a certain color or size) and ends with the experience of having the intended image. This capacity, like most of our cognitive capacities, exhibits intentionality, coherence, pragmatic evaluability, reliability, and productivity. Since intentionality underwrites each of the other basic general properties except productivity, I shall focus primarily on that.

Now suppose neuroscientists want to understand more precisely, in low-level neural terms, what the human capacity to generate images *is* in a way that sheds light on the intentionality of the capacity. What kind of account must they come up with, and what kind of account are they likely to get?

First questions first. What kind of account must they come up with? The answer has two parts. As far as I can see, neuroscientists are going to have to come up with an account that closely mirrors the kind of account proposed by information processing theorists such as Kosslyn. That is, they will have to identify states (now in neural terms rather than information processing terms) that figure in the characteristic beginning and end states of the ordinary capacity. And since both the beginning state and the end state are intentional and, hence, involve an attitude, and have both content and significance, the neural description will have to include reference to properties that can do the job representational states are supposed to do in information-processing accounts. How is this possible, given that I have barred representations *per se* from the neural level? True, all references to representations *per se* have been barred; however, since features such as attitude, objective content, and significance are not supposed to be *basic* (that is, lacking a naturalistic supervenience base), it is possible that the neural level might include, if not representations themselves, then the naturalistic properties that determine what it is to be a representation. The first part of the answer, then, is that the sought-after neural description must include reference to properties capable of determining the various features of intentional states: their attitude, objective content, and significance.

The second requirement is that mere reference to such supervenience base properties is not enough. Reference to such properties must also be *explanatory*. It must lead to understanding.

Having considered what a satisfactory neural account must be like, let us now consider what we are likely to get. To simplify the discussion, let us assume that there is no multiple neural realizability over persons and over occasions. The first point to note is that if events at the neural level consist of groups of neurons firing in certain ways, then any first-order psychoneural correlations will be to *determinate* (types of) exercises of image generation rather than to the *determinable* types of states described above. Thus, imagine an individual—Joe—with very limited imaging ability. Joe can image only in black and white, and he can image only pine trees and apples, and these only as small or large, right-side-up or tilted, at the center of his imagistic "field," and with a medium degree detail. Then the folk-psychological states relevant to image generation in Joe for which we are likely to get first-order neural correlates will be either intention states specifying particular objects to be imaged in particular ways (at particular sizes, orientations, etc.) or states involving an imagistic experience of those particular objects.

Next question: In view of what neuroscientists are likely to get at the neural level, will they be able to get what they need to answer Q1 about image generation? I don't see how. All three key features of intentional states—attitude, objective content, and significance—seem to pose difficulties. Both attitude and significance require high-level computational notions not available at the neural level. And owing to the way cognitive scientists are currently thinking about content determination (as described in chapter 6), the chances that the supervenience-base properties of objective content will be located solely in the brain seem extremely remote.

But there are more serious problems still. Suppose I am simply wrong on this point. Suppose that we can identify neural states that determine the attitude, the objective content, and the significance of the various determinate mental states. The account would still be unsatisfactory, because it would not fill the second requirement. It would not be explanatory. Suppose it is rumored that a neuroscientist has discovered the answer to Q1 for image generation, and he has arrived at your campus for a lecture. You eagerly ask him a question: "Tell me, Professor X, when your subject Joe images a small pine tree at an angle in the center of his imagistic 'field,' what is going on at the neural level that explains the intentionality of Joe's imaging?" Professor X consults his table of psychoneural correlations and replies, in deep, serious tones. "I'm so glad you asked that. The explanation is simple. When Joe exercises his imaging capacity in that way his brain is moving from neural state N624 to neural state N1009." "Thank you, sir; that's very enlightening," you reply, as your mind draws a complete blank. Of course, if you *knew* that N624 was a composite of states that determined the attitude, objective content, and significance of Joe's intending to image a small pine tree at a tilt, then you might, in fact, feel enlightened. But then, of course, the explanation would not lie solely at the neural level. It would consist of an account at the neural level plus what philosophers of science call "bridge statements," which in this case make reference to *representational and computational properties*. I conclude, therefore, that explaining intentionality exclusively at the neural level is a hopeless enterprise.

Thus far I have appealed only to intentionality (and, indirectly, to reliability) in making the case for the information processing ineliminability thesis. Where do multiple realizability and capturing the generalizations come in?

Both Fodor (1981c) and Pylyshyn (1984) argue that descriptions at the neural level could never replace information processing accounts for purposes of explanation because the former simply can't "capture" the relevant generalizations. In order to understand this claim we need to lay a bit of groundwork. In particular, we need to get clear on what a generalization is, what the "relevant" generalizations are that presumably can't be captured, and what "capturing" amounts to.

Assume that a generalization is a kind of proposition that one can express in a "generalization sentence" using quantifiers such as 'all' and 'most'. And assume that generalizations describe regularities or patterns in nature which involve particular properties picked out by the predicates used in the generalization sentence. I take it that the "relevant" generalizations are the generalizations to be found in the information processing theories that cognitive scientists ultimately accept. In fact, from the standpoint of the present reconstruction, these generalizations are, for the most part, nothing but the answers to the basic questions of the field. This last point allows us to see why the issue of "capturing" the generalizations is relevant to the debate over information processing ineliminability. It is relevant because the debate concerns whether Q1–Q4 can be answered at the neural level. Since cognitive science can presumably answer these questions, and the answers constitute a set of generalizations, one way to frame the debate is to ask whether these information processing generalizations can be "captured" at the neural level. (Note, though, that this is only one way of framing the debate, since it presupposes that any explanatory set of answers will be relevantly similar to the cognitivist answers. It is possible, at least in principle, that completely explanatory answers could be given at the neural level but that these would not "capture" the generalizations formulated at the information processing level.)

Suppose now that cognitive scientists have identified a certain generalization which makes reference to computational processes and representational states and which therefore is expressed at the level of information processing. What would it mean for a neuroscientist to "capture" this information-processing generalization (IPG)? There are two things this claim might mean in this context, and these are not always clearly distinguished in the literature:

(a) IPG would be "captured" at the neural level if it could be *expressed* in a generalization statement at the neural level; or

(b) IPG would be "captured" at the neural level if another generalization —NG—could be discovered which, roughly speaking, identifies the same pattern as IPG describes, albeit with reference to different properties. (More about this shortly).

I shall call sense a "expressive capture" and sense b "reductive capture."

Most of the arguments in the literature are concerned with reductive capture. But in the light of our discussion about intentionality it should be clear that only sense a is really relevant. Even if neuroscientists could capture the information-processing generalizations of cognitive science at the neural level in sense b, this would not suffice to explain what cognitive scientists are interested in explaining. The reason is that NG, insofar as it makes no reference to computational and representational properties *per se*, could not answer the basic questions of the field in a way that accounted for the basic general properties of cognition. I shall take it, then, that the thesis of information-processing ineliminability has been sufficiently justified and, hence, that the following assumption can be added to our set of methodological assumptions for cognitive science.

M11[n]   Information-processing theories of the cognitive mind/brain can explain certain features of cognition that cannot be explained by means of lower-level neuroscientific accounts. Such theories are, thus, in principle, explanatorily ineliminable.

But what about reductive capture? Independent of any concern with explanatory eliminability, does it seem likely that neuroscientists could "capture" information-processing generalizations in sense b at the neural level? I am skeptical, but since nothing turns on the matter for my purposes let me simply indicate what I take to be the lay of the land. I will begin by saying a bit more about the generalizations to be captured and about what is involved in reductive capture.

Consider how Kosslyn answers Q2′ with respect to image generation. In schematic form, the resulting generalization looks roughly like this:

KG   (s)(t)(o)(p) (If a normal typical subject s has ⟨Generate an image of o with properties p⟩ in his or her "intention box" at t, then s will generate a surface representation of o with properties p by doing … shortly after t.)

According to Kosslyn's model, the instructions to the imaging system can (but need not) specify not only the object to be imaged but also various properties of the image, such as size, orientation, location in the "imagistic field," and level of detail. For the sake of a simpler exposition, I have collected all these parameters under the variable 'p' above. The ellipsis in the generalization is to be filled in with something like the flow chart given in figure 1.5.

Now what does it mean for one generalization G1, at one level of description L1, to capture another generalization G2, at another level of description L2? One possibility is this:

(1) Either G1 and G2 share the same domain or there is a function f mapping objects in the domain of G2 to objects in the domain of G1 where the value of the function will be an object that realizes the object constituting the argument of the function. Thus,

f(domain of G2) = domain of G1.

(2) For each predicate in the canonical statement of G2 there exists a predicate in the canonical statement of G1 that is, roughly speaking,

extensionally equivalent within the specified domains. More precisely, if the extension of the G2 predicate is a set A, then there exists a G1 predicate whose extension is either A itself or f(A).

(3) G1 and G2 have the same logical form.

Applying this conception of reductive capture to our sample generalization KG, we see that the reductive capture of KG by NG will require at least the following:

(1') The neural generalization NG must quantify over persons, occasions, and contents or over things which realize persons, occasions, and contents.

(2') There can be no multiple neural realization across persons or occasions. Furthermore, the neural descriptions of the various states involved in imaging must be just as *articulated* as the information-processing descriptions. Thus, if a person's surface representation can differ with respect to size, orientation, location, level of detail, and so forth, there must be distinct properties at the neural level corresponding to these features. And if image generation involves manipulation of the *parts* of the surface representation, this part-whole structure must be reflected in the underlying neural states as well. In other words, in Fodor's (1981c) terms, the neural descriptions cannot be "fused."

(3') Neural generalizations cannot "crosscut" information-processing ones.

Skepticism about whether the neural level has the theoretical resources to formulate generalizations which reductively capture information-processing generalizations is based on the belief that one or another of (1')–(3') cannot be satisfied. Most of the emphasis in the literature has been on the possibility of multiple neural realization, a possibility that undercuts (2'). Since this is an empirical matter and the facts are far from in, I prefer to focus on other aspects of the problem—in particular, those aspects that concern content. If what is required to capture a generalization such as KG is that the neural generalization actually quantify over contents themselves, then the matter is settled: Reductive capture is impossible, for contents simply don't exist at the neural level. I have made life a bit harder for the skeptic by allowing the reductionist to quantify over objects that realize contents rather than over the contents themselves. But then we get back to an earlier objection: Insofar as content determination for the mental representation system is not solely "in the head," even this weaker sort of quantification over content will be ruled out. Furthermore, there is serious question whether there will be properties at the neural level (where formal computational notions are just as absent as representational ones) to underwrite the compositional structure of the representations invoked in generalizations such as KG. In short, although the case against reductive capture is not iron-clad, the situation looks very unpromising.

Epilogue: Some Challenges for the Future

Books of this sort often end by making pronouncements about the future of the field that has been described (Norman 1981; Gardner 1985; Haugeland 198S). I will not try to buck this trend. This epilogue, therefore, consists of my personal list of challenges cognitive science must face if it is to remain viable. If there is an overall theme to this list, it is the need to integrate theories that focus on different aspects of mind and to integrate theories from different subdisciplines.

(1) The domain of cognitive science consists of the human cognitive capacities, and methodological assumptions M1 and M2 tell us that cognition is sufficiently autonomous from the surrounding cultural and social context and from other aspects of mind that, to a large extent, it can be studied in isolation. As the basis of a short-term research strategy, I have no quarrel with this claim. But it is essential that cognitive scientists not forget the qualification in these assumptions. Cognition can, be studied in isolation to a *large* extent, but not *completely*. Much of human cognizing takes place in social or cultural contexts. And, in fact, much important human cognizing—such as doing science—is social in its very nature (Smolensky 1988). In addition, cognition is connected in important ways with affect, motivation, personality, and consciousness (Norman 1981; Gardner 1985; Johnson-Laird 1988). In the long run, therefore, cognitive scientists must seek to develop theories of cognition that will integrate with the outer and inner contexts in which human cognizing takes place.

It is particularly important to integrate our theories of cognition with a theory of consciousness, as some cognitive scientists such as Johnson-Laird (1988) are beginning to do. We have seen that one of the facts about cognition that cognitive scientists seek to understand is that our ordinary cognitive capacities are intentional. But the intentional states that make up the beginning and/or end points of our cognitive capacities are states of which we are aware. The content of such states is handled at the information-processing level by positing representations which themselves have content. Their "attitude" is handled by the computational relations to which the underlying representations are subject. But what about the fact that these states are conscious? What does that come to in information-processing terms?

(2) Cognitive science assumes that the human mind/brain is a computational device, but we have seen that the notion of a computer employed by

cognitive science is relatively vague and open-ended. Two architecturally more specific conceptions have been employed in research to date (conventional computers and connectionist computers); however, both seem to have limitations. Conventional devices are slow, ill suited for modeling certain aspects of cognition (such as pattern recognition), fault intolerant, and neurally implausible. Connectionist machines cannot (as yet, anyway) handle high-level sequential cognitive tasks or account for the productivity and systematicity of human cognition. In addition, although they are more neurally plausible than conventional machines, their architecture differs in significant respects from brain architecture. (See Smolensky 1988 for a nice table summarizing the similarities and differences.) But if the mind/brain is neither a conventional nor a connectionist device, then what kind of computer is it? The second challenge for cognitive science is to answer this question—that is, to develop a conception of a kind of computer that is truly neurally plausible.

(3) According to cognitive science, the cognitive mind/brain is a device that has states or contains within it entities that are representations. There is much, however, about these representations that is poorly understood. Cognitive scientists are beginning to develop hypotheses about what kinds of representations are implicated in what sorts of cognitive tasks but the nature of the mental representation system itself is almost a complete mystery. Is MRS a homogeneous language of thought, or does it consist in various subsystems distinguished by something like modality (e.g., imagistic versus propositional representation)? What is the semantics of MRS? How is the content of MRS determined?

The challenge of understanding mental representation lies not just in answering such questions but in figuring out how to go about answering them. In particular, are there empirical findings that could be brought to bear to constrain answers to these questions? I have suggested that certain very general features of the semantics of MRS can be inferred on the basis of certain very general features of our cognitive capacities (section 5.3). In like fashion, I believe that these posited general features of the semantics of MRS—selectivity, diversity, complexity, and so forth—can be used to constrain and evaluate proposed theories of content determination. But is this the best we can do?

There are other problems associated with developing a semantics for MRS. Specific hypotheses about the content of mental representations are often based on content attributions made in the idiom of folk psychology. But a number of philosophers, particularly Burge (1979) and Stich (1983), have argued that the attribution of propositional-attitude content is subject to a variety of contextual pressures. In particular, it is claimed that propositional attitude attributions are relative to the observer (Stich) and to the language community (Burge). In contrast, cognitive scientists generally assume that the semantics of MRS is objective and independent of the social or linguistic context of the subject. But does this discrepancy between content attribution at the folk-psychology level and content attribution at the information-processing level raise an insoluble epistemic and methodological obstacle to the study of MRS?

(4) The last challenge is sociological rather than conceptual. I have suggested that, in order to be successful, cognitive science must move toward a less isolated, more integrated conception of its subject matter. Such a desideratum underscores the importance of a multidisciplinary and, in fact, an interdisciplinary approach to the study of cognition in which disciplinary boundaries and loyalties are less important than what aspect of the cognitive domain is being worked on (Gardner 1985). But there are major institutional obstacles in the way of serious interdisciplinary research—departmental structure, hiring and promotion practices, and so forth. The challenge is, thus, to continue to resist and fight against these conservative forces, working toward an institutional structure that facilitates rather than impedes the research that cognitive scientists have mapped out for themselves.

Appendix: Characterizing an Immature Science

The history of modern philosophy of science can be divided into three periods: the hegemony of the logical positivist tradition from the 1920s to the late 1950s, the more or less radical response to the logical positivist tradition from the late 1950s through the 1960s (what Suppe [1977] calls the "Weltanschauungen analyses"), and the current period of diversity and eclecticism. In each of these periods, views have been advanced that, either directly or indirectly, address the question of how best to characterize the fundamental commitments shared by a scientific community. In this appendix I will consider a representative view from each period and assess it in terms of the desiderata described in chapter 1. Section A.1 will briefly consider the logical positivist tradition, section A.2 will consider Thomas Kuhn's challenge to this tradition, and section A.3 will take a careful look at a promising post-positivist proposal: the view of Larry Laudan.[1] The mode of my exploration will, naturally enough, be dictated by the purposes at hand. Thus, I will be engaged in a process of sifting and sorting, and, in general, attempting to distinguish what is sound (coherent, clear, plausible) in the texts under consideration from what is not, and what is relevant to my purposes from what is not. As I indicated in chapter 1, the bottom line of these explorations will be that a new proposal is required. However, this new proposal (detailed in section 1.1) will be built on the insights assembled from a careful study of past efforts.

A.1 The Logical Positivist Tradition

From the 1920s until, roughly, the early 1960s, research in philosophy of science was dominated by an approach to science that grew out of work by the so-called logical positivists. Extrapolating somewhat from Suppe 1977, I shall call this approach "the received view."[2]

Although the received view is no longer so universally well received as it once was, having been subjected to fairly serious revision by sympathizers as well as radical challenge by critics, it nevertheless constitutes an appropriate starting point for our inquiries. It is difficult to arrive at an adequate understanding of subsequent developments in philosophy of science without understanding what was being reacted against. In addition, certain features of the received view are far from dead, as a glance at current journals, popular textbooks, or the relatively recent volume *Current Research in Philosophy of Science* (Asquith and Kyburg 1979) will readily reveal.

In his highly stimulating study of alternative contemporary schools of metascience, Radnitzky (1973, p. 19) alludes to the fact that a philosophical school or tradition can be viewed from a variety of different "altitudes." That is, it can be described more or less abstractly and with more or less detail depending on the purposes at hand. From a relatively low "altitude," the received view can be seen to encompass a fairly large body of evolving doctrine on such topics as the structure of scientific theories, the nature of explanation, confirmation and induction, the nature of scientific laws, and the reduction of one theory to another. For our purposes, such a detailed description is unnecessary. This is because we are interested not so much in the detailed doctrines which the adherents of the received view developed about the nature of science as in the sort of *approach* they took to their subject matter. This approach can be summed up in two tenets:

(1) The principal objects of study for the philosopher of science are the "products" of science—its theories, hypotheses, laws, explanations, models, etc.

(2) The principal aim of philosophy of science is to propose a theory of the "good-making" characteristics of the various products of science.

In an early paper (1938), Rudolph Carnap, one of the leading exponents of logical positivism, makes the focus on the products of science quite explicit:

The task of analyzing science may be approached from various angles.... We may, for instance, think of an investigation of scientific *activity*. We may study the historical development of this activity. Or we may try to find out in which way scientific work depends upon the individual conditions of the men working in science, and upon the status of the society surrounding them. Or we may describe procedures and appliances used in scientific work. These investigations of scientific activity may be called history, psychology, sociology, and methodology of science. The subject matter of such studies is science as a body of actions carried out by certain persons under certain circumstances.... We come to a theory of science in another sense if we study not the actions of scientists but their results, namely, science as a body of ordered knowledge. Here, by 'results' we do not mean beliefs, images, etc., and the behavior influenced by them. That would lead us again to psychology of science. We mean by 'results' certain linguistic expressions, viz., the statements asserted by scientists. The task of the theory of science in this sense will be to analyze such statements, study their kinds and relations, and analyze terms as components of those statements and theories, as ordered systems of those statements.   (pp. 42–43)

Twenty-two years later, the point is repeated by Ernest Nagel in his preface to a popular anthology of writings in philosophy of science:

[Much] is gained in the way of clarifying the aims of philosophical analysis by limiting the philosophy of science to a group of related questions that arise in attempting to understand *the intellectual products* of scientific inquiry as embodied in explicitly formulated statements. (Danto and Morgenbesser 1960, p. 13; my emphasis)

A study of some of the principal texts in the philosophy of science of the 1960s and the early 1970s provides further evidence for the product orientation of the received view. Of the seven substantive chapters in Hempel's (1966) classic *Philosophy of Natural Science*, two are on the problem of testing or confirming scientific hypotheses, one is on laws and their role in scientific explanation, one is on the structure of scientific theories, one is on the nature of scientific concepts, and one is on the nature of scientific reduction (specifically, the reduction of terms and the reduction of laws). Nagel's (1961) *Structure of Science* contains six chapters on metascientific topics and eight on issues related to specific disciplines such as physics, biology, and history. The six metascientific chapters include two on scientific explanation, one on scientific laws, and three on scientific theories (one on their structure, one on their cognitive status, and one on the nature of reduction of one theory to another). Brody's (1970) anthology of readings in philosophy of science has three major parts: part I, on explanation and prediction; part II, on the structure and function of scientific theories; and part III, on the confirmation of scientific hypotheses. These books are typical.

In view of the received view's preoccupation with the "good-making" characteristics of science, its focus on intellectual products is, perhaps, understandable. But from the perspective of the post-Kuhnian era it can be seen that this narrow focus had some clearly undesirable consequences. Whole facets of science were taken out of the purview of philosophy and relegated to the psychologist, the social scientist, or the historian. And even topics that were deemed properly philosophical often received one-sided treatment.

A case in point—and one relevant to our concerns—is how the received view dealt with the existence and the significance of distinct scientific fields. In the first place, because the logical positivists were obsessed with the idea of promoting the unity of science, advocates of the received view tended to play down the importance of divisions within science. Campbell (1921), for example, in his classic text *What Is Science?*, argues that "science is a single whole" and that "the divisions between its branches are largely conventional and devoid of ulterior significance" (p. 13). Secondly, where the significance of branches of science was acknowledged, such branches were usually identified with the body of theory accepted by scientists within that branch. For instance, at one point in his 1959 book *A Philosopher Looks at Science*, Kemeny comments:

We do not have as complete a picture of the structure of Science [as we do of the color continuum], since our knowledge of theories is incomplete. Scientists will study a group of phenomena which seem related, and try to connect them by means of a theory. Sometimes they fail, and at other times they succeed. In the latter case, we have a branch of Science. But there is a great deal of arbitrariness in this procedure.   (p. 179)

A similar identification of branches of sciences with their theories is to be found in Kemeny and Oppenheim's famous 1955 paper "On reduction." Reduction is first defined as a relation between theories. Subsequently, Kemeny and Oppenheim suggest that there is a natural way of extending their account so that it makes sense to talk about the reduction of one branch of science to another. This natural way turns out to be identifying any given branch with its "theoretical body" (p. 314).

It appears, then, that insofar as a proposal emerges from the logical positivist tradition for characterizing an individual science or field, it is that, from the standpoint of philosophy of science, a field should be described in terms of its prevailing body of theory. It should be clear that this proposal is completely unsuitable for our purposes. Although there is no lack of theories within cognitive science (given a suitably generous notion of theory), because of the immaturity of the field, the theories of cognitive science do not, at this point, command much consensus. Hence, if a transdisciplinary framework of commitments for cognitive science exists, as I am supposing, it must take some other form.

A.2   Kuhn's Notion of a Paradigm

In our quest for a suitable metatheoretic unit of analysis, Kuhn's notion of a paradigm merits close attention for several reasons. First, Kuhn's views in general, particularly those articulated in his book *The Structure of*

Scientific Revolutions (1970a; henceforth, *SSR*), are widely known and have been extremely influential. As a result, there have been a variety of attempts to describe or analyze particular scientific fields in terms of the notion of a paradigm.[3] In psychology, for example, such analyses have been attempted for Wundtian structural psychology, neo-behaviorism, and cognitive psychology.[4] This fact itself provides a certain *prima facie* argument for taking Kuhn's views seriously. More important, however, a number of the psychologists who have turned to Kuhn for help in conceptualizing various areas of psychology have done so because they regard the modes of description provided by the received view as inadequate, just as I do. Lachman, Lachman, and Butterfield (1979), for example, who make the notion of a paradigm the central organizing principle of their textbook on cognitive psychology, motivate their choice as follows:

The knowledge that a field claims at any point in its development cannot be unified, at that time, by a correct account of the phenomenon it studies; for that only becomes available much later.... What, then, does? It is our premise that the data, experiments, and theory of a developing field can only be fully understood by reference to the paradigmatic commitments of its practitioners. A dynamic field of science is held together by its *paradigm*.   (p. ix)

In other words, because cognitive psychology is still developing, they regard any description in terms of a finished product as untenable. Similarly, Kessel (1969) argues that the "standard" empiricist view of science cannot provide an account of the tacit "premises" or "presuppositions" which play a significant role at all levels of scientific activity. For this, he claims, we must turn to the views of Kuhn.

Kuhn's conception of a paradigm merits close attention, then, not only because it has gained wide currency but also because—if we take seriously the reasoning of others who have been attracted to the notion—it promises to provide us with a framework capable of handling the commitments of an immature science such as cognitive science. Unfortunately, however, evaluating Kuhn's central notion is no easy matter. One of the central criticisms of *SSR* has been that Kuhn's use of the term 'paradigm' suffers from excessive looseness and even inconsistency. Shapere (1964), for example, accuses Kuhn of putting forth a notion so broad that "anything that allows science to accomplish anything can be a part of (or somehow involved in) a paradigm" (p. 385). Masterman (1970) goes so far as to claim that Kuhn uses the term 'paradigm' in twenty-one different senses.[5] Kuhn himself, in his later writings,[6] has admitted to using the term in *two* very different ways, for which he has since provided new labels (viz. 'disciplinary matrix' and 'exemplar'). Such criticisms are of concern to us because if they are correct they suggest that the Kuhnian notion of a paradigm may be inadequate for our purposes simply on the grounds that it does not satisfy our desideratum of soundness. Thus, our first task must be to determine whether Kuhn even provides us with a clear notion or set of notions suitable for assessment. What we shall discover is that, insofar as we can extract a clear conception from the text, the Kuhnian notion of a paradigm will be a far less radical departure from traditional thinking than it has seemed to many of its adherents.

The view presented in *SSR* is, fundamentally, a theory of scientific change. Arguing against the so-called received view that regarded scientific development as the cumulative process by which facts, theories and methods are "added, singly and in combination, to the ever growing stockpile that constitutes scientific technique and knowledge" (Kuhn 1970a, p. 2),[7] Kuhn proposes, instead, that such cumulative growth is characteristic of only one of the four stages of scientific inquiry, namely, the period of "normal science." It is not true of the immature periods of science— the period of "indiscriminate fact finding" and the period of "multiple schools"—which typically preceed the period of normal science; nor is it true of the period of "crisis and revolution," which typically follows the period of normal science.

Kuhn's basic insight, and the one that serves as the organizing principle for his entire account, is that effective scientific research (that is, research which appears to "progress" and add to our store of knowledge of facts and theories) can take place only within a framework of shared commitments of a certain sort, the locus of which is what Kuhn calls a "scientific community." What distinguishes the various stages of scientific inquiry is the presence or absence, the precise nature, and the status of this framework. Roughly speaking, the earliest period of indiscriminate fact finding is characterized by the absence of such a framework. During the subsequent period of multiple schools, such frameworks have been adopted and they guide research, but they differ in certain important respects from the frameworks that guide normal science research, and, in addition, each competing school has its own. During periods of normal science, there is widespread agreement on a single framework and the character of this framework is such that it guides research in a particularly effective way.

Finally, during periods of crisis and revolution, this single shared framework is threatened and may, ultimately, give way to an alternative.

In Kuhn's original book, the role of this framework of shared commitments is, of course, played by the notion of a "paradigm." It is presumably the absence or presence of a paradigm that distinguishes the "pre-paradigmatic" period of the schools from the period of normal science (although, as we shall see, the text is somewhat confusing on this point). It is commitment to the same paradigm that allows a scientific community to engage in progressive and coherent research. And it is paradigms that are questioned and overthrown during periods of crisis and revolution. Thus the "burden" of Kuhn's original account is clearly placed on the notion of a paradigm (Shapere 1964).

But what, precisely, is a paradigm? This is a question to which Kuhn, unfortunately, never provides a very clear answer. That *SSR* contains numerous inconsistencies and confusions regarding what a paradigm is should be obvious to anyone who reads the text closely. It seems to me, however, that from the start Kuhn provides us with a fairly clear *functional characterization* (in terms of its role in science) of a paradigm. It is only when he tries to spell out what *sort* of thing (characterized intrinsically) plays this functional role that difficulties begin to emerge.

Kuhn first introduces the notion of a paradigm in the context of his discussion of normal science. Although the relevant passage is rather long, it will be useful for present purposes to quote it in its entirety:

In this essay, 'normal science' means research firmly based upon one or more past scientific achievements, achievements that some particular scientific community acknowledges for a time as supplying the foundation for its further practice. Today such achievements are recounted, though seldom in their original form, by science textbooks, elementary and advanced. These textbooks expound the body of accepted theory, illustrate many or all of its successful applications, and compare these applications with exemplary observations and experiments. Before such books became popular early in the nineteenth century (and until even more recently in the newly matured sciences), many of the famous classics of science fulfilled a similar function. Aristotle's *Physica*, Ptolemy's *Almagest*, Newton's *Principia* and *Opticks*, Franklin's *Electricity*, Lavoisier's *Chemistry*, and Lyell's *Geology*—these and many other works served for a time implicitly to define the legitimate problems and methods of a research field for succeeding generations of practitioners. They were able to do so because they shared two essential characteristics. Their achievement was sufficiently unprecedented to attract an enduring group of adherents away from competing modes of scientific activity. Simultaneously, it was sufficiently open-ended to leave all sorts of problems for the redefined group of practitioners to resolve.

Achievements that share these two characteristics I shall henceforth refer to as 'paradigms', a term that relates closely to 'normal science'. By choosing it, I mean to suggest that some accepted examples of actual scientific practice—examples which include law, theory, application, and instrumentation together—provide models from which spring particular coherent traditions of scientific research. (p. 10)

Now, it seems perfectly clear from this passage *roughly* what sort of thing a paradigm is supposed to be. It is a specific scientific achievement (or set of scientific achievements) that plays a certain functional role in inquiry: It (a) gives rise to a particularly coherent and "progressive" tradition of scientific research (at least partly) in virtue of (b) the fact that it has attracted a group of adherents and (c) the fact that it is sufficiently open-ended to leave all sorts of problems for these adherents to solve. The important point to note is that in this initial formulation paradigms are essentially characterized in terms of their generative role vis-à-vis normal science. This fact is important, on my view, because one can view this initial characterization as, in some sense, setting the stage and defining the terms of Kuhn's subsequent elaboration of the notion of a paradigm in the rest of *SSR*. That is, one can take it as a significant part of Kuhn's project to flesh out more precisely *how* paradigms play the generative role that has been envisioned for them. In view of the claims that commitment to a paradigm somehow "gives rise" to periods of normal research and the claim that such normal research is characterized by both its coherence (single-mindedness) and its effectiveness (progressiveness), a number of questions naturally arise. What is it about a paradigm that leads to research in the first place? That is, in what respects is it open-ended? What lends this research its coherence or unity? What makes it particularly effective or progressive? What *kind* of thing is a paradigm? How do paradigms differ from the sorts of things to which "pre-paradigmatic" schools are committed such that research generated by the latter falls to have the coherence and progressiveness characteristic of normal reseach? I take it that much of what goes on in the initial chapters of *SSR* constitutes Kuhn's attempt to answer these various questions. I also take it that the soundness (i.e., coherence, clarity, consistency) of Kuhn's conception of a paradigm is in large measure a function of how successful this attempt is. As we shall see, although *SSR* is suggestive on a number of points, it appears to be virtually impossible to wrest anything like an internally adequate account from its pages.

It will be useful to begin our discussion of the details of Kuhn's views on paradigms and normal science by considering his contrast between normal science and the science of the schools. On the standard exegesis of Kuhn, pre-normal science is distinguished from normal science by the fact that the latter is somehow rooted in a paradigm whereas the former is not. This exegesis is clearly supported by certain passages in the text. For example, in describing "the route to normal science" Kuhn sketches the history of physical optics and claims that, from Newton to the present, physical optics reveals "the usual developmental pattern of mature science," namely "the successive transition from one paradigm to another via revolution" (p. 12). Before Newton, however, the pattern is very different. In particular, on Kuhn's view, "no period between remote antiquity and the end of the seventeenth century exhibited a single generally accepted view about the nature of light. Instead there were a number of competing schools and subschools...." (p. 12) The inference is clear: Mature science involves paradigms whereas the science of the schools does not.

Two features of Kuhn's discussion of pre-normal science raise questions about this reading, however. The first is that Kuhn describes what unites members of a "school" during periods of immature science in a way very similar to the way he describes what unites a research community during periods of normal science. He suggests, for example, that every school will be committed to "some implicit body of intertwined theoretical and methodological belief that permits selection, evaluation, and criticism" (p. 17). And later, in discussing the transition from pre-normal science to normal science in the study of electricity, he remarks that both the fluid theory of electricity (held by a school of electricians) and the Franklinian paradigm (later held by the entire group of electricians) functioned similarly in guiding their respective research programs. Both "suggested which experiments would be worth performing and which, because directed to secondary or to overly complex manifestations of electricity, would not" (p. 18). The situation gets even more confusing when we read such things as the following:

The history of electrical research in the first half of the eighteenth century provides a more concrete and better known example of the way a science develops before it acquires its *first universally received* paradigm.   (p. 13; my emphasis)

In parts of biology—the study of heredity, for example—the first universally received paradigms are still more recent; and it remains an open question what parts of social science have yet acquired *such* paradigms at all. (p. 15; my emphasis)

What is confusing about such passages is that the qualifications 'universally received' and 'such' suggest that before a science has its first universally received paradigm it has something which is not universally received but is a paradigm nonetheless. In other words, it suggests that the schools of immature science also have paradigms.[8]

Although some aspects of Kuhn's discussion introduce some confusion as to the precise role of paradigms in distinguishing between pre-normal and normal science, still the gist of what Kuhn wants to say about the transition from immature to mature science seems clear enough. Such a transition occurs when, first, one of the multiple competing schools achieves a high degree of *success* in formulating a theory and explaining a significant set of facts in the domain in question and, second, this achievement is recognized by virtually all the interested parties.[9] Both the fact of a significant achievement in solving a certain set of scientific problems and the cessation of competing views on foundational and theoretical matters are essential, on Kuhn's view, for normal science to proceed, for normal science is characterized by a certain narrow-minded focus which is possible only if the research scientist has supreme confidence in what he is doing and only if his attention is not diverted by controversies over foundational issues stirred up by those with radically different approaches to the subject matter. These points are brought out most clearly in Kuhn's discussion of the transition between pre-normal and normal science in the study of electricity:

What the fluid theory of electricity did for the subgroup that held it, the Franklinian paradigm later did for the entire group of electricians.... Only the paradigm did the job far more effectively, partly because the end of interschool debate ended the constant reiteration of fundamentals and partly because the confidence that they were on the right track encouraged scientists to undertake more precise, esoteric and consuming sorts of work. Freed from the concern with any and all electrical phenomena, the united group of electricians could pursue selected phenomena in far more detail, designing much special equipment for the task and employing it more stubbornly and systematically than electricians had ever done before. Both fact collection and theory articulation became highly directed activities. (p. 18)

Note that we have here a partial answer to the question of how paradigms give rise to periods of normal science. Because paradigms are, "by definition" as it were, scientific contributions that have achieved both success and recognition, they engender in the scientists committed to them a degree of confidence that leads to both a significant investment of resources and a certain narrowness of focus. Although these two factors are certainly not sufficient to bring about the sort of effective and progressive research that characterizes normal research, one can certainly see how they might contribute to the single-mindedness of the effort involved. This account tells us very little, however, about the intellectual role that paradigms are supposed to play. How is it that they give rise to research in the first place? What is it about a paradigm that controls the direction of this research? To answer these questions, Kuhn must say something more in *substantive* terms about the kind of things they are.

If we consult the Kuhnian text in an effort to determine more precisely the sort of thing Kuhn takes paradigmatic scientific achievements to be, three possible candidates emerge: scientific theories, certain "networks" of commitments held by scientists (which Kuhn often refers to as "rules" of a certain sort), and particular instances of scientific research that consist primarily in the *application* of a theory to some set of observations. Let us examine what he has to say about each of these.

Paradigms as Theories

Supporting the view that theories are kinds of or aspects of paradigmatic scientific achievements is Kuhn's discussion of the nature of normal science in the third chapter of *SSR*. Normal science, according to Kuhn, is "mop-up work." It is not aimed at "call[ing] forth new sorts of phenomena" or at "invent[ing] new theories." Instead, "normal-scientific research is directed to the articulation of those phenomena and theories that the paradigm already supplies" (p. 24). To be more precise, normal science consists of both "factual scientific investigation" and "theoretical investigation." The former has "only three normal foci." The first is "that class of facts that the paradigm has shown to be particularly revealing of the nature of things" (p. 29). The second consists of "those facts that, though often without much intrinsic interest, can be compared directly with predictions from the paradigm theory" (p. 29). And the third is the "empirical work undertaken to articulate the paradigm theory, resolving some of its residual ambiguities and permitting the solution of problems to which it had previously only drawn attention" (p. 29).

Theoretical investigation also has a number of different facets. A small part of theoretical work consists simply in "the use of existing theory to predict factual information of intrinsic value" (p. 30). A larger part consists in "manipulations of theory undertaken, not because the predictions in which they result are intrinsically valuable, but because they can be confronted directly with experiment" (p. 30). Finally, there are also theoretical problems of "paradigm articulation," that is, problems concerned with clarifying the theory by reformulation.

Of the six specific kinds of normal science investigation that Kuhn describes, five involve the use of a scientific theory in some essential way. Since normal science is supposed to be the working out of a paradigm, Kuhn's detailed account of the nature of normal science strongly suggests that theories (with their associated predictions) are, at least, key constituents of paradigms. This picture also supplies a fairly adequate account of what it is about paradigms that leads to research in the first place and what it is that leads to research marked by coherence and effectiveness. The first problem is explicitly addressed by Kuhn in chapter 3 of *SSR* ("If the paradigm represents work that has been done once and for all, what further problems does it leave the united group to resolve?"—p. 23). His answer is that when a paradigm makes its first appearance and is accepted by the relevant research group in question, it is often exceedingly limited in both scope and precision. It is at the start more a promise of success than a completed achievement. Normal science research is then the result of attempts by the research community to actualize the promise represented by the theory by extending its scope empirically and increasing its precision theoretically. Furthermore, what gives such research its coherence is that it is focused on a single theory. What makes it effective is less clear, although the key again seems to be that normal science is research based on a theory that has already achieved some measure of success. Insofar as this success leads to a narrowing of focus and a channeling of resources, the probability of continued success is enhanced. Furthermore, initial success provides some reason to believe that the theory is on the right track empirically and, hence, that nature will cooperate in further research along the same lines.

Paradigms as Rules

A very different view is suggested by Kuhn's discussion of "rules" and their role in normal science in the subsequent two chapters. Rules are first assigned a place in the Kuhnian scheme in the context of Kuhn's comparison of normal science to puzzle-solving. The problems of normal science share a number of important characteristics with puzzles, according to Kuhn. Two of these are of particular importance. First, puzzles have definite solutions. Second, to classify as a puzzle a problem must be associated with "rules that limit both the nature of acceptable solutions and the steps by which they are to be obtained" (p. 38). The relevance to normal science is this:

If we can accept a considerably broadened use of the term 'rule'—one that will occasionally equate it with 'established viewpoint' or with 'preconception'—then the problems accessible within a given research tradition display something much like this set of puzzle characteristics.   (p. 39)

These "rules" fall into four main categories:

"explicit statements of scientific law and about scientific concepts and theories"

"a multitude of commitments to preferred types of instrumentation and to the ways in which accepted instruments may legitimately be employed"

"the higher level, quasi-metaphysical commitments" that concern what sorts of entities the universe contains, what ultimate laws and fundamental explanations must be like, and what (at least, some) legitimate research problems consist in

those commitments "without which no man is a scientist" that concern the fundamental aims and the fundamental methods of science.   (pp. 40–42)

Note that it is far from clear how *these* "rules" are supposed to play their assigned role in puzzle-solving. *How* do they "limit both the nature of acceptable solutions and the steps by which they are to be obtained"? Kuhn's talk about "puzzle-solving" is suggestive, but at this point in his discussion it is far too vague to be very illuminating.

Nevertheless, Kuhn's motivation for the analogy seems clear. He intends the likening of normal science to puzzle-solving to provide us with some account of why normal science research is so effective and progressive (the only problems worked on are those guaranteed to have a solution) as well as what gives it its coherence (the research program is focused on a single set of problems and attempts to solve these problems in a particular way). And since we have previously been told that it is commitment to a paradigm that makes normal science so effective and coherent, it is natural to assume that Kuhn's network of "rules" *is* the paradigm. However, Kuhn soon disabuses us of this assumption. Although a discussion of puzzles and of rules can serve to illuminate the nature of normal scientific practice, "in another way, that illumination may be significantly misleading" (p. 42).

Though there obviously are rules to which all the practitioners of a scientific specialty adhere at a given time, those rules may not by themselves specify all that the practice of those specialists has in common.... That is why, at the start of this essay, I introduced shared paradigms rather than shared rules, assumptions, and points of view as the source of coherence for normal research traditions. *Rules*, I suggest, *derive from paradigms*, but paradigms can guide research even in the absence of rules. (p. 42; my emphasis)

Paradigms as Theory Applications

But if a paradigm is not the network of commitments—conceptual, theoretical, instrumental, and methodological—that Kuhn calls "rules," then what is it? It is something far more *concrete*, according to Kuhn in chapter 5 of *SSR*:

Close historical investigation of a given specialty at a given time discloses a set of recurrent and quasi-standard *illustrations* of various theories in their conceptual, observational, and instrumental applications. These are the community's paradigms, revealed in its textbooks, lectures, and laboratory exercises. (p. 43)

Kuhn's reason for identifying paradigms with such concrete instances of research is closely tied to his interest in making commitment to a paradigm psychologically instrumental in the generation of normal scientific research. He notes, for example, that any given scientific subspecialty is always *taught* and *learned* by means of such concrete examples. Furthermore, when scientists communicate their research to one another, it is always in this concrete form (p. 46). Of course, these facts by themselves do not dictate any particular psychological model for how normal research gets generated. Given such concrete examples of research, scientists could proceed in a variety of ways. Consistent with the view that a paradigm is primarily a scientific theory, one might argue that scientists proceed by abstracting this theory from the concrete research example and then producing new research by either further empirical application of the theory or further theory articulation as suggested by Kuhn's account of normal science in chapter 2. Or, consistent with the view that a paradigm consists of a set of "rules," scientists might proceed by abstracting from the concrete research example both a set of puzzles and a set of rules to guide them in their solution. New research would then simply be generated by doing the relevant problem solving. Kuhn, however, rejects both of these pictures for the simple reason that he is skeptical that scientists abstract anything at all. Instead he argues that scientists produce new instances of scientific research by somehow "modeling" them directly on the paradigmatic achievement without the intervention of anything like a set of rules.[10] However, what this process of direct modeling is supposed to come to remains totally mysterious and vague.[11] The difficulty is that without a more satisfactory elaboration of what Kuhn has in mind it is completely unclear how, or even whether, paradigms as theory-applications can satisfy the functional role that paradigms are supposed to play. What is it about such paradigms that generates a normal science research tradition? What would give such a tradition its coherence and effectiveness?

Let us take stock. To be adequate for our purposes Kuhn's notion of a paradigm must satisfy two desiderata: it must be sound (that is, clear, consistent, and coherent), and it must be suitable for the characterization of an immature science such as cognitive science. Although the notion has been invoked by psychologists to characterize various subfields of psychology, two immediately evident features of Kuhn's account should give us pause: the fact that Kuhn does not seem to use the term 'paradigm' in a consistent way and the fact that, on the standard account of Kuhn's theory of scientific change, the presence of a paradigm is what is supposed to *distinguish* the period of normal science (i.e., mature science?) from the period of multiple schools (i.e., immature science?). The first feature raises questions concerning the soundness of Kuhn's account whereas the second raises questions concerning its applicability to cognitive science.

However, neither feature should be regarded as decisive. This is particularly true of the second. As we saw, even Kuhn is of two minds as to whether "schools" of science have paradigms. Furthermore, it is not all that clear that only mature sciences are capable of normal science in the sense of coherent, effective research activity.

The first feature is more troublesome. But even here the notion of a paradigm might be saved for our purposes. Even if there is not a *single* coherent account of what a paradigm is and how it gives rise to normal science, one of Kuhn's three senses, taken individually, might do the trick. Unfortunately, this turns out not to be the case. Of the three views, the only one that provides a clear account of how a paradigm gives rise to normal science is the view that paradigms are theories. But this view is clearly inadequate for our purposes, because it fails to satisfy the immaturity desideratum. Thus, although at the outset Kuhn's notion seems to promise a radical break from the product-oriented approach of the received view, in fact we are back just where we started. It is thus with interest that we turn to Kuhn's later work to see if any advances can be made.

In a series of papers written around 1969[12] Kuhn attempts to reply to some of the criticisms directed at *SSR*—especially the charge of systematic ambiguity in his treatment of the notion of paradigm. The result is a number of changes in his position that are of interest to us. First, he radically alters his functional characterization of a paradigm, divorcing it from its close association with normal science and marrying it instead to the notion of a scientific community. Second, he attempts to rescue his notion of a paradigm from the charge of systematic ambiguity by distinguishing two new notions—*disciplinary matrix* and *exemplar*—each of which is supposed to assume some of the jobs formerly associated with the notion of a paradigm. Finally, he reassigns the role formerly held by paradigms with respect to generating normal science research to exemplars and attempts to answer the question of how exemplars give rise to normal science research by an elaboration of his views on modeling.

Paradigms are now seen as fundamentally what is shared by a scientific community. Kuhn recognizes that in order to avoid the problem of circularity (defining a paradigm as what the members of a scientific community share and a scientific community as a group of researchers that share a paradigm) he must ultimately find a way of identifying scientific communities independently. At this point, however, he is content to mention various techniques being explored by sociologists of knowledge which may eventually lead to a solution of this problem.[13]

An important consequence of this change, which Kuhn explicitly recognizes, is that the distinction between pre-normal and normal science can no longer be drawn in terms of the absence or presence of a paradigm. Every scientific community, including the schools of pre-normal science, is now said to possess a paradigm. What then characterizes the transition to the maturity of normal science? Kuhn's revised answer is that it is no longer simply the acquisition of a paradigm; rather, it is the acquisition of a paradigm with a specific "nature" or of a particular *sort*.

Before we can inquire into precisely what sort that is supposed to be, we must lay out Kuhn's new distinction between disciplinary matrices and exemplars. In the postscript to *SSR* (1970a, p. 175), Kuhn now admits that the term 'paradigm' was used in two essentially different ways. One was to refer to "the entire constellation of beliefs, values, techniques, and so on shared by the members of a given community." The other was to refer to one particular element of this constellation, namely the concrete puzzle-solutions previously discussed as theory-applications. The first, similar but not identical to what Kuhn formerly called "rules," he now dubs a "disciplinary matrix"; the second he calls "exemplars."

More specifically, a disciplinary matrix is a constellation of commitments shared by a specific scientific community that can account for "the relative fullness of their professional communication and the relative unanimity of their professional judgments" (postscript, p. 182) and which is relevant to the functioning of the scientific community as a "producer and validator of sound knowledge" (1977, p. 298). Its central elements include the following:

Symbolic generalizations, such as '$f = ma$' or 'elements combine in constant proportion by weight.' These have two important properties for Kuhn's purposes. They are expressions which are already formal or which can be readily cast in a form that allows for the application of logic and mathematics. And they "are not so much generalizations as generalization-sketches, schematic forms whose detailed symbolic expression varies from one application to the next" (1977, p. 465). For example, for the problem of free fall, '$f = ma$' becomes '$mg = md^2s/dt^2$'; for the simple pendulum, it becomes '$mg \sin \theta = -md^2s/dt^2$', and so forth.

Models, by which Kuhn seems to mean beliefs about what some set of natural phenomena are *like* ("heuristic" models), or beliefs about what they *really are* ("metaphysical" models). An example of the first is the belief that a gas behaves *like* a collection of microscopic billiard balls; an example of the second is the belief that the heat of a body *is* the kinetic energy of its constituent particles. Like the "higher-level, quasi-metaphysical commitments" that constituted one kind of "rule" in *SSR*, such models putatively "help to determine what will be accepted as an explanation and as a puzzle-solution" and "assist in the determination of the roster of unsolved puzzles and in the evaluation of the importance of each" (postscript, p. 184).

Exemplars—the concrete problem-solutions that students encounter in their scientific education (in the laboratory, on examinations, and in textbooks) and which professional scientists encounter in their post-educational careers (in the periodical literature) which show them by example how their job is to be done (postscript, p. 187). Exemplars are important because they illustrate, roughly, how the symbolic generalizations of the field are to be applied to nature. (I shall say more about how they are supposed to do this shortly.)[14]

We are now in a position to return to the question raised previously: What *sort* of paradigm must be acquired in order for a scientific community to make the transition to normal research? The few scattered passages where Kuhn explicitly addresses this question in his post-*SSR* papers are clearly reminiscent of *SSR* passages already discussed. He writes, for example:

What changes with the transition to maturity is not the presence of a paradigm but rather its nature. Only after the change is normal puzzle-solving research possible. Many of the attributes of a developed science which I have above [i.e., in *SSR*] associated with the acquisition of a paradigm I would therefore now discuss as consequences of the acquisition of the sort of paradigm that identifies challenging puzzles, supplies clues to their solution, and guarantees that the truly clever practitioner succeed. (postscript, p. 179)

And, echoing Kuhn's earlier views on the importance of having a successful and open-ended theory, we find the following:

... a field [which aims to explain in detail some range of natural phenomena] first gains maturity when provided with a theory and technique which satisfy the four following conditions. First is Sir Karl [Popper]'s demarcation criterion without which no field is potentially a science; for some range of natural phenomena concrete predictions must emerge from the practice of the field. Second, for some interesting sub-class of phenomena, whatever passes for predictive success must be consistently achieved.... Third, predictive techniques must have roots in a theory which, however metaphysical, simultaneously justifies them, explains their limited success, and suggests means for their improvement in both precision and scope. Finally, the improvement of predictive technique must be a challenging task, demanding on occasions the very highest measure of talent and devotion. (1970b, pp. 245–246)

Again, as in *SSR*, Kuhn's statements leave us with more questions than answers. Precisely what component of a disciplinary matrix is it that identifies challenging puzzles, provides clues to their solution, and so on? And what does this have to do with extending the predictive power and range of a theory? A clue to a possible answer can be found in the passage immediately following the one just quoted:

These conditions are, of course, tantamount to the description of a good scientific theory.... With such a theory in hand the time for steady criticism and theory proliferation has passed. Scientists for the first time have an alternative which is not merely aping what has gone before. They can instead apply their talents to the puzzles which lie in what Lakatos now calls the 'protective belt.' One of their objectives then is to extend the range and precision of existing experiment and theory as well as to improve the match between them. Another is to eliminate conflicts both between the different theories employed in their work and between the ways in which a single theory is used in different applications.... These puzzles and others like them constitute the main activity of normal science. (Kuhn 1970b, p. 246)

What this passage suggests is that the sort of puzzle-solving which Kuhn takes to be characteristic of normal science may be far more specific than his discussion of puzzle-solving in *SSR* led us to believe. That is, what Kuhn has been calling the "puzzles" of normal science may consist primarily in the problems of theory articulation and further empirical application originally discussed in chapter 3 of *SSR*. Precisely why such puzzles are not available to the schools of pre-normal science is not entirely clear, but one might conjecture this: Prior to achieving significant *empirical success* with a theory, the efforts of the research community will be devoted primarily to the search for such a theory. And, obviously, the problem of constructing a theory that is successful will not be the kind of problem Kuhn would consider a puzzle. There are few constraints on what can count as a solution, and there is no guarantee that a solution even exists. In contrast, given a theory which has achieved some measure of success, the problems of theory articulation and further empirical application are far more clearly defined.[15]

This interpretation is further supported by Kuhn's discussion of the role of exemplars in normal science. Recall that exemplars are important for Kuhn because they teach the scientist, roughly, how the symbolic generalizations of his disciplinary matrix are to be applied to nature. Kuhn frequently refers to exemplars as "puzzle-solutions." And he spends considerable time describing the process of normal science as one in which "scientists solve puzzles by modeling them on previous puzzle-solutions" (postscript, p. 189), where the "previous puzzle-solutions" he has in mind are clearly exemplars. If we now look more closely at what precisely exemplars are supposed to teach the student of science and the scientist, we find the following. According to Kuhn, exemplars illustrate what sort

of experimental phenomena the symbolic generalizations of the disciplinary matrix can be applied to, what form the schematic symbolic generalizations must take for purposes of application, and how these symbolic
generalizations must be manipulated to actually carry out the application.[16] If this is what exemplars do in their role of puzzle-solutions, then
the corresponding "puzzles" must obviously be something like: What kind
of empirical phenomena can the symbolic generalizations of the disciplinary matrix apply to? What specific form must these generalizations take
for purposes of novel application? How must these generalizations be
manipulated to actually carry out the application? Note that these are
all problems that could fall under the heading of theory articulation
and further empirical application as originally discussed in chapter 3 of
SSR.[17]

The above account solves many of the difficulties we found in Kuhn's
original discussion. We now have at least the outlines of a coherent picture
which can make sense of much of what Kuhn has said about normal
science, puzzle-solving, theories, rules, and concrete problem-solutions.
Moreover, while Kuhn still insists that scientists learn to generate new
research by "modeling" it on the previously learned exemplars (which bear
a "similarity relation" to the newly generated applications), this view of the
psychological mechanisms underlying the generation of normal science no
longer must bear the main burden of his account. I have argued that a
satisfactory account of what a paradigm is (or, on the new view, what a
mature paradigm is) must tell us how such paradigms play the role they
do in normal science. It must tell us how paradigms give rise to research
in the first place, what gives that research its coherence, and what makes
it particularly effective. On the reconstructed, revised view I have provided
for Kuhn, he can answer as follows: When a scientific community reaches
maturity, it finds itself in possession of a disciplinary matrix (consisting of
symbolic generalizations which have been successfully applied to some
range of phenomenon) as well as the set of applications themselves. The
fundamental research problems to which the normal scientific endeavor
will be directed are set by the conjunction of a set of abstract formalisms
and the specification of a set of phenomena in nature, picked out by the
exemplars. Specifically, those problems consist in figuring out how to
extend the application of the formalisms to additional phenomena of
roughly the sort to which they have already been applied. What gives

coherence to the whole enterprise is that it centers exclusively on the general symbolic generalizations provided by the disciplinary matrix and the sort of phenomena specified by the exemplars. What makes it *effective* is that the exemplars also provide clues as to how the problems of further application are to be solved. They do this by providing an example of how the general formalisms must be converted into more specific ones and how the relevant observation sentences are to be derived from the specific formalisms. Kuhn's "modeling" hypothesis might still enter in as an account of how scientists are able to make use of these clues. But note that this specific hypothesis about the psychological mechanism whereby exemplars make normal research so effective is really quite independent of the general account. Thus, we can accept the general account even if we continue to have reservations about Kuhn's talk of "modeling" and "similarity relations."

It was concluded above that Kuhn's original (*SSR*) notion of a paradigm was both too confused and too traditional to be of much use for our purposes. What of the revised notions of a disciplinary matrix and an exemplar? It should be evident that, although Kuhn's general account is now more coherent, the new notions do not, in fact, represent much of a departure from traditional units of analysis, despite their newly acquired labels. One of the three major components of a disciplinary matrix consists of a set of symbolic generalizations (which is, at the very least, a theory stripped of its interpretation), and exemplars are specific applications of these generalizations to some particular experimental or observational phenomenon. Moreover, the most coherent account that we can eke out of the text of how paradigms give rise to and guide normal research assigns a central role to the successful theory and its applications. Thus, for reasons similar to those discussed above, Kuhn's revised notion of a paradigm seems equally unsuitable for a description of cognitive science.

Though Kuhn's proposed units of analysis may be unsuitable. they are nevertheless suggestive. This becomes particularly apparent if we look at the use to which Kuhn's proposals have been put by those psychologists who have forayed into the realm of meta-theory. Palermo (1971), for example, defines a paradigm as follows:

... the consensually agreed upon *modus operandi* of a mature scientific discipline. It consists of the conceptions of the nature of the theory to be used in guiding research, the types of problems worthy of investigation, the research methods appropriate to investigating those problems, and even, on occasion, the instrumentation which is required.   (p. 136)

According to Segal and Lachman (1972, p. 46–47), when a graduate student learns a paradigm, he learns what constitutes an appropriate data base, what constitutes proper methodology, and what sorts of concepts are most appropriate for describing that chunk of reality which makes up the subject-matter domain. Weimer and Palermo (1973) specifically state that paradigms are not scientific theories and mention with approval Kuhn's revised notions of disciplinary matrix and exemplar. However, when they come to actually describing Wundtian psychology and neo-behaviorism in supposedly Kuhnian terms, we get an account that is not strictly Kuhnian. In particular, Wundtian psychology is described in terms of its methodology, aim, preferred instrumentation, and associated set of metaphysical directives. Neo-behaviorism is described in terms of its metaphysical directives and exemplars, where the latter are taken to be techniques and instrumental procedures (Weimer and Palermo 1973, pp. 221–228). Lachman, Lachman, and Butterfield (1979, pp. 28–33) also explicitly deny that paradigms are theories, identifying the former, instead, as "the common set of ideas a subgroup of scientists brings to their subject matter." Specifically, paradigms are said to include intellectual antecedents, pre-theoretical ideas (notions about "the reality" underlying the subject matter), a subject matter, a set of concepts and terminology (which reflect the scientists beliefs about "the basic properties of the system they are studying"), preferred analogies, and a research methodology.[18]

Of the various descriptions, suggestions, and hints that Kuhn gives concerning what kind of thing a paradigm is, the above characterizations most closely fit Kuhn's original discussion of "rules." The "rules" that Kuhn had in mind were supposed to include, among other things, commitments to preferred types of instrumentation and to the ways in which these should be employed, as well as the higher-level, quasi-metaphysical commitments concerning what sorts of entities the universe contains, what ultimate laws and fundamental explanations must be like, and what a legitimate research problem might consist in.

Describing a field such as cognitive science in terms of the above sort of "disciplinary matrix" (which is not, of course, the same as Kuhn's sort) certainly has possibilities. But, at the moment, we are dealing with merely a suggestion. If we are to take the suggestion seriously, a number of points will require elaboration:

Precisely what should be included under such a revised conception of a matrix so that the result will be applicable to an immature field such as cognitive science?

How might commitment to such a matrix account for the coherence and unity underlying the various research endeavors that make up a field such as cognitive science?

Would such a matrix be useful in assessing the viability of a field such as cognitive science in the face of the various challenges and critiques issued in recent years?

A.3 Laudan's Notion of a Research Tradition

We have seen that neither Kuhn's original idea of a paradigm nor its progeny, exemplars and disciplinary matrices, can constitute a suitable unit of analysis for our purposes. In this section, I will consider another unit of analysis proposed in the context of recent work in philosophy of science: Larry Laudan's conception of a *research tradition*. Like Kuhn's proposals, Laudan's view (in unmodified form) will, ultimately, prove to be unsatisfactory, but studying its strengths and weaknesses will be useful for developing a more acceptable notion.

Before I describe Laudan's proposal, let me say something about the context in which it was developed. Although many of Kuhn's insights were well received by philosophers of science,[19] one aspect of the Kuhnian position prompted a strong negative reaction. This was Kuhn's apparent challenge to the deeply held conviction (at least, among philosophers of science) that scientific change is fundamentally rational. Not so, Kuhn seemed to argue.[20] Although normal science is eminently rational, the process whereby a prevailing paradigm is replaced by a new paradigm, according to Kuhn, is more like a revolution than an orderly deliberation. Here are two of *SSR*'s more provocative passages:

Like the choice between competing political institutions, that between competing paradigms proves to be a choice between incompatible modes of community life. Because it has that character, the choice is not and cannot be determined merely by the evaluative procedures characteristic of normal science, for these depend in part upon a particular paradigm, and that paradigm is at issue.   (p. 94)

As a consequence, techniques of persuasive argumentation become more important than "the impact of nature and logic." Further,

Paradigms are not corrigible by normal science at all. Instead, as we have already seen, normal science ultimately leads only to the recognition of anomalies and to crises. And these are terminated, not by deliberation and interpretation, but by a relatively sudden and unstructured event like the gestalt switch.   (p. 122)

Clearly, passages such as these could not be tolerated very long by philosophers of science committed to the essential rationality of science. The reaction was threefold: Kuhn was labeled an irrationalist in no uncertain terms,[21] the basis of his claims was given careful scrutiny (Scheffler 1967; Shapere 1964, 1966), and, most important, steps were taken to develop an alternative account of scientific change that preserved his historical outlook without giving up the rationality of science. It is in the context of the latter that Laudan's unit of analysis was proposed.

In *Progress and Its Problems*, Laudan (1977) proposes a theory of research traditions the aim of which is to "begin afresh" to analyze the rationality of science.[22] Although Laudan is highly critical of Kuhn for supposedly arguing that science is fundamentally an irrational enterprise, there is, nevertheless much that is Kuhnian in Laudan's book. In particular, I believe that Laudan shares with Kuhn the picture of science I sketched in section 1.1. To say that Laudan shares this picture with Kuhn is not, of course, to say that he adopts Kuhn's *detailed* views of the nature of frameworks of shared commitments (FSCs), FSC-guided science, and FSC-choosing science. In fact, *Progress and Its problems* can be viewed as adopting the broad outlines of Kuhn's view, as specified by this picture, but offering an alternative conception of the details.

Before look at Laudan's proposal, let me say something about what I intend to do in this section. Of the various metascientific views examined in this appendix, Laudan's comes the closest to being useful for our purposes. Yet it is still not exactly right. Thus, in the same way that Laudan attempts to revise Kuhn, I will propose a revision of Laudan. My discussion will fall into two parts. First, I will provide a quick overview of Laudan's proposal, largely in his own terms. Second, I will review the proposal once more, this time more critically and with an eye to the desiderata outlined in section 1.1. During this phase of the discussion, a number of shortcomings will emerge to which I will respond by a series of constructive suggestions and reconstructions. These suggestions and reconstructions form the basis of my notion of a research framework presented in section 1.1.

At the heart of Laudan's proposal is a unit of analysis reminiscent of Kuhn's "rules": the notion of a *research tradition*. According to Laudan, it is a research tradition that constitutes the FSC of a scientific community, that somehow shapes FSC-guided science, and that is endorsed or rejected during periods of FSC-choosing science. What precisely is this new unit of analysis? On Laudan's view, a research tradition is a set of general assumptions that fall into two classes: *metaphysical* assumptions and *methodological* assumptions. The metaphysical assumptions do two things: they specify "in a general way, the types of fundamental entities which exist in the domain or domains within which the research tradition is embedded" (p. 79) and they outline "the different modes by which these entities can interact" (p. 79). The methodological assumptions specify "the appropriate methods to be used for investigating the problems and constructing the theories" in the domain of the research tradition (p. 80). These methodological principles will be "wide-ranging in scope, addressing themselves to experimental techniques, modes of theoretical testing and evaluation, and the like" (p. 79).

For Kuhn, the elements that constitute an FSC are unchanging. That is, any modification of these elements will *ipso facto* result in a different FSC. Laudan disagrees with this point on the grounds that it does not do justice to the historical record. On his view, if one looks at the great research traditions in the history of science, one finds many cases where scientists claiming to adhere to a particular tradition (such as Aristotelianism, Cartesianism, Darwinism, or Freudian psychology) take issue with some of its basic doctrines. To handle such situations, Laudan proposes that research traditions can *evolve*. The fundamental assumptions that constitute the research tradition can change gradually without the tradition's being abandoned. That is, from one stage to the next, *some* of the fundamental assumptions can change so long as *most* of them remain the same in order to preserve the identity of the tradition.

FSC-guided science consists, fundamentally, in problem-solving, on Laudan's view.[23] In particular, it consists in the efforts of scientists to develop theories that solve the problems associated with the research tradition in question. The problems of a research tradition fall into two groups: empirical problems and conceptual problems. Empirical problems are questions or phenomena or statements (it is not clear which—see below) that concern the world and are unexpected, peculiar, or problematic given "our theoretical presuppositions about the natural order" (p. 15). Conceptual problems, in contrast, are "higher order"; that is, they concern the well-foundedness of the theories devised to solve the empirical problems. The idea here is that scientific attempts to solve a set of empirical problems typically take place in the context of previous theoretical attempts to solve that very set of problems—attempts which may have resulted in theories that were flawed in various ways. Thus, in proposing a new, more adequate theory, the scientist must not only respond to the empirical problems at hand but also attempt to solve the conceptual problems associated with the older (presumably inadequate) theory.

Given this conception of FSC-guided science, what precisely does the "guiding" by the FSC (i.e., the research tradition) come to on Laudan's account? To put the question slightly differently: How does a research tradition contribute to the coherence of the FSC-guided science that takes place under its aegis? Laudan attributes four "roles" to research traditions vis-à-vis the theories developed in conjunction with them: a "problem-determining role," a "constraining role," a "heuristic role," and a "justificatory role." Of these, the first three are relevant for understanding the guiding function of a research tradition. Basically, the view is that a research tradition contributes to the coherence of its associated research in three ways: First, it strongly influences the range of the *problems*, both empirical and conceptual, that the FSC-guided science aims to solve. This is its "problem-determining role." Second, it imposes negative constraints on the kinds of *theories* that are considered to be acceptable solutions to those problems. This is its "constraining role." Third, it provides "vital clues for theory construction" (p. 90). This is its "heuristic role."

The aim of FSC-guided science is to develop increasingly adequate theories. The adequacy of a theory is determined by its "problem-solving effectiveness." To understand how Laudan defines problem-solving effectiveness we must take a closer look at his view of empirical problems. Empirical problems can be taxonomized, according to Laudan, in terms of their status relative to some theory T. We thus get the following:

Unsolved problems   These are problems not solved by T and not solved by any other competing theory.

Solved problems   These are problems solved by T.

Anomalous problems   These are problems not solved by T that have been solved by some competing theory.

Laudan now defines problem-solving effectiveness as follows:

The overall problem-solving effectiveness of a theory is determined by assessing the number and importance of the empirical problems which the theory solves and deducting therefrom the number and importance of the anomalies and conceptual problems which the theory generates.   (p. 68)

Note that unsolved problems (in the sense defined above) do not count against a theory. The adequacy of a theory is only judged relative to its competitors, and since (by definition) if a problem is "unsolved" for theory T it is also unsolved for all competitors of T, counting unsolved problems against a theory will not be a way to distinguish between it and its competitors.

Theories within a research tradition are thus evaluated by their comparative adequacy, where adequacy is measured in terms of problem-solving effectiveness. What about the research tradition itself? Are there any appraisal measures relevant to choosing one research tradition over another? Again problem-solving effectiveness is the key notion. Two measures are relevant to the comparative assessment of two research traditions. First, scientists can assess the overall *adequacy* of the research tradition by looking at the adequacy (i.e., problem solving effectiveness) of its most recent theory (or theories). Second, scientists can look at the history of the research tradition and measure its *rate of progress* (that is, the degree of adequacy of its theories as a function of time). According to Laudan, the first measure is relevant to the question of whether a research tradition should be *accepted* relative to another; the second is relevant to whether it should be *pursued*. At a given moment of time, research tradition X might not be as adequate as competing tradition Y, but yet it might exhibit more "promise" and hence seem to be worth pursuing. On Laudan's view, one should cash in such vague talk about promise by looking at the comparative rates of progress of the two traditions.

That, in a nutshell, is Laudan's view. How does it measure up to our desiderata? The first point to note is that, with respect to the immaturity desideratum, Laudan's proposed unit of analysis fares better than those discussed thus far. Recall that our working assumption regarding immature science has been this: Whatever else the FSC of an immature field is like, it can be said with confidence that commitment to the FSC of an immature field does not involve commitment to some *specific* set of scientific theories or hypotheses. Yet each of the proposed units of analysis discussed thus far exhibits such theory-centeredness. A branch of science, on the logical positivist view, is both individuated and identified with some particular theory; and a Kuhnian paradigm (as well a disciplinary matrix and an exemplar) either is identical to a theory, contains a theory as one of its elements, or consists in the application of a theory. In contrast, Laudan's research tradition is not theory-centered in the same way. Although research traditions may be "associated" with series of particular theories and may, even in some sense "inspire" and "guide" them, they are not identical to such series, nor do they contain any significant part of them. Thus, for the first time in our discussion, we have found a unit of analysis that satisfies our crucial immaturity desideratum.

Unfortunately, however, we are not yet home free. Laudan's proposal suffers from a host of difficulties when assessed relative to our other desiderata.

Consider, for example, soundness. Do the concepts or claims of the view suffer from any internal difficulties? For the most part, Laudan's concepts and claims are relatively clear. There are, however, three problems. The first is a problem of omission. A research tradition, on Laudan's view, is a set of assumptions which tell the scientists working in that tradition something about the sorts of theories they should be developing and the sorts of methods they should use in developing and empirically supporting those theories. Note, however, that a research tradition does not say anything about what *phenomena* those theories are supposed to be theories of. This is a serious omission, on my view. It is certainly not the case that a scientist takes the domain to be defined by *whatever* the metaphysical and methodological assumptions might apply to; that is to put the cart before the horse. Rather, the scientist begins with at least a rough conception of what he or she wants to understand and then attempts to develop theories, in accordance with something like Laudan's metaphysical and methodological assumptions, in order to arrive at that understanding.

Although Laudan does not include any domain-specifying assumptions in his notion of a research tradition, he recognizes (at least implicitly) that much of what he has to say makes sense only if one assumes that every research tradition is, in fact, associated with a domain of inquiry. For example, here is his "working definition" of a research tradition: "... a research tradition is a set of general assumptions about the entities and processes *in a domain of study*, and about the appropriate methods to be used for investigating the problems and constructing the theories *in that domain*" (p. 81; my emphasis). Similarly, when discussing the empirical problems addressed by a given research tradition, Laudan again invokes the idea of an associated domain: "Empirical problems are thus *first order problems*; they are substantive questions about the objects *which constitute the domain* of any given science." (p. 15; second emphasis is mine)

The idea of an associated domain also plays a crucial role in Laudan's account of FSC-choosing science. Recall that the appraisal measure of problem-solving effectiveness requires the notion of an anomaly, for the problem-solving effectiveness of any theory T is the difference, roughly, between the number of empirical problems solved and the number of anomalies and conceptual problems generated by T. But what is an anomaly? An anomaly is an empirical problem not solved by T but solved by some competitor to T. And what kinds of theories count as competitors to T? The only possible answer is: theories that share *the same domain*.

These critical considerations give rise to the following obvious constructive suggestion:

LL1   To be completely described, a research tradition should include not only a set of metaphysical and methodological assumptions but also a set of domain-specifying assumptions.

A second area of weakness in Laudan's account can be found in his talk about problems. As we have seen, both the notion of a problem in general and the distinction between empirical and conceptual problems play important parts in Laudan's account. However, as they stand, neither the general nor the specific notions are rendered clearly enough in Laudan's discussion to bear the burden he assigns to them.

For a proposal that takes one of its major contributions to be an elaboration of the problem-solving view of science, Laudan's has amazingly little to say about what a problem is. Worse yet, he seems to use the term in two quite distinct senses. On the one hand, empirical problems are problems in the sense of something requiring explanation or understanding. On the other hand, conceptual problems are problems in the sense of a difficulty or an obstacle—something not to be explained but to be surmounted or eliminated.

Things get even more confusing if we focus exclusively on his view of empirical problems. Roughly speaking, an empirical problem is something requiring explanation. But what kind of something? Close inspection of the text reveals that Laudan sometimes identifies an empirical problem with a question,[24] sometimes with a fact, phenomenon, datum or state-of-affairs,[25] sometimes with a statement (about the phenomena requiring explanation),[26] and sometimes with a task.[27]

This sort of confusion is easily avoided. One need simply preserve all the relevant distinctions and be clear in one's use of terminology. As a start, I propose the following:

LL2

(1) We typically use the word 'problem' to refer to one of two kinds of things: a difficulty to be overcome or a task to be performed, subject to certain fairly well-defined constraints, where the correct way to carry out the task is not obvious. Since the word 'difficulty' is perfectly serviceable in this context, let us refer to problems in the sense of difficulties simply as "difficulties" and reserve the word 'problem' for tasks of the relevant sort.

(2) Intellectual problems, including many scientific problems, are question-answering tasks. That is, the task the scientist sets for him- or herself is to answer certain sorts of questions about the world (or, at least, questions about what he or she takes the world to be). The scientist believes the world to be made up of myriads of *empirical phenomena*. These putative empirical phenomena can be described in *empirical statements*. They also give rise to *empirical questions*, such as why such-and-such an empirical phenomenon occurs at t or why it has these-and-those properties. Roughly speaking, an *empirical problem* is, then, the task of answering an empirical question about some putative empirical phenomenon.

The third problem with Laudan's theory of what an FSC is concerns his claim that research traditions can evolve. Laudan believes that the history of science is better served if a research tradition is the kind of thing that can evolve. And he may be quite right about this. He recognizes, however, that to make such a claim cogently requires an account of why the change in question counts as one and the same research tradition's evolving rather than one research tradition's being replaced by another. One quite unproblematic way in which this can happen is that, while the foundational assumptions of the tradition remain the same, the theories being developed in terms of those assumptions change. But Laudan wants to maintain that a research tradition can evolve in a more fundamental sense: by "a change of some of its most basic core elements" (p. 96).

Prima facie the claim is puzzling, for it would seem that there is no other way to *individuate* a research tradition other than by the foundational assumptions that constitute it. But how then can a change in the "core elements" of a research tradition constitute the evolution of one and the same research tradition rather than the replacement of one tradition by another? Here is Laudan's response:

> A partial answer to the question comes from recognizing that *at any given time* certain elements of a research tradition are more central to, more entrenched within, the research tradition than other elements. It is these more central elements which are taken, at that time, to be most characteristic of the research tradition. To abandon them is indeed to move outside the research tradition, whereas the less central tenets can be modified without repudiation of the research tradition. Like Lakatos, then, I want to suggest that certain elements of a research tradition are sacrosanct, and thus cannot be rejected without repudiation of the tradition itself. But unlike Lakatos, I want to insist that *the set of elements falling in this (unrejectable) class changes through time.* (p. 99)

Let us call a research tradition at a time an "instantiation" of a research tradition. Then, Laudan seems to be maintaining the following.

SRTE   (STRONG MODEL OF RESEARCH TRADITION EVOLUTION)

(1) The foundational assumptions of a research tradition's instantiation can be distinguished into those that are "central" and those that are not central. (Let us call the latter "peripheral" foundational assumptions.)

(2) A foundational assumption may change its status from central to peripheral (or vice versa) from one instantiation of a research tradition to the next.

(3) Central foundational assumptions are "sacrosanct." That is, to reject an assumption at time t which is central to a research tradition at t is to reject the research tradition itself.

(4) Peripheral foundational assumptions are not "sacrosanct." That is, to reject at time t an assumption which is peripheral to a research tradition at t is not to reject the research tradition itself; rather, it is to effect an evolution of the research tradition.

Figure A.1
How a research tradition can evolve on the "strong" evolutionary model.

Two striking consequences follow from these assumptions. First, *any* foundational assumption of a research tradition is, in principle, *revisable*. This is so because any foundational assumption can always be demoted from central to peripheral (from one instantiation to the next), from which status it can be revised (or rejected) without rejecting the research tradition itself. In addition. there is a sense in which any foundational assumption is *unrevisable*. This is because any foundational assumption can be central in some instantiation of the research tradition. In that case it would be unrevisable because rejection of that assumption *at that time* would result in rejection of the research tradition itself. (I am, of course, not talking about unrevisability *per se*.) For example, suppose that we are presented with the series of research-tradition instantiations depicted in figure A. 1. In this series, FA1 is both unrevisable and revisable. It is unrevisable because at time t1 it is central and, hence, sacrosanct. That is, to reject FA1 at time t1 would be to reject the research tradition itself. However, it is also revisable because at time t2 it has been demoted to the status of being a peripheral assumption; hence, it can be rejected at t3 without jeopardizing the research tradition.

I have called this picture of how a research tradition can evolve the "strong model of research tradition evolution." How satisfactory is it? There is at least one serious difficulty on my view: There is no clear sense to the claim that one and the same research tradition is evolving. Figure B.1 shows us several research-tradition *instantiations* and a research-tradition *series*. But where or what is the research tradition itself? Another way to put the point is this: A series of research-tradition instantiations counts as *evolving* for Laudan because each subsequent member of the series differs from the previous member by only a few (or a small fraction of the) foundational assumptions. (As Laudan says: "From one stage to the next, there is preservation of most of the crucial assumptions of the research traditions". (p. 98) But if the only constraint on change within an evolutionary research-tradition series is that neighboring research-tradition instantiations must share *most* of their foundational assumptions, then it is quite possible for two research-tradition instantiations within the same series to differ *radically*. For instance, a research-tradition series might look like this:

$$\langle FA1, FA2, FA3, FA4 \rangle, \langle FA5, FA2, FA3, FA4 \rangle, \langle FA5, FA6, FA3, FA4 \rangle,$$

$$\langle FA5, FA6, FA7, FA4 \rangle, \langle FA5, FA6, FA7, FA8 \rangle, \ldots$$

In other words, given such a minimal constraint, it is quite possible for there to be a research-tradition series in which the first research-tradition instantiation and the last have nothing in common. But in that case it seems quite counterintuitive to say that the entire process is just the evolution of the first instantiation, or even to consider the first and the last research-tradition instantiations as parts of the same research tradition, for there is no *tradition* that is preserved in any meaningful sense.[28]

The fact that Laudan's strong model of research tradition evolution is unsatisfactory does not mean that we have to abandon the idea of evolution in this context. There is an alternative way of making sense of the claim that research traditions evolve which is not subject to the above two difficulties. This "weak model of research-tradition evolution" takes seriously Laudan's suggestion that the foundational assumptions of a research tradition fall into two classes: those that are sancrosact (or unrevisable) and those that are revisable. However, it denies the two features of Laudan's "strong" evolutionary model that seem to get it into trouble: that a foundational assumption can change its status from central to peripheral (and, hence, from unrevisable to revisable) and that, as a consequence, all foundational assumptions are, in principle, revisable. The alternative view is this:

LL3 (WEAK MODEL OF RESEARCH TRADITION EVOLUTION)

(1) The foundational assumptions of a research tradition can be distinguished into those that are unrevisable and those that are revisable (with respect to the tradition).

(2) The status of an unrevisable foundational assumption cannot change (to revisable) throughout the evolution of the research tradition.

(3) Any given research tradition can manifest itself in various versions, where what *distinguishes* the versions is that they differ with respect to the revisable assumptions whereas what makes them all versions of the *same* research tradition is that they share the sancrosact assumptions.

(4) The evolution of a research tradition will consist in the fact that changes from one instantiation to the next are relatively minimal and the fact that every instantiation will be an instantiation of some version of the research tradition.

LL3 not only solves the difficulty that plagues the Strong Model of Research Tradition Evolution; it also seems to have some applicability to cognitive science, for it turns out that the central concept of one of the "metaphysical" (i.e. substantive) assumptions of cognitive science— namely, the concept of a computer—is open-ended in a quite striking way. As chapter 3 ("The Computational Assumption") makes clear, cognitive scientists maintain that the cognitive mind is a certain kind of computer, but, at the same time, no one has a very precise idea of what in general a computer is. Computer scientists are, however, beginning to know a lot about specific kinds of devices that qualify as computers, and this knowledge is continuously changing over time. Furthermore, if we look at the comparatively short history of cognitive science, we find that at different points in that history the theories of cognition that have been developed model the cognitive mind on correspondingly different kinds of computational devices. Initially, researchers believed that the cognitive mind was a computer because they believed that the cognitive mind was a conventional general-purpose computational device. In recent years, the concept of a computer relevant to cognitive science has become far richer and more eclectic. In particular, cognitive scientists are now taking seriously the view that, instead of (or in addition to) being a general-purpose conventional computer, the cognitive mind might be a collection of special-purpose conventional devices or a nonconventional, connectionist device.[29] The point is that if the unit of analysis we are using to characterize cognitive science is one that is capable of evolution (in the sense of the weak model), we can capture the situation I have just described in a rather neat way. We can claim that, although the research tradition itself has remained unchanged throughout the history of the field (insofar as both early and contemporary cognitive scientists are committed to the assumption that the cognitive mind is a kind of computer), some evolution of that research tradition has taken place. The specific *kinds* of computers in terms of which cognition has been modeled have changed considerably.

In light of these considerations, I propose that we understand Laudan's claims about the evolution of research traditions in the weak sense of LL3.

Let us now consider Laudan's proposal in the light of our "coherence" desideratum. Is it reasonable to suppose that commitment to a Laudan-style research tradition can contribute in some significant way to the coherence of the research associated with that tradition? Although Laudan does not talk about the coherence of research within a research tradition *per se*, we can easily infer what he would say, at least roughly, from his discussion of the "guiding" functions of a research tradition—both about what such coherence comes to and about how it gets produced. He would undoubtedly claim that the scientific activities that take place within a research tradition are coherent in two respects: they are directed at solving a coherent set of empirical problems and they issue in a coherent set of theories. This coherence gets produced as follows: The empirical problems constitute a coherent set because they are "at least partially and in outline" delimited by the research tradition; the theories constitute a coherent set because their content is constrained and guided by that same research tradition. Let us see if we can make these suggestions more precise. I will first consider the coherence of a research tradition's theories and then the coherence of its empirical problems.

Laudan talks about a research tradition "constraining" and "providing vital clues for" the construction of its associated theories. Since, taken literally, such talk makes no sense (research traditions are abstract objects and hence can't *do* anything), he must clearly have something like this in mind: *Commitment* by a scientific community to a research tradition as a framework of research constrains and provides clues for the theory construction that takes place within that framework.

How, then, does such a commitment affect the character of research done within the relevant community? There are two stories to be told here, one for the constraining function of a research tradition and one for the heuristic function. The constraining story posits a *rational* relation between commitment to the research tradition and the mode in which theory construction is carried on. The heuristic story posts a more *inspirational or suggestive* one.

The constraining story goes like this: Suppose a scientific community is committed to a certain research tradition, RT, as a framework of research.

Then that community will have as a goal to develop only theories sanctioned by RT. Suppose further that the scientific community believes that a theory is sanctioned by RT just in case it satisfies certain *constraints*. Then, being rational, the community will try to develop only theories that satisfy the endorsed constraints. Finally, to the extent that the community is successful in carrying out its intentions, the theories it develops will, in fact, satisfy the constraints in question, and will hence exhibit a certain coherence.

The heuristic story is somewhat different. Instead of positing a rational relation between commitment to a research tradition as a framework for research and the mode of development of the associated theories, we now posit an inspirational or suggestive one. The heuristic story goes like this: Suppose a scientific community is committed to a certain research tradition, RT, as a framework of research. As a consequence, when that community tries to develop theories to solve the empirical problems associated with RT, this commitment will tend to give rise to theoretical ideas that trade on the metaphysical and methodological assumptions of RT. Hence, insofar as the theories associated with RT are inspired by the assumptions of RT, they will exhibit a certain coherence.

What we have thus far is a plausible but somewhat sketchy reconstruction of Laudan's view of how commitment to a research tradition might contribute to the coherence of its associated theories. To fill in the stories with more detail, we need to ask two questions, one about the constraining role of a research tradition and one about its heuristic role:

• What, precisely, are the constraints that determine whether or not a theory is sanctioned by RT?

• How, precisely, will the theoretical ideas that tend to be developed by the scientific community trade on the assumptions of RT?

In discussing the "constraining role" of the research tradition, Laudan gives several examples, all of which are designed to show that "the research tradition within which a scientist works precludes him from adopting specific theories which are *incompatible* with the metaphysics or methodology of the tradition" (p. 89). He writes:

If the ontology of the research tradition denies the existence of forces acting-at-a-distance, then it clearly rules out as unacceptable any specific theory which relies on noncontact action. It was precisely for this reason that "Cartesians" such as

Huygens and Leibniz (committed to an ontology of pushes and pulls) found Newton's theory of celestial mechanics so otiose. Einstein's theory of the equivalence of matter and energy excludes from consideration any specific theory which postulates the absolute conservation of mass.   (p. 89)

This passage suggests that the constraint imposed by a research tradition on its associated theories is the constraint of *consistency*. That is, Laudan seems to be attributing the following belief to the scientific community: A theory T is sanctioned by RT just in case T is consistent with the metaphysical and methodological assumptions of RT. I take it that this constitutes the answer to our first question.

Note that a constraint of consistency is an exceedingly weak and purely negative mode of influence for a research tradition to exert on its associated theories, for basically it allows the construction of any sort of theories whatsoever except those that come into explicit contradiction with the assumptions of the research tradition. In particular, a theory could satisfy such a constraint while making reference to entities and processes wildly different from those posited by the metaphysical assumptions of RT just so long as it was logically possible for both sets of entities and processes (those posited by the theory and those posited by the metaphysical assumptions of RT) to exist side by side.

A more positive influence is exerted by the research tradition in its heuristic function. Precisely what Laudan wants to say here is far from clear, but the examples he gives suggest something like the following: Although a scientific community is not *constrained* by its commitment to RT to develop theories which refer to the sorts of entities and processes posited by the metaphysical assumptions of RT, it will often be *inspired* to do so. That, I take it, is Laudan's answer to our second question.

For example, according to Laudan, Franklin's important theoretical insight that electrical charge must be conserved "emerged as an almost inevitable result of Franklin's thinking about the relations between his emerging theory and its parent research tradition" (p. 90). Carnot "almost certainly would not have enunciated" his theory of steam engines without the inspiration provided by his commitment to the research tradition of the caloric doctrine of heat and its assumption that heat is "a conserved substance capable of flowing from one point to another without loss of its quantity" (p. 91). Finally, there is the case of Descartes. According to Laudan:

When Descartes attempted to develop a theory of light and colors, he had already defined his general research tradition. In brief, it amounted to the assertion that the only properties which bodies can have are those of size, shape, position, and motion. The research tradition did not, indeed could not, specify precisely what sizes, shapes, positions, and motions particular bodies could exhibit. But it did make it clear that any specific physical theory, in optics or elsewhere, would have to deal exclusively with these four parameters.   (p. 91)

As a result, Descartes' research tradition "directed the construction of Cartesian theories in a number of subtle and important ways" (p. 91).

We now have before us a reasonably detailed reading of Laudan's proposal concerning how a research tradition can affect the coherence of its associated theories. How satisfactory is it from our point of view? The view seems to me to be basically on the right track. I would, however, introduce one amendment. I believe that the constraining role of a research tradition is far stronger than Laudan takes it to be. In particular, I want to suggest that formulating theories in terms of the entities and processes posited by the metaphysical assumptions of a research tradition is not merely something that *tends to happen*; it is rather a mode of theory construction *required* by commitment to the research tradition. That is, it is a product of the constraining role of the research tradition rather than of its heuristic role.

My reason for suggesting this modification of Laudan's view is this. Let us call a theory that makes substantial reference to the entities and processes of the sort posited by the metaphysical assumptions of a research tradition an "ontologically compliant" theory (relative to that tradition) and a theory that does not make such substantial reference an "ontologically deviant" theory (relative to that tradition). The point then is that if constructing ontologically compliant theories were merely a tendency rather than a requirement we should expect the theories associated with a research tradition to include far more ontologically deviant theories than they typically do.

Ontologically deviant theories are certainly absent in the case of cognitive science. The principle "metaphysical" assumptions (although I will not call them that) of cognitive science are that the cognitive mind is a representational device and that it is a computational device. If all that is *required* of cognitive scientists to be doing cognitive science is that they develop theories that are *consistent* with this assumption (with the key ideas of representation and computation functioning merely as a source of inspiration rather than as a constraint), we ought to find at least some theories that are universally taken to be clear cases of cognitive science research but that offer an account of the human cognitive capacities quite distinct from the information-processing account. But we don't find this. I conclude therefore that the constraining role of the research tradition of cognitive science requires more than mere consistency with the metaphysical assumptions of the field. In addition, it requires that any theory sanctioned by cognitive science must answer the empirical questions associated with the field by reference to the sorts of entities and processes posited by the metaphysical assumptions of that tradition.[30]

Let me now try to summarize the position I have been developing.

LL4

(1) The coherence of theories associated with a given research tradition is due primarily to the fact that a research tradition "imposes" certain constraints on what can count as an associated theory.

(2) To say that a research tradition "imposes" certain constraints on its associated theories really comes to this: Research traditions function as FSCs for scientific communities. Commitment to a given research tradition as a framework for research by a scientific community means that the community takes it as a goal to develop only theories that satisfy certain constraints that make reference to the assumptions of the research tradition. Given this goal attribution, we can explain the coherence of the associated theories by making the further assumptions that the community will try to carry out its goal and that it will be largely successful in doing so. The resulting theories will then be coherent in the sense that they will, for the most part, in fact satisfy the adopted constraints.

(3) There are two constraints that scientific communities typically adopt. It is typically assumed that a theory T will be a member of the set of theories associated with a given research tradition RT only if T is consistent with the metaphysical and methodological assumptions of RT and T makes significant reference to the entities and processes posited by the metaphysical assumptions of RT.

Thus far in discussing Laudan's handling of the coherence problem I have focused exclusively on Laudan's view of how research traditions contribute to the coherence of their associated *theories*. Let us now turn to the parallel question of how they contribute to the coherence of their associated *empirical problems*. What sense can we make of Laudan's view on this question, and how satisfactory is it?

Laudan states his view this way:

> Among the other roles of a research tradition, it is designed to delimit, at least partially and in outline, *the domain*[31] *of application* of its constituent theories. It does this by indicating that it is appropriate to discuss certain classes of empirical problems.... Either the ontology or the methodology of the research tradition can influence what are to count as legitimate problems for its constituent theories. (p. 86)

Following our suggestion LL2, let us take an empirical problem to be the task of answering an empirical question about some putative empirical phenomenon. The set of empirical problems associated with a given research tradition will then be determined by the set of empirical *questions* associated with that research tradition. Our query then becomes: How can a research tradition, in Laudan's sense, determine the set of empirical questions associated with a research tradition even "partially and in outline"? It can do so in two ways, according to Laudan: by means of constraints imposed by the methodological assumptions of the research tradition and by means of constraints imposed by the metaphysical assumptions.

Note that there are strong parallels between the way a research tradition delimits its theories and the way it delimits its empirical problems. For one thing, as in the case of the constraining and heuristic roles of a research tradition, the problem-determining role must be understood psychologically. To say that a research tradition determines the class of empirical problems associated with it is thus really to say that commitment to a research tradition by a scientific community makes a difference to what class of empirical problems the community considers to be associated with the research tradition. Furthermore, I would like to suggest that the relation of "determination" Laudan attributes to research traditions vis-à-vis their associated empirical problems is, once again, the constraint relation. Thus, a research tradition "determines" its associated empirical problems in the sense that the scientific community that endorses the research tradition uses the assumptions of the tradition to impose certain constraints on what can count as a legitimate empirical problem within that tradition.

What are these constraints? Laudan's suggestion regarding the problem-determining role of the methodological assumptions seems reasonably clear:

... if ... the *methodology* of a research tradition specifies— as it usually will— certain experimental techniques which alone are the legitimate investigational modes for determining what are the data to be explained, then it is clear that only "phenomena" which can be explored by those means can, in principle, count as legitimate empirical problems for theories within that tradition. (pp. 86–87)

As an example Laudan cites the case of nineteenth-century phenomenological chemistry, adherents of which believed that "the only legitimate problems to be solved by the chemist were those that concerned the *observable* reactions of chemical reagents" (p. 87). Reconstructed in our terminology, I take it that Laudan is suggesting this:

EQ1   An empirical question EQ is a member of the set of empirical questions associated with a given research tradition RT only if EQ is answerable by methods sanctioned by the methodological assumptions of RT.

What about the problem-determining role of the metaphysical assumptions? Here the text gets a bit more opaque. According to Laudan, the *ontology* of a research tradition may "exclude certain situations from, or include them within, the appropriate domain" (p. 87). He gives two examples to illuminate this claim:

... the rise of the Cartesian mechanistic research tradition in the seventeenth century radically transformed the accepted problem domain for optical theories. It did so by arguing, *or rather simply postulating*, that problems of perception and vision—problems which had classically been regarded as legitimate empirical problems for any optical theory—should be relegated to psychology and to physiology.... (p. 87)

A different kind of example is provided by late nineteenth-century physics, where the subtle fluid tradition (of Faraday, Maxwell, Hertz, and others) countenanced as legitimate empirical problems queries about the properties of the electromagnetic aether.... With the emergence of special relativity theory, however, a new research tradition and its related ontology cut out from the domain of the empirical problem of physics all questions about the elasticity, density, and velocity of the aether—questions which had been central *empirical* problems between 1850 and 1900. (pp. 87–88)

Although there is much that is unclear about these passages (for example, precisely what are the empirical problems in the two cases, and how exactly do the ontological assumptions perform their constraining function?), my guess is that Laudan has something like the following in mind:

EQ2   An empirical question EQ is a member of the set of empirical questions associated with a given research tradition RT only if EQ is answerable by a theory sanctioned by the metaphysical assumptions of RT.

I have now reconstructed Laudan's view of problem determination as requiring two *necessary* conditions (EQ1 and EQ2) for an empirical question belonging to the set of empirical questions associated with a research tradition. The term 'determination', however, suggests the idea of sufficiency. A natural suggestion is to regard EQ1 and EQ2 as jointly sufficient but individually necessary for the task. Laudan's view on the coherence of the empirical problems associated with a research tradition then becomes this:

PDV (LAUDAN'S PROBLEM-DETERMINATION VIEW)

(1) The coherence of the empirical problems associated with a given research tradition is due primarily to the fact that the research tradition "imposes" certain constraints on what can count as an associated empirical question.

(2) The research tradition "imposes" certain constraints in the sense that, in selecting empirical problems to work on, the scientific community committed to the research tradition makes use of these constraints.

(3) There are two constraints that scientific communities typically adopt. It is generally assumed that an empirical question EQ is a member of the set of empirical questions associated with a given research tradition RT if and only if (a) EQ is answerable by methods sanctioned by the methodological assumptions of RT and (b) EQ is answerable by a theory sanctioned by the metaphysical assumptions of RT.

How satisfactory is PDV when assessed in terms of our coherence desideratum? There are two difficulties, both of which concern the constraint principles articulated in (3). The first difficulty is that the constraint principles are too weak; the set of empirical problems associated with a given research tradition is typically *smaller* than that specified by (3). In particular, the set of empirical problems associated with a given research tradition will typically not include all the empirical questions answerable by reference to the entities and processes posited by the metaphysical assumptions of that tradition. For one thing, the set of empirical problems associated with a research tradition will certainly concern only empirical phenomena that are within the domain of the field. Furthermore, even if we couple (3) with a restriction to the domain, the result may be too weak, for research traditions often focus only on particular questions concerning their domain.

Such additional restrictions are certainly manifest in the case of cognitive science. Roughly speaking, the domain-specifying assumption of cognitive science is that the domain consists of the human cognitive capacities, and the principle "metaphysical" assumptions are that the cognitive mind is a representational device and that it is a a computational device. If the empirical questions (and, hence, empirical problems) of the field were determined solely by these two assumptions (plus the methodological assumptions), the class of questions posed by cognitive scientists would be much larger than it, in fact, is. For example, it would include these questions: Why do people exercise their capacities when they do? How did the human cognitive capacities evolve throughout the history of the species? What will the human cognitive capacities be like in the year 2500? But such questions are not, in fact, part of the current research program of cognitive science.

The second difficulty with Laudan's view of the problem-determining role of a research tradition is that (3) is also too strong. That is, it rules out questions that may legitimately be asked within a research tradition. This is because clause b requires that answers to empirical questions make reference to the entities and processes posited by the metaphysical assumptions of the research tradition. But research traditions typically include questions of another sort as well—"low-level" questions about the precise *nature* and *extent* of the domain under study which can be answered without resort to underlying entities and mechanisms.

For example, cognitive scientists not only want to know *how* a person typically perceives, or speaks a language, or remembers, in representational and computational terms; they also want to know precisely *what* the capacities for perception, language production, and memory are. Since questions of this sort are answerable by describing, in commonsense psychological terms, precisely how a person with the capacity in question typically responds (either behaviorally or mentally) given certain instructions and under various task and stimulus conditions, they will not require reference to what is going on at the so-called subpersonal level of the mind, where the representations and computations of cognitive science are presumably located. Hence, if reference to the representational and computational resources of the mind were required of every answer to a legitimate question of the field, such questions would be ruled out.

I am dubious that any fiddling with the constraint principles in PDV will solve the two difficulties discussed above. Nevertheless, it is still possible to maintain that a research tradition, in some sense, determines the set of empirical problems associated with it. We can do so by substituting the following suggestion for Laudan's view:

LL5

(1) There are two kinds of empirical questions associated with a given research tradition: basic empirical questions and derivative empirical questions. A *basic* empirical question is one that can be raised about phenomena in the domain prior to any research concerning those phenomena (within the framework of the research tradition). A *derivative* question is one that arises only once the research process is underway, since it is typically a question prompted either by data gathered in the course of research or by specific hypotheses or theories formulated in response to such data.

(2) The set of basic empirical questions associated with a research tradition are determined by that research tradition simply by virtue of being a *part* of that tradition. That is, to be completely described, a research tradition should contain not only domain-specifying assumptions, metaphysical assumptions, and methodological assumptions but also a list of basic questions. In this way, commitment to a research tradition will *ipso facto* entail commitment to a set of basic questions.

(3) The derivative empirical questions are determined by a research tradition in a more complex fashion. By virtue of its commitment to a research tradition, the relevant scientific community will be committed to pursuing a set of basic empirical questions. Research on these questions will result in data collection and theory construction of a sort sanctioned by the metaphysical and methodological assumptions of the research tradition. These research processes will, in turn, give rise to certain derivative questions.

With the modifications suggested above, Laudan's notion of a research tradition can satisfy our desiderata of soundness, immaturity, applicability, and coherence. The final desideratum to be considered is what I have called "the assessability desideratum": It must be reasonable to suppose that cognitive scientists' awareness of their commitment to a framework of shared commitments of the proposed kind could contribute to their ability to assess the various challenges and critiques that have been leveled against cognitive science in recent years. Since we will not actually be considering the challenges and critiques of cognitive science in this book, the question of whether Laudan's conception of a research tradition satisfies the desideratum of assessability will not receive as thorough a treatment as it deserves. It is important, however, to treat it at least minimally, for one of the principle background motivations of this project is to develop at least some of the apparatus necessary for assessing the viability of cognitive science. And this means, among other things, that we must assure ourselves that the kind of FSC we choose in order to capture the commitments of cognitive science could, in principle, be used for purposes of assessment.

In order for a theory of FSC-choosing science to be useful for purposes of scientific assessment—either the evaluation of some episode in the history of science or the adjudication of some contemporary controversy—it must specify at least two things: a set of norms relevant to the evaluation of the FSC in question and a set of conditions of satisfaction for each proposed norm. Laudan's theory of how research traditions are chosen certainly includes a normative theory in this sense. In particular, he claims that research traditions can be assessed in terms of two norms: whether they are *acceptable* and whether they are *rational to pursue*. And he proposes specific conditions of satisfaction for both of these norms based on his notion of problem-solving effectiveness. Clearly, then, the notion of a research tradition goes hand in hand with *a* normative theory. But is it adequate, and (more particularly) would it help us to adjudicate the current controversy over the scientific merits of cognitive science?

Although Laudan's proposed normative theory (as sketched just above) has much to recommend it, it also has its share of difficulties. I will focus on two sets of difficulties, one with the way Laudan defines problem-solving effectiveness and one with the role he assigns to problem-solving effectiveness vis-à-vis his two norms.

Recall that the problem-solving effectiveness of a theory is determined by assessing (a) the number and importance of the empirical problems the theory solves and (b) the number and importance of the anomalies and conceptual problems the theory generates, and substracting (b) from (a). There are at least two difficulties here.

The first is that Laudan's notion of problem-solving effectiveness makes use of the idea of a *solved* empirical problem. However, Laudan's view of what counts as a solution to an empirical problem is both confused and mistaken. It is confused because there is text which suggests that he thinks that what counts as a solution to an empirical problem is both *relative* to a particular scientific community (and, hence, subject to change over time) (p. 22) and *objective* (and, hence, universal) (p. 25). Clearly he cannot have it both ways. Furthermore (and this is a point for which Laudan has frequently been criticized), insofar as he takes the standards relevant to solving a problem to be objective, he claims that they have nothing to do with truth or confirmation (pp. 22–23). Rather, his view is that "generally, any theory, T, can be regarded as having solved an empirical problem, if T functions (significantly) in any schema of inference whose conclusion is a statement of the problem" (p. 25). In other words, the criteria for solving an empirical problem, on Laudan's view, are purely formal, amounting to something like entailment. But surely this cannot be correct, for— whatever one may think of truth and confirmation in science—Laudan's suggestion flies directly in the face of scientific practice. If scientists functioned in accordance with Laudan's suggestion, they would never have any reason to worry about testing their theories by seeking out empirical evidence. But clearly they do worry about doing this. Hence, empirical problem solution must require something more than derivation of the relevant problem statement from the proposed theory.

Second, insofar as problem-solving effectiveness is a *quantitative* measure, based in part on the *number* of problems solved, it requires some way of *individuating* problems so that we can count them. But Laudan provides us with no such criterion of individuation. Furthermore, it is far from clear what such a criterion would look like. Suppose that scientists are interested in explaining a set of data that can be represented by a mathematical function. Does this mathematical function represent many problems to be solved (corresponding to the many data points), or just one? Or suppose we take an empirical problem to be an empirical statement that satisfies certain other conditions (such as oddness), as Laudan suggests. Are problems then identical only to logically simple statements, or are they also identical to logically compound statements? That is, if P1 is an empirical statement (and, hence, a problem) and P2 is an empirical statement (and, hence, a problem), then is (P1 and P2) also an empirical problem? Laudan does not seem to worry about such questions.

Clearly the notion of problem-solving effectiveness needs some work. Let us assume, however, at least for purposes of discussion, that a more adequate conception can be developed, and turn our attention to Laudan's normative theory at a grosser level.

Laudan claims that there are two norms relevant to the assessment of both theories and research traditions: acceptability and rational pursuability. It seems clear that both are relevant to the assessment of *theories*, but I have my doubts as to whether both are relevant to the assessment of *research traditions*. The reason for these doubts is that there seem to be only two ways to accept a research tradition. One can accept some set of theories developed within the framework of the research tradition or one can accept the research tradition as a framework for research, but in neither case does one to have an independent notion of *accepting a research tradition*. The first case simply amounts to theory acceptance *tout court*, and the second is equivalent to a decision to *pursue* the research tradition. In any event, even if some independent sense can be given to the idea of accepting a research tradition, the norm that is most relevant to our concerns (namely, the viability of an immature research tradition such as cognitive science) is certainly rational pursuability. I shall therefore focus exclusively on this norm.

Let me begin by making a few preliminary observations. Laudan discusses rational pursuability as if it were an absolute (i.e., nonrelative) notion, but this does not seem right. Rather, let me suggest that it is rational (or irrational) to pursue something only in relation to some goal. The implicit goal in this case would, I take it, be the relevant scientific community's desiring to understand or explain some particular set of phenomena.

Furthermore, there are several distinct senses (kinds? modes?) of rationality that can be invoked with respect to research traditions. Some are purely psychological, in that they simply impose requirements on the agent; others are objective, in that they require that the world be a certain way; others are both psychological and objective. As a first step toward understanding Laudan's conception of rational pursuability, it is useful to determine which sense of rationality he has in mind.

Psychologically, we can say that it is minimally rational for a scientific community to pursue some research tradition RT_1 if the following conditions are met:

WPRP (WEAK PSYCHOLOGICAL RATIONAL PURSUABILITY)   Suppose:

(1) Scientific community SC desires goal G (i.e., to understand and explain some set of phenomena D).

(2) SC believes that the research traditions available for accomplishing G are $RT_1, \ldots, RT_n$.

(3) SC believes that the best available research tradition is RT_1.

Then, it is rational for SC to pursue research tradition RT_1.[32]

Note that this form of rationality is extremely minimal. The rationality of SC's pursuing RT_1 follows simply from the fact that SC has certain beliefs, but nothing is said about the epistemic status of these beliefs. A stronger but still purely psychological form of rational pursuability results from adding the requirement that SC believes that the beliefs alluded to in (2) and (3) are justified (or true). Further strengthening requires the addition of an objective component. That is, we need to say not only that SC *believes* that the beliefs alluded in (2) and (3) are justified (or true) but also that these beliefs are *in fact* justified (or true).

As it turns out, Laudan is not interested in any form of psychological rationality. Rather, he is concerned with a more "objective" sense of rationality which is independent of the particular beliefs of the scientific community in question. That is, he seems to be asking the following question: Given that a scientific community desires to understand and explain some set of phenomena D, what conditions must the research tradition *itself* satisfy, in order for it to be rational for SC to pursue that research tradition?

Laudan's answer is that "it is always rational to pursue any research tradition which has a higher rate of progress than its rivals" (p. 111). In reconstructed form, I take Laudan to be suggesting the following:

ORP (OBJECTIVE RATIONAL PURSUABILITY) (LAUDAN'S VERSION)   Suppose:

(1) Scientific community SC desires goal G (i.e., to understand and explain some set of phenomena D).

(2) The research traditions available to SC are $RT_1, \ldots, RT_n$.

(3) RT_1 has a higher rate of progress than any of its rivals.

Then, it is rational for SC to pursue RT_1.

When we are dealing with objective rationality, it does not follow that the scientific community (or the agent, in general) is irrational if the suggested conditions are met but the scientific community (agent) fails to pursue the targeted research tradition (action). Even if a scientific community did not do the rationally optimal thing, it still may have acted rationally in the psychological sense (that is, in the sense that its choice was a consequence of its beliefs and desires).

What should we think about ORP? First, an obvious and minor point. Clearly, it would not be rational to pursue RT_1 if the domain of RT_1 did not match the domain relevant to the community's goal. For example, suppose that the goal of the scientific community was to understand human cognition but the domain of RT_1 was continental drift! Thus, we also need an analogue to the psychological condition (2) to restrict the available research traditions to those that are available *for accomplishing goal G.*

There is, however, a far more important way in which ORP is inadequate. Suppose that the scientific community in question had some reason to believe that RT_1 could *never* accomplish the goal of understanding and explaining domain D. In that case, surely it would not be rational to pursue RT_1 even if the above minor condition were met and RT_1 had a higher rate of progress than any of its rivals. What sort of reason might this be? Suppose that RT_1 were foundationally flawed in some way—that is, that there were serious difficulties with respect to the explanatory power, soundness, or truth of its metaphysical and methodological assumptions. In this case, there would be good reasons to believe that a research program built on RT_1 could never succeed. But then, *ceteris paribus*, it would not be rational to pursue the tradition in question.[33] Note that this suggestion has a strong kinship with Laudan's claim that "conceptual problems" in a theory count against the overall merit (i.e., the problem-solving effectiveness) of that theory. This is precisely the sort of argument that we find in the current controversy over the scientific viability of cognitive science. Dreyfus (1979), Dreyfus and Dreyfus (1986), Haugeland (1978), Searle (1980a, 1980b), and, on occasion, the Churchlands (P. S. 1980a, 1980b; P. M. 1981) argue, in effect, that it is not rational to pursue cognitive science. Why? Although Dreyfus (1979) does argue against AI on the based of its lack of progress, other sorts of reasons are given as well. These include the following: (a) that there are numerous phenomena that legitimately belong within the domain of cognitive science that it cannot at present (or ever) adequately explain,[34] (b) that cognitive science does not cohere well with the theories and findings of presumably "neighboring" sciences, such as evolutionary biology and neuroscience,[35] and (c) that cognitive science is committed to one or more "foundational" assumptions that are false, such as the assumption that mental processes are computational processes.[36] Whether any of these challenges succeed is not, at present, the issue. Rather, the point is that (a)–(c) all rest their cases on the adequacy of the research tradition itself rather than on how research within the research tradition has progressed. More specifically, (a) is supposed to impugn the explanatory power of the assumptions that make up cognitive science's research tradition, (b) is supposed to question their soundness (no metaphysical assumption of a research tradition can be sound unless it "coheres" with the assumptions of neighboring sciences), and (c) clearly counters their truth.

It looks, then, as if ORP should be replaced with this:

RORP (OBJECTIVE RATIONAL PURSUABILITY) (REVISED VERSION)   Suppose:

(1) Scientific community SC desires goal G (i.e., to understand and explain some set of phenomena D).

(2) The research traditions currently available to SC are $RT_1, \ldots, RT_n$.

(3) The domain of RT_1 corresponds, at least roughly, with D.

(4) RT_1 has a higher rate of progress than any of the other research traditions that are available and relevant to the pursuit of G.

(5) RT_1 is not foundationally flawed (that is, its foundational assumptions are not unsound, untrue, or without sufficient conceptual resources to explain D).

Then, it is rational for SC to pursue RT_1.

In developing RORP, I have focused on articulating a set of *sufficient* conditions for rational pursuability, following Laudan's original suggestion. Let me now raise the question of whether these are the sort of conditions we want. There are different reasons why someone might be interested in a theory of appraisal for research traditions. Laudan is interested primarily because he wants to be able to rationally reconstruct the reasons why, historically, scientists decided to pursue some particular research tradition rather than another. In view of such an interest, an emphasis on sufficiency makes perfect sense, for in this case one wants to identify the set of reasons that should have been (or, if the scientists were acting rationally, were actually) sufficient for the scientists to make the choice.

However, my interest in a theory of scientific rationality is somewhat different. Rather than being concerned with a rational reconstruction of why linguists, psychologists, and AI researchers opted to become cognitive scientists in the first place, I am interested primarily in assessing current challenges and critiques of the field. And for this purpose, knowing the *necessary* conditions for rational pursuability is more important. The reason is that challenges to a research tradition typically take the following form (at least, implicitly):

It is not rational to pursue research tradition RT because RT does not satisfy certain *necessary* conditions of rational pursuability.

As a consequence, the question of interest to us is this: Which (if any) of the conditions listed in RORP not only is part of a jointly sufficient set of conditions for rational pursuability but is also individually necessary?

The answer is that all the conditions *except* Laudan's are necessary. That is, it is rational for a scientific community to pursue a particular research tradition RT_1 only if the domain of RT_1 corresponds (at least roughly) with the domain the scientific community seeks to understand and only if RT_1 is not foundationally flawed in some way. But do we want to say that it is rational to pursue RT_1 only if it outscores its rivals with respect to rate of progress? I think not. What if RT_1's rate of progress was equal to that of its rivals? What if we had some reason to believe that the rivals' rate of progress was only temporary and that RT_1 had more "promise"?[37] We probably want it to be the case that a research tradition which is rational to pursue must meet *some* minimal requirement with respect to its research track record, but precisely how to combine considerations of adequacy, rate of progress, and promise is not at all obvious.

Clearly, a theory of appraisal for research traditions will be far more complex than Laudan's proposal suggests. Nevertheless, despite both Laudan's and my cursory discussion of the topic, I hope the reader is persuaded that the notion of a research tradition is amenable to normative treatment, and that, in particular, it is amenable in a way that could contribute to the assessment of the challenges and critiques that have been leveled against cognitive science in recent years. I conclude, therefore, that the notion of a research tradition, in amended form, satisfies the assessability desideratum.

The modifications, corrections, and additions advanced in this section were all introduced as modifications, corrections, and additions to Laudan's notion of a research tradition. Taken as a whole, however, the suggested changes seem sufficiently great to warrant the claim that we now have in hand a new kind of FSC. I call this new unit of analysis a *research framework*. In chapter 1 I assemble and, in some cases, elaborate on the suggestions developed in connection with my critical analysis of Laudan's theory of research traditions to develop a theory of research frameworks suitable for discussing the case of cognitive science case.

Notes

Introduction

1. See P. S. Churchland 1980a,b; Haugeland 1978; Searle 1980a, 1980b, 1983; P. M. Churchland 1981; Dreyfus 1979; and Turvey et al. 1981.

2. An example of this sort of response to a critique of cognitive psychology can be found in Von Eckardt 1984, where I consider some arguments put forth by P. S. Churchland. Churchland (1980a) criticizes cognitive psychology on two grounds: because on her view it is committed to the assumption that mental representations are exclusively sentence-like (sententialism) and because it is committed to the truth of commonsense or folk psychology (commonsense foundationalism). I argue that neither attribution is correct, and, hence, that Churchland's arguments against the viability of cognitive psychology are misdirected. In her more recent work, Churchland (1986) seems to accept my point, at least for sententialism, for she explicitly notes that "there are many cognitive psychologists who do not adhere to the sentential theory and who investigate cognitive capacities while awaiting the development of a nonsentential theory of representations" (p. 387). She thus redirects her criticisms against a certain prominent *view* of cognitive psychology, which she associates with Fodor and Pylyshyn.

3. Certain remarks made by Stevan Harnad, the editor of *The Behavioral and Brain Sciences*, at the University of Rochester Cognitive Science Curriculum Conference in 1982, suggest such a view. In response to a claim made by Greg Carlson that cognitive science presupposes a representational theory of mind, Harnad says the following: "… if it is in fact the case that some representational theory of mind has to be correct for cognitive science to exist, you have a very strange kind of science here. It depends on the truth of a certain class of theories. That seems to be a unique case." (Lucas and Hayes 1982, p. 40)

Harnad is, of course, completely correct that cognitive science would be a "strange kind of science" if its existence depended on the *truth* of some representational theory (in the sense that if no representational theory of mind were true the field would cease to exist). But if he is read as responding to the claim that cognitive science presupposes (at least, tentative) *commitment* to the truth of a representational theory (rather than simply presupposing the truth of such a theory itself), the situation is quite different.

4. The views of two such philosophers—Thomas Kuhn and Larry Laudan—are discussed in appendix. Other prominent philosophers of science who accept the framework hypothesis are Imre Lakatos (1968, 1970) and Stephen Toulmin (1972). A philosopher who questions it is William Bechtel (private correspondence). Specifically, Bechtel suggests that the recent history of science (especially the history of cell biology and molecular biology) reveals that a conceptual foundational consensus is often not necessary in order for disciplinary development to occur. It should be noted that my claims along these lines are quite modest. I am neither endorsing the framework hypothesis for all of science nor claiming that a common framework of commitments is necessary for the development of cognitive science. Instead, I simply want to maintain that, *as a matter of fact,* (a) the cognitive science community currently shares a significant number of assumptions as to what questions cognitive science is trying to answer and how, generally speaking, it is supposed to answer them; and (b) in a sense to be spelled out in chapter 1, these assumptions guide research in the field.

5. For example, one might argue as follows:

ARGUMENT FROM SUCCESS

(1) To date, the scientific community has been extremely successful in its efforts to carry out the objectives of research program RP.
(2) Therefore, it is not the case that RP will eventually fail.
(3) *Failure Principle* If the foundational assumptions of a research program are false, the research program will eventually fall, no matter how ingenious and strenuous the research effort.

(4) Therefore, the foundational assumptions of RP are true.

The conclusion is a straightforward deductive inference from premises 2 and 3 and the logical rule of *modus tollens*. In contrast, the inference from premise 1 to premise 2 is inductive. Hence, the argument as a whole is clearly nondemonstrative. However, since successful attempts to meet the objectives of a research program over time provide significant evidence in support of its ultimate overall success, they also provide significant evidence in support of its foundational assumptions.

ARGUMENT FROM FAILURE

(1) To date, the scientific community has failed dismally in its efforts to carry out the objectives of research program RP.

(2) Therefore, it is not the case that RP will eventually succeed.

(3) *Success Principle* If the foundational assumptions of a research program are true and the research effort is sufficiently ingenious and strenuous, the research program will eventually succeed.

(4) Therefore, either the foundational assumptions of RP are not true or the research effort has not been sufficiently ingenious or strenuous.

(5) The research effort has been sufficiently ingenious and strenuous.

(6) Therefore, the foundational assumptions of RP are not true.

The logical structure of this argument is similar to the first in containing an inductive step from premise 1 to premise 2 and in making use of *modus tollens* to move from premises 2 and 3 to premise 4. This time, though, there is an added complication. To conclude that the foundational assumptions of RP are not true, we must rule out an alternative explanation for the failure: namely, that the research effort associated with RP has not been sufficiently ingenious and strenuous. Thus, again, the argument is nondemonstrative. The point is, however, that, even if this argument, like the argument from success, is nondemonstrative, the fact that a research program's track record has been none too good does constitute evidence against the truth of its foundational assumptions. And this is all we need to show that the foundational assumptions of a research program are not metaphysical.

6. 'Normal' here is supposed to contrast with 'pathological', whereas 'typical' is supposed to contrast with 'idiosyncratic'.

7. Of the three areas of disagreement, this is the most controversial. My sense is that AI researchers tend to want to include the study of machine intelligence (*per se*, not just as a tool for the study of human cognition) within the purview of cognitive science, whereas most other cognitive scientists believe that the focus should be on human cognition. In the literature, the view that cognitive science is the study of intelligence in general, including machine intelligence, is held by Simon (1981a), Norman (1981), Partee, Peters, and Thomason (1985), and Pylyshyn (1984). The view that cognitive science is restricted to the study of human cognition is advocated by Walker (1978), Johnson-Laird (1981), Gardner (1985), and Stillings et al. (1987).

8. Most cognitive scientists do not include either the study of animal cognition or the study of the emotions within cognitive science. However, investigations of both areas using a cognitive science approach have recently met with a certain amount of success. See, for example, Roitblat, Bever, and Terrace (1984) on animal cognition and Oatley (1987), Oatley and Johnson-Laird (1987), and Ortony, Clore, and Collins (1988) on the emotions. By a "cognitive science approach" I mean an approach defined by the substantive and methodological assumptions of the research framework of cognitive science, as I will characterize them in chapters 3–9.

9. I also do not intend to suggest that the ANTCOG research program can be carried out autonomously (that is, without reference to data usually associated with the non-ANTCOG research programs). For example, information on how human cognition typically develops

or how it can go awry can be very useful (and may, even, be indispensable) in developing models of adult, normal, typical cognition.

Chapter 1

1. Talk of "theories" is, of course, common among both philosophers of science and scientists; however, the notion of a scientific theory played an especially important role in the analysis of science provided by the logical positivist tradition. See Suppe 1977. The related notions of "paradigm," "exemplar," and "disciplinary matrix" are found in the writings of Kuhn (1970a, 1970c, 1977). "Explanatory ideals," "research programs," "fields," and "research traditions" are constructs introduced by Toulmin (1972), Lakatos (1968, 1970), Darden and Maull (1977), and Laudan (1977), respectively.

2. The term 'domain' is used in at least two distinct ways in the philosophy-of-science literature. I (and Laudan) use it to refer to a *set of phenomena* about which there are scientific problems or questions. In contrast, Shapere (1977, p. 521), who has made an important contribution to our understanding of domains and their role in science, uses the term to refer to a *body of related information* about which there are scientific problems. In my terms, this is equivalent to equating the domain with my identification and property domain-specifying assumptions rather than with what those assumptions are *about*.

3. These do not exhaust the class of theoretical problems, on Shapere's (1977) view. In fact, he suggests that it may not be possible to give a complete classification of such problems (p. 534).

4. Giere does not do this in his 1979 book.

5. Giere considers the option of including statements defining some population of models rather than the models themselves as one component of a scientific theory, and rejects it because "it puts too much emphasis on matters linguistic" (1988, p. 85). I'm not sure I understand his reasoning here. There is certainly something wrong with considering a theory to be (even in part) a set of sentences, since that makes it impossible to have the same theory expressed in more than one language. But this objection does not apply if we consider a theory to be a set of statements or propositions (which are, presumably, language-neutral) rather than a set of sentences.

6. Joe Mendola reminds me that 'metaphysical' is often used simply as a contrast with 'epistemic'. Thus, in this sense, to say that a statement is "metaphysical" is simply to say that it concerns the nature of the world, as opposed to saying that it concerns what we know about the world and how we know it. This usage is irrelevant to the dispute in question because on this sense of 'metaphysical' both substantive assumptions and specific theories are metaphysical.

7. The one exception to this might be the research framework of quantum physics, but even in this case the domain is universal only if we are restricting ourselves to the *natural* world.

8. A natural suggestion is to consider the "unrevisable" assumptions the "metaphysical" ones. But although these assumptions are not revisable while one is doing FSC- guided science, they are revisable in the context of FSC-choosing science. It is precisely such revision that is at issue when scientists consider discarding one research framework in favor of another.

9. Another philosopher of science who has taken the view that science is often regulated by metaphysical frameworks is Agassi (1964). His view is curious in that, although he seems to agree with me that metaphysical doctrines playing such a role can be ultimately rejected on empirical grounds (in his case because a metaphysical "interpretation" of a body of known facts can be developed into a scientific theory that is defeated by a crucial experiment), he persists in calling them "metaphysical." Why is not at all clear. Some passages suggest that he has Walsh's second feature in mind: "Metaphysical theories are views about the nature of

things...." (p. 191); "My own use of the word 'metaphysics' in the present essay is in its traditional ... sense. Metaphysical doctrines are to be found, first and foremost, in Aristotle's *Metaphysics*, especially in Book Alpha: all is water; atoms and the void; matter and form; etc." (p. 193). But if Agassi does have Walsh's second feature in mind, then the substantive assumptions of most research frameworks are still not metaphysical, because they are not general enough.

10. Although the notion of a research framework was developed in order to handle the case of an immature science (i.e., cognitive science), the reader may wonder at this point whether it might not apply to mature science as well, and, if it does, what distinguishes immature and mature science. I will address these questions shortly.

11. Not all answers to questions are explanations, but which ones are need not concern us here.

12. I owe the third and fourth points to Jeffrey Poland.

13. In chapter 9 I will discuss how the question of revising our ordinary conceptual scheme manifests itself in the case of cognitive science.

14. For the sake of simpler prose, I will often refer to the research under discussion as "Kosslyn's." It should be understood, however, that much of it was done in collaboration with others.

15. Unless otherwise specified, the work to be described is reported in Kosslyn 1980.

16. Much more will be said about these representations in section 5.2.

17. In making his theory/model distinction, Kosslyn claims that there are two kinds of models: *general* and *specific*. "Specific models are designed to account for performance in a particular task, whereas general ones embody the set of principles that should account for performance in all tasks in a given domain" (Kosslyn, Pinker, Smith, and Shwartz 1979, p. 540). For some reason, however, Kosslyn countenances only one kind of theory, although "a complete cognitive theory ... would allow us to explain performance in all the tasks in the domain of the theory by specifying the ordered sequence in which operations process particular data-structures when people perform a given task" (Kosslyn 1980, p. 118). On my view, there is nothing about a model as opposed to a theory that makes the former uniquely suitable for "capturing" how a person accomplishes a particular task. Thus, in the interests of a logically more complete taxonomy, Kosslyn should distinguish between specific and general theories as well as between specific and general models.

18. Both the query and the first part of my answer are due to Pat Manfredi.

19. Both questions are discussed in Kosslyn 1980, the first in chapter 9 and the second on pp. 268–276 and pp. 463–464.

Chapter 2

1. The view that the domain of cognitive science includes machine intelligence can be found in Norman 1981, in Partee, Peters, and Thomason 1985, and in Pylyshyn 1984.

2. This is not to say, of course, that the study of intelligence in the elitist sense should not be a *part* of cognitive science. I—and probably Sternberg—would argue that it should be. The point is rather that the study of what makes a person intelligent in the sense of "smart" does not *exhaust* the research program of the field.

3. In his original paper, Turing (1950) suggests that the somewhat vague and ill-defined question "Can machines think?" should be replaced by a more precise question framed in terms of an "imitation game." The imitation game goes like this: There are three players, a, b, and c. Player a is an individual of type X (man or machine), player b is an individual of

type Y (woman or person), and player c is an interrogator. Player c cannot see either a or b, and communication takes place by typed messages. The interrogator's aim is to guess which of a and b is of type X and which is of type Y. Player a's aim is to fool the interrogator into thinking he/she/it is of type Y; player b's aim is to help the interrogator to guess the truth. There are two versions of the game. In the man/woman version, type X is a man and type Y is a woman. In the machine/person version, type X is a machine and type Y is a person. Turing's criterion for machine intelligence is that a machine is intelligent if, when playing the machine/person imitation game, it can fool the interrogator as often as a man can when paying the man/woman imitation game. Other writers simplify the criterion somewhat—in particular, Block (1981b, p. 7) claims that the machine passes the test "just in case the judge cannot tell which are the machine's answers and which are those of the person."

4. He doesn't actually say the latter, though I take it that this is what he has in mind.

5. Cummins (1983) makes a similar point, although, for some reason, he restricts himself to those cases in which only the output is intentional. He writes: "What makes a capacity cognitive is that the outputs are cognitions" (p. 53). This is clearly too restrictive to cover all the cognitive capacities.

6. The expression 'conditions of satisfaction' is ambiguous as between the *requirement* and the *thing required*. Searle (1983, p. 13) writes: "... for example, if I believe that it is raining then the conditions of satisfaction of my belief are that it should be the case *that it is raining* (requirement). That is what my belief requires in order that it be a true belief. And if my belief actually is a true belief then there will be a certain condition in the world, namely the condition *that it is raining* (thing required), which is the condition in the world which actually satisfies my belief."

7. The term 'intrinsic intentionality' is not always used in this sense. Van Gulick (1988) points out that Searle, who is largely responsible for the intrinsic/derived distinction, uses the term to contrast with three different nonequivalent terms: (1) 'derived intentionality', (2) 'relational intentionality', and (3) 'observer-relative intentionality'. To distinguish these three contrasts, it is essential to recognize that an intentional state has two important distinct features: content, and significance for someone or something. For any specific (or subkind of) intentional state X, two general questions can be raised, corresponding to each of these features: In virtue of what does X have the content it has? For whom or what does X have significance? Contrasts 1 and 2 both concern the nature of content determination for X (that is, the first question), whereas contrast 3 pertains to the question of significance (that is, the second question). More specifically, the contrasts can be distinguished in terms of the issue each raises:

(a) *intrinsic versus derived*   whether the content determination for X is not consciously endowed by an intentional agent or whether it is

(b) *intrinsic versus relational*   whether the content determination of X is solely a function of intrinsic properties of the system (or person) in which X occurs or whether relational properties are also relevant

(c) *intrinsic versus observer-relative*   whether X has significance for its "containing" system or whether X has significance *only* for some observer system.

The question of content determination will be discussed in greater detail in chapters 6 and 7. The question of significance will be discussed in chapter 8.

8. See Searle (1983, pp. 61–62) on this point.

9. Although Haugeland's idea is applicable to the present context, it was originally intended to solve a slightly different (though related) problem: how to apply the notion of an "intentional black box" (IBB) to a person. An object "is interpreted" as an IBB, according to Haugeland (1978, p. 219), just in case, roughly speaking, its inputs and outputs can be interpreted as quasilinguistic representations and "it is shown empirically that under the interpretations the actual outputs consistently make reasonable sense in the context (pattern) of actual prior inputs and other actual outputs." Haugeland wants his notion of an IBB to

apply to a person; but, as it stands, it does not, since a person's inputs and outputs (if he or she has them at all) are perceptual stimuli and actions, respectively, and not quasilingistic representations. It is at this point that his suggestion enters the picture.

10. My rejection of Chomsky's stronger notion of productivity in the present context (that is, in the context of characterizing properties of our *ordinary* cognitive capacities) does not mean that I reject his account at the information-processing level. From a computational point of view, a very plausible explanation of the productivity (in the weak sense) of our ordinary cognitive capacities is that such capacities are information-processing capacities and the latter involve transformations over an (in principle) unbounded number of representations. The point is that when Chomsky's account is located at the information-processing level it is not subject to my objection, for theoretical baggage is now quite appropriate.

11. They continue: "Notice that this is still true even on the assumption that my grandmother's favorite metal is gold and there *are* laws about gold. This is because *being my grandmother's favorite metal* and *being gold* are different properties and the laws about gold would continue to hold even if my grandmother's taste in metals were to change." (pp. 146–147).

Chapter 3

1. This is not to say that all cognitive science research is framed in explicitly representational or computational terms, or even that all cognitive scientists believe that detailed computational models can fruitfully be developed at this stage in the game. As I note in section 3.3, many cognitive scientists engage in "architecturally neutral" research—research that is consistent with the idea that the mind/brain is a computer in a very general sense but which makes no specific architectural assumptions about what that computer is like.

2. The qualification 'to a large extent' is there because not all of our cognitive capacities consist *solely* of computational capacities, on the cognitivist approach. Both input and output capacities (such as perception and intentional action, respectively) reach out into the world, and, hence, must include a transduction component (which may not be strictly computational).

3. For example, Richards (1936) distinguished the 'vehicle' and the 'tenor' of a metaphor, and Black (1954) introduced the terminology of 'focus', 'frame', 'primary subject', and "subsidiary subject'.

4. In simple cases such as 'man is a wolf' there is a great temptation to locate the incongruity in the violation of a semantic selection restriction. The difficulty is that this view relies on a particular approach to semantics and does not generalize to all cases of metaphor. For examples, the metaphor "I shall kill two birds with one stone" does not involve any violation of selection restriction (birds are the kind of things that can be killed with a stone). It makes perfect sense when read literally, and it might well be true on some occasion. However, as Kittay (1987) points out, such cases do not count against the claim that metaphorical understanding is prompted by a perceived incongruity. The incongruity is simply not located *within* the sentence; rather, it is to be found *between* the sentence and some element of the surrounding (implicit or explicit) context.

5. According to Black (1954), each of these alternatives is associated with a different version of the substitution view. His labeling of these versions is somewhat unfortunate. The version that assumes that the intended proposition is an explicit comparison (e.g., man is like a wolf in being fierce) is, quite naturally, called "the comparison view." However, the alternative version that assumes that the intended proposition is a simple attribution (e.g., man is fierce) is, like the genus it falls under, also called "the substitution view." I have no doubt that Black recognized the distinction between the more general view and this version. (He refers to the latter as "a substitution view (of the sort previously considered)" (p. 71).) However, a label

like "simple attribution view" for the specific version would have helped keep the distinction clear.

6. Thus, the comparison view, for example, is taken to hold that the metaphorical meaning of a simple 'A is B' metaphor is identical to the literal meaning of either 'A is like B' (*tout court*) (Fogelin 1988) or 'A is like B in such- and-such respects' (Black 1954). The interaction view is taken to include the claim that what the recipient constructs during the act of metaphorical understanding is the metaphorical meaning of the metaphor (Black 1954; Kittay 1987). For critical discussion of these assumptions, see Davidson 1978, Searle 1979, and Fogelin 1988.

7. For helpful reviews of this literature, see Thagard 1988 and Hall 1989.

8. There is general agreement that the core of analogical reasoning is a process of mapping. However, the questions of precisely how the source and target domains are to be represented and what is involved in the mapping process (in particular, what constraints are involved) remain in dispute.

9. The role of metaphor and analogy in science has also been discussed by Hesse (1966), Barbour (1974), MacCormac (1976), Kuhn (1979), and Nersessian (1988 and forthcoming).

10. This could be either a first-order similarity in which the nonmetaphorical and metaphorical subjects share the same properties or a second-order similarity in which they share similar properties (Sellars 1967).

11. Boyd (1979, p.360) focuses not only on a statement akin to my C1 ("the claim that thought is a kind of "information processing," and that the brain is a sort of "computer") but also on a number of more specific analogies between aspects of the cognitive mind/brain and computers (for example, "the suggestion that certain motoric or cognitive processes are 'pre- programmed' ").

12. The terms 'connectionism' and 'connectionist' were first introduced by Feldman (1981; see also Feldman and Ballard 1982) and are sometimes used (as in Rumelhart et al. 1986) to refer to a specific *kind* of massively parallel computational system rather than to the entire class of such systems. (Rumelhart et al. call the general class "parallel distributed processing" systems. They are also sometimes called "neural nets.") However, in the past few years, Feldman's terminology seems to have gained ground as the generic terminology of choice. (See, for example, Tienson 1987, Pinker and Mehler 1988, McClelland 1989, Pfeifer et al. 1989, and Bechtel and Abrahamson 1990.) I shall follow this general trend and, hence, refer to all massively parallel computational systems (as described in section 3.4) as "connectionist" machines.

13. In section 3.3 I will distinguish these two. Strictly speaking, the class of conventional computers will turn out to be broader than the class of von Neumann computers.

14. The descriptions to be provided make use of the notions of a set, a Cartesian product, and a function from a Cartesian product onto a set. Readers not familiar with these notions may find the following preliminary definitions helpful.

A *set* is a collection of objects usually characterized by a predicate which is said to define the set. Sets will be denoted by capital letters. The objects in a set are called the *members* or *elements* of the set. To denote set membership I will use the standard symbol '$\in$'. Thus, if $A = \{1,2,3\}$, then $1 \in A$.

If A and B are sets, then the *Cartesian product* of A and B, notated as '$A \times B$', is the set of all ordered pairs $\langle a,b \rangle$ such that $a \in A$ and $b \in B$.

If A and B are sets, then a *function f from A onto B* is a rule that associated to each element of A a *unique* element of B. Such a function will be represented as '$f: A \rightarrow B$'. Since the Cartesian product of two sets is itself a set, we can have a function that maps from the Cartesian product of two sets onto a third set, thus: $f: D \times E \rightarrow F$.

15. Newell (1990) points out that the concept of computational architecture as "fixed structure," especially in a natural system, is a relative notion. Change is constantly occurring on

different time scales, during performance, knowledge acquisition, skill acquisition, and development. Thus, structure is only fixed relative to a time scale—typically, the time scale of performance and knowledge acquisition. As Newell puts it, "fixed structure means changing relatively slowly" (p. 81).

16. For a useful description of the various computational levels of description in a digital system, see Siewiorek et al. 1982 and Newell 1990.

17. Given that the architecture of a device is described in one way, it is not always obvious whether a description at another "level" is also applicable. For example, Nelson (1987) cites findings by Arthur Burks and associates (Burks and Wang 1957; Burks, Goldstine, and von Neumann 1946) that show that stored-program digital computers are, structurally, finite-state automata. This is, however, far from obvious.

18. One prominent exception is Nelson (1989)—but even he admits that finite-state automata may be more useful for "helping establish the plausibility of the computationalist hypotheses than at constructing explanatory models for cognitive science" (p. 407).

19. As I shall make clear shortly, by claiming that minds have internalized rules I am not claiming that they must have something analogous to a *stored* program. I take it that rules that are hard-wired also count as "internalized" in the relevant sense.

20. This ambiguity is reflected in a number of recent reference books. For example, the *Encyclopedia of Computer Science and Engineering* (Ralston and Reilly 1983) adopts the semantic sense. Data are "facts or are believed to be or said to be facts which result from the observation of physical phenomena," and information is "data which is used in decision-making" (pp. 715–716). In contrast, the *Dictionary of Computing* (Oxford University Press 1986) adopts the formal sense, in which information consists of "collections of symbols", where symbols are "patterns that carry meaning" (p. 182), and data is characterized as "information that has been prepared, often in a particular format, for a specific purpose" (p. 90) A third reference book, the *Computer Dictionary and Handbook* (Sippl and Sippl 1972) provides two entries for the term 'information'. In one, 'information' is defined as a "set of symbols"; in the other, it is "the meaning assigned to data by the known conventions used in its representation" (p. 211). Finally, the *Dictionary of Computers, Data Processing, and Telecommunications* (Rosenberg 1984) treats information semantically and data formally.

21. The question of whether data and information consist of form or content is not the only point of dispute in the literature on these concepts. Some authors use the concepts interchangeably; others take pains to distinguish them. Among those who consider data and information to be different, some take data to be a subset of information (Oxford University Press 1986); others regard information as a subset of data (Ralston and Reilly 1983). Some impose certain epistemic requirements on one or both (Ralston and Reilly 1983; Sippl and Sippl 1972; Dretske 1981); others do not (Oxford University Press 1986). Unless I indicate otherwise, I will be using the terms (a) interchangeably and (b) without any epistemic restrictions. Item b means, in particular, that something can be a datum or a piece of information whether or not it is known or believed or used, and that, in addition, information is not necessarily true.

22. My thanks to Pat Manfredi for clarifying this point.

23. This is the reason it is a mistake to identify the distinction between architecture, as fixed structure, and content, as variable data, with the distinction between hardware and software. For example, Laird, Newell, and Rosenbloom's (1987) system SOAR consists of a software architecture programmed in Common LISP, itself a software architecture, which runs on a hardware architecture (Newell 1990).

24. My example is a bit misleading, since all LISP functions are ultimately (at the primitive level) defined in terms of operations on list structures. For a more detailed but still nontechnical discussion of the characteristics of LISP, see Haugeland 1985, chapter 4.

25. Henceforth, I shall use the term 'data structures' to cover both complex, structured representations and simple data representations.

26. The above conception of a conventional machine is closely related to ideas found in Pylyshyn 1984 ("symbol processing devices"), Haugeland 1981 ("semantic engines"), Haugeland 1985 ("GOFAI"—Good Old-Fashioned AI), Dennett 1986 ("High Church Computationalism"), and Fodor and Pylyshyn 1988 ("classical architecture"). It differs from Newell's (1980, 1990) conception of a "physical symbol system" (in his 1990 book Newell just calls it a "symbol system") in that conventional machines need not be universal whereas physical symbol systems (symbol systems) always are; otherwise it is very similar. It also differs from the sort of device employed in Smolensky's (1988) "symbolic paradigm" and Clark's (1989) "semantically transparent systems", because both of the latter involve restrictions on how data structures represent what they represent. In particular, both "symbolic paradigm" devices and "semantically transparent systems" must represent objects in terms of "the same concepts as the ones used to consciously conceptualize the task domain" (Smolensky 1988, p. 5). In contrast, no such restrictions are associated with the idea of a conventional machine.

27. See chapter 5 for further discussion of this point.

28. Arguments in favor of using connectionist models for cognitive science research rather than conventional ones can be found in Anderson and Hinton 1981, Churchland 1986, Feldman 1983, McClelland, Rumelhart, and Hinton 1986, Tienson 1987, Churchland and Sejnowski 1989, and Clark 1989. Arguments in support of conventional models and against the adequacy of connectionist ones can be found in Fodor and Pylyshyn 1988, Pinker and Prince 1988, and Lachter and Bever 1988.

29. My description of McCulloch-Pitts neural nets is based on Minsky 1967. The neural net is a precursor of modern connectionist devices.

30. Both M-P and connectionist networks are sometimes called "neural" nets because they are similar to real neural nets in certain gross respects. However, there are also many important differences. Smolensky (1988, p. 9) summarizes the similarities and differences between cerebral cortex and connectionist systems.

31. My discussion is based on the general framework for parallel distributed processing sketched in Rumelhart, Hinton, and McClelland 1986.

32. In current connectionist models, the nature of this teaching input is determined by the human model builder (or programmer), not by the connectionist system itself. This constitutes a major weakness in current models.

33. A recent survey of learning rules can be found in Hinton 1989.

34. As I noted above, the devices that I call FSAs are called "finite state automata with output" (FSOs) by Nelson (1987). Thus, Nelson frames the dispute with Pylyshyn over symbol processing as a dispute over the capacities of FSOs rather than FSAs (as he defines them). Note also that both Nelson and I use the word 'symbol' to mean something that can symbolize or represent, with no restriction imposed on what is symbolized or represented. This is in contrast with a more restricted use, as in Smolensky 1988, where something is a symbol only if it refers to "essentially the same concepts as the ones used to consciously conceptualize the task domain" (p. 5). Newell (1990) also uses the term in a more restricted sense, as referring to something like primitive representations (that is, simple representational components in larger representational structures).

35. The proof goes, roughly, like this: The key idea, according to Nelson (1987), is that of a logical net—"a systematic interconnection of logic switches, ANDS, ORS, NOTS, and DELAYS." Any logical net is a FSA (in my sense) (Burks and Wang 1957; Nelson 1968), and a von Neumann machine is a logical net (Burks and Copi 1956).

36. Although connectionist units aren't computers in the sense of C2, they clearly "compute" in the sense of automatically performing numerical calculations. Thus, rather than make the notion of a computer an all-or-none affair, it seems appropriate to distinguish between simple *computing units* (devices which perform input-output operations that are semantically inter-

pretable) and genuine computers (in the spirit of C2), and to regard connectionist units as the first but not the second.

37. Fodor's claim is actually a good deal richer than this. He argues that the input systems are *modules* in the following senses: they are domain specific, their operation is mandatory, there is only limited access to the mental representations they compute, they are fast, they are informationally encapsulated, they have "shallow" outputs, they exhibit characteristic and specific breakdown patterns, and the ontogeny of input systems exhibits a characteristic pace and sequencing.

38. I pick this date because Fodor 1983 developed out of a graduate course on cognitive theory taught in 1980 and because most of the important early works on connectionism hover around this date (e.g. Rumelhart 1977; Grossberg 1978, 1980; Hinton and Anderson 1981; McClelland and Rumelhart 1981; Rumelhart and McClelland 1982; Feldman and Ballard 1982).

Chapter 4

1. This result depends on the conception of a computer we have adopted. There are other conceptions which would not yield the same result. For example, on Newell's (1990) view, a computer is an input-output device capable of producing many functions where some inputs provide a specification of the function to be performed. Such a device need not be representational. Simply imagine a machine whose inputs and outputs are nonsymbolic (say, coins and soda cans, respectively) and whose mechanism does not involve the storing or manipulation of anything remotely representational.

2. For example, one additional assumption is that the property or relation of a mental representation that determines its representational object (or content) must be naturalistic— that is, nonsemantic and non-intentional. This constraint is not satisfied by ordinary computers because their representations have the content they do at least partly in virtue of the intentions of the user or designer (and, hence, in virtue of an intentional property). Their content is partly determined by the functional role of the representation, as Cummins (1989) and Haugeland (1985) have emphasized, but functional role in itself cannot determine the sort of unique interpretation we typically attribute. To arrive at a unique interpretation, we must consider what the designer had in mind or what the user wants to do. This is not to say, of course, that a computer *could* not have representations of the sort that humans have. If cognitive scientists are right, then humans are computers of this kind. It is simply to make the obvious point that not all computers have representations that are naturalistically determined simply by virtue of their being computers.

3. Since completing this chapter, I have discovered that several other writers have used Peirce's semiotic theory to a similar end. See, for example, Pearson 1982 and Fetzer 1988.

4. The majority of references to Pierce's work will be to his collected papers (Hartshorne, Weiss, and Burks 1931–1958). Where this is the case, I will follow the standard practice of referring to specific passages by volume number and paragraph number (e.g., 5.346). Texts other than the collected papers will be cited in the usual way.

5. In a letter to Lady Welby (December 23, 1908), Peirce writes that the dynamical object (here he calls it the "dynamoid object") "may be a Possible [by which he means a quality such as whiteness, beauty] ... an Occurrence (Existent thing or Actual fact of past or future)... [or] a Necessitant [laws, habits, continua, and whatever is expressible in a universal proposition]" (Hardwick 1977, pp. 83–84).

6. A number of commentators (see, for example, Pharies 1985) hold that the immediate object of a nonmental representation is an idea or a concept—in particular, the mind's own representation of the dynamical object of the representation in question. I do not think this view is correct, for it would make the immediate object equivalent to the interpretant. It is a

much more plausible reading of the text to regard the immediate object as a "slice" of reality—namely, that bundle of properties picked out by our representation of the object itself, as is suggested by Hookway (1985) and Savan (n.d.).

7. Peirce's notion of a habit-change will loom large in my discussion of the interpretant for mental representation in chapter 8.

8. In fact, my own explication will reveal that Peirce's characterization is not entirely accurate. It will turn out that, whereas the subrelation between the representation and interpretant *is* triadic in the sense that it cannot be understood without reference to the object, the subrelation between the representation and the object is only sometimes triadic. Specifically, it is triadic when the ground of the representation-object relation is conventional; however, it is dyadic when the ground is iconic or indexical. It is, of course, quite possible that I have not fully understood the sense in which Peirce intends representation to be essentially triadic.

9. The third kind of icon is a *metaphor*, a sign that represents "the representative character of a representamen by representing a parallelism in something else" (2.277).

10. At one point Peirce distinguishes between genuine and degenerate symbols. Only the former "has a general meaning." "There are two kinds of degenerate symbols, the *Singular Symbol* whose Object is an existent individual, and which signifies only such characters as that individual may realize; and the *Abstract Symbol*, whose only Object is a character." (2.293).

11. This is where the triadicity of the representation-object relation comes in. See section 4.2 and note 8.

12. This problem will be discussed at greater length in the next section.

13. Naturalism will be discussed in greater detail in chapter 7. Note that a naturalistic mode of grounding representation does not necessarily exclude *intensional* properties and relations which are not *intentional*. This is an important point to make in this context because, as Robert Meyers has pointed out to me, Peirce's notion of a habit is closely connected with the idea of a law and laws are counterfactual supporting and, hence, intensional.

14. Peirce does not really make it clear what the content of this thought is. There are two obvious possibilities. One is that the interpreting thought is a representation of the content of R (i.e., that it is something like a translation). The other is that it is akin to a metastatement about the original representation (i.e. with the content): that R represents O. There are passages in the Peircian corpus that suggest both of these. The translation view is suggested by the following: "... by the *meaning* of a term, proposition, or argument, we understand the entire general intended interpretant...." (5.179) In contrast, the metastatement view can be found in one of Peirce's discussions of the interpretant of a thought: "... as the [interpreting] thought is determined by a previous thought [i.e., the mental representation] of the same object, it only refers to the thing through denoting this previous thought" (5.285).

15. This is not to say that Peirce's semiotic framework is without its weaknesses. For example, there are two quite glaring omissions: Peirce's neglect of representational *systems* (which have both a syntax and a compositional semantics), as opposed to single cases of representation, and his failure to say anything about how *false* representation is possible. Also, I certainly do not believe that we should be constrained, *a priori*, by Peirce's taxonomy of kinds of ground.

16. This will be discussed in chapter 8.

Chapter 5

1. The use of 'system' here is not meant to suggest that our mental representations are all of a piece—all language-like (or "propositional"), for example. MRS may contain many different subcodes, each with its own formal and semantic characteristics.

2. Dennett (1977, p. 75) is also in agreement on this point. He writes that "cognitivist theories are or should be theories of the subpersonal level, where beliefs and desires disappear to be replaced with representations of other sorts on other topics."

3. Since this version of the attitude-representation identification assumption is open to counterexamples (propositional attitudes that are not correlated with mental representations and mental representations that are not correlated with propositional attitudes), Fodor (1987, pp. 20–26) modifies it to hold only of what he calls "core" propositional attitudes, where a core propositional attitude is one that plays a role in a mental process. Thus the slogan becomes "No Intentional Causation without Explicit Representation."

4. This point will be discussed further in chapter 9.

5. This is not to say that there are no serious *methodological* problems in identifying the representation bearers of the MRS. See Dennett 1987, p. 145.

6. Putnam (1986, p. 101) identifies a very similar assumption as "the working hypothesis of cognitive psychology today." His formulation goes like this: "The mind uses a formalized language, or something analogous to a formalized language, both as medium of computation and medium of representation." Putnam's formulation, of course, belongs to that version of the cognitive science research framework that assumes the cognitive mind/brain to be a conventional computer.

7. My discussion of data structures is based on the wonderfully lucid exposition of Wirth (1976).

8. Note that an instance of a data structure is not yet a spatiotemporal particular. As I will use the term, an instance is more specific than a data type but more abstract than a spatiotemporal particular. It is, in fact, a *kind* of spatiotemporal particular which constitutes a subkind of the data type.

9. See, however, Kosslyn and Hatfield 1984, where a very different approach to mental representation is advocated.

10. They also discuss the role of node labels in connectionist machines. But since node labels so obviously won't do to endow connectionist representations with structure (since they are not even a property of connectionist devices, but only a property of their *description*), I have omitted them from my discussion.

11. Smolensky (1987) makes a similar point, although there are several important differences between his argument and mine. First, his argument is not in terms of microfeature components but in terms of what he calls symbolic-level components (see note 34 to chapter 3, above). Specifically, Smolensky argues that the representation of the concept *cup with coffee* contains ("in an approximate sense") a representation of the concept *coffee* and a representation of the concept *cup*. Second, he claims that these component representations are context-sensitive, and that this is why they are components of the complex representation only "in an approximate sense" (See Fodor and McLaughlin 1990 for criticism of this aspect of his view), whereas, as far as I can see, microfeature representations are perfectly context- free. Note, however, that, although Smolensky and I are in agreement that example 2 illustrates how a distributed connectionist representation can be a complex representation with representational parts, we disagree as whether this sort of complexity is sufficient for constituent structure. Smolensky seems to think that it is; I think that it is not, as I will argue shortly.

12. I intend here to include relations of the networks to their environments. For some suggestions as to how connectionist representations might be grounded, see Goschke and Koppelberg 1990.

13. See Smolensky 1991 for another proposal concerning how connectionist networks might have constituent structure; see Fodor and McLaughlin 1990 for arguments against its viability.

14. In contexts where it does not matter, I occasionally omit the subscript.

15. See, for example, Mathews 1986, p. 122.

16. Note that talk about representing₀ an object is sometimes quite misleading, for some representation bearers of MRS (like some expressions of natural language) may have meaning because they serve certain semantic *functions*, not because they are semantically related to any representational object. Examples of function words in English are 'of', 'the', and 'and'. MRS undoubtedly includes analogues to such words.

17. This is not to say that, *methodologically*, we must first have our semantics completely in place before tackling the content-determination problem. Clearly, the two theories must be developed in tandem. However, it remains true that we cannot develop a theory of the ground of MRS unless we know what semantic properties we are grounding (whereas, presumably, the reverse does not hold). Rather, the semantics for MRS will be developed primarily with an eye to what we want to *explain* (namely, properties of one or another of the human cognitive capacities) rather than to the nature of the ground.

18. Block (1986) attempts to preserve the distinction between the two kinds of theory by distinguishing between reductionistic and nonreductionistic semantics, where the former is equivalent to a TCD. This has the virtue of vindicating current usage and marking the distinction at the same time. However, I think the danger of confusion is, at present, sufficiently high that a more radical terminological revision is called for.

19. Lacking a canonical way of *theoretically* representing specific mental representations, cognitive scientists usually resort to referring to primitive mental representations in terms of their English translations. Thus, when Kosslyn claims that there is a long-term memory file containing the representation

size:medium

he means that there is a representation with unknown formal characteristics that expresses the same content as the English phrase 'size:medium'. And this is all he means. The fact that this phrase, in English, has a certain orthography is not supposed to have any implications for the formal characteristics of the MRS representation. (See Palmer 1978 for an interesting discussion of this point.) Note that solving the theoretical notation problem by this sort of translation device in effect appropriates the semantics of whatever English is employed in the theoretical description as the semantics of MRS.

20. Assumptions similar to these are included in Lloyd's (1987, p. 26) list of "relatively untendentious properties of representations in general". (See also Lloyd 1989, pp. 11–17.) Lloyd's list also includes a number of other assumptions which are not, strictly speaking, semantic.

21. There may, of course, also be other dimensions of meaning (such as Kaplan's [1977, 1979] notion of *character*, which is a function from context to intensions).

22. As in the case of the natural-language representational system, there may be a few kinds of simple representations, akin to proper names and demonstratives, that simply pick out an object itself without doing so under an aspect.

23. Of course, the nature of the object itself (that is, what a concept *is*) may also differ on each view, but this does not detract from the main point.

Chapter 6

1. Two exceptions are the views of Millikan (1984, 1986, 1989a, 1989b, 1990) and Lloyd (1989), each of which has an interpretative component.

2. For a survey of the current state of the art, see Poland (forthcoming).

3. This follows Kim 1984 very closely, although it is not a direct quote.

4. Post (1987) and Poland (forthcoming) suggest a similar restriction in their discussions of supervenience.

5. I am indebted to Poland's (forthcoming) discussion of the importance of an explanatory component in an adequate characterization of physicalism for a number of the ideas expressed in this paragraph.

6. Fodor (1984, p. 233) makes an even stronger claim. He suggests that theories based on resemblance and theories based on causality are the only two kinds of TCDs that have ever been proposed.

7. The only critical discussions I have been able to unearth directed specifically at Palmer's view are the commentaries by Nelson (1982) and Rozeboom (1982) on Roitblatt's (1982) version of that view. General discussions of TCDs based on similarity can be found in Cummins 1989 and Fodor 1984.

8. In the interest of readability, I shall sometimes drop the subscript in 'representation$_o$'. The reader is reminded, however, that I am here concerned only with what makes a representation bearer a representation$_o$, not with what makes it a representation. The latter question will be discussed in chapter 8.

9. This is my gloss of Palmer's position. What he says is this: "The nature of representation is that there exists a correspondence (mapping) from objects in the represented world to objects in the representing world such that at least some relations in the represented world are structurally preserved in the representing world" (pp. 266–267). I take it that structural preservation of D by G requires a relation of isomorphism between the G set and the D set of relations.

10. This is somewhat simplified, since Goodman allows for the elements of the relations themselves to consist of sequences of elements which can, in turn, consist of sequences of elements, and so on. Elements that cannot be further dissolved in this way are called the *ultimate factors* of the original n-tuple. Goodman's definition of isomorphism is then formulated in terms of these ultimate factors: "A relation R is isomorphic to a relation S in the sense here intended if and only if R can be obtained by consistently replacing the ultimate factors in S" (p. 14). The idea of consistent replacement also requires modification: "Consistent replacement requires only that each not-null ultimate factor be replaced by one and only one not-null element; that different not-null ultimate factors be always replaced by different not-null elements; and that the null class be always replaced by itself" (p. 14).

11. A number of the classic papers on functionalism can be found in Block 1980a.

12. The idea of a functional role is standardly made more precise as follows (Lewis 1970; Block 1980b). Suppose S is a system with mental states $(s_1, \ldots, s_n)$. Let T be a psychological theory of S that specifies the causal relations among its mental states, inputs, and outputs. We can then represent T as:

$$T(s_1, \ldots, s_n).$$

I shall call such a theory a *functional theory* of S. Next reformulate T as a single, very long, conjunctive sentence, replace each internal state term in T with a variable indexed to the state, and prefix the appropriate number (i.e., n) of existential quantifiers. The result is what is known as the *Ramsey sentence* of the theory (named after the British logician)—viz.,

$$Ex_1, \ldots, x_n T(x_1, \ldots, x_n).$$

The point of transforming T in this way is to pick out the internal states of the system *solely* in terms of their causal relations to inputs, outputs, and other mental states. The *property* of being one of the states whose functional role is specified by T can now be defined by means of the property-abstraction operator "%". Given an open sentence 'Fy', we can *refer* to the property *expressed* by 'Fy' thus: %y, Fy. This refers to (rather than expresses) the property of being F, and it means the same as 'the property of being a y that is F'. For example, given the open sentence 'x is red', we can refer to the property of being red by writing "%x, x is red'. Replacing 'F' in this schema with our Ramsey sentence, we can now refer to the property of being an instance y of an internal state type x_i which has the functional role attributed to x_i by T as follows:

%y[Ex$_1$,...,Ex$_n$T(x$_1$,...,x$_n$) & y is a token of x$_i$],

where 'y' ranges over state tokens. Following Block (1978), let us call an expression of this sort "the Ramsey functional correlate of state s_i, with respect to theory T."

The claim of functionalism, stated more precisely, is then this:

There exists a class of mental state types M and a functional theory T of M such that, for each mental state type s in M, the property of being an instance of s is identical to the Ramsey functional correlate of s, with respect to T.

13. Most philosophers who endorse the conceptual-role approach are also "two-factor" theorists (e.g., Field [1977, 1978], McGinn [1982], Loar [1981, 1982], Block [1986]). That is, they believe that there are two factors determining the content of MRS: conceptual role and causal relations to the environment (in the sense endorsed by the causal historical and indicator approaches discussed below). In what follows, I will concentrate exclusively on conceptual role.

14. Cummins (1989, p. 122) claims that conceptual-role theories "provide us with no hint as to why being a node in a network of computational or causal relations should make something a representation or endow it with a particular content." But this is clearly false; although not all discussions of the conceptual-role approach give the isomorphism explanation sketched above, some surely do (e.g., Fodor 1990c; Field 1978).

15. I say "usually nonformal" because a data structure or a connectionist node can, of course, also be the *object* of a mental representation.

16. This isn't quite right, but it will do for our purposes. It's not quite right because Cummins wants to impose a few additional constraints on the isomorphism. The problem with the theory as it stands—and this is a point that applies also to the conceptual-role version—is that mere isomorphism is too weak to ground the semantic selectivity of mental representation. It simply allows for too many representation bearer–object pairings. Cummins is, ultimately, willing to live with a fair bit of non-uniqueness, but even he draws the line at complete representational promiscuity. See Cummins 1989, pp. 102–108, for a discussion of this problem.

17. Devitt seems to accept some form of the attitude-representation identification thesis as discussed in section 5.1. Thus, he feels free to move between propositional-attitude talk ("grounding thoughts" and "identity beliefs") and MRS talk. Because it simplifies the task of exposition, I will follow him in this practice. However, it should be understood that, ideally, a TCD for MRS would not include any reference to folk-psychological entities such as "thoughts" or "beliefs."

18. My thanks to Michael Devitt for clarifying this case for me.

19. The other obvious candidate, of course, is Dretske's (1981) view.

20. Fodor (1987, p. 126) grants that the notion of an "intact" organism is a promissory note.

21. By the "thought box" Fodor means the "box" in which thoughts occur to one, not the "box" in which beliefs are formed.

22. See Godfrey-Smith 1989.

23. This is a reconstruction. Fodor gives several formulations (1987, pp. 107–108; forthcoming) of the semantic version of the asymmetrical dependence relation, not all of which say the same thing, on my view, and not all of which work.

Given that one is after an asymmetrical dependence relation between misrepresentational and representational *tokenings* (rather than misrepresentational tokenings and the existence of content, another possibility Fodor flirts with), there are at least four options: (a) that the *existence* of misrepresentations is dependent on the existence of representations, but not vice-versa: (b) that the *possibility* of misrepresentations is dependent on the possibility of representations, but not vice-versa; (c) that the existence of misrepresentations is dependent on the possibility of representations, but not vice-versa; and (d) that the possibility of misrepresentations is dependent on the existence of representations, but not vice versa. Only option c works, on my view. Options a and d fail because *actual* representational tokenings are not required for there to be an actual or a possible misrepresentation. All that is required is that the representational expression that is misused have a content. But actual representational tokenings are not required for there to be content. Consider, for example, representational expressions that have content innately. I would also argue that option b fails, although this may be more controversial. It fails because its nondependency clause is false. Just as the possibility of misrepresentational uses depends on the possibility of representational uses, so the possibility of representational uses depends on the possibility of misrepresentational uses. This is because a representational use is possible only if the expression in question has content, and if that is the case then a misrepresentational use is also possible. It is not possible for me to represent a horse by tokening ⟨horse⟩ unless it is also possible for me to represent a cow (as a horse) by tokening ⟨horse⟩.

24. Again I have changed Fodor's formulation. He expresses his conditions thus:

In a world where B-caused 'A' tokens are wild (and express the property A), the nomic relations among properties have to be such that

1. A's cause 'A''s.
2. 'A' tokens are *not* caused by B's in nearby worlds in which A's *don't* cause A's.
3. A's cause 'A''s in nearby worlds in which B's don't cause 'A''s. (Fodor 1987, p. 109)

I find good old-fashioned counterfactual talk just as clear, if not clearer, than talk about nearby possible worlds. In addition, I have replaced Fodor's 'A''s with '∂#$''s so that when these tokens are referred to in conditions 1–3 there is no temptation to think of them as having any representational content above and beyond what the conditions specify. The change to 'X''s and 'Z''s instead of 'A''s and 'B''s is simply to emphasize the fact that these letters are functioning as *variables*.

Fodor initially (1987, p. 109) claims that 1–3 are merely *necessary* conditions. However, later on the same page he says that he is inclined to think that "asymmetric dependence is both necessary *and* sufficient for wildness".

25. For some recent criticisms of Fodor's view, see Cummins 1989, Baker 1989, Wagner (unpublished), and Fodor 1990b.

26. This is Fodor's (1987) view. In a recent essay (1990b), Fodor proposes two new (and presumably improved) versions of his view. The first—still a pure indicator (informational) view—modifies his causal theory in two respects. First, he drops the attempt to identify circumstances in which it is semantically necessary that *all* F instantiations cause G instantiations, simply requiring instead that F instantiations cause G instantiations. Second, he formulates his view in terms of nomic relations among properties rather than causal relations among individuals. Thus, the reformulated view comes down to this: A representation bearer RB's having some nonsemantic property G expresses the property F in a subject S if (1') there is a nomic relation between the property of being an F and the property of being a cause of G instantiations and (2') if there are nomic relations between other properties and the property of being a cause of G instantiations, then the latter nomic relations depend asymmetrically upon the former (see p. 93). Asymmetrical dependence then gets cashed out as follows: "... if the nomic relation between P1 and P2 is asymmetrically dependent on the nomic relation between P3 and P4 then, *ceteris paribus*, breaking the relation between P3 and P4 would break the relation between P1 and P2" (p. 95). Fodor claims that the second modification helps the theory avoid some of the objections raised against the original (1987) version.

In the second version of his TCD, Fodor (1990b) combines the indicator approach with the causal historical approach. In particular, he adds a causal historical condition to 1' and 2' above, viz. (3') some F instantiations actually cause G instantiations.

27. Although she probably shouldn't, as Cummins (1989) points out, Millikan is committed to giving a naturalistic account of intentionality. On the standard view that explanations are statements or propositions, explanations *per se* have no place in a naturalistic account, although the *processes* such explanations describe can have such a place (assuming, of course, that these processes themselves are naturalistic). However, as John Post (in private correspondence) has noted, recently several philosophers have tried to develop theories of explanation according to which explanation is an objective relation among the phenomena being explained rather than something epistemic and intensional. (See Kitcher and Salmon 1989.) Millikan could vindicate her talk of "normal explanation" by appealing to such theories.

28. This is not to say, however, that there are not important differences between the signs of MRS and public languages, on the one hand, and the signs involved in animal communication, on the other. One important difference, according to Millikan, is that the former, but not the latter, are used by "interpreting" devices that are capable of *identifying* the representation being responded to. (See Millikan 1984, pp. 239–244, for a discussion of what such acts of identifying come to.) A terminological point is relevant here. In her book, Millikan reserves the term 'representation' for intentional icons that can be identified in her sense. However, in Millikan 1989a, where she tries to join issue with the current debate on content determination for MRS, she follows the practice of using 'representation' more broadly, and she explicitly notes that she is now using 'representation' where in the book she used 'intentional icon'.

29. Note that I am using lower-case letters (e.g. 'rb') as variables and upper-case letters (e.g. 'RB') as constants.

Chapter 7

1. For an example from Millikan's work, see note 27 chapter 6 (above). Another example can be found in Dretske 1981. Indicator theories, in general, are plagued with the problem of handling the selectivity of mental representations. The difficulty is that any given representation will be involved in many more causal relations (both synchronic and diachronic) than it has representational objects. Dretske (1981, p. 115) attempts to handle the problem of synchronic selectivity by relegating the irrelevant conditions on which the representation depends to the status of a *channel of communication* or, simply, *channel conditions*, where a channel of communication is "that set of existing conditions (on which the signal depends) that either (1) generate no (relevant) information, or (2) generate only redundant information (from the point of view of the receiver)." However, as Loewer (1987) points out, Dretske also says that whether or not a given condition is included in the set of channel conditions "is a question of degree, a question about which people (given their different interests and purposes) can reasonably disagree, a question that may not have an objectively correct answer" (Dretske 1981, pp. 132–133). Loewer (1987, p. 291) is understandably surprised by this remark:

If what counts as channel conditions is relative to interests and purposes, then the information carried by a signal is likewise relative. He [Dretske] seems to be admitting that intentional notions are involved in the characterization of information. I do not know whether this relativity to interests undermines Dretske's attempt to construct a physicalistic account of intentionality in terms of information.... However, it is clear that it would be fatal to Dretske's project if in specifying the information carried by r's being G the property G or the channel conditions are themselves characterized in intentional or semantic terms.

2. See also Stampe 1977, p. 48; Field 1978, p. 78; Stalnaker 1984, p. 6; Millikan 1984, p. 87; Schiffer 1987, p. 10; Lloyd 1987, p. 23; Lloyd 1989, pp. 19–20; and Loewer 1987, pp. 287, 288.

3. The hedges "roughly speaking" and "for the most part" are included because contemporary physicalists tend to believe that this hierarchy is much messier than was originally envisioned (as, for example, in Oppenheim and Putnam 1958). Note also that not all physicalists take the relevant kind of supervenience to be Kim's strong supervenience.

4. Mentions of some form of the circularity argument can be found in Field 1978 (p. 52), Schiffer 1987 (p. 13), and Loewer 1987 (p. 291).

5. The reference is to the work of Paul Grice (1957, 1969). According to Schiffer (1987, pp. 11–12), the Gricean program, or "Intention-Based Semantics" (IBS), proceeds in two stages. In the first stage, the IBS theorist seeks "to identify speaker-meaning—a person's meaning that such-and-such, or that so-and-so is to do such-and-such—with a species of intentional behavior that does not itself presuppose any of the semantic concepts in question." In the second stage, the theorist seeks "to define the meaning of linguistic items in terms of speaker-meaning, thereby completing the reduction of the semantic to the psychological. Here the theorist will avail himself of an ancillary concept of *convention*, itself already defined, in wholly nonsemantic terms, as various kinds of self-perpetuating regularities in behavior." Schiffer's work constitutes an excellent example of both options. Schiffer 1972 is an attempt to work out the details of the Gricean program whereas Schiffer 1987 argues that the program is not viable.

6. Internalism differs not only in name but also in substance from other related formulations in the literature. A standard way of formulating the doctrine of individualism is, in effect, to restrict the ground of MRS to properties whose attribution does not *entail* the existence of anything outside the head. I prefer my formulation because it is stricter. The standard formulation would allow *probabilistic* indicator accounts, such as Lloyd's (1989), to be treated as individualistic; but cutting the pie in that way would violate the widely accepted intuition that individualism deals exclusively with properties and relations "in the head."

7. This follows Burge (1986a, pp. 5–6) closely, but it is not an exact quote.

8. See Burge 1986a, p. 7.

9. Ibid.

10. Such a construal seems to coincide, at least to some extent, with Burge's conception of individualism. In explicating what he means by the term 'individualism', Burge (1986a) says (p. 4) that current individualistic views have tended to take one of two forms. One of these forms "makes a claim of *supervenience*: an individual's intentional states and events (types and tokens) could not be different from what they are, given the individual's physical, chemical, neural, or functional histories, where these histories are specified non-intentionally and in a way that is independent of physical or social conditions outside the individual's body." Such a supervenience claim corresponds exactly with claiming, in my terms, that the ground of MRS satisfies the constraint of Internalism.

11. See Stich 1983. In their cognitive science textbook, Stillings et al. (1987) cite Stich's position as one that has "gained much favor within cognitive science" (p. 337).

12. Stich's formulation of the Principle of Autonomy and his argument in support of this principle refer to psychology rather than cognitive science. I do not think he would object to my restatement, however, although he would probably object to the use to which I have put his argument.

13. Of course, the two sets of thought experiments also differ in the uses to which they are put. Putnam's and Burge's thought experiments are used to argue *against* any TCD that takes the ground of MRS to be solely internal. In contrast, I am viewing Stich's argument as an argument *for* such a ground.

14. The latter is an allusion to Burge's (1979) 'arthritis' thought experiment. See section 7.4.

15. I shall define a *narrow* information-processing capacity as one that is purely computational and, hence, one that can be viewed as a function from a representational state to a

representational state. The *broad* information-processing capacities will include all narrow information- processing capacities but will also include input and output capacities that reach out into the world beyond the skin.

16. The phrase "and this difference in ground results in a difference in content" is necessary because the supervenience of MRS-SEMPROP on the ground for MRS allows for the possibility of something like multiple realization: two representations with the same content but different grounds. However, what Fodor cares about is not that *this* kind of ground difference be reflected in the causal powers of the representations in question, but only that ground differences that underly content differences are so reflected. I am grateful to Phil Hugly for drawing this point to my attention.

17. Reminder: The angle-brackets convention picks out mental representations in terms of both structure and content. Thus, '⟨I want an aluminum can⟩' is intended to designate the MRS expression that has, roughly, the same structure and meaning as the English sentence 'I want an aluminum can'. However, where structure and content come apart, as they do in the twin cases, structure takes precedence. That is why the representations of both twins are designated in the same way. Obviously, if we actually knew the morphological and syntactic structure of MRS, we could avoid the above content/structure ambiguity by using something akin to a real quote convention. But things are not that simple, alas.

18. Fodor's (1987) suggestions are (1) that the difference between E1's being EP1 and E2's being EP2 counts as a difference in relevant effects only if these effects result from causal powers that supervene on the local microstructure of C1 and C2 (p. 44) and (2) that the difference counts as a difference in relevant effects only if these effects result from causal powers whose own source is related to those causal powers by either a causal mechanism or a fundamental law (p. 41). Although suggestion 1 may well hold true for mental representations, it is not generally true, as Fodor's planet case makes clear. Why Fodor (1991) says no more about suggestion 2 is not clear, but it may be because he now feels that it begs the question.

19. He makes this strategy quite explicit in Fodor 1991 (see p. 12)—but it is also at work in Fodor 1987.

20. CPDC captures Fodor's basic idea, but it is admittedly a bit vague. However, to spell out exactly what Fodor (1991) is driving at turns out to be a bit tricky. Precisely what does it mean, on Fodor's account, for the relation between a given causal property and its associated effect property to be "conceptually necessary" or "mediated by a conceptually necessary relation"? Fodor's "Condition C" suggests that the relevant conceptually necessary relation is that "causes that differ in that one [individual] has CP1 where the other has CP2 have effects that differ in that one has EP1 where the other has EP2" (p. 16). Or, to put the whole requirement schematically:

C* The difference between E1's being EP1 and E2's being EP2 counts as a difference in relevant effects only if it is not conceptually necessary that (a) if C1 has CP1 (rather than CP2) then E1 will occur and have EP1 (rather than EP2) and (b) if C2 has CP2 (rather than CP1) then E2 will occur and have EP2 (rather than EP1).

But this is not really what Fodor wants. For example, in the Burge ⟨aluminum⟩ case, Fodor wants it to be the case that the fact that Actual A seeks aluminum cans whereas Counterfactual A seeks twalum cans does not count as a difference in *relevant* effects because the relations between the twins' respective ⟨aluminum⟩ representations and their ensuing can-seeking behavior are conceptually necessary. But if we understand this claim in terms of the above schema, then we get the following: The difference between engaging in aluminum-can-seeking behavior as opposed to twalum-can-seeking behavior does not count as a difference in relevant effects because it is conceptually necessary that if a person's ⟨aluminum⟩ representation refers to aluminum (rather than twalum) then that person will engage in aluminum (rather than twalum) can-seeking behavior; and it is conceptually necessary that if a person's

⟨aluminum⟩ representation refers to twalum (rather than aluminum) then that person will engage in twalum (rather than aluminum) can-seeking behavior. The difficulty is that it is not conceptually necessary (or necessary in any sense at all) that the twins' aluminum representations lead to *any* can-seeking behavior *whatsoever*. Rather, what is conceptually necessary is that *if* the representations give rise to the appropriate kind of can-seeking behavior, *then*, if the causally relevant representation expresses the proposition that the thinker wants an aluminum can, the can-seeking behavior will be aluminum-can-seeking behavior; whereas if the causally relevant representation expresses the proposition that the thinker wants a twalum can, then the can-seeking behavior will be twalum-can-seeking behavior.

Thus what Fodor needs instead of his condition C is this:

C** The difference between E1's being EP1 and E2's being EP2 counts as a difference in relevant effects only if it is not conceptually necessary that (a) if C1 has CP1 (rather than CP2) and C1's being CP1 causes either E1's being EP1 or E1's being EP2, then E1 will be EP1; and (b) it is not conceptually necessary that if C2 has CP2 (rather than CP1) and C2's being CP2 causes either E2's being EP1 or E1's being EP2, then E2 will be EP2.

CPDC allows a conceptual relation to be one that is "mediated by a conceptually necessary relation." This broader construal of 'conceptual' is motivated by the following kind of case, suggested to Fodor by Steve Stich. (I have changed the actual example.) Suppose Bush's favorite kind of can is an aluminum can. Then Actual A will be engaging in Bush's-favorite-can-seeking behavior while Counterfactual A will not. Is that a difference in relevant effects? If the only reason for answering "no" is that the relation between this effect and its cause is conceptually necessary, then we must answer "yes," for it is certainly not conceptually necessary that if Actual A's representation refers to aluminum and causes some sort of appropriate can-seeking behavior then it will cause Bush's-favorite-can-seeking behavior.

But the day can still be saved if we allow for conceptual mediation. Let us say that the relation between C1's having CP1 and C2's having some effect property G is "mediated by a conceptually necessary relation" just in case there exists an effect property EP1 such that to have EP1 is (contingently) to have G and the relation between C1's having CP1 and E1's having EP1 is conceptually necessary. Then engaging in Bush's-favorite-can-seeking behavior will not count as a relevant effect, because the relation between Actual A's having a representation that refers to aluminum (C1's having CP1) and his subsequent can-seeking behavior being Bush's-favorite-can-seeking behavior (E1's being G) will be conceptually mediated. For there is an effect property (namely, Actual A's can-seeking behavior being aluminum can-seeking behavior) which is such that to engage in this behavior is (contingently) to engage in Bush's-favorite-can-seeking behavior, and the relation between having a representation that refers to aluminum and this behavior is conceptually necessary, as we saw above.

21. More precisely (in terms of the characterization in note 20): Being an H particle does not count as a relevant effect property vis-à-vis the causal powers of Fodor's coin toss, because it is conceptually necessary that if Fodor's coin lands heads up (rather than tails up) and its landing heads up causes all the particles in the universe to become either H particles or T particles, then the particles will become H particles. In contrast, it is not conceptually necessary that if a heavenly body is a planet (rather than something else) and its being a planet causes it to move either in a Keplerian or a non-Keplerian orbit, then its motion will take the form of a Keplerian orbit.

22. The test also seems to be violated by some versions of the indicator view. It is certainly violated by Fodor's (1990b) new "combined" indicator/causal historical view (see note 26 to chapter 6 above). Fodor (1990b, pp. 114–116) also claims that on his pure indicator theory—either the 1987 version discussed in Chapter 6 or the updated (1990b) version mentioned in note 26 to chapter 6—⟨water⟩ here on Earth would represent H_2O while ⟨water⟩ on Twin Earth would represent XYZ because the application of ⟨water⟩ to XYZ is asymmetrically dependent on the application of ⟨water⟩ to H_2O. If he is right about this (and

I am not completely convinced), then these versions of the indicator theory would also violate the Methodological Individualism* test.

23. Van Gulick (1989) and Burge (1989) also use Davidson's position to raise questions about Fodor's claim. A similar point is made by Egan (1991, p. 190), who notes that causation (including mental causation) is a relation between state or event *tokens*, not types.

24. Al Casullo has pointed out to me that the *status* of the key mediating assumptions in each case is somewhat different. The assumption leading to the possibility of insignificant content is (at least on my reconstruction of the foundations of cognitive science) a foundational assumption, whereas the assumption leading to ungraspable natural-language meaning is merely a currently popular theory of reference. What one is to make of this difference in status is not entirely clear.

25. Narrow and broad content differ both semantically and in ground. Fodor distinguishes the two semantically by making use of a rough-and-ready version of possible-world semantics. In particular, he views the narrow content of a sentence-like representation R as a function from R and a context (world) to a set of truth conditions (intension), where the latter is itself a function from possible worlds to truth values. The broad content of R is then the function you get when you fix the value of the context (when you specify a world)—namely, simply a function from R to a set of truth conditions. Thus, on this view, when A and Counterfactual A both have ⟨aluminum⟩ representations, the narrow contents of these representations are the same, whereas the broad contents are different (since the twins live in different worlds).

Fodor's (1987) indicator view is supposed to be an account of how the context relevant to content gets fixed. It is thus a story that belongs to the TCD concerning broad content. He says virtually nothing about the ground of narrow content, but presumably on his account the ground of the narrow content of the representation ⟨aluminum⟩ would be whatever it is in a person's information-processing apparatus that results in ⟨aluminum⟩'s being in the perceptual belief box whenever the person perceives something with the observable properties of aluminum—in other words, whatever it is in the twins' information-processing mechanisms that results in ⟨aluminum⟩ in Actual A being caused by the presence of aluminum and ⟨aluminum⟩ in Counterfactual A being caused by the presence of twalum.

Chapter 8

1. The two I shall consider stem from rather late in Peirce's career (1903 and later). The putative solution I shall not consider is found in a paper called "Some Consequences of Four Incapacities," published in the *Journal of Speculative Philosophy* in 1868. Here is the relevant passage from that work: "... if a train of thought ceases by gradually dying out, it freely follows its own law of association as long as it lasts, and there is no moment at which there is not a thought which interprets or repeats it. There is no exception, therefore, to the law that every thought-sign is translated or interpreted in a subsequent one, unless it be that all thought comes to an abrupt and final end in death." (5.284) On the cognitivist view, this ploy would certainly not work, for insofar as representations are realized by computational structures they cannot be gradually diminished and still retain their identity as representations.

2. Cummins (1983) does not address the question of what the respective grounds of the higher-order representations are (that is, in virtue of what R_2, R_3, etc. represent$_o$ what they do). Whether the account of the ground of MRS offered in Cummins 1989 (summarized in section 6.3 above) will do the trick remains to be seen.

3. The terminology and the examples are from Palmer 1978. I summarize Palmer's view in section 6.2.

4. Palmer (1978, p. 265) puts the point this way: "It is axiomatic within an information-processing framework that one cannot discuss representation without considering processes.... There is an important sense in which the only information contained in a representation is that for which operations are defined."

5. Something like this idea of dependency is found in the works of a number of other writers. For example, Newell's (1980, p. 58) definition of "designation" reads as follows: "An entity X designates an entity Y relative to a process P, if, when P takes X as input, its behavior depends on Y." Rozeboom (1982, p. 386) writes: "R' symbolizes/signifies/stands for T' only if it does so for some organism O at a time t by somehow standing proxy for T' in O's occurrent or dispositional functioning at t."

6. Pat Manfredi (private correspondence) has objected that if all interpretant representations are discharged in *non-intentional*, external outputs, then the cognitive science conception of the interpretant will fail because it will not "fix an interpretation" for a representation. Perhaps he is right, but I do not think the point is obvious. Presumably, to fix an interpretation for R means to determine a highly *specific* significance for R (as opposed to some other representation R'). I am fully in accord with Manfredi that determinate computational processes that issue in non-intentional, external outputs may well suffer from a problem of "indeterminacy," but it is less obvious to me that this kind of indeterminacy constitutes a serious problem for a theory of the interpretant. We clearly want mental representations to have reasonably specific *content*, but it may be less important for them to have equally specific significance. Why isn't it enough for a representation to have a specific content and for this content to simply *be* significant?

7. See Dretske 1981, pp. 214–215, for a nice statement of this point.

Chapter 9

1. In saying that part of the exercise of a capacity occurs "in the head" I do not mean to be saying anything about content determination. Certain portions of our ordinary input and output capacities exist "in the head" in the sense that certain portions of the causal chains that underwrite those capacities take place in the head rather than in the environment (at least, if we bracket any considerations of content determination).

2. Gardner (1985, p. 41) considers these two assumptions taken together to be one of the five "key features" of cognitive science. He puts the point this way: "Though mainstream cognitive scientists do not necessarily bear any animus against the affective realm, against the context that surrounds any action or thought, or against historical or cultural analyses, in practice they attempt to factor out these elements to the maximum extent possible."

3. This is not an insignificant simplifying assumption. There is a large literature on problems associated with "reducing" ordinary objects and actions to scientifically recognized phenomena. See, for example, Armstrong (1961), Smart (1963), Jackson (1977), and McGinn (1983) on ordinary objects and Goldman (1970, 1990) on actions.

4. Reminder: Reference to a "_____ box," with the blank filled in by an intentional attitude, is just a place holder for the as-yet-unknown computational relation or "location" at the information-processing level that is assumed to correspond to the attitude at the folk-psychological level.

5. To anticipate, there are two principal difficulties. First, neuroscientists are beginning to develop "high-level" neural theories that are both computational and representational. Second, many of the findings generated by neuropsychology and neurology concern how human information processes can fail, and these findings bear on what information processing in normal individuals is like. In sum, theories at the information-processing level can derive both from research in the non-neural cognitive sciences and from research in the neurosciences.

6. That they are *purely* functional in character seems to me not as obvious as it once was thought to be. The formal computational aspect of information processing is clearly functional, but are all aspects of representations (including the properties that determine content) functional? Fortunately, for the purposes at hand, this question need not be answered here.

7. Richardson (1979, p. 557) makes the same point.

8. It is, actually, not completely obvious to me that Fodor himself wants to draw an isolationist methodological moral from the supposition of multiple neural realizability. Nonetheless, for convenience, I will continue to refer to the argument as Fodor's. In the quoted paper Fodor is primarily concerned with arguing against the "reducibility" of psychology, and elsewhere (1968a) he explicitly endorses the constraint thesis.

9. He, in fact, takes multiple realizability in general to argue against the *lawfulness* of correlations between psychological kinds and neurological kinds, rather than against their mere existence.

10. See also McClelland and Rumelhart 1986.

11. The importance of the second path of influence has been emphasized by Fodor (1968a, p. 110) and Gardner (1985, p. 287).

12. For example, in Churchland 1980a she gives the following quote from a paper of mine to support the claim that "the functionalist naturally enough sees the appropriate research strategy as exclusively top down" (p. 187):

... in general, research must proceed from psychology to neurology. The reason is simple. We will not be in a position to discover how language-responsible cognitive structure is realized neurologically until we know what is so realized. In other words, evidence of the neurological realization of language-responsible cognitive structure cannot be properly evaluated except in the context of linguistic and psycholinguistic models of language responsible cognitive structure.   (Von Eckardt Klein 1978a, p. 5)

This much certainly sounds pretty top-downy, but what Churchland omits from the quote indicates clearly that I was *not*, at the time, endorsing a top-down position. What precedes the first phrase in the quoted passage is this: "Although neurological evidence may lead to insights as to the most appropriate functional theory and certainly must be consistent with such theories, ...'   Furthermore, in another paper in the same volume I investigate the use of neurological evidence to support functional localization claims and argue, as my main point, that "the deficit method of functional localization is a valid method *only* if it is utilized in a research context in which neurology, linguistics, and psycholinguistics *interact significantly*" (Von Eckardt Klein 1976b, p. 30; second emphasis not in original).

13. See also Norman 1981, p. 6; Marr 1982, p. 20; Mandler 1984, p. 310; Stillings et al. 1987, p. 263; and Churchland and Sejnowski 1989, p. 45.

14. See, especially, her discussion of the work of Pellionisz and Llinas (Churchland 1986, pp. 412–458).

Appendix

1. The units of analysis to be discussed do not by any means exhaust the set of possible candidates. Conspicuously absent from my discussion are Lakatos' (1968, 1970) notion of a *research programme*, Darden and Maull's (1977) idea of a *field*, and Toulmin's conception of a *discipline* committed to an *explanatory ideal*, all of which are interesting and suggestive.

2. Suppe (1977, p. 3) uses the term to refer to a certain view of the nature of scientific theories that grew out of the logical positivist tradition, viz. that they should be construed as "axiomatic calculi which are given a partial observational interpretation by means of correspondence rules." In contrast, I shall use the term more loosely to designate the whole gamut of doctrines

that accompanied this view of scientific theories, including doctrines of the nature of science as well as of the proper role of the philosopher vis-à-vis science.

3. See Gutting 1980 for selected articles.

4. See Palermo 1971 and Weimer and Palermo 1973 for putatively Kuhnian analyses of Wundtian structural psychology and behaviorism, and Palermo 1971 and Lachman et al. 1979 for a Kuhnian description of cognitive psychology. For applications of Kuhn's ideas to other areas of psychology, see Peterson 1981. Critical remarks concerning such applications can be found in Warren 1971 and Koch 1976. As we shall see, it is debatable how true these analyses actually are to the notion of a paradigm found in the Kuhnian text.

5. This claim is patently absurd. Kuhn certainly *describes* paradigms in many different ways—in terms of intrinsic properties (what *sort* of scientific entity they are), in terms of functional properties (what role they play in scientific inquiry), and metaphorically (what they are similar to)—but that fact alone does not mean that the term has more than one sense. I can describe a pencil in hundreds of different ways, given enough time and imagination, but surely 'pencil' is not 100 ways ambiguous. Furthermore, many of the quotes Masterman gives to support her claim of multiple ambiguity make no mention of paradigms and, in fact, are not referring to paradigms at all.

6. See, in particular, Kuhn 1970b, Kuhn 1977, and the postscript in Kuhn 1970a.

7. For the remainder of the section, I will refer to passages in *SSR* only by page number.

8. This is, in fact, the view that Kuhn explicitly adopts in his later writings. See the postscript in *SSR* (p. 179).

9 Note that Kuhn's notion of universal allegiance requires some specification of what the relevant universe is. Presumably, it will be something like all scientists working on the same subject matter (no matter what their "school" affiliation). But specifying a subject matter independent of any theory or approach may involve considerable difficulties.

10. Much of Kuhn's argument against the claim that scientists abstract "rules" from particular applications of theory to evidence seems to be based on two rather questionable assumptions: (1) that in order to use a set of rules a person must use them *consciously* (or, at least, must be able to make them explicit) and (2) that rules involve the specification of necessary and sufficient conditions. (See pp. 44–45 of *SSR* for the relevant passages.) Note that assumption 2 does not even seem to fit with Kuhn's own characterization of what these rules consist in. The following are then cited as some of the reasons for believing that rules are not involved in how a paradigm "determines" normal science:

• that discovering rules that have guided particular normal-scientific traditions has always been extremely difficult ("the discovery is very nearly the same as the one the philosopher encounters when he tries to say what all games have in common"—p. 46)
• that scientists never learn concepts, laws, and theories in the abstract but always in terms of their specific applications
• that scientists "are little better than laymen at characterizing the established bases of their field, its legitimate problems and methods" (p. 47).

None of these reasons cuts any ice if we assume, *contra* Kuhn, that rules can be abstracted and used unconsciously and that they can take forms other than a specification of a set of necessary and sufficient conditions.

11. Kuhn's idea seems to be that the paradigmatic application of theory to observations bears some sort of *resemblance relation* to the various research problems and problem solutions that arise within a single normal-scientific tradition. Modeling then somehow involves exploiting this relation in order to generate new instances of theory application. The "somehow," however, is left to our imagination.

12. This includes the postscript written for the second edition of *SSR* and two papers with some overlapping content: Kuhn 1970b (actually completed in 1969) and Kuhn 1977 (which consists of a paper originally read at a conference in 1969).

13. See references in Kuhn 1977, p. 461.

14. In both Kuhn 1970c and the postscript, though not in Kuhn 1977, a fourth element is mentioned (making the parallel to *SSR*'s characterization of "rules" even closer)—namely, shared values. I omit this in my discussion because the sorts of values which Kuhn specifically mentions will generally be held by groups far larger than a particular research community (for example, all scientists or all natural scientists) and, hence, will not serve to identify and distinguish the latter. These values include that prediction should be accurate, that quantitative predictions are preferable to qualitative ones, that an adequate theory should permit the formation and solution of puzzles, and that an adequate theory will be simple, self-consistent, plausible, and compatible with other theories currently deployed. Note that even where Kuhn mentions this fourth element, he claims that he is not giving an exhaustive list of disciplinary matrix components (though there is no indication of what more he might want to include).

15. There are still many loose ends in this account. What is the role of models, for example, in setting and constraining such puzzles? And what, precisely, provides the scientist with a guarantee that the puzzles' solutions are to be found? As far as I can see, there are only two possible sources of such a guarantee: the truth of the theory and the total empirical adequacy of a theory. (Certainly mere success will not do, for a theory can be predictively adequate in a limited domain and fall miserably outside that domain.) But it is doubtful that either of these would be acceptable to Kuhn.

16. See "postscript," pp. 188–189, and Kuhn 1977, pp. 466–472, for relevant passages. There is also another way in which exemplars show the scientist how symbolic generalizations are applied to nature, according to Kuhn: Not only do they function as models for research, they also are supposed to supply the *interpretation* for the uninterpreted symbolic generalizations. Thus they are claimed to play the role classically played by "correspondence rules." See Suppe 1977, p. 484, for a nice critical discussion of this and Kuhn's other claims about exemplars.

17. I have been assuming that when Kuhn talks of "symbolic generalizations" and when he talks of "theories" he has in mind roughly the same thing, although it may be that, for him, theories are *interpreted* symbolic generalizations, where the interpretation is provided by the exemplars. (See the preceding note.)

18. To be fair, it should be pointed out that Lachman et al. claim that this is how *they* will use the term 'paradigm'. Furthermore, they mention that a number of other philosophers of science (including Lakatos [1970], Toulmin [1972], and Shapere [1977]) have tried to articulate alternative conceptions of the "systems of assumption in science larger than formal theories," and that "their treatment of the information- processing paradigm and its properties does not require a choice among the formulations that presently exist or are currently under development" (p. 23). On the other hand, they do specifically credit Kuhn with developing the concept of a scientific paradigm (p. ix), and they do not seem to recognize that their own version of what a paradigm is may differ in important ways from Kuhn's.

19. For example, the following two claims were extremely influential: that what is characteristic and important about science becomes apparent only when science is viewed *dynamically* (that is, in terms of its patterns of growth, development, or change), and that individual scientists do not work in isolation, either from each other or from the past (rather, scientific research typically occurs in both a sociological and an intellectual context, and that it thereby gains both continuity and coherence over time).

20. I say "apparent" and "seemed" because it is not entirely clear to what extent Kuhn in fact held the view that was attributed to him. The attribution was certainly not without cause, as the passages to be quoted indicate. On the other hand, Kuhn (1970b) has since argued that he was seriously misunderstood. The important point for our purposes is that, among the philosophers of science who are of concern here, Kuhn was universally *read* as advocating an irrational picture of science. See the following note for some relevant quotations from Kuhn's critics.

21. Thus Scheffler (1967, pp. 74–89) classes Kuhn with those critics of the traditional view of science whose work has tended to "call into question the very conception of scientific thought as a responsible enterprise of reasonable men." Lakatos (1970, p. 93) writes that "for Kuhn scientific change—from one 'paradigm' to another—is a mystical conversion which is not and cannot be governed by rules of reason and which falls totally within the realm of the (*social*) *psychology of discovery*." In the same spirit, Toulmin (1972, p. 102) claims that for Kuhn the "merits of intellectual 'revolutions' cannot be discussed or justified in rational terms—since no common set of procedures for judging this rationality are acceptable, or even intelligible, to both sides in the dispute." Shapere (1971, p. 707) accuses Kuhn of relativism: "In emphasizing the determinative role of background paradigms, and attacking the notion of theory- (or paradigm-) independent 'facts' (or any such independent factors or standards whatever), Kuhn appears to have denied the possibility of reasonable judgment, on objective grounds, in paradigm choice; there can be no good reason for accepting a new paradigm, for the very notion of a 'good reason' has been made paradigm-dependent." Laudan (1977, p. 3) characterizes Kuhn as a historian who has argued "not merely that certain decisions between theories in science have been irrational, but that choices between competing theories, in the nature of the case, must be irrational."

22. All references to Laudan's work in this section will be to Laudan 1977. I will therefore give only page numbers when citing his work in the text.

23. Laudan acknowledges that science has a wide variety of aims. However, he contends (p. 12) that "a view of science as a problem-solving system holds out more hope of capturing what is most characteristic about science than any alternative framework has."

24. "The first and essential acid test for any theory is whether it provides acceptable answers to interesting questions; whether, in other words, it provides satisfactory solutions to important problems." (p. 13)

25. "More generally, anything about the natural world which strikes us as odd, or otherwise in need of explanation, constitutes an empirical problem." (p. 15).

"... a fact only becomes a problem when it is treated and recognized as such...." (p. 16).

"... the only empirical data which can count as anomalies [i.e. as one type of problem] are those which...." (p. 26)

26. "A problem need not accurately describe a real state of affairs to be a problem." (p. 19).

"... a theory may solve a problem so long as it entails even an approximate statement of the problem." (p. 22)

27. "Kepler's problem of finding the law for the motion of Mars...." (p. 35)

28. Laudan (p. 99) is quite cheerful about the possibility that the earliest and the latest research instantiation in a research-tradition series will have "many discrepancies," but he doesn't seem to face up to the possibility of a complete transformation.

29. See chapter 3 above for an elaboration of these distinctions.

30. Actually, Laudan toys with this position in his discussion of the Descartes case (quoted above). Recall that, according to Laudan, Descartes knew, as a result of his commitment to the Cartesian research tradition, that his optical theories "would have to be" constructed along certain lines (p. 91). The phrase 'would have to be' here suggests not simply that commitment to the Cartesian research tradition naturally gave rise to a certain way of developing an optical theory but rather that Descartes' commitment *constrained* the form his theories could take. And this is just the point I want to make.

31. Use of the term 'domain' in this context is confusing to say the least. Either it is an instance of Laudan's occasional tendency to equate empirical problems with empirical phenomena or he takes it that the "domain of application" of a theory is not, strictly speaking, a domain in our sense (namely, a set of phenomena) but rather a set of empirical problems about such a domain.

32. I am obviously assuming that some sense can be made of a scientific community's having beliefs and desires.

33. Patrick Franken (private correspondence) suggests that there are circumstances under which it might still be rational to pursue RT: for example, if RT were the only or the best "game in town" and researchers believed that temporary pursuit of RT was likely to bring them *closer* to the goal G (for whatever reason) despite the fact that RT itself could never succeed.

34. Examples of such phenomena are the rotation of images, right-hemisphere functioning, intelligent behavior of preverbal humans and nonverbal animals (P. S. Churchland 1980a,b), moods and skills (Haugeland 1978), the understanding of language (Searle 1980b, 1983), and intentionality (Searle 1980a).

35. See P. M. Churchland 1981.

36. For example, Dreyfus (1979) and Turvey et al. (1981) criticize the foundational assumption that mental processes are computational processes.

37. Laudan claims that the notion of a high comparative rate of progress makes explicit "what has been implicitly described in scientific usage as 'promise'" (p. 112). But this is surely nonsense, since a high comparative rate of progress pertains to the past and "promise" pertains to the future. If anything, "promise" should be explicated as an expected *future* high comparative rate of progress.

Glossary

Abbreviations

ANTCOG	The subsidiary research program within cognitive science that studies adult normal typical cognition.
FSC	Framework of shared commitments.
I&P	"Individualism and Psychology" (Burge 1986a)
MRS	The mental representation system.
MRS-SEMPROP	The set of all the various semantic properties associated with MRS.
RF	Research framework.
SSR	*The Structure of Scientific Revolutions* (Kuhn 1970a)
TCD	Theory of content determination.
TE, TE′	Two particular thought experiments due to Burge. (See sections 7.2 and 7.3 above for details.)
⟨···⟩	A convention for designating mental representations so as to reveal both their content and their structure.

Technical Terms

Note. Terms italicized in entries are defined elsewhere in this glossary.

Analog computer A computer that represents information primarily by means of a continuously varying magnitude (such as voltage), where any change in the value of that magnitude is computationally significant.

Applicability desideratum A condition desirable for a *PS unit of analysis* to satisfy, viz. that the unit of analysis must fit the specific kinds of explanations and theories typically found in cognitive science.

Architecturally neutral research Research on the nature of human cognition that presupposes no (or very few) assumptions about the computational architecture of the mind/brain.

Architecturally specific research Research on the nature of human cognition that presupposes a relatively specific hypothesis as to what the computational architecture of the mind/brain is like.

Array An *n*-dimensional arrangement of individual data representations, all of which belong to the same type.

Assessment desideratum A condition desirable for a *PS unit of analysis* to satisfy, viz. that the unit of analysis must identify those properties of a *framework of shared commitments* that are normatively relevant for assessing the adequacy of frameworks of the type in question.

Asymmetrical dependence According to Fodor (1987, 1991), the relation that holds between "wild" tokenings of a representation (namely, those irrelevant to fixing its content) and relevant tokenings, viz. that wild tokenings are dependent on relevant tokenings in a way that relevant tokenings are not dependent on wild tokenings. See section 6.5 above.

Attitude-representation identification assumption The claim, due to Fodor (1975, 1987), that for any organism O and any (type of) propositional attitude A to a proposition P there will exist a (type of) computational relation CR and a (type of) representation R such that R means that P and O will have (a token of) A just in case O bears CR to (a token of) R.

Basic empirical questions One component of a *research framework*. The basic empirical questions of a scientific field are the fundamental questions about the domain that research in the field is designed to answer.

Basic general properties of cognition Properties ascribed to the cognitive capacities of normal, typical adults by the *property assumption* of the *research framework* of cognitive science. These properties include that all the capacities are *intentional*, that virtually all of the capacities are *pragmatically evaluable*, that when successfully exercised all of the evaluable capacities exhibit *coherence*, that most of the capacities are *reliable*, and that many of the capacities are *productive*.

Biological function view An approach to developing a *theory of content determination* for the mental representation system whose core idea is the following: Suppose that there exists a family of *intentional icons RB*, one of whose members is RB, and a set of world affairs *O*, one of whose members is O; that there exists a normal mapping relation M between *RB* and *O* which pairs RB with O; and that among the *proper functions* of the interpreter device for *RB* are various *relational proper functions* adapted to the members of *RB*, including some *adapted relational proper functions* adapted to RB. Then:

• RB *represents$_0$* world affairs O if for each member rb of *RB* and each member o of *O* paired with rb it is a *normal condition*, according to the most proximate *normal explanation*, of the interpreter of *RB* performing some of its proper functions (including its rb-adapted relational proper functions) that rb is paired with o; and, hence, if it is a normal condition, according to the most proximate normal explanation, of the interpreter of RB performing some of its proper functions, including its RB-adapted relational proper functions, that RB is paired with O.

• RB represents$_o$ the command *bring it about that O* if for each member rb of *RB* and each member o of *O* paired with rb it is an adapted relational proper function of the interpreter of rb, relative to rb, to bring it about that o, and o is the last member of the series of world affairs rb is supposed to map onto and to produce; and, hence, if it is an adapted relational proper function of the interpreter of RB, relative to RB, to bring it about that O, and O is the last member of the series of world affairs RB is supposed to map onto and to produce.

Bottom-up approach An approach to the study of cognition that attempts to develop information-processing answers to the basic questions of cognitive science by starting with findings from neuroscience and working up to an information-processing description.

Broad information-processing capacity The extended input-output sequence in which *narrow information-processing capacities* are embedded. Such capacities may include distal stimuli on the input end and motor movements with characteristic environmental consequences on the output end.

Causal historical view An approach to developing a *theory of content determination* for MRS whose core idea is that a token designational expression RB designates a representational object O if there is a certain sort of causal chain (a *d- chain*) connecting RB with O. Such d-chains are made up of three sorts of links: *groundings*, abilities to designate, and *reference borrowings*.

Causal theory of reference A type of *theory of content determination* for natural language, usually associated with Kripke (1972) and Putnam (1975), according to which referring expressions, such as proper names and natural-kind terms, attach to the world, not by means of any implicit description associated with the referring expressions, but rather by means of causal links to the objects and phenomena being referred to.

Co-evolutionary approach An approach to the study of cognition that attempts to develop information-processing answers to the basic questions of cognitive science by using both psychological and neuroscientific findings in whatever order seems the most theoretically fruitful.

Coherence   A property exhibited by an evaluable cognitive capacity such that when the capacity is successfully exercised its beginning state bears a certain systematic relation to its end state.

Coherence desideratum   A condition desirable for a *PS unit of analysis* to satisfy, viz. that the unit of analysis must be such that commitment to a *framework of shared commitments* of the proposed kind by a scientific community contributes in some significant way to the coherence of research associated with the framework in question.

Compiler   A program that translates instructions written in a *high-level language* into a sequence of *machine code* instructions prior to their execution.

Compositional semantics   A form of *semantics* for a representational system whose rules indicate how the meanings of complex expressions are determined by the meanings and formal "arrangement" of the constituents of these expressions.

Computer   A device capable of automatically inputting, storing, manipulating, and outputting information in virtue of inputting, storing, manipulating, and outputting representations of that information. These information processes occur in accordance with a finite set of rules that are *effective* and which are, in some sense, in the machine itself.

Conceptual role view   An approach to developing a *theory of content determination* for MRS whose core idea is that a *representation bearer* RB *represents*$_o$ a proposition P if that representation bearer belongs to a causal network of representation bearers RBNet, P belongs to a logical network of propositions PNet, and there exists an isomorphism between RBNet and PNet such that RB maps onto P.

Conditions of satisfaction   According to Searle (1981), conditions specified by the content of a propositional attitude that can either be satisfied or not, depending on how the world is. What satisfaction comes to depends on the nature of the propositional attitude. For example, the conditions of satisfaction associated with a belief are conditions under which the belief is true; the conditions of satisfaction associated with a perception are conditions under which it is veridical.

Connectionist computer A computer, consisting of a collection of simple computing units linked into a network, that is capable of modifying the pattern of connectivity of those units. As I use the term, the class of connectionist computers includes both "localist networks" and "parallel distributed processing networks." (See section 3.4 and table 3.1 for more detail.)

Constituent structure A form of structure possessed by some representation bearers such that (a) they have parts that are also representation bearers (and, hence, parts that have content) and (b) these parts are formally related to one another in such a way that the "arrangement" typically has semantic consequences.

Constraint stance The view that information-processing theories of cognition need not be constrained by the findings of neuroscience.

Conventional computer A kind of computer the paradigm of which is the *von Neumann computer*. The points of similarity and difference between a conventional computer and a basic von Neumann machine are as follows: Like a basic von Neumann machine, a conventional computer has distinct components for memory, processing, and input-output; has a set of basic operations defined over data representations; and computes its input-output functions by executing its basic operations in accordance with a program. However, unlike a basic von Neumann machine, a conventional computer can have an enhanced set of basic operations, can have a non–von Neumann control structure, can operate on data structures rather than simple data representations, can be general-purpose or special-purpose, can have programs that are stored or wired in, can have multiple memories and processers, can involve processing that is either strictly serial or partly parallel, and need not have a separate executive or control unit.

Data structure A set of single data representations, often of a characteristic type, structured in a particular way.

D-chain According to Devitt (1981), the sort of causal chain whose existence constitutes the *ground* (in my sense) of a token designational expression designating some representational object. D-chains are made up of *groundings*, abilities to designate, and *reference borrowings*.

Derivative empirical questions Questions that arise in the course of scientific research once the *basic empirical questions* of a *research framework* have been constrained by its *substantive assumptions* or once data have been collected and hypotheses formulated in answer (or partial answer) to those basic questions.

Descriptive argument   An argument that cognitive science is, in fact, committed to some particular assumption.

Determinable process   According to Newell (1980), a type of computational operation or a series of computational operations of the sort specified by an algorithm that, typically, include certain determinable features such as variable inputs or branching structures.

Digital computer   A computer that represents information primarily by means of discrete units, such as zeros and ones.

Disciplinary matrix   A kind of *PS unit of analysis*, proposed in the "Postscript" of Kuhn 1970a, that consists of symbolic generalizations, "models," exemplars, and shared values. For details see section A.2 of the appendix.

Distributed representation   A form of representation, found in *connectionist computers*, in which the *representation bearer* consists of activation of a set of nodes rather than a single node.

Domain of inquiry   A set of phenomena grouped together for purposes of scientific inquiry.

Dynamic data structure   A *data structure* that can vary in size during computation.

Effective procedure   A set of rules that tell us, from moment to moment, precisely how to behave, and which are so explicit that they can be followed mechanically—that is, without the use of understanding or interpretation. (After Minsky 1967.)

Encapsulated capacity   A capacity whose exercise always proceeds in a certain specified way without regard to the goals and general "knowledge" of the person exercising that capacity.

Erotetic approach to explanation   An approach to the nature of explanation that treats explanations as, fundamentally, answers to questions.

Execution behavior of a process   According to Newell (1980), a type of computational operation or series of computational operations that constitutes the specification of a *determinable process* (algorithm) with various determinable features. In other words, an execution behavior of a process is a possible computational path through a determinable process.

Exemplar   According to Kuhn (1970a), a concrete problem solution encountered by students in their scientific education and by professionals scientists in their post-educational careers that shows them by example how their work is to be done. Exemplars constitute one of the elements of a *disciplinary matrix* and are claimed by Kuhn (in the "Postscript" of *SSR*) to be one of the things he had in mind by *paradigm* in the original text of *SSR*.

Explanandum   What an explanation explains.

Explanans   The part of an explanation that does the explaining.

Explanatory ineliminability   The quality or state of being subject to explanations that are not eliminable. The "information processing ineliminability thesis" says that there are questions about cognition of central interest to cognitive science that can be answered at an information-processing level but cannot be answered at the neural level.

Explanatory primacy view   The view that X is a natural kind just in case there exists a set of *explananda* of interest to some community of scientists associated with X and there exists a set of properties shared by all and only instances of X the attribution of which (in conjunction with appropriate true auxiliary hypotheses) truly explains those explananda.

Expressive capture   "Capturing" an information-processing generalization at the neural level by actually expressing it at that level.

External factor   A property or relation whose instantiations exist, at least in part, outside the head.

Fetch-execute cycle   A cycle of instructions that allows programs input and stored in a *von Neumann computer* to be executed. The instructions are as follows: Determine the next instruction in the program. Transfer a copy of the instruction to the central processing unit. Execute the instruction. Return to first step.

Finite-state automaton   A "black box" that takes in input and generates output as a function of its internal states.

Folk psychology   A set of assumptions about the nature of the mind embodied in the ordinary ways we describe and explain our mental states and behavior.

Framework of shared commitments   A framework of commitments shared by a scientific community that gives coherence to research carried out by that community.

FSC-choosing science   Scientific activities that pertain to choosing a *framework of shared commitments*.

FSC-guided science   Scientific activities that occur within and are in some sense "guided by" a *framework of shared commitments*.

Functional role   The causal or computational relations of a state or entity, such as a mental representation.

Functional role view   An approach to a *theory of content determination* for the mental representation system whose core idea is that the semantic properties of mental representations are determined by their *functional role*.

Fundamental data structure   A data structure that is fixed in size.

General-purpose computer   A computer that, for all practical purposes, can compute any computable function.

Ground   The properties or relations that determine the fact that a representation or representations *represent$_o$* the object (or express the content) they do. The general ground for the mental representation system consists of a set of properties that constitute a minimal *strong supervenience* base for *MRS-SEMPROP*. The individual ground for some specific semantic property belonging to the set MRS-SEMPROP is that member of the general ground for the MRS upon which that property individually supervenes.

Grounding (of a representation bearer in an object)   According to Devitt's (1981) *causal historical view*, an episode in which a person perceives the object in question and, as a consequence, comes to have a "grounding thought"—that is, a thought that includes a token of the relevant representation bearer (typically, of a "demonstrative" sort).

Grouping assumption   An assumption that belongs to the *pretheoretic specification of the domain* component of a *research framework*. It claims that the phenomena picked out by the *identification assumption* make up a theoretically coherent set of phenomena or a "system."

High-level language   A programming language whose control structure and *data structures* are designed to suit the programmer rather than the available hardware. A high-level language must be translated into *machine code* by a *compiler* or an *interpreter*.

Icon   In Peirce's theory of representation, a sign that represents its object in virtue of being similar to it in some respect.

Identification assumption An assumption that belongs to the *pretheoretic specification of the domain* component of a *research framework*. It claims that the domain of the research framework consists of phenomena of some specified kind.

Immaturity desideratum The condition that instances of a *PS unit of analysis* must be adoptable by an immature scientific community.

Index In Peirce's theory of representation, a sign that represents its object in virtue of an "existential" or real connection.

Indicator view An approach to developing a *theory of content determination* for the mental representation system whose core idea is that a *representation bearer* RB *represents$_o$* an object O if RB is related to O by certain counterfactual and probabilistic relations. Various versions of this approach have been developed by Dretske (1981, 1986a, 1986b), Fodor (1987, 1991), Harnad (1990), Lloyd (1987, 1989), Stalnaker (1984), and Stampe (1977). Fodor's (1987) indicator view is this: A representation bearer RB's having some nonsemantic property G (say, being a *data structure* of a certain sort) expresses the property F in a subject S if (1) all F instantiations cause G instantiations in S when F instantiations are causally responsible for psychophysical traces to which S stands in a psychophysically optimal relation and (2) if non-F instantiations cause G instantiations then they are "wild" (that is, their doing so is *asymmetrically dependent* upon F instantiations causing G instantiations).

Intentional Having content or being "about" something.

Intentional Icon According to Millikan (1984), a kind of representation that is "articulate" and whose instantiations always mediate between producer and interpreter devices. Intentional icons come in two forms: indicative and imperative.

Interaction view The view, due to Black (1954), that understanding a metaphor consists in using a set of commonly held beliefs about the *metaphorical subject* to shed light on the *nonmetaphorical subject*.

Internal factor A property or relation whose instantiations exist solely "in the head" of a subject.

Internalism The view that the *ground* of the content of human mental representations consists only of *internal factors*.

Interpretant   In Peirce's theory of representation, the "mental effect" in the mind of an interpreter of a sign that makes the sign significant for that interpreter.

Interpretant representations   Representations involved in the set of possible determinate computational processes assumed by cognitive science to constitute the *interpretant* of a given representation.

Interpretational view   Otherwise known as "interpretational semantics." An approach to developing a *theory of content determination*, due to Cummins (1989), whose core idea is that a *representation bearer* RB *represents_o* an object O if RB is an argument or a value of some computational function g, O is an argument or a value of some other function h, and there exists a structure-preserving interpretation function I from g to h that pairs RB with O.

Interpreter   (1) In Peirce's theory of representation, a person or thing that supplies the *interpretant* of a representation. (2) A program that translates instructions written in a *high-level language* into *machine code* one by one as those instructions are being executed.

Intertheoretic identity   The identity of an entity or a state posited by one theory with an entity or a state posited by a different theory.

Isolationist stance   The view that information-processing theories of cognition need not be constrained by the findings of neuroscience.

Language community determination thesis   The view, suggested by one of Burge's (1979) thought experiments, that the *external* relation of belonging to some particular language community counts as a factor in determining the *ground* of the mental representation system even when every other *internal* and external factor is controlled for.

Liberal view   The view that a natural kind is any kind picked out by a predicate in a scientific law belonging to our ultimate science.

Linking assumption   An assumption that belongs to the *substantive assumptions* of a *research framework*. It says that the domain picked out by the domain-specifying assumptions (see *pretheoretic specification of the domain*) of the research framework constitutes, or is substantially like, a system of some specified sort.

Localist representation   A form of representation in connectionist networks in which one node functions as the representation bearer for the representation in question.

Machine code   A programming language whose instructions can be directly "understood" (i.e. acted upon) by a computer.

Matrix   An *array* whose constituents are themselves arrays.

Metaphorical subject   The object designated (or property expressed) by the B term in a simple sentential metaphor of the form 'A is B'.

Metaphorical term   The B term in a simple sentential metaphor of the form 'A is B'.

Methodological assumptions   One of the four components of a *research framework*. The methodological assumptions specify, in very general terms, the appropriate ways to go about studying the domain of the framework.

Methodological Individualism*   The view that an acceptable ground for the human mental representation system consists of either *internal* or *external naturalistic* factors so long as such factors satisfy the following restriction: If two token representations are ground-distinct, and this difference in ground results in a difference in content, these representations must also differ in their causal powers to produce relevant effects across nomologically possible contexts.

Microstructure view   The view that X is a natural kind just in case there exists a set of *explananda* concerning the causal powers of instances of X and there exists a microstructure, shared by all and only instances of X, the attribution of which (in conjunction with appropriate true auxiliary hypotheses) truly explains those explananda.

M-P neural net   A collection of simple *finite-state automata* of a specific sort linked together in such a way that outputs from one automaton become inputs to another. (See section 3.4 or table 3.1 for more detail.)

Multiple realizability   The state of being realizable in multiple ways. For example, functional states are said to be realizable by many different kinds of physical states.

Narrow information-processing capacity   An information-processing capacity that is purely mental, involving a transformation from one representational state to another. (Contrasts with *broad information capacity*.)

Naturalism   The view that an acceptable *ground* for the human mental representation system consists exclusively of properties that are *naturalistic*.

Naturalistic   Neither semantic nor *intentional*.

Nonmetaphorical subject   The object designated by the A term in a simple sentential metaphor of the form 'A is B'.

Nonmetaphorical term   The A term in a simple sentential metaphor of the form 'A is B'.

Normal condition   According to Millikan (1984), a condition mentioned in a *normal explanation* of a *proper function* of a biological phenomenon (organism, system, or state or activity of an organism or system). The normal conditions are the conditions that obtained historically when ancestors of the phenomenon in question performed the function properly (that is, in a way that contributed to the survival and proliferation of the relevant biological family of phenomena).

Normal explanation   According to Millikan (1989a, p. 284), a form of explanation associated with any *proper function* that explains the performance of that function in a system S "telling how it was (typically) historically performed on those (perhaps rare) occasions when it was properly performed" (that is, performed in a way that contributed to the survival and proliferation of the relevant biological family of phenomena). All normal explanations include information about the structure of S, about the *normal* conditions under which the proper function has historically been performed ("these conditions being uniform over as large a number of historical cases as possible" [Millikan 1984, p. 33]), and about natural laws mediating between this structure, these conditions, and actual performance of the function. Normal explanations can be more or less proximate. A more proximate explanation is the least detailed normal explanation possible.

Normative argument   An argument that cognitive science ought, on grounds of rationality, to accept a certain assumption.

Paradigm   A *PS unit of analysis* that functions as the *framework of shared commitments* of any scientific community engaged in effective scientific research, according to Kuhn (1970a). Precisely what paradigms *are* is controversial; see section A.2 of the appendix for my interpretation.

Parallel computer   A computer that is capable of performing more than one operation at a time.

Physicalism   The view that, roughly speaking, everything is physical. Current conceptions of physicalism make three assumptions: (1) that, to a reasonable approximation, nature is organized in a hierarchy of ontological levels such that any given level will (for the most part) *supervene* on the level immediately below; (2) that the lowest level of the hierarchy consists of the entities and properties of physics; and (3) that supervenience is a transitive relation. Thus, physicalism, in its current manifestation, claims that everything is physical in the sense that everything ultimately supervenes on the physical.

Pragmatic evaluability A property of human cognitive capacities, viz. that they can be exercised with varying degrees of success.

Pretheoretic specification of the domain One of four kinds of assumptions that make up a *research framework*. The pretheoretic specification of the domain includes an *identification assumption, property assumptions*, and a *grouping assumption*. These pick out a certain domain for study, ascribe certain pretheoretic properties to this domain, and claim that this domain constitutes a theoretically coherent set of phenomena, respectively.

Principle of autonomy The doctrine, due to Stich (1983), that the states and processes that are relevant to cognitive science are those that *supervene* on the current internal physical state of the organism.

Productive Capable of producing novel instances. A cognitive capacity is productive in the sense that once a person has the capacity in question, he or she is typically in a position to exercise it in a practically unlimited number of novel ways.

Proper function According to Millikan (1984), a capacity of a biological phenomenon that contributed historically to the survival and proliferation of the ancestors of the phenomenon in question. There are many different subspecies of proper functions. A "relational proper function" is a proper function "to do or produce something that bears a specific relation to something else" (Millikan 1984, p. 39). An "adapted relational proper function" is a relational proper function adapted to some particular adaptor.

Property assumptions One of four kinds of assumptions included in the *pretheoretic specification of the domain*. Such assumptions claim that the phenomena picked out by the *identification assumption* have certain specified properties.

Propositional attitude A mental state that can be analyzed into an "attitude" component (e.g., perceiving, remembering, or intending) and a "content" component (e.g., that there is milk in the refrigerator).

PS unit of analysis A unit of analysis intended to be used for the characterization of "chunks" of science. The notions of theory (logical positivists), *paradigm* (Kuhn), and *research tradition* (Laudan) are all PS units of analysis.

Psychologically efficacious Able to make a psychological difference. According to Peirce, a representation is significant for a subject S only if it is psychologically efficacious for S in an appropriate way—that is, only if it can make a difference to either the internal states or the external behavior of S in ways that depend on the content or the referent of the representation.

Rational reconstruction The description of some phenomenon (typically, a conception or a set of assumptions) with attention not only to what it is actually like but also to what it should, on rational grounds, be like.

Record An n-dimensional *data structure* whose components may be of multiple types.

Reductive capture "Capturing" an information-processing generalization at the neural level by discovering a neural generalization that, roughly speaking, identifies the same pattern that the information processing generalization describes (albeit with reference to different properties).

Reference borrowing In Devitt's (1981) *causal historical view*, a means of passing on a designating ability from one person to another.

Reliable To say that a cognitive capacity is reliable is to say that, typically, it is exercised successfully (at least to some degree) rather than unsuccessfully.

Represents$_o$ The aspect of the representation relation between a *representation* and its object (or content) that is purely objective (i.e., independent of the representation's having significance for someone).

Representation According to Peirce's theory of representation, an entity or a state that has the following four essential properties: it is realized by a *representation bearer*, it *represents$_o$* one or more objects, its representation$_o$ relations have a *ground*, and it is interpretable by (that is, it functions as a representation for) some currently existing *interpreter*.

Representational version of TE (TE') A version of Burge's thought experiment TE (TE') described in terms of mental representations instead of propositional attitudes.

Representation bearer   The aspect of a representation—usually non-intentional and nonsemantic—that "bears" the representational properties of the representation. For example, the representation bearer of the inscription

dog

is a pattern of ink marks.

Research framework   Both a unit of analysis for characterizing scientific fields or research programs and a type of *framework of shared commitments* that scientific communities may hold in common. A research framework consists of four components: the *pretheoretic specification of the domain*, a set of *basic empirical questions*, a set of *substantive assumptions*, and a set of *methodological assumptions*. A specific research framework may consist entirely of unrevisable assumptions or of a mix of unrevisable assumptions and revisable assumption "slots." In the latter case, filling the revisable assumption slots with specific assumptions results in a *research-framework version*.

Research-framework version   A set of specific *research-framework* assumptions.

Research tradition   A *PS unit of analysis*, proposed by Laudan (1977), that consists of a set of metaphysical assumptions and a set of methodological assumptions. See section A.3 of the appendix for more detail.

Revised basic questions   The set of questions that result when the *basic questions* of a *research framework* are constrained by the *substantive assumptions* of the framework.

Semantic selectivity   A hypothesized property of human mental representations—viz. that, out of the numerous objects to which each representation bears a relation of some sort, only a very few (typically only one or two) are *represented$_o$*.

Semantic diversity   A hypothesized property of human mental representations—viz. that, as a class, they possess many different kinds of representational objects.

Semantic complexity   A hypothesized property of most human mental representations—viz. that, individually, they have several representational objects. For example, most representations are assumed to have something like a sense and something like a referent.

Semantic evaluability   A hypothesized property of human mental representations—viz. that, depending on the context in which they are tokened, they can be assigned a value such as true or false, vacuous or nonvacuous, or accurate or inaccurate.

Semantics   The rules that specify the interpretations of a systematically related set of representations.

Serial computer   A computer that is capable of performing its operations only one at a time.

Schema S   A schema used by Fodor (1991) to elucidate the idea of two things' having the same causal powers. See figure 7.4.

Soundness desideratum   The condition that a *PS unit of analysis* and its accompanying theory of science must be free of internal difficulties such as excessive vagueness and inconsistency.

Special-purpose computer   A computer designed for a limited number of applications.

Stored-program computer   A *conventional computer* capable of executing programs temporarily stored in memory.

Structural isomorphism view   An approach to developing a *theory of content determination* for the mental representation system whose core idea is that a *representation bearer* RB *represents$_o$* a representational object O under some aspect D if there exists a set *G* of relations that constitute RB and a set *D* of relations that constitute O such that *G* is isomorphic to *D*.

Subroutine   A miniprogram stored in memory that can be "called up" as necessary by a single instruction in a larger program.

Substantive assumptions   One of the four components of a *research framework*. The substantive assumptions constrain what counts as an acceptable possible answer to any of the *basic empirical questions* of the framework by claiming that the domain under study is, or is substantially like, a system of some specified kind. The substantive assumptions of a research framework fall into two groups: *linking assumptions* and *system assumptions*.

Substitution view   The view that metaphorical understanding consists in the recovery of an underlying literal proposition. For example, if the metaphor has the form 'A is B', the underlying literal proposition might be taken to be that A has such-and-such B-like properties or that A is like B in such-and-such respects.

Supervenience, strong A relation of determination between families of properties defined by Kim (1984). A family A strongly supervenes on a family B just in case, necessarily, for each x and each property A_i, in A, if x has A_i, then there is a property B_j, in B, such that x has B_j, and necessarily if any y has B_j, it has A_i.

Symbol (1) In common and philosophical usage, a representation of any sort—that is, something that stands for or represents something else. (2) In Peirce's theory of representation, a sign that represents its object in virtue of a convention. (3) In connectionist writings, a form of representation used in *conventional* models of cognition.

Syntactic theory of mind The view, due to Stich (1984), that cognitive science can accomplish its explanatory goals by regarding the mind as a purely syntactic engine.

System assumptions A set of assumptions belonging to the *substantive assumptions* of a *research framework*. The system assumptions claim that systems of a certain specified kind have certain specified properties.

Theory-constitutive metaphor According to Boyd (1979), a metaphor used in the context of scientific research whose function is to introduce new theoretical terminology by encouraging scientific exploration of previously unknown similarities and differences between the *nonmetaphorical subjects* and the *metaphorical subjects*.

Theory of content determination A theory describing the *ground* of the semantic properties of a system of representation.

Top-down approach An approach to the study of cognition according to which one should develop information-processing answers to the *basic questions* of cognitive science by initially considering only findings that pertain to the functioning of the "whole" subject (on the basis of either ordinary reflection and observation or psychological experimentation) and by only subsequently, after an adequate theory has been constructed and tested, determining how the posited information-processing structures and processes are realized in the brain by considering findings from neuroscience.

Turing machine A *finite-state automaton* associated with an external storage or memory medium that takes the form of an indefinitely long two-way tape with squares from which input symbols are read and on which output symbols are written.

Turing test   A test devised by Turing (1950) to determine whether a computer can think. An interrogator asks questions of a person and of a computer. The computer's aim is to fool the interrogator into thinking it is a person; the person's aim is to help the interrogator guess the truth. This is called the "imitation game." Turing proposed that a computer is intelligent if, when playing the imitation game, it can fool the interrogator as often as a man could when playing a similar game against a woman.

Type-individuate   To distinguish between types of entities of a given sort (for example, mental representations) on the basis of some principle in such a way that the principle determines when two or more tokens of this sort of entity belong to the same type and when they belong to a different type. For example, to type-individuate mental representations in terms of their causal powers, as Fodor (1987) suggests, is to count token mental representations as belonging to the same type when they have the same causal powers and as belonging to a different type when they have different causal powers.

Universal Turing machine   A *Turing machine* that is capable of "imitating" any other Turing machine by, in effect, getting a description of that machine as part of its input.

Virtual machine   A computer whose software allows it to function as if it were a different type of machine—for example, one with an extended instruction set, the capability of manipulating more complex data structures, or a different control structure.

von Neumann computer   A general-purpose, *stored-program computer* pioneered by John von Neumann and co-workers and described in Burks, Goldstine, and von Neumann 1946. A von Neumann computer has the following properties: (1) It has four principal functional parts: a memory, a control unit, an arithmetic/logic unit, and input-output devices. The control unit and the arithmetic/logic unit together constitute the central processing unit (c.p.u.). (2) It is a stored-program computer. (3) The memory is large but finite, consisting of a long string of storage locations each of which has a unique address. (4) The function of the control unit is to read and execute instructions from the program stored in memory, either by moving data between memory and a temporary register within the c.p.u. or by activating the arithmetic/logic unit. The program is executed one instruction at a time by repeating a *fetch-execute cycle* until the program is completed. (5) The arithmetic/logic unit is made up of various hard-wired circuits capable of performing the basic arithmetic and logical operations of the machine.

Wired-program computer   A *conventional computer* whose programs are wired into its hardware in such a way that they cannot be altered by the computer itself.

References

Achinstein, P. 1971. *Law and Explanation*. Oxford University Press.

Achinstein, P. 1983. *The Nature of Explanation*. Oxford University Press.

Agassi, J. 1964. The nature of scientific problems and their roots in metaphysics. In *The Critical Approach to Science and Philosophy*, ed. M. Bunge. Free Press.

Anderson, J. A., and Hinton, G. E. 1981. Models of information processing in the brain. In *Parallels Models of Associative Memory*, ed. G. E. Hinton and J. A. Anderson. Erlbaum.

Anderson, J. R. 1976. *Language, Memory, and Thought*. Erlbaum.

Armstrong, D. M. 1961. *Perception and the Physical World*. Routledge and Kegan Paul.

Asquith, P. D., and Kyburg, H. E., eds. 1979. *Current Research in Philosophy of Science*. Philosophy of Science Association.

Baker, L. R. 1989. On a causal theory of content. In *Philosophical Perspectives*, ed. J. E. Tomberlin. Ridgeview.

Barbour, I. 1974. *Myths, Models, and Paradigms*. Harper and Row.

Beardsley, M. C. 1958. *Aesthetics: Problems in the Philosophy of Criticism*. Harcourt, Brace.

Beardsley, M. C. 1962. The metaphorical twist. *Philosophy and Phenomenological Research* 22: 293–307. Reprinted in Johnson 1981.

Bechtel, W. 1987. Connectionism and the philosophy of mind: An overview. *Southern Journal of Philosophy* 26, Supplement: 17–41.

Bechtel, W., and Abrahamson, A. 1991. *Connectionism and the Mind: An Introduction to Parallel Processing in Networks*. Blackwell.

Bernstein, I. L. 1978. Learned taste aversions in children receiving chemotherapy. *Science* 200: 1302–1303.

Bieri, P. 1988. Thinking machines: Some reflections on the Turing Test. In *Interpretation in Context in Science and History*, ed. P. Bieri and B. Harshav. Duke University Press.

Black, M. 1954. Metaphor. *Proceedings of the Aristotelian Society* 55: 273–294. Reprinted in Black 1962 and Johnson 1981.

Black, M. 1962. *Models and Metaphors*. Cornell University Press.

Black, M. 1977. More about metaphor. *Dialectica* 31: 431–457. Reprinted in Ortony 1979.

Block, N. 1978. Troubles with functionalism. In *Perception and Cognition: Issues in the Foundations of Psychology, Minnesota Studies in the Philosophy of Science*, vol. 9, ed. C. W. Savage. University of Minnesota Press.

Block, N., ed. 1980a. *Readings in Philosophy of Psychology*, vol. 1. Harvard University Press.

Block, N. 1980b. Introduction: What is functionalism. In *Readings in Philosophy of Psychology*, vol. 1. Harvard University Press.

Block, N. 1981. Psychologism and behaviorism. *Philosophical Review* 90: 5–43.

Block, N. 1983. Mental pictures and cognitive science. *Philosophical Review* 42: 499–541.

Block, N. 1986. Advertisement for a semantics for psychology. In *Midwest Studies in Philosophy, Studies in the Philosophy of Mind*, vol. 10, ed. P. A. French, T. E. Uehling, Jr., and H. K. Wettstein. University of Minnesota Press.

Block, N. 1987. Functional role and truth conditions. *Proceedings of the Aristotelian Society* Supplement 61: 157–181.

Boden, M. 1981. *Minds and Mechanisms: Philosophical Psychology and Computational Models*. Cornell University Press.

Boyd, R. 1979. Metaphor and theory change: What is "metaphor" a metaphor for? In *Metaphor and Thought*, ed. A. Ortony. Cambridge University Press.

Brody, B., ed. 1970. *Readings in the Philosophy of Science*. Prentice-Hall.

Bromberger, S. 1965. An approach to explanation. In *Studies in Analytical Philosophy*, ed. R. J. Butler. Blackwell.

Burge, T. 1979. Individualism and the mental. *Midwest Studies* 4: 73–121.

Burge, T. 1982a. Two thought experiments reviewed. *Notre Dame Journal of Formal Logic* 23: 284–293.

Burge, T. 1982b. Other bodies. In *Thought and Object*, ed. A. Woodfield. Oxford University Press.

Burge, T. 1986a. Individualism and psychology. *Philosophical Review* 95: 3–45.

Burge, T. 1986b. Cartesian error and the objectivity of perception. In *Subject, Thought, and Context*, ed. J. MacDowell and P. Pettit. Oxford University Press.

Burge, T. 1989. Individuation and causation in psychology. *Pacific Philosophical Quarterly* 70: 303–322.

Burks, A., Goldstine, H. H., and von Neumann, J. 1946. Preliminary discussion of the logical design of an electronic computing instrument. Institute for Advanced Study, Princeton.

Burks, A., and Wang, H. 1957. The logic of automata. *Journal of the Association for Computing Machinery* 4: 193–218, 279–297.

Campbell, N. R. 1921. *What Is Science?*. Methuen. Reprint: Dover, 1953.

Carnap, R. 1938. Logical foundations of the unity of science. In *Foundations of the Unity of Science*, Vol. 1, ed. O. Neurath, R. Carnap, and C. Morris. University of Chicago Press.

Carnap, R. 1947. *Meaning and Necessity: A Study in Semantics and Modal Logic*. University of Chicago Press. Second enlarged edition: 1956.

Chandor, A., Graham, J., and Williamson, R., eds. 1977. *A Dictionary of Computers*. Penguin.

Chomsky, N. 1965. *Aspects of the Theory of Syntax*. MIT Press.

Chomsky, N. 1968. *Language and Mind*. Harcourt Brace Jovanovich.

Churchland, P. M. 1981. Eliminative materialism and the propositional attitudes. *Journal of Philosophy* 78: 67–90.

Churchland, P. M. 1982. Is thinker a natural kind? *Dialogue* 21: 223–238.

Churchland, P. M. 1990. Cognitive activity in artificial neural networks. In *Thinking: An Invitation to Cognitive Science*, vol. 3, ed. D. N. Osherson and E. E. Smith. MIT Press.

Churchland, P. S. 1980a. A perspective on mind-brain research. *Journal of Philosophy* 77: 185–207.

Churchland, P. S. 1980b. Language, thought, and information processing. *Nous* 14: 147–170.

Churchland, P. S. 1986. *Neurophilosophy: Toward a Unified Science of the Mind/Brain*. MIT Press.

Churchland, P. S., and Sejnowski, T. J. 1989. Neural representation and neural computation. In *Neural Connections, Mental Computation*, ed. L. Nadel, L. A. Cooper, P. Culicover, and R. M. Harnish. MIT Press.

Clark, A. 1989. *Microcognition: Philosophy, Cognitive Science, and Parallel Distributed Processing*. MIT Press.

Copi, I. M. 1954. Essence and accident. *Journal of Philosophy* 51: 706–719.

Crick, F. H., and Asanuma, C. 1986. Certain aspects of the anatomy and physiology of the cerebral cortex. In *Parallel Distributed Processing: Explorations in the Microstructure of Cognition*, vol. 2: Psychological and Biological Models, ed. J. L. McClelland, D. E. Rumelhart, and the PDP Research Group. MIT Press.

Cummins, R. 1975. Functional analysis. *Journal of Philosophy* 72:741–760.

Cummins, R. 1977. Programs in the explanation of behavior. *Philosophy of Science* 44: 269–287.

Cummins, R. 1983. *The Nature of Psychological Explanation*. MIT Press.

Cummins, R. 1989. *Meaning and Mental Representation*. MIT Press.

Danto, A., and Morgenbesser, S., eds. 1960. *Philosophy of Science*. Meridian.

Darden, L., and Maull, N. 1977. Interfield theories. *Philosophy of Science* 43: 44–64.

Davidson, D. 1978. What metaphors mean. *Critical Inquiry* 5: 31–47. Reprinted in Johnson 1981.

Davidson, D. 1980. Actions, reasons, and causes. In *Essays on Actions and Events*, ed. D. Davidson. Clarendon.

Dennett, D. C. 1975. Why the law of effect will not go away. *Journal of the Theory of Social Behavior* 5: 169–188. Reprinted in Dennett 1978a.

Dennett, D. C. 1977. A cure for the common code? *Mind* 86: 265–280. Reprinted in Block 1981a and Dennett 1978a.

Dennett, D. C. 1978a. *Brainstorms: Philosophical Essays on Mind and Psychology*. MIT Press.

Dennett, D. C. 1978b. Artificial intelligence as philosophy and psychology. In *Brainstorms*, ed. D. C. Dennett. MIT Press.

Dennett, D. C. 1986. The logical geography of computational approaches: A view from the East Pole. In *The Representation of Knowledge and Belief*, ed. R. Harnish and M. Brand. University of Arizona Press.

de Sousa, R. 1984. The natural shiftiness of natural kinds. *Canadian Journal of Philosophy* 14: 561–580.

Devitt, M. 1981. *Designation*. Columbia University Press.

Devitt, M., and Sterelny, K. 1987. *Language and Reality*. MIT Press.

Dietrich, E. 1989. Semantics and the computational paradigm in cognitive psychology. *Synthese* 79: 119–141.

Dretske, F. 1981. *Knowledge and the Flow of Information*. MIT Press.

Dretske, F. 1983. Precis of *Knowledge and the Flow of Information*. *Behavioral and Brain Sciences* 6: 55–63.

Dretske, F. 1986a. Misrepresentation. In *Belief*, ed. R. Bogdan. Oxford University Press.

Dretske, F. 1986b. Aspects of cognitive representation. In *Problems in the Representation of Knowledge and Belief*, ed. M. Brand and R. Harnish. University of Arizona Press.

Dreyfus, H. 1979. *What Computers Can't Do*. Harper and Row.

Dreyfus, H., and Dreyfus, S. 1986. *Mind over Machine*. Free Press.

Egan, M. F. 1991. Must psychology be individualistic? *Philosophical Review* 100: 179–203.

Farah, M. J. 1984. The neurological basis of mental imagery: A componential analysis. *Cognition* 18: 245–272.

Farah, M. J. 1986. The laterality of mental image generation: A test with normal subjects. *Neuropsychologia* 24: 541–551.

Farah, M. J. 1988. Is visual imagery really visual? Overlooked evidence from neuropsychology. *Psychological Review* 95: 307–317.

Farah, M. J., Gazzaniga, M. S., Holtzman, J. P., and Kosslyn, S. M. 1985. A left hemisphere basis for visual mental imagery? *Neuropsychologia* 23: 115–118.

Farah, M. J., Levine, D. N., and Calvanio, R. 1988. A case study of mental imagery deficit. *Brain and Cognition* 8: 147–164.

Feldman, J. A. 1981. A connectionist model of visual memory. In *Parallel Models of Associative Memory*, ed. G. E. Hinton and J. A. Anderson. Erlbaum.

Feldman, J. A. 1983. Introduction: Advanced computational models in cognition and brain theory. *Cognition and Brain Theory* 6: 1–3.

Feldman, J. A. 1989. Neural representation of conceptual knowledge. In *Neural Connections, Mental Computations*, ed. L. Nadel, L. A. Cooper, P. Culicover, and R. M. Harnish. MIT Press.

Feldman, J. A., and Ballard, D. H. 1982. Connectionist models and their properties. *Cognitive Science* 6: 205–254.

Fetzer, J. H. 1988. Signs and minds: An introduction to the theory of semiotic systems. In *Aspects of Artificial Intelligence*, ed. J. H. Fetzer. Kluwer.

Field, H. 1977. Logic, meaning and conceptual role. *Journal of Philosophy* 74: 379–409.

Field, H. 1978. Mental representation. *Erkenntnis* 13: 9–61. Reprinted in Block 1981a.

Fodor, J. A. 1968a. *Psychological Explanation: An Introduction to the Philosophy of Psychology*. Random House.

Fodor, J. A. 1968b. The appeal to tacit knowledge in psychological explanation. *Journal of Philosophy* 65: 627–640.

Fodor, J. A. 1975. *The Language of Thought*. Crowell.

Fodor, J. A. 1981a. Methodological solipsism considered as a research strategy in cognitive psychology. In *Representations*, ed. J. A. Fodor. MIT Press.

Fodor, J. A. 1981b. Special sciences. In *Representations*, ed. J. A. Fodor. MIT Press.

Fodor, J. A. 1981c. Computation and reduction. In *Representations*, ed. J. A. Fodor. MIT Press.

Fodor, J. A. 1983. *The Modularity of Mind*. MIT Press.

Fodor, J. A. 1984. Semantics, Wisconsin style. *Synthese* 59: 231–250.

Fodor, J. A. 1985a. Narrow content and meaning holism. Unpublished manuscript.

Fodor, J. A. 1985b. A presentation to the National Science Foundation Workshop on Information and Representation. In *Report of Workshop on Information and Representation.*, ed. B. H. Partee, S. Peters. and R. Thomason. Unpublished.

Fodor, J. A. 1987. *Psychosemantics*. MIT Press.

Fodor, J. A. 1990a. A theory of content, I: The problem. In *A Theory of Content and Other Essays*, ed. J. A. Fodor. MIT Press.

Fodor, J. A. 1990b. A theory of content, II: The theory. In *A Theory of Content and Other Essays*, ed. J. A. Fodor. MIT Press.

Fodor, J. A. 1990c. Fodor's guide to mental representation: The intelligent Auntie's vademecum. In *A Theory of Content and Other Essays*, ed. J. A. Fodor. MIT Press.

Fodor, J. A. 1991. A modal argument for narrow content. *Journal of Philosophy* 88: 5–25.

Fodor, J. A. Forthcoming. Information and representation. In *Information, Language, and Cognition*, ed. P. Hanson. University of British Columbia Press.

Fodor, J. A., and McLaughlin, B. P. 1990. Connectionism and the problem of systematicity: Why Smolensky's solution doesn't work. *Cognition* 35: 183–204.

Fodor, J. A., and Pylyshyn, Z. W. 1981. How direct is visual perception? Some reflections on Gibson's "Ecological Approach". *Cognition* 9: 139–196.

Fodor, J. A., and Pylyshyn, Z. W. 1988. Connectionism and cognitive architecture: A critical analysis. In *Connections and Symbols*, ed. S. Pinker and J. Mehler. MIT Press.

Fogelin, R. 1988. *Figuratively Speaking*. Yale University Press.

Foss, D. J., and Hakes, D. T. 1978. *Psycholinguistics: An Introduction to the Psychology of Language*. Prentice-Hall.

Freedman, A., ed. 1989. *The Computer Glossary*, fourth edition. American Management Association.

Frege, G. 1952. On sense and reference. In *Translations from the Philosophical Writing of Gottlob Frege*, ed. P. Geach and M. Black. Oxford University Press.

Freyd, J. J. 1987. Dynamic mental representations. *Psychological Review* 94: 427–438.

Garcia, J., Ervin, F. R., and Koelling, R. A. 1966. Learning with prolonged delay of reinforcement. *Psychonomic Science* 5: 121–122.

Gardner, H. 1985. *The Mind's New Science*. Basic Books.

Garnham, A. 1985. *Psycholinguistics: Central Topics*. Methuen.

Giere, R. 1979. *Understanding Scientific Reasoning*. Holt, Rinehart and Winston.

Giere, R. 1988. *Explaining Science: A Cognitive Approach*. University of Chicago Press.

Gleitman, H. 1981. *Psychology*. Norton.

Godfrey-Smith, P. 1989. Misinformation. *Canadian Journal of Philosophy* 19: 533–550.

Godman, A., ed. 1984. *Cambridge Illustrated Thesaurus of Computer Science*. Cambridge University Press.

Goldman, A. I. 1970. *A Theory of Human Action*. Princeton University Press.

Goldman, A. I. 1990. Action and free will. In *Visual Cognition and Action: An Invitation to Cognitive Science*, vol. 2, ed. D. N. Osherson, S. M. Kosslyn, and J. M. Hollerbach. MIT Press.

Goodman, N. 1951. *The Structure of Appearance*. Bobbs-Merrill.

Goodman, N. 1955. *Fact, Fiction, and Forecast*. Bobbs-Merrill.

Goodman, N. 1968. *Languages of Art*. Bobbs-Merrill.

Goschke, T., and Koppelberg, D. 1990. The concept of representation and the representation of concepts in connectionist models. In Report No. 36, University of Bielefeld Center for Interdisciplinary Studies Research Group on Mind and Brain.

Gould, I. H., ed. 1971. *IFIP Guide to Concepts and Terms in Data Processing*. North-Holland.

Grice, H. 1957. Meaning. *Philosophical Review* 66: 377–388.

Grice, H. 1969. Utterer's meaning and intentions. *Philosophical Review* 78: 147–177.

Grossberg, S. 1978. A theory of visual coding, memory, and development. In *Formal Theories of Visual Perception*, ed. E. L. J. Leeuwenberg and H. F. J. M. Buffart. Wiley.

Grossberg, S. 1980. How does the brain build a cognitive code? *Psychological Review* 87: 1–51.

Gutting, G., ed. 1980. *Paradigms and Revolutions*. University of Notre Dame Press.

Hall, R. P. 1989. Computational approaches to analogical reasoning: A comparative analysis. *Artificial Intelligence* 39: 39–120.

Hardwick, C. S., ed. 1977. *Semiotics and Significs: The Correspondence between Charles S. Peirce and Victoria Lady Welby*. Indiana University Press.

Harman, G. 1982. Conceptual role semantics. *Notre Dame Journal of Formal Logic* 23: 242–256.

Harnad, S. 1990. The symbol grounding problem. *Physica D* 42: 335–346.

Hartshorne, C., Weiss, P., and Burks, A., eds. 1931–58. *Collected Papers of Charles Sanders Peirce*. Belknap Press of Harvard University Press.

Haugeland, J. 1978. The nature and plausibility of cognitivism. *Behavioral and Brain Sciences* 2: 215–260.

Haugeland, J., ed. 1981. *Mind Design.* MIT Press.

Haugeland, J. 1985. *Artificial Intelligence: The Very Idea.* MIT Press.

Hempel, C. 1966. *Philosophy of Natural Science.* Prentice-Hall.

Henle, P. 1958. Metaphor. In *Language, Thought, and Culture,* ed. P. Henle. University of Michigan Press.

Hesse, M. B. 1966. The explanatory function of metaphor. In *Models and Analogies in Science,* ed. M. B. Hesse. University of Notre Dame Press.

Hinton, G. E. 1981. Implementing semantic networks in parallel hardware. In *Parallel Models of Associative Memory,* ed. G. E. Hinton and J. A. Anderson. Erlbaum.

Hinton, G. E. 1989. Connectionist learning systems. *Artificial Intelligence* 40: 185–234.

Hinton, G. E., and Anderson, J. A., eds. 1981. *Parallel Models of Associative Memory.* Erlbaum.

Hinton, G. E., McClelland, J. L., and Rumelhart, D. E. 1986. Distributed representations. In *Parallel Distributed Processing: Explorations in the Microstructures of Cognition,* vol. 1: Foundations, ed. D. E. Rumelhart, J. L. McClelland, and the PDP Research Group. MIT Press.

Holyoak, K. J., and Thagard, P. 1989. Analogical mapping by constraint satisfaction. *Cognitive Science* 13: 295–355.

Hopkin, D., and Moss, B. 1976. *Automata.* North-Holland.

Jackson, F. 1977. *Perception.* Cambridge University Press.

Johnson, M., ed. 1981. *Philosophical Perspectives on Metaphor.* University of Minnesota Press.

Johnson-Laird, P. N. 1983. *Mental Models.* Harvard University Press.

Johnson-Laird, P. N. 1988. *The Computer and the Mind: An Introduction to Cognitive Science.* Harvard University Press.

Johnson-Laird, P. N., and Wason, P., eds. 1977. *Thinking,* Cambridge University Press.

Kaplan, D. 1977. Demonstratives. Unpublished manuscript.

Kaplan, D. 1979. On the logic of demonstratives. In *Contemporary Perspectives in the Philosophy of Language,* ed. P. A. French, T. E. Uehling. Jr., and H. K. Wettstein. University of Minnesota Press.

Keil, F. 1981. Constraints on knowledge and cognitive development. *Psychological Review* 88: 197–227.

Kemeny, J. G. 1959. *A Philosopher Looks at Science.* Van Nostrand.

Kemeny, J. G., and Oppenheim, P. 1955. On reduction. *Philosophical Studies* 7: 6–19.

Kessel, F. S. 1969. The philosophy of science as proclaimed and science as practiced: 'identity' or 'dualism'? *American Psychologist* 25: 999–1005.

Kim, J. 1984. Concepts of supervenience. *Philosophy and Phenomenological Research* 45: 153–176.

Kitcher, P., and Salmon, W. C., eds. 1989. *Scientific Explanation.* University of Minnesota Press.

Kitty, E. F. 1987. *Metaphor.* Clarendon.

Koch, S. 1976. Language communities, search cells, and the psychological studies. In *Nebraska Symposium on Motivation 1975: Conceptual foundations of psychology,* ed. J. K. Cole and W. J. Arnold. University of Nebraska Press.

Kosslyn, S. M. 1980. *Image and Mind*. Harvard University Press.

Kosslyn, S. M. 1988. Seeing and imagining in the cerebral hemispheres: A computational approach. In *Readings in Cognitive Science: A Perspective from Psychology and Artificial Intelligence*, ed. A. Collins and E. E. Smith. Morgan Kaufmann.

Kosslyn, S. M., Brunn, J., Cave, K. R., and Wallach, R. W. 1984. Individual differences in mental imagery ability: A computational analysis. In *Visual Cognition*, ed. S. Pinker. MIT Press.

Kosslyn, S. M., and Hatfield, G. 1984. Representation without symbol systems. *Social Research* 51: 1019–1045.

Kosslyn, S. M., Holtzman, J. D., Gazzaniga, M. S., and Farah, M. J. 1985. A computational analysis of mental image generation: Evidence from functional dissociations in split-brain patients. *Journal of Experimental Psychology: General* 114: 311–341.

Kosslyn, S. M., Margolis, J. A., Barrett, A. M., Goldknopf, E. J., and Daly, P. 1990. Age differences in imagery abilities. *Child Development* 61: 995–1010.

Kosslyn, S. M., Pinker, S., Smith, G. E., and Shwartz, S. P. 1979. On the demystification of mental imagery. *Behavioral and Brain Sciences* 2: 535–581.

Kosslyn, S. M., and Shwartz, S. P. 1977. A simulation of mental imagery. *Cognitive Science* 1: 265–295.

Kripke, S. 1972. *Naming and Necessity*. University Press.

Kuhn, T. 1970a. *The Structure of Scientific Revolutions*. University of Chicago Press.

Kuhn, T. 1970b. Reflections on my critics. In *Criticism and the Growth of Knowledge*, ed. I. Lakatos and A. Musgrave. Cambridge University Press.

Kuhn, T. 1977. *The Essential Tension*. University of Chicago Press.

Kuhn, T. 1979. Metaphor in science. In *Metaphor and Thought*, A. Ortony. Cambridge University Press.

Lachman, R., and Lachman, J. L. 1982. Memory representations in animals: Some metatheoretical issues. *Behavioral and Brain Sciences* 5: 380–381.

Lachman, R., Lachman, J. L., and Butterfield, E. C. 1979. *Cognitive Psychology and Information Processing*. Erlbaum.

Lachter, J., and Bever, T. G. 1988. The relation between linguistic structure and associative theories of language learning: A constructive critique of some connectionist learning models. In *Connections and Symbols*, ed. S. Pinker and J. Mehler. MIT Press.

Laird, J. E., Newell, A., and Rosenbloom, P. S. 1987. Soar: An architecture for general intelligence. *Artificial Intelligence* 33: 1–64.

Lakatos, I. 1968. Criticism and the methodology of scientific research programmes. *Proceedings of the Aristotelian Society* 69: 149–186.

Lakatos, I. 1970. Falsification and the methodology of scientific research programmes. In *Criticism and the Growth of Knowledge*, ed. I. Lakatos and A. Musgrave. Cambridge University Press.

Laudan, L. 1977. *Progress and Its Problems*. University of California Press.

Lewis, D. 1970. Psychophysical and theoretical identifications. In *Readings in Philosophy of Psychology*, vol. 1, ed. N. Block. Harvard University Press.

Linsky, B. 1982. Is transmutation possible? *Philosophical Studies* 41: 367–381.

Lloyd, D. E. 1987. Mental representation from the bottom up. *Synthese* 70: 23–78.

Lloyd, D. E. 1989. *Simple Minds*. MIT Press.

Loar, B. 1980. Syntax, functional semantics and referential semantics. *Behavioral and Brain Sciences* 3: 1.

Loar, B. 1981. *Mind and Meaning.* Cambridge University Press.

Loar, B. 1982. Conceptual role and truth conditions. *Notre Dame Journal of Formal Logic* 23: 272–283.

Loewer, B. 1982. The role of "conceptual role semantics." *Notre Dame Journal of Formal Logic* 23: 305–315.

Loewer, B. 1987. From information to intentionality. *Synthese* 70: 287–317.

Lucas, M., and Hayes, P., eds. 1982. *Proceedings of the Cognitive Curriculum Conference.* University of Rochester.

Lycan, W. G. 1981. Form, function, and feel. *Journal of Philosophy* 78: 24–49.

Lycan, W. G. 1987. *Consciousness.* MIT Press.

MacCormac, E. 1976. *Metaphor and Myth in Science and Religion.* Duke University Press.

Mandler, G. 1984. Cohabitation in the cognitive sciences. In *Methods and Tactics in Cognitive Science*, ed. W. Kintsch, J. R. Miller. and P. G. Polson. Erlbaum.

Marr, D. 1982. *Vision: A Computational Investigation into the Human Representation and Processing of Visual Information.* Freeman.

Masterman, M. 1970. The nature of a paradigm. In *Criticism and the Growth of Knowledge*, ed. I. Lakatos and A. Musgrave. Cambridge University Press.

Mathews, R. J. 1971. Concerning a "linguistic theory" of metaphor. *Foundations of Language* 7: 413–425.

Mathews, R. J. 1986. Does psychology need exact semantics? In *Meaning and Cognitive Structure: Issues in the Computational Theory of Mind*, ed. Z. W. Pylyshyn and W. Demopoulos. Ablex.

Maynard, J. 1975. *Dictionary of Data Processing.* Newnes-Butterworths.

McClelland, J. L. 1981. Retrieving general and specific knowledge from stored knowledge of specifics. In *Proceedings of the Third Annual Meeting of the Cognitive Science Society.*

McClelland, J. L. 1989. Parallel distributed processing: Implications for cognition and development. In *Parallel Distributed Processing: Implications for Psychology and Neurobiology*, ed. R. G. M. Morris. Clarendon.

McClelland, J. L., and Rumelhart, D. E. 1981. An interactive activation model of context effects in letter perception: Part I. An account of basic findings. *Psychological Review* 88: 375–407.

McClelland, J. L., and Rumelhart, D. E. 1986. A distributed model of memory. In *Parallel Distributed Processing: Explorations in the Microstructures of Cognition*, vol. 2, ed. J. L. McClelland, D. E. Rumelhart, and the PDP Research Group. MIT Press.

McClelland, J. L., Rumelhart, D. E., and Hinton, G. E. 1986. The appeal of parallel distributed processing. In *Parallel Distributed Processing: Explorations in the Microstructures of Cognition*, vol. 1, ed. D. E. Rumelhart, J. L. McClelland and the PDP Research Group. MIT Press, A Bradford Book.

McClelland, J. L., Rumelhart, D. E., and the PDP Research Group, eds. 1986. *Parallel Distributed Processing: Explorations in the Microstructures of Cognition*, vol. 2: Psychological and Biological Models. MIT Press.

McCulloch, W. S., and Pitts, W. 1943. A logical calculus of the ideas immanent in nervous activity. *Bulletin of Mathematical Biophysics* 5: 115–133.

McGinn, C. 1982. The structure of content. In *Thought and Content*, ed. A. Woodfield. Oxford University Press.

McGinn, C. 1983. *The Subjective View: Secondary Quality and Indexical Thoughts.* Clarendon.

McGuiness, C. 1986. Problem representation: The effects of spatial arrays. *Memory and Cognition* 14: 270–280.

McLaughlin, B. P. 1987. What is wrong with correlational psychosemantics. *Synthese* 70: 271–286.

Meadows, A. J., Gordon, M., and Singleton, A. 1984. *Dictionary of Computing and New Information Technology*. Kogan Page.

Mellor, D. H. 1977. Natural kinds. *British Journal for the Philosophy of Science* 28: 299–312.

Miller, J. R., Polson, P. G., and Kintsch, W. 1984. Problems of methodology in cognitive science. In *Methods and Tactics in Cognitive Science*, ed. W. Kintsch, J. R. Miller, and P. G. Poison. Erlbaum.

Millikan, R. 1984. *Language, Thought, and Other Biological Categories*. MIT Press.

Millikan, R. 1986. Thoughts without laws: Cognitive science without content. *Philosophical Review* 95: 47–80.

Millikan, R. 1989a. Biosemantics. *Journal of Philosophy* 86: 281–297.

Millikan, R. 1989b. In defense of proper functions. *Philosophy of Science* 56: 288–302.

Millikan, R. 1990. Compare and contrast: Dretske, Fodor, and Millikan on teleosemantics. *Philosophical Topics* 18: 151–162.

Minsky, M. 1967. *Computation: Finite and Infinite Machines*. Prentice- Hall.

Mook, D. G. 1987. *Motivation: The Origin of Action*. Norton.

Nadel, L., Cooper, L. A., Harnish, R. M., and Culicover, P. 1989. Introduction: Connections and computations. In *Neural Connections, Mental Computation*, ed. L. Nadel, L. A. Cooper, P. Culicover, and R. M. Harnish. MIT Press.

Nagel, E. 1961. *The Structure of Science*. Harcourt Brace.

Neisser, U. 1967. *Cognitive Psychology*. Prentice-Hall.

Nelson, R. J. 1968. *Introduction to Automata*. Wiley.

Nelson, R. J. 1982. On the content of representations. *Behavioral and Brain Sciences* 5: 384.

Nelson, R. J. 1987. Machine models for cognitive science. *Philosophy of Science* 54: 391–408.

Nelson, R. J. 1989. *The Logic of Mind*. Kluwer.

Nersessian, N. 1988. Reasoning from imagery and analogy in scientific concept formation. In *PSA 1988*, vol. 1, ed. A. Fine and J. Leplin. Philosophy of Science Association.

Nersessian, N. 1990. Methods of conceptual change in science: Imagistic and analogical reasoning. *Philosophica* 45: 33–52.

Newell, A. 1980. Physical symbol systems. *Cognitive Science* 4: 135–183.

Newell, A. 1982. The knowledge level. *Artificial Intelligence* 18: 87–127.

Newell, A. 1986. The symbol level and the knowledge level. In *Meaning and Cognitive Structure: Issues in the Computational Theory of Mind*, ed. Z. W. Pylyshyn and W. Demopoulos. Ablex.

Newell, A. 1990. *Unified Theories of Cognition*. Harvard University Press.

Newell, A., Shaw, J. C., and Simon, H. A. 1958. Elements of theory of human problem solving. *Psychological Review* 65: 151–166.

Newell, A., and Simon, H. A. 1976. Computer science as empirical inquiry: Symbols and search. *Communications of the Association for Computing Machinery* 19: 113–126. Reprinted in Haugeland 1981.

Norman, D. A. 1981. What is cognitive science? In *Perspectives on Cognitive Science*, ed. D. A. Norman. Ablex.

Oatley, K. 1987. *Best Laid Schemes: A Cognitive Psychology of Emotions.* Harvard University Press.

Oatley, K., and Johnson-Laird, P. N. 1987. Towards a cognitive theory of emotions. *Cognition and Emotion* 1: 29–50.

Oppenheim, P., and Putnam, H. 1958. Unity of science as a working hypothesis. In *Minnesota Studies in the Philosophy of Science*, vol. 2, ed. H. Feigl, M. Scriven, and G. Maxwell. University of Minnesota Press.

Ortony, A., ed. 1979. *Metaphor and Thought.* Cambridge University Press.

Ortony, A., Clore, G. L., and Collins, A. 1988. *The Cognitive Structure of Emotions.* Cambridge University Press.

Osherson, D. N., and Lasnik, H., eds. 1990. *Language: An Invitation to Cognitive Science*, vol. 1. MIT Press.

Oxford University Press. 1986. *Dictionary of Computing*, second edition.

Palermo, D. 1971. Is a scientific revolution taking place in psychology? *Science Studies* 1: 135–155.

Palmer, S. E. 1978. Fundamental aspects of cognitive representation. In *Cognition and Categorization*, ed. E. Rosch and B. B. Lloyd. Erlbaum.

Partee, B. H., Peters, S., and Thomason, R. 1985. Report of Workshop on Information and Representation. Unpublished.

Pearson, C. 1982. The cognitive sciences: A semiotic paradigm. In *Language, Mind, and Brain*, ed. T. W. Simon and R. J. Scholes. Erlbaum.

Peterson. G. L. 1981. Historical self-understanding in the social sciences: The use of Thomas Kuhn in psychology. *Journal of the Theory of Social Behaviour* 11: 1–31.

Pfeiffer, R., Schreter, Z., Fogelman-Soulie, F., and Steels, L., eds. 1989. *Connectionism in Perspective.* North- Holland.

Pharies, D. A. 1985. *Charles S. Peirce and the Linguistic Sign.* Benjamins.

Pinker, S., and Mehler, J., eds. 1988. *Connections and Symbols.* MIT Press.

Pinker, S., and Prince, A. 1988. On language and connectionism: Analysis of a parallel distributed processing model of language acquisition. In *Connections and Symbols*, ed. S. Pinker and J. Mehler. MIT Press.

Platt, M. 1983. Explanatory kinds. *British Journal for the Philosophy of Science* 34: 133–148.

Poland, J. Forthcoming. *Physicalism: The Philosophical Foundations.* Oxford University Press.

Post, J. 1987. *The Faces of Existence.* Cornell University Press.

Putnam, H. 1975a. Is semantics possible? In *Mind, Language and Reality: Philosophical Papers*, vol. 2, ed. H. Putnam. Cambridge University Press.

Putnam, H. 1975b. Philosophy and our mental life. In *Mind, Language and Reality: Philosophical Papers*, vol. 2, ed. H. Putnam. Cambridge University Press.

Putnam, H. 1975c. The meaning of 'meaning'. In *Language, Mind and Knowledge*, ed. K. Gunderson. University of Minnesota Press.

Putnam, H. 1986. Computational psychology and interpretation theory. In *Meaning and Cognitive Structure: Issues in the Computational Theory of Mind*, ed. Z. W. Pylyshyn and W. Demopoulos. Ablex.

Rosenberg, J. M. 1984. *Dictionary of Computers, Data Processing, and Telecommunications.* Wiley.

Rozeboom, W. W. 1982. The logic of representation. *Behavioral and Brain Sciences* 5: 385.

Rumelhart, D. E. 1917. Toward an interactive model of reading. In *Attention and Performance VI*, ed. S. Dornic. Erlbaum.

Rumelhart, D. E., Hinton, G. E., and McClelland, J. L. 1986. A general framework for parallel distributed processing. In *Parallel Distributed Processing: Explorations in the Microstructures of Cognition*, vol. 1, ed. D. E. Rumelhart, J. L. McClelland, and the PDP Research Group. MIT Press.

Rumelhart, D. E., Hinton, G. E., and Williams, R. J. 1986. Learning internal representations by error propogation. In *Parallel Distributed Processing: Explorations in the Microstructures of Cognition*, vol. 1, ed. D. E. Rumelhart, J. L. McClelland, and the PDP Research Group. MIT Press.

Rumelhart, D. E., and McClelland, J. L. 1982. An interactive activation model of context effects in letter perception: Part 2. The contextual enhancement effect and some tests and extensions of the model. *Psychological Review* 89: 60–94.

Rumelhart, D. E., McClelland, J. L., and the PDP Research Group, eds. 1986. *Parallel Distributed Processing: Explorations in the Microstructures of Cognition*, vol. 1: Foundations. MIT Press.

Rumelhart, D. E., and Norman, D. A. 1988. Representation in memory. In *Steven's Handbook of Experimental Psychology*, second edition, vol. 2, ed. R. C. Atkinson, R. J. Herrnstein, G. Lindzey, and R. P. Luce. Wiley.

Rumelhart, D. E., Smolensky, P., McClelland, J. L., and Hinton, G. E. 1986. Schemata and sequential thought processes in PDP models. In *Parallel Distributed Processing: Explorations in the Microstructures of Cognition*, vol. 2, ed. J. L. McClelland, D. E. Rumelhart, and the PDP Research Group. MIT Press.

Salmon, M. H. 1984. *Introduction to Logic and Critical Thinking*. Harcourt, Brace, Jovanovich.

Savan, D. No date. *An Introduction to C. S. Peirce's Semiotics*. Unpublished manuscript, Toronto Semiotic Circle.

Schank, R. C., and Abelson, R. P. 1977. *Scripts, Plans, Goals, and Understanding*. Erlbaum.

Scheffler, I. 1967. *Science and Subjectivity*. Bobbs- Merrill.

Schiffer, S. 1981. Truth and the theory of content. In *Meaning and Understanding*, ed. H. Parret and J. Bouverese. De Gruyter.

Schiffer, S. 1987. *Remnants of Meaning*. MIT Press.

Schneider, W. 1987. Connectionism: Is it a paradigm shift for psychology? *Behavior Researh Methods; Instruments and Computers* 19: 73–83.

Searle, J. R. 1979. Metaphor. In *Expression and Meaning*, ed. J. Searle. Cambridge University Press.

Searle, J. R. 1980a. Minds, brains, and programs. *Behavioral and Brain Sciences* 3: 417–457.

Searle, J. R. 1980b. The background of meaning. In *Speech Act Theory and Pragmatics*, ed. J. R. Searle, F. Kiefer, and M. Bierwisch. Reidel.

Searle, J. R. 1981. The intentionality of intention and action. In *Perspectives on Cognitive Science*, ed. D. A. Norman. Erlbaum.

Searle, J. R. 1983. *Intentionality*. Cambridge University Press.

Segal, E. M., and Lachman, R. 1972. Complex behavior or higher mental processes: Is there a paradigm shift? *American Psychologist* 27: 46–55.

Segal, G. 1989. Seeing what is not there. *Philosophical Review* 98: 189–214.

Sejnowski, T. J. 1986. Open questions about computation in cerebral cortex. In *Parallel Distributed Processing: Explorations in the Microstructures of Cognition*, vol. 2, ed. J. L. McClelland, D. E. Rumelhart, and the PDP Research Group. MIT Press.

Sejnowski, T. J., and Rosenberg, C. R. 1986. NETtalk: A parallel network that learns to read aloud. Technical Report JHU/EECS-86/01, Johns Hopkins University.

Sejnowski, T. J., and Rosenberg, C. R. 1987. Parallel networks that learn to pronounce English text. *Complex Systems* 1: 145–168.

Sejnowski, T. J., and Rosenberg, C. R. 1988. Learning and representation in connectionist models. In *Perspective in Memory Research and Training*, ed. M. Gazzaniga. MIT Press.

Sellars, W. 1967. Scientific realism or irenic instrumentalism: A critique of Nagel and Feyerabend on theoretical explanation. In *Philosophical Perspectives: Metaphysics and Epistemology*, ed. W. Sellars. Ridgeview.

Shapere, D. 1964. The structure of scientific revolutions. *Philosophical Review* 73: 383–394.

Shapere, D. 1966. Meaning and scientific change. In *Mind and Cosmos: Explorations in the Philosophy of Science*, ed. R. Colodny. University of Pittsburgh Press.

Shapere, D. 1977. Scientific theories and their domains. In *The Structure of Scientific Theories*, ed. F. Suppe. University of Illinois Press.

Shapiro, S. C. 1979. The SNePs semantic network processing system. In *Associative Networks*, ed. N. V. Findler. Academic Press.

Shapiro, S. C., and Rapaport, W. J. 1987. SNePs considered as a fully intensional propositional semantic network. In *The Knowledge Frontier: Essays in the Representation of Knowledge*, ed. N. Cercone and G. McCalla. Springer-Verlag.

Siewiorek, D. P., Bell, C. G., and Newell, A. 1982. *Computer Structures: Principles and Examples*. McGraw- Hill.

Simon, H. A. 1981a. Cognitive science: The newest science of the artificial. In *Perspectives On Cognitive Science*, ed. D. A. Norman. Ablex.

Simon, H. A. 1981b. *The Sciences of the Artificial*. MIT Press.

Sippl, C. J., and Sippl, C. P. 1972. *Computer Dictionary and Handbook*. Howard W. Sams.

Smart, J. J. C. 1963. *Philosophy and Scientific Realism*. Routledge and Kegan Paul.

Smith, E. E., and Medin, D. L. 1981. *Categories and Concepts*. Harvard University Press.

Smolensky, P. 1987. The constituent structure of connectionist mental states: A reply to Fodor and Pylyshyn. *Southern Journal of Philosophy* 26, Supplement: 137–161.

Smolensky, P. 1988. On the proper treatment of connectionism. *Behavioral and Brain Sciences* 11: 1–74.

Smolensky, P. 1991. Connectionism, constituency and the language of thought. In *Meaning in Mind: Fodor and His Critics*. ed. B. Loewer and G. Rey. Blackwell.

Spencer, D. D. 1980. *The Illustrated Computer Dictionary*. Charles E. Merrill.

Stalnaker, R. 1984. *Inquiry*. MIT Press.

Stampe, D. W. 1977. Toward a causal theory of linguistic representation. In *Midwest Studies in Philosophy: Studies in the Philosophy of Language*, vol. 2, ed. P. A. French, T. E. Uehling, Jr., and H. K. Wettstein. University of Minnesota Press.

Sterelny, K. 1983. Natural kind terms. *Pacific Philosophical Quarterly* 64: 110–125.

Sterelny, K. 1990. *The Representational Theory of Mind: An Introduction*. Blackwell.

Sternberg, R. 1984. Towards a triarchic theory of human intelligence. *Behavioral and Brain Sciences* 7: 269–315.

Stich, S. 1983. *From Folk Psychology to Cognitive Science: The Case Against Belief.* MIT Press.

Stillings, N., Feinstein, M. H., Garfield, J. L., Rissland, E. L., Rosenbaum, D. A., Weisler, S., and Baker-Ward, L. 1987. *Cognitive Science: An Introduction*. MIT Press.

Suppe, F. 1977. *The Structure of Scientific Theories.* University of Illinois Press.

Swinney, D. A. 1979. Lexical access during sentence comprehension: Re(consideration) of context effects. *Journal of Verbal Learning and Verbal Behavior* 18: 645–659.

Tarski, A. 1954. Contributions to the theory of models, I, II. *Indigationes Mathematicae* 16: 572–588.

Thagard, P. 1988. Dimensions of analogy. In *Analogical Reasoning*, ed. D. H. Helman. Kluwer.

Tienson, J. 1987. An introduction to connectionism. *Southern Journal of Philosophy* 26, Supplement: 1–16.

Toulmin, S. 1972. *Human Understanding.* Princeton University Press.

Turing, A. 1950. Computing machinery and intelligence. *Mind* 59: 433–460.

Turvey, M. T., Shaw, R. E., Reed, E. S., and Mace, W. M. 1981. Ecological laws of perceiving and acting: In reply to Fodor and Pylyshyn. *Cognition* 9: 237–304.

Van Gulick, R. 1988. Consciousness, intrinsic intentionality, and self-understanding machines. In *Consciousness and Contemporary Science*, ed. T. A. Marcel and E. Bisiach. Oxford University Press.

Van Gulick, R. 1989. Metaphysical arguments for internalism and why they don't work. In *Rerepresentation*, ed. S. Silvers. Kluwer.

Von Eckardt, B. 1984. Cognitive psychology and principled skepticism. *Journal of Philosophy* 81: 67–88.

Von Eckardt Klein, B. 1978a. What is the biology of language? In *Explorations in the Biology of Language*, ed. E. Walker. Bradford Books.

Von Eckardt Klein, B. 1978b. Inferring functional localization from neurological evidence. In *Explorations in the Biology of Language*, ed. E. Walker. Bradford Books.

von Frisch, K. 1967. *The Dance Language and Orientation of Bees.* Belknap Press of Harvard University Press.

Wagner, S. Theories of Mental Representation. Unpublished manuscript.

Walker, E. 1978. Cognitive Science, 1978: Report of the State of the Art Committee to the Advisors of the Alfred P. Sloan Foundation. Unpublished.

Walsh, W. H. 1967. Nature of metaphysics. In *The Encyclopedia of Philosophy*, ed. P. Edward. Macmillan.

Warren, N. 1971. Is a scientific revolution taking place in psychology—Doubts and reservations. *Science Studies* 1: 407–413.

Weik, M. H. 1977. *Standard Dictionary of Computers and Information Processing.* Hayden.

Weimer, W. B., and Palermo, D. S. 1973. Paradigms and normal science in psychology. *Science Studies* 3: 211–244.

Wilde, D. U. 1973. *An Introduction to Computing: Problem-Solving, Algorithms and Data Structures.* Prentice-Hall.

Wirth, N. 1976. *Algorithms + Data Structures = Programs.* Prentice-Hall.

Wittgenstein, L. 1961. *Tractatus Logico-philosophicus.* Routledge and Kegan Paul. Republished with a new translation by D. F. Pears and B. F. McGuinness. Originally published in 1922.

Yuille, A. L., and Ullman, S. 1990. Computational theories of low-level vision. In *Visual Cognition and Action: An Invitation to Cognitive Science*, vol. 2, ed. D. N. Osherson, S. M. Kosslyn, and J. M. Hollerbach. MIT Press.

Sumpplementary Readings

Section 1.2	Kosslyn 1980; Kosslyn, Pinker, Smith, and Shwartz 1979
Section 2.2	Searle 1983, chapter 1–3
Section 2.3	P. M. Churchland 1982
Section 2.4	Cummins 1975
Section 3.1	Black 1954; Boyd 1979
Section 3.3	Newell 1980
Section 3.4	Bechtel and Abrahamson 1991
Section 5.1	Rumelhart and Norman 1988
Section 5.2	Kosslyn 1980, pp. 136–147; Fodor and Pylyshyn 1988; Smolensky 1987
Section 6.1	Kim 1984
Section 6.2	Palmer 1978
Section 6.3	Block 1986; Cummins 1989, chapter 8
Section 6.4	Sterelny 1990, chapter 6
Section 6.5	Fodor 1987, chapter 4; Dretske 1983
Section 6.6	Millikan 1989a
Section 7.2	Burge 1986a
Section 7.3	Stich 1983, pp. 160–170
Section 7.4	Fodor 1987, chapter 2; Fodor 1991
Section 9.4	Stich 1983, pp. 170–183; Fodor 1981c
Section A.2	Kuhn 1970a, chapters 2–5
Section A.3	Laudan 1977, chapters 1–4

Index

Action. *See* Behavior, intelligent
Animal cognition, 398n8
ANTCOG (adult, normal typical
  cognition), 6–7, 46, 48, 54–55, 57, 90,
  92–95, 106, 305, 311–313, 332, 398n9
Anthropology, 1–2
Artificial intelligence (AI), 59, 112, 117, 167,
  311, 398n7. *See also* Computer science,
  role of
Assumption(s)
  combined linking, 303
  computational, 50, 97–141
  computational linking, 98
  computational system, 104–116, 139, 141
  domain specifying, 31, 47–48, 57–91,
    372–373. *See also* Domain
  foundational, 4, 18, 29. *See also*
    Framework of shared commitments
    (FSC)
  grouping [D3], 19, 48, 57, 82–91
  identification [D1], 19, 47, 57–72
  linking, 22, 50, 97–98, 139, 140, 143–145,
    303, 309, 434
  as metaphysical, 4–5, 23–24, 399n6, 399n8,
    399n9
  methodological [MA], 18, 24, 53–56, 92,
    303–339, 341, 373, 384, 435
  property [D2], 19, 47, 57, 72–82, 437
  representational [SA2], 50–53, 143–145,
    190, 192–195
  representational system, 50–51, 143,
    158–159
  revisable/unrevisable, 18, 46
  substantive, 5, 8–10, 22–23, 28–29, 50–53,
    92, 97, 106, 108, 161, 440
  system [C2], 22, 97, 441
  working, 14, 32
Asymmetrical dependence. *See* Fodor, J. A.,
  on asymmetrical dependence
Autonomy, principle of, 254–262

Ballard, D. H., 325
Basic questions. *See* Questions, basic
  (empirical)
Bechtel, W., 308, 397n4
Behavior
  intelligent, 59–64
  of a process, 291
Biological function. *See* Content
  determination, biological function
  approach to
Black, M., 99–100, 402n5, 433
Block, N., 409n18
Boyd, R., 102–104, 403n11, 441

Burge, T.
  descriptive argument against internalism,
    251–253
  discourse similarity argument, 243–249
  on Fodor, 417n23
  language community determination thesis,
    263–264, 434
  on Marr's theory of early vision, 251–253
  on propositional attitude content, 343
  simple thought experiment argument
    against internalism, 241–249
  on Stich's normative argument for
    internalism, 259–262
Butterfield, E. C., 366

Carnap, R., 346
Casullo, A., 417n24
Causal historical approach to content
  determination. *See* Content determina-
  tion, causal historical approach to
Causal Powers Difference Condition
  (CPDC), 271–272, 415n20
Causal theory of reference, 214–215,
  277–278, 427
Chomsky, N., 81–82, 179, 402n10
Churchland, P. M., 85–97
Churchland, P. S., 16–17, 136, 324, 327,
  330–331, 397n2, 419n12
Cognitive capacity, 47–50, 65–66, 191,
  303–310, 332, 341–342
  basic general properties of, 426
  coherence of, 47–48, 54, 72, 77–82, 93–94,
    305, 307, 315–316, 332–333, 428
  as a computational capacity. *See*
    Assumptions, computational
  intentionality of, 47–48, 63, 66, 73–82,
    314–316, 333–335
  as natural kind, 82–91
  pragmatic evaluability of, 47–49, 54, 72,
    75–76, 93–94, 305, 307, 314–315,
    332–333, 437
  productivity of, 48, 54, 73, 81–82, 93–94,
    179–182, 305, 307, 316, 333, 402n10, 437
  reliability of, 48, 54, 73, 81, 9–94, 305, 307,
    317, 332–333, 438
Cognitive science, 1, 14, 30. *See Also*
  Assumption(s), domain specifying,
  methodological, substantive
  evolution of, 138–141
  example of, 32–45
  future of, 9, 341–343
  general characterization of, 45–56
  research framework of, 45–56, 70, 92, 106,
    139–141, 161, 182, 190, 233, 264, 276,